A Voice for Mothers

A Voice for Mothers

The Plunket Society and Infant Welfare, 1907–2000

Linda Bryder

AUCKLAND UNIVERSITY PRESS

First published 2003
Auckland University Press
University of Auckland
Private Bag 92019
Auckland, New Zealand
http://www.auckland.ac.nz/aup

ISBN 1 86940 290 1

Publication is assisted by the History Group, Ministry for Culture and Heritage.

Designed and typeset by Amy Tansell
Printed by Astra Print, Wellington

Contents

This is essentially a woman's matter. Surely as mothers, we should have some voice in what so intimately concerns us.

Plunket Society to Chief Health Officer, Thomas Valintine, arguing the case for society's right to control infant welfare, 1911, Plunket Society Archives, AG7 5-36.

Foreword

Most New Zealanders, or their mothers, have retained their 'Plunket Baby Record Book' as a treasured memento of an important life stage. Our family is no exception. As a shy young Danish immigrant in the 1950s my mother recalls with pleasure her visits to the Plunket nurse in Auckland, Sister Aileen Rountree, whom she describes as 'just lovely, so reassuring'. My own experiences with Plunket nurse Yvonne Robinson in the 1990s were equally positive. Many New Zealanders share this opinion. After I had spoken about the Society at a medical history conference in 1994, one member of the audience wrote to me in the following terms: 'Congrats on sticking up for Plunket. My mother brought up eight kids with Plunket assistance – she thought they were excellent. And Heaven help anyone who tried to <u>impose</u> any notions on my mother.' Plunket nurses have not always had a good historical press. In this book I am not 'sticking up for Plunket', and yet the research gave me great respect for the women who fought so hard for the service and the nurses whom they employed.

I wish to thank the Auckland branch of the Plunket Society and in particular its former president and treasurer, Averill Matthews, who alerted me to the existence of historical records then held at the branch's headquarters in Auckland. As a medical and social welfare historian I was fascinated by these records, which formed the basis of *Not Just Weighing Babies: Plunket in Auckland, 1908–1998*. The research undertaken for this book prompted me to explore the 'full story' and I am grateful to the Plunket Society's national office staff, in particular John Thompson, Paul Baigent, Graig Pollock and Gail Max for their helpfulness and friendliness, and for allowing me access to the Society's voluminous records. Thanks also to former Plunket nurse Joyce Powell for sharing with me her personal experiences and allowing me access to her taped interviews with other Plunket nurses. I am also grateful to broadcaster Jim Sullivan for having the foresight to create a Plunket Society oral history archive, held at the Turnbull Library. Helpful comments and feedback were received from Plunket's former medical and assistant medical directors, David Geddis and

Ian Hassall. In particular I was buoyed by Ian Hassall's encouragement and enthusiasm for my project.

There are various institutions and their staff I wish to thank such as Archives New Zealand, Alexander Turnbull Library, Auckland Museum Library, Auckland Public Library, and the University of Otago Medical School library. Special thanks go to the staff of the Hocken Library of the University of Otago, and to Chief Archivist Stuart Strachan and his wife Jean, who have always shown me such wonderful hospitality when I have visited their city. I was privileged to know the late David McDonald, the Hocken's incomparable reference librarian, and to benefit from his vast knowledge. I am grateful to the University of Auckland for the award of a Staff Research Grant to aid this research. Thanks also to the Wellcome Institute Library and the Highgate Literary and Scientific Institution in London, and to the Wellcome Trust for a Short-term Travel Grant enabling me to visit London. For the right to reproduce photographs and cartoons I am grateful to Archives New Zealand, the Turnbull Library, Hocken Library, *Metro*, the Auckland Museum, Barry Gustafson, the Plunket Society and its Auckland branch. Thanks also to Plunket nurse Ripeka Mokaraka for her friendliness and helpfulness in identifying individuals in recent photographs held at Plunket's national office.

Finally I wish to thank my partner Derek Dow for his unfailing support and encouragement and my sons Dennis and Martin. I knew this research must have rubbed off when Dennis came home from school one day having chosen to do a school project on Truby King!

Linda Bryder

Introduction

The motto of the Royal New Zealand Plunket Society has always been 'to help the mothers and save the babies'.[1] The society was founded in 1907 as part of a Western-world infant welfare movement that aimed to improve the survival and fitness of future citizens in the interests of 'national efficiency'. The diagnosis of the problem and the solutions put forward were the same everywhere: mothers were ignorant of the correct methods of child-rearing and needed to be educated. To that end, clinics were set up and nurses employed to monitor infant health and provide advice. Although the movement was medically inspired, in New Zealand's case principally by Dr Frederic Truby King, it was generally organised and maintained by voluntary groups of women, sometimes with government support. In Britain, however, by the 1920s, the services had largely been taken over by the Ministry of Health's medical officers and local authorities, while by the 1930s the American movement was dominated by paediatricians in their private clinics. By contrast, in New Zealand the movement continued much longer to be controlled by women in a voluntary capacity and run by nurses with little medical supervision. It also remained rare in providing free services to almost all Pakeha women, and later Maori and Pacific Island women, without the stigma of charity. With ever-increasing subsidies from the state (from a third of its costs in 1914 to 78 per cent by 2001),[2] and with its many clinics and six baby ('Karitane') hospitals, it remained a society run by women for women. Men were involved – as fathers, handymen, and medical, legal and financial advisers – but they took a back seat until relatively recently.

Plunket has often been heralded as New Zealand's most successful voluntary organisation and certainly its most famous. Returning from an overseas trip in 1923, Dr Ada Paterson expressed her surprise at the praise she had heard of Plunket wherever she went: 'After a year's investigations, I have come back more than ever impressed with the great value of Dr King's work'.[3] In 1930 the Mayor of Wellington claimed that, along with New Zealand's troops and the All Blacks, Plunket had advertised the dominion.[4] Shortly after the Second World War, Elizabeth Bryson, a Scottish doctor who had practised in New Zealand for more than 30 years, visited Britain where she gave a talk on 'Women in New Zealand'. The one thing, she claimed, of which New Zealand women could really boast was the work they had done, and were still doing, in connection with the care of mothers and babies. New Zealand had the lowest infant death rate in the world, and that it had dropped from 40.57 per 1000 live births in 1906–10 to 9.5 by 1936–40. Pointing out that many causes contributed to this record, such as 'virility of race, climate, absence of densely populated areas', she nevertheless argued that the major part of the credit had to go to the work of the Plunket Society, 'carried to a noteworthy conclusion by the New Zealand women'.[5] A member of the Legislative Council, Mary Patricia Anderson from Greymouth, similarly referred to Plunket in 1949 as 'one noble character of our New Zealand public life whose work now resounds around the world, and whose efforts to promote health and happiness for all classes of people in this and other lands makes me proud to be a New Zealander'.[6] These views were reinforced by a constant stream of over-seas visitors who came to observe the society's work. In 1952 Dr Jean Mackintosh, Director of Maternal and Child Welfare for the English city of Birmingham, told delegates at a Plunket Society conference in New Zea-land that she had needed little persuasion to visit because, for more years than she could remember, New Zealand – and specifically the Plunket Society – had been held up to the rest of the world as an example of what could be done in maternal and child health.[7]

Plunket was usually given the credit for New Zealand's low infant death rates during the first half of the twentieth century, a source of great national pride. As Bryson noted, and as has been pointed out by historians who have examined the early twentieth-century infant welfare movement, in New Zealand as elsewhere, there were other factors involved in the decline. One important factor was the reduction in family size: women who married in 1880 averaged 6.5 live births when their families were completed and their 1923 equivalents 2.4.[8] The extension of the general education of girls has also been considered critical. For New Zealand, the availability of food and the lack of overcrowding were undoubtedly also significant. Philippa Mein Smith has argued convincingly that the infant welfare movement was a consequence rather than a cause of the mortality decline.[9] Yet, as French historian Catherine Rollet has postulated, that does not mean the movement had no effect on mortality rates.[10] Milton Lewis held that the infant welfare movement in Sydney, with its emphasis on hygiene and

breastfeeding, probably did contribute to fewer deaths.[11] It is also probable
that ready access, via the Plunket Society, to advice on breastfeeding and
hygiene in the home contributed to New Zealand maintaining its record of
the lowest infant mortality in the world at a time when the major cause of
infant death was of digestive origin. Breastfeeding was a known protective
against infant diarrhoea or gastro-enteritis.[12]

During the second half of the twentieth century New Zealand could no
longer claim this record. This was partly because the rest of the Western
world caught up: thanks to improved infant feeding formulae, higher standards of domestic hygiene including refrigeration, antibiotics and improved
methods of rehydration, infant diarrhoea was no longer the killer of former
years. Other causes of death began to assume a greater importance, and
here New Zealand's record was not so good – cot deaths, accidents in the
home and on the roads, child abuse and diseases for which some other
countries were more effectively immunised all took their toll. Plunket
nurses continued to offer support and assistance at an individual level, but
wider social, political and economic changes affected overall infant health.
This did not mean that the Plunket Society was failing the country. Plunket
became involved in research, funding visits from overseas experts, mass
immunisation campaigns, the detection of abuse, accident prevention
campaigns and counselling and support for cot deaths. Cutbacks and targeting of services were regretted by the society at a time when support
was considered more important than ever. Yet changes in the organisation
itself and in late twentieth-century society meant that it lost its status as
a powerful and confident women's movement demanding resources for
infant and child welfare.

Plunket was always concerned with more than preventing deaths. It
viewed itself as a 'Health Society' and aimed to provide support for
parents.[13] The support of 'ordinary' mothers and fathers who had no previous experience of child-rearing because they themselves came from small
families was a feature that ensured loyalty to the society from a large proportion of the public. Also, Plunket provided an organisational framework
for women to come together and be involved in public issues. Through
this they gained mutual support and a collective identity. In 1959 Plunket's
Medical Director, Dr Neil Begg, claimed that Plunket was 'fairly bursting
at the seams', with about 600 branches and 250 Mothers' Clubs: 'Each one
of these has a considerable sphere of influence and the sum of their
opinions is a tremendous public force'.[14]

The Plunket Society has always had its critics. The Health Department

resented a portion of the health budget going to a nursing service over
which it had no control, and some members of the medical profession resented the fact that parents consulted Plunket nurses rather than doctors,
to the detriment, they believed, of infant health. The emergence of a new
child psychology in the 1950s, which promoted more permissive and child-
centred child-rearing, saw Plunket nurses accused of being old-fashioned
in their promotion of routines in child care and breastfeeding. In the 1970s,
inspired by social control models of history and the new women's history, specifically work on the rise of 'the cult of motherhood', Professor
Erik Olssen discussed the ideology underlying Truby King's child-rearing
advice.[15] In a ground-breaking article, he argued that the aim was to turn
out self-controlled citizens who would be good factory workers and soldiers, governed by the clock and 'programmed for capital accumulation':
'the baby thrived only because it had learned to be obedient to the mother,
the [Plunket] Society, the dictates of science and the imperatives of time as
defined in a capitalist society'.[16] The mother became subject to the control
of outside experts, and 'the Society's success in defining motherhood and
home-making as women's only legitimate activity transformed these tasks
into straitjackets . . . for some the new precision of these roles constituted
a form of imprisonment, a cage from which mental breakdown marked an
increasingly common avenue of escape'.[17] These criticisms will be addressed and discussed in the course of the book.[18]

This history sets out to place Plunket in the context of three broad
themes: the relationship between the voluntary sector and the state in the
provision of welfare, the development of paediatrics as a specialty and
changing trends in infant health, and the relationship between health
providers and their clients, the mothers. Underlying these themes are the
ways in which the New Zealand experience paralleled or differed from that
of comparable countries such as Britain and the United States.

The 'mixed economy of welfare' and 'maternalist welfare'

Recent historical scholarship in Europe and the United States has pointed
to the continuing role of the non-state sector in providing welfare, resulting in a 'mixed economy of welfare' or 'welfare pluralism'.[19] Assessing the
relationship between the voluntary sector and the state not only places a
new perspective on the state's role, it also negates the older view of a linear
progression from the 'individualism' of the nineteenth century to the 'col-
lectivism' of the mid-twentieth century.[20] Much has been written on the

rise of the welfare state in New Zealand, but little on the voluntary sector.[21] This history explores the way in which the women who ran Plunket succeeded in retaining control of an important area of welfare in the face of Health Department opposition, despite the fact that they had no technical expertise or training in providing health services.

'Maternalist welfare' is the label given to the early twentieth-century movement that evolved in the Western world, including New Zealand, whereby voluntary networks of women controlled welfare services relating to women and children.[22] They did this as an act of citizenship, in the firm belief that, as educated women and as mothers, such control was their duty and their right. [23] Maternalism empowered these women. Some historians have claimed that maternalism flourished in weak welfare states,[24] but, as Philippa Mein Smith has argued, the New Zealand and Australian cases show that maternalism could co-exist with a pronounced paternalist welfare system.[25] This can be seen particularly in the continuing strength of the Plunket Society during the reign of New Zealand's first Labour government, 1935–49, which established the welfare state. Its policies, which included free maternity care, family allowances and housing for families, and gender-differentiated minimum wages, assumed a view of women as wives and mothers rather than as equal citizens.[26] Maternalists appeared to be comfortable with that interpretation of welfare, and the Plunket Society did not suffer. Just as Anne Digby found in relation to the earlier maternalist movement in Britain, the maternalists appealed successfully to male policy-makers precisely because they were able to ground their policies in sexual difference, and in the perpetuation of 'traditional' roles for women: the body politic remained paternalistic.[27] Although a strong paternalist welfare state did not preclude the existence of maternalist welfare, conversely the residual welfare system of late twentieth-century New Zealand coincided with the collapse of maternalism. From around the 1970s the maternalist consensus collapsed, with implications for the Plunket Society.

Paediatrics as a specialty and changing trends in infant health

There are few academic histories of paediatrics, with the notable exception of that by Sydney Halpern on the rise of the profession in the United States and, more recently, an edited volume by Alexandra Stern and Howard Markel on aspects of paediatrics in the United States since 1880.[28] Although there were local differences in numbers and professional status, Western child-health professionals were confronted with similar issues. The history of paediatrics in New Zealand is part of a bigger story. As the major provider of infant health services, the Plunket Society attempted to keep up to date with international trends in paediatrics. A study of its medical advisers and their preoccupations therefore provides an understanding of changing trends in paediatrics. Plunket's success in accessing most mothers and babies also afforded an opportunity to gather research data.

During the first half of the twentieth century paediatricians in New Zealand were struggling to become established as a profession. In Britain the term 'paediatrics' had come into currency only when the British Paediatric Association adopted it at its founding meeting in 1928.[29] New Zealand established its own Paediatric Society in 1947. There had, however, been professional rivalry between Plunket nurses and doctors from the outset. The early agreement that nurses would only treat 'mere infantile ailments, eg simple diarrhoea, indigestion or colic, such as would ordinarily be dealt with by the mother or grandmother, without calling in a doctor' did not help.[30] The Karitane hospitals often provided the arena in which the battles were fought, and yet they were also important sites for professional advancement. Medical disputes with Plunket reached a height in the 1930s. They were ostensibly about Plunket's feeding practices, but beneath the surface lay issues of power and control. In 1938 Dr Ian Ewart of Wellington complained that 'New Zealand was the only country where nurses prescribed for babies'.[31] In 1958 Dr Harold Turbott, shortly to be New Zealand's Director-General of Health, maintained that 'It is this virtual exclusion of the medical profession from well-baby care and its provision mainly through a voluntary organised nursing service, which is anomalous in our land'.[32] Yet some doctors were supportive throughout, becoming the society's medical advisers. Paediatrician Dr Helen Deem, Plunket's Medical Adviser from 1939 to 1955, stated after a decade in the job that she had remained only because she was convinced that the society was 'doing a really worthwhile job for the mothers and babies of the country'.[33] From the 1950s, when Plunket appeared to be threatened by a state takeover, paediatricians aligned themselves with Plunket, perhaps seeing a possible role within the system. Plunket supported the establishment of New Zealand's first Chair of Paediatrics at Otago University in 1967. The politics of the relations between various health providers are therefore far from straightforward.

The professionals and the mothers

The feminist movement of the 1970s and the new social history based on social constructionist models gave rise to a view that the Plunket Society was oppressive of women. Imposing 'expert' medical advice on women supposedly undermined their confidence in their parenting skills.[34] Impressionistic accounts of mothers' responses cast doubt on these interpretations, as do the surveys on client responses to Plunket nurses, which became increasingly frequent from the 1950s. The surveys usually produced the same results: most women appreciated the advice and reassurance provided by the nurses, whereas a minority resented or dismissed advice. The surveys showed that women usually made up their own minds and that they displayed more 'agency' than the social control models allowed for. These responses will be addressed, and the nurses will be given a 'voice' in discussing the interaction between the two parties. One recurrent complaint was that nurses could not possibly understand unless they had children of their own. This perhaps validates the claim among the women who founded Plunket that, as mothers, they were capable of acting as Plunket nurses. Nursing has often been portrayed as an extension of a woman's caring and nurturing role within the family.[35] Who better fitted this model than the Plunket nurse with her obvious love of babies? This was an exclusively female branch of nursing, and nothing came of the suggestion by Plunket's Director of Nursing in 1973 that the society should seriously consider employing male nurses to 'bring a new aspect to the Society's work'.[36] Yet Plunket nurses displayed more than 'motherly instincts'; they were health professionals who, through their contact with mothers and babies, were often the first to detect potentially serious problems.

The surveys paid close attention to the interaction with Maori and Pacific Islanders, as a result of the Plunket Society's monocultural image, perpetuated in part by an unsympathetic Health Department.[37] The history of the relationship between Plunket and Maori is complex.[38] The department and Plunket reached an agreement early on that departmental, not Plunket, nurses would deal with Maori infant health. Maori women were entitled to use the Plunket clinics, though few did so. The segregated service was more than an administrative agreement: there was little pressure to change it at the local level. Other groups were set up for Maori, such as the Women's Health League from the 1930s, but these were not resourced to the same extent as Plunket. With Maori urbanisation in the post-Second World War period, the segregated service could no longer be sustained. Yet Plunket's attempts to combat the 'stigma of racialism' by including Maori mothers in the 1960s were regarded by Director-General of Health Harold Turbott as 'empire building'.[39] From the 1980s Plunket had to confront this issue publicly to retain credibility in a self-consciously multicultural society.

This is a history of the politics of infant health and welfare in twentieth-century New Zealand. It is also a history of the Royal New Zealand Plunket Society. Although it is not an institutional history of Plunket, it does focus on the society as the major provider of well-infant health care throughout most of the century.[40] In 1975 Plunket's President Joy Reid referred to the Minister of Health's veiled threats about the society's future – 'He mentioned infant welfare', she said, 'and obviously there's no other infant-care organisation.'[41] In 2001 Prime Minister Helen Clark stated, 'It is a truism that the future of our country lies with our children and young people. As a nation, we need to give some very serious thought to how we can give them better support.'[42] Different groups of people have grappled with these issues in different ways over the past hundred years. This book examines those efforts.

CHAPTER 1

Founding the Society for Promoting the Health of Women and Children

Politicians and doctors define the problem

New Zealand had the lowest recorded infant mortality in the world at the beginning of the twentieth century, but this did not appear to be a cause of self-congratulation. John Findlay, Attorney-General and leader of the Legislative Council from 1906 to 1911, explained in 1907 that, although the infant death rate was lower in New Zealand than elsewhere, it was not declining. In 1904 it was 71 per 1000 births; in 1897 it had been 72.[1] At the same time the fertility rate was declining, which gave rise to 'reflection and anxiety', according to New Zealand's Governor, Lord Ranfurly.[2] These matters were publicly discussed in the early part of the century because of prevailing concerns – not confined to New Zealand – about 'national efficiency'. New Zealand saw itself as part of the great British Empire and Anglo-Saxon race: population issues were viewed in terms of imperial strength. In a 1904 memorandum on infant life preservation, Premier Richard John Seddon declared, 'Babies are our best immigrants', echoing the conclusion of a recent report on declining birth rates in New South Wales.[3] Given their geographical position, these young British colonies were particularly worried about a potential influx of Asians. For Seddon, 'In the younger colonies of the Empire population is essential and if increased from British stock the self-governing colonies will still further strengthen and buttress our great Empire. In British interests it is clearly undesirable that the colonies should be populated by the inferior surplus of people of older and alien countries.'[4] Immigration policies were restricted accordingly but there were also attempts to build up the local white population to fill the spaces.

The origins of the infant welfare movement in Britain have been traced to the South African War of 1899–1902, in which it was discovered that up to a third of the recruits were unfit for military training owing to physical defects. There was a public outcry and army records were said to show that there had been deterioration in health during the previous 50 years (i.e. coinciding with a period of urbanisation). This resulted in the setting up of the Inter-departmental Committee on Physical Deterioration, which reported in 1904. In the event no deterioration was found, but it did reveal extensive ill health among the poorer sectors of society. The report focused in particular on infants and children, the next generation of fighters and workers. It was shown that the death rate among infants had not declined as had general death rates over the previous half-century. The infant welfare movement in Britain was launched as a result of a concern for national efficiency, especially in the light of declining British military and economic power compared with Germany, the United States and Japan.[5] Nor was Britain alone in this concern. As Alisa Klaus has written, Fascists and Fabians alike advocated public programmes to protect maternal and child life and to encourage child-bearing for the sake of national strength.[6]

In New Zealand, political interest in the high infant death rates is evident in the debates surrounding a 1904 bill to set up maternity hospitals for poor but respectable working-class wives and as training schools for midwives. Although the focus was maternity services, it was infant rather than maternal health that was the central concern. Introducing the bill into Parliament, Seddon stated that the 'deaths at maternity are alarming', and went on to point out that during the period 1894–1903, there had been 20,487 deaths among children aged five and under, and 15,767 under the age of one year. He added that he was still awaiting information about the deaths of mothers. Introducing the bill into the Legislative Council, Attorney-General Albert Pitt explained that the aim of registering and training midwives was to reduce infant deaths. He repeated Seddon's statistics on infant mortality and added that 'in addition, no doubt many of the mothers died in childbirth'.[7]

In 1908 Seddon's successor as Prime Minister, Sir Joseph Ward, addressed a meeting presided over by the Governor of New Zealand, Lord Plunket, to set up a voluntary society to protect infant life in Auckland. Ward declared that he knew of no matter more urgent. Putting aside sentimentalism, and approaching it from a 'mercenary point of view', he calculated that 'every human being in the Dominion was valued at about £250'.[8] A few months earlier a member of the Legislative Council voiced similar sentiments when supporting an amendment to the Infant Life Protection Act: 'The real reason for our solicitude is not murdered babes. It is that population, which is decreasing, is indispensable to national safety and national progress. We must have soldiers and workers, or our prosperity will be imperilled and our industry will decay.'[9] In a health promotion poster issued in 1909, the newly appointed Chief Health Officer, Dr Thomas

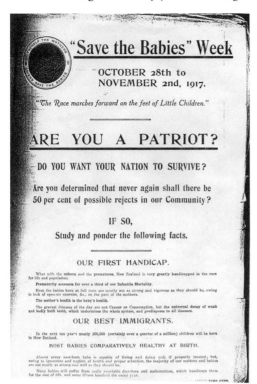

"Save the Babies" Week poster, 1917. The 'following facts' included the statements that the 'mother's health is the baby's health' and 'owing to ignorance and neglect of health and proper attention, the majority of our mothers and babies are not nearly as strong and well as they should be'. Hocken Library, University of Otago, AG7/119

Valintine, devoted a section to 'Assets versus Liabilities', placing the value to the country of each healthy young adult at over £300, and each 'unhealthy wastrel and dependent [*sic*] who has to be kept by the public' as a 'grave liability'. A government poster succinctly summarised the belief during the First World War, using a military image, 'The Race marches forward on the feet of Little Children'.[10] Warfare had provided a major impetus for the infant welfare movement in Britain. In New Zealand, too, records of army recruits in the First World War showed up poor health. The Army Medical Board had rejected 31 per cent of those examined; many more 'unfits' reached England.[11] The publicity surrounding this gave added impetus, and political respectability, to the infant welfare movement.

These concerns must be viewed in the context of contemporary attitudes which regarded the environment and 'the laws of Nature' (or becoming 'more sensible, normal and healthy in our habits')[12] as more important than heredity. Some commentators followed the teachings of late nineteenth-century social Darwinism that nature should be allowed to take its course in wiping out the less fit members of the society, and that social policy should not pander to the survival of the weak but rather should prevent them from propagating. Marsden MP Frank Mander, for example, put forward the eugenist view that 'consumptives and imbeciles and weaklings, who cannot possibly rear healthy children, should not be allowed to marry'. He believed the proposed free maternity homes were not a good thing, because they might lead to 'propagating a lot of criminal children, who would be better out of the world altogether'.[13] This, however, appears to have been a minority view. Environmentalism was much more to the fore among 'progressive' thinkers of the early twentieth century.

One of these was London-trained Dr William Collins – a new member of the Legislative Council, Seddon's physician and a friend of Dr James Mason, first Chief Health Officer of New Zealand from 1900 to 1909. Collins argued that children were born 'full of possibilities for good health or ill health and for good or evil', and that it was the state's responsibility to ensure that they did not grow up to become inmates of general or mental hospitals.[14] He believed that, although all instincts of 'criminal stock' could not be eradicated in one generation, it was possible to change the mental condition of the child through the environment, and so lessen the hereditary taint.[15] This was a view shared by the doctor who was to become the leader and figurehead of the infant welfare movement in early twentieth-century New Zealand, Dr Frederic Truby King, then Medical Superintendent of Seacliff Mental Asylum.[16]

What aspects of the environment required modifying? In his 1907 annual report, Mason analysed the 1811 infant deaths during the past year. Of these, 861 were due to 'diarrhoea, enteritis and marasmus', which, he claimed, 'often spells nothing more than bad feeding'. In Mason's view 'bad feeding' was caused by ignorance, 'want of care' and the quality of the milk supply. The solution was knowledge, 'love' and a clean milk supply.[17] There was nothing original in this analysis. Any New Zealander with an interest in the subject would be aware of a recent book by the English medical officer, Dr George Newman, *Infant Mortality. A Social Problem*, published in 1906.[18] Indeed, Collins and Findlay cited Newman's book during the parliamentary debates.[19]

Although child-rearing may have been perceived as a women's sphere and previously a private affair, the early twentieth-century concern for the future of the race and empire elevated it to a matter of national importance, discussed at length by the country's leaders who, as fathers themselves, claimed to have a special grasp of the issue. For example, Liberal MP for Christchurch city, Thomas Taylor, stated in 1904, 'Most members of the

House – with the exception of one or two bachelors (and bachelors have no right to be counted at all) – most men out of their own experience will have seen how the average mother, a woman of education, well trained and well cared for, lacks education in regard to one of the most important, if not the most important, of her duties in life, when for the first time she handles her own offspring, in the most clumsy manner – does not know quite which is the head end and which is the foot end of the baby.'[20] During the 1907 discussions on infant life protection in the Legislative Council, 56-year-old prominent Auckland citizen, Seymour George, stated modestly, 'I am speaking, I may say, with some little knowledge. I have a large family myself, and my children are all grown-up young men and young women, and they are very healthy people.' He proceeded to claim that deaths were caused 'through ignorance'. His own children were brought up on milk and had nothing to eat or drink but milk until they were over twelve months of age.[21] Sixty-two-year-old George Jones pointed out that he was the father of ten children, nine of whom were living 'and in that respect I can put myself in competition with the Hon. Mr George'. He mocked George's self-proclaimed expertise in child-rearing: 'Here we have a gentleman in Chamber who can rock the cradle, fill the bottle, mix the food, and make a fortune all at once'. The *New Zealand Observer* also picked up on George's 'touching exposition of the subject before the Legislative Council' which 'mark[ed] him out as an authority on "baby" topics'.[22] Yet Jones too went on to expand on the 'teachings of medical science' in child-rearing.[23]

The problem was perceived to be ignorance of 'the laws of nature', which could be remedied through the teaching of scientific principles. The most 'natural' form of infant feeding was of course breastfeeding and this was strongly promoted by early twentieth-century environmentalists. Medical studies conducted in Europe since the 1880s had shown that breast milk was a protective factor against infantile diarrhoea, the major cause of infant deaths.[24] In his 1906–7 annual report, Mason cited the Health Officer for Liverpool, England, who had calculated that the rate of deaths for breast-fed infants was 20 per 1000 from infantile diarrhoea, while among those fed on artificial foods and cow's milk it was a staggering 440 per 1000.[25]

Breastfeeding did not just prevent deaths in infancy. Truby King had a particular interest in psychiatry, not only as medical superintendent of a mental asylum, but also as lecturer in mental diseases at Otago University and member of the Psychological Association. He argued that breastfeeding 'formed the best means of prophylaxis against the infantile cerebropathies', by which he was referring to the development of 'idiots, imbeciles and epileptics'. He cited Professor Ernesto Lugaro who, in his 1909 text *Modern Problems in Psychiatry*, argued that these conditions might be the result of lesions in the brain following infantile cerebral disease.[26] King included breastfeeding among the factors tending to 'reduce the supplies of populations in asylums, hospitals, benevolent institutions, goals and slums' and to contribute to 'a very remarkable improvement . . . in the physical, mental and moral condition of the whole community'.[27]

Although it is not known how many women breastfed in early twentieth-century New Zealand, many expressed the view that the number was declining. At least one MP believed that the 'great bulk of the mothers' did not breastfeed.[28] Dr Collins estimated in 1907 that about 80 per cent did not 'suckle' their infants.[29] The trend was perceived as a public issue. In 1904 Legislative Council member William Beehan commented on the disinclination of many present-day mothers to 'suckle their young', which was the greatest cause of infant mortality.[30] Collins explained that many women objected to breastfeeding, no matter how much the doctor urged it.[31] Seymour George claimed they objected that it 'put their figures out of shape' and that it was inconvenient.[32]

Other medical authorities commented on the trend. Writing on infant diarrhoea in his annual report for 1906–7, Christchurch sanitary inspector, R. J. McKenzie, claimed that 'the most grave responsibility rests on the mothers who, from carelessness, ignorance, or selfishness, do not feed their children at the breast'. He thought that the absence of breastfeeding was understandable (though perhaps not justifiable) in the manufacturing districts in England, where women were largely employed in factories, but that the neglect was 'less excusable' in New Zealand where few mothers were wage-earners.[33] Dr Joseph Frengley, Assistant Chief Health Officer, claimed it was the 'so-called upper classes, Society women, . . . Social parasites' who did not breastfeed. In his view, 'the working women, the true mothers, the women with the breasts', had no trouble. He was satisfied that it was a mistake 'from the natural point of view' to keep alive babies who could not be suckled by their mothers: 'If we only bred from the mothers who can suckle their babies we should soon have proper motherhood'.[34] At the inaugural meeting of the Auckland Society for the Protection of Infant Life in 1908 Dr Arthur Marsack stated that 'Any woman who could nurse her child, and would not, took the risk of being morally guilty of homicide by omission'.[35]

According to these observers, this failure to breastfeed was compounded by their ignorance of 'the rudimentary art of preparing food for their offspring'.[36] Thomas Kelly complained that 'the great bulk of mothers gave condensed milk or starchy food to infants under twelve months, which it was very well known infants could not digest'.[37] Attorney-General John Findlay claimed there was no excuse for 'dietetic disease', the major cause of infant death, since the methods of child-rearing were no longer 'haphazard, but have been reduced, as any well-instructed book will tell you, to an exact science'. He asserted that any 'long-experienced physician' could speak of the 'appalling' ignorance of many 'well-intentioned' mothers.[38] Seymour George lamented that young wives did not even know how to cook dinner for their husbands yet were responsible for infant health: 'The result is that many children die in the early stages of life'.[39] He claimed it was 'the duty of the State' to teach young girls housewifery, so that 'their husbands and families should not suffer from food badly cooked – a matter that is often the beginning of disease in people'.[40]

The Liberal government, which had been in power since 1891, did not shy away from acting upon recommendations and using the powers of the state to intervene in the lives of individuals for the greater public good.[41] According to Findlay, 'the first duty of the state [was] to increase the number of your good citizens'.[42] State intervention into the lives of certain infants had begun with the Infant Life Protection Act of 1896, reflecting similar trends in Britain.[43] A response to the scandals surrounding 'baby-farming', it required the licensing and police inspection of homes for children under five living away from their natural parents. By 1907, however, there were only four police matrons undertaking the inspections for the whole of New Zealand. The 1907 amendment to the 1896 Infant Life Protection Act had two parts. The first proposed that responsibility for overseeing the homes be transferred from the police to the Education Department and that trained nurses be employed to undertake the inspections. The second part followed British legislation passed that year concerning the notification of births. It proposed that the time limit for registering births be reduced from the current 62 days (under the 1876 Health Act), so that nurses could reach all new-born babies as quickly as possible. The resultant legislation reduced the time to 72 hours after a birth in a city or borough and 21 days in any other case. The stated aim was to reduce infant mortality among illegitimate children in particular, which was much higher than among legitimate children. To environmentalists, illegitimate children were also 'social capital'.[44]

In the discussions of the 1907 amendment, it was explained why women were more appropriate inspectors of homes than male police officers or even doctors. Despite all the talk of maternal ignorance, it appears that the experience of motherhood counted for a good deal. Findlay maintained that the medical profession 'have not the chance of knowing the thousand-and-one things which an intelligent and experienced mother has learnt in the upbringing, training, and feeding of her infant children'.[45] Nor did he believe that the majority of nurses had the appropriate skills: 'Most of them are young women who have had very little experience of the training of children. Certainly they have one thing in their favour – the maternal instinct – which we do not find in the breast of the police constable', yet for inspection of the homes he would prefer 'persons who had brought up families of their own'.[46] Others also believed that instinct and practice would make women better inspectors.[47] Dismissive of the work of the medical profession in the area, Irish-born John Barr spoke of 'the mother's instincts or a mother's heart'. He referred to St Pancras, London, where schools of nursing for mothers were being set up, including 'mothers' meetings': 'We sometimes hear the term "mothers' meeting" used in a frivolous way, but these are true mothers' meetings, where real, practical mothers exchange their confidences and opinions, and where they help each other'. In his view, 'It is the true-hearted home-making woman who will control the destinies of this young country'.[48] According to the diagnosis offered by male politicians and doctors, women were both the cause of, and the solution to, this particular health problem.

Dr Frederic Truby King and paediatrics

Philippa Mein Smith has commented that Dr Frederic Truby King 'in reality . . . knew little about babies'.[49] Yet his name became so widely associated with the infant welfare movement in New Zealand that he was the first New Zealand private citizen to receive a state burial when he died in 1938. He had become a national hero, and more than 50 years later would be included in a list of the twenty most influential people in twentieth-century New Zealand.[50] One of New Zealand's most eminent historians, Sir Keith Sinclair, described Truby King as 'arguably the most influential man in Pakeha society' in the early to mid-twentieth century.[51] The explanation for this apparent discrepancy is that, although Truby King was not a trained paediatrician, he was an intellectual and a fanatical enthusiast: once he had decided to make infant health his chosen area he read avidly and travelled widely, rubbing shoulders with world authorities in the new and growing profession of paediatrics. As a mark of his acceptance within that

LEFT: This postage stamp featuring Sir Frederic Truby King was issued on 14 May 1957, to celebrate the fiftieth anniversary of the founding of the Plunket Society.

BELOW: Truby King joins eminent child-health specialists at the Inter-allied Red Cross Conference at Cannes, April 1919. Standing: Dr Fritz Talbot; sitting from left: Professor Luther Emmett Holt, Sir Arthur Newsholme, Dr Samuel Hamill, Dr Frederic Truby King. Alexander Turnbull Library, National Library of New Zealand, Te Puna Matauranga O Aotearoa (ATL), C-26096-1/2

international community, he was made an honorary member of the American Pediatric Society in 1919.[52] He was invited to London during the First World War by Lord William Lee Plunket (Governor of New Zealand 1904–10), Lady Victoria Plunket, Major Evelyn Wrench and Miss Winifride Wrench of the Overseas Club, to set up an infant welfare centre under the auspices of the newly formed Babies of the Empire Society. This became the Mothercraft Training Society, which established a clinic in Earl's Court, London. The clinic thrived, in 1925 moving to bigger premises at Cromwell

House, Highgate. It grew to be an important model for infant welfare work in Britain, under the patronage of the Duchess of York, later Queen Elizabeth, wife of King George VI. It produced its own child-rearing manual which has been described as 'the major source of orthodoxy on infant care and management for the next thirty years'.[53] Truby King kept in close contact with the London Society. Immediately after the First World War, while still in London, he was invited along with Sir Arthur Newsholme[54] and Professor H. R. Kenwood, to represent the British Empire at the Child Welfare Section of the Inter-allied Red Cross Conference at Cannes, organised by an American paediatrician, Professor Emmett Holt.

Born near New Plymouth in Taranaki in 1858, King graduated in medicine at Edinburgh University in 1886 with first class honours and was awarded the Ettles Scholarship as the most distinguished graduate of his year. Two years later he was awarded the first Bachelor of Science in Public Health, a degree the university had instituted during his studentship. Alexander Simpson, Professor of Midwifery and Diseases of Women and Children at the University of Edinburgh, noted in a testimonial that, as a student, he had taken a 'high place' in his department.[55] Truby King returned to New Zealand in 1888 with his Glasgow-born wife, Isabella Cockburn Millar (known as Bella), and acted as medical superintendent of Wellington Public Hospital until 1889, when he was appointed medical superintendent of Seacliff Mental Asylum near Dunedin, at the time the largest mental hospital in the colony. Attached to the hospital was a large farming estate of 900 acres, and administration of this was one of Truby King's responsibilities. He gained a reputation for 'scientific farming' and his interest in animal husbandry led him to investigate human nutrition.[56]

Frederic Truby King and his wife Isabella in the garden of their Seacliff residence, 1904–7.
ATL, F-43223-1/2

He was particularly concerned with the rate of mortality among calves from scouring (a disease similar to diarrhoea in babies). Through studying tracts on artificial feeding systems, he brought about a significant reduction in cattle deaths.[57]

It appears that Truby King's lifelong interest in paediatrics stemmed at least partly from the physical condition of his adopted daughter, Mary. Originally called Esther, Mary was the second daughter of an attendant at Seacliff, Eliza Gordon ('Leilah') and co-worker William Gordon. After developing diabetes, Gordon returned to his mother's house. Since Leilah Gordon no longer had any family living in Dunedin, she was left in financial difficulties and was vulnerable to pressure when the Kings, now both in their mid-forties, offered to adopt baby Esther in 1904.[58] Isabella later explained that Mary was a 'very delicate baby . . . almost a skeleton' and was bottle fed with a mixture of cow's milk and cane sugar. She was not happy with Mary's progress. Frustrated by her husband's apparent lack of concern, she remarked, 'Fred, you're more interested in your animals than your own child', and suggested that he should devise a more suitable food, as he had done for his animals.[59] Thus he began to study the methods used for feeding infants in other parts of the world.

His enthusiasm for promoting infant welfare more generally appears to have stemmed partly from a colleague at Seacliff, Dr Alexander Falconer. Later medical superintendent of Dunedin Hospital (1910–27) and Ashburn Hall (1927–47), Falconer had been appointed assistant medical officer to Seacliff Asylum in 1898 after qualifying in medicine at Otago University. After serving in the South African War, Falconer took the public health course at University College London. He later explained how Professor

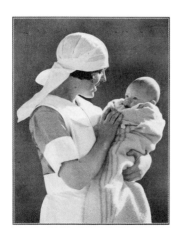

The King's adopted daughter, Mary Truby King, trained as a Karitane nurse in Auckland in 1925. Her continued involvement with the Plunket Society included the authorship of a textbook, *Mothercraft* (1934), and *Truby King, the Man: A Biography* (1948). She eventually married Anthony White, and settled in Australia, where she had two sons. *1908–1929 Twenty One Years*

Kenwood had laid particular stress on infant mortality in the course and had taken the students to see Dr G. F. McCleary's milk depot for infants at Battersea, London, in 1903. McCleary, the local medical officer of health, had set up the first milk depot in London in 1902; the idea had originated in France.[60] McCleary's scheme also involved the appointment of 'health visitors' to advise women on infant care in their own homes.[61] Keen to establish a similar depot in Dunedin, before returning to New Zealand in 1905, Falconer had written to McCleary asking for a copy of his second annual report. Back at Seacliff, Falconer alerted Truby King to trends in Britain and to current writings of American paediatricians. Falconer later claimed that McCleary's work at the Battersea milk depot had a direct influence on the infant welfare movement in New Zealand.[62]

Like many of his contemporaries, King was convinced by the arguments of national efficiency: as he declared in 1910, 'the destiny of the race is in the hands of its mothers'.[63] He was also, as noted earlier, an environmentalist. He believed that changing methods of child-rearing had far-reaching potential: 'the first five or six years of a child's life are by far the most momentous years of existence, because during this period the whole future being – potentialities of body, mind, and even character – are mainly determined'.[64] Truby King claimed to see in the asylum the end products of faulty feeding and used his annual reports as medical superintendent to expound his child-rearing ideas. For instance, in 1910 he wrote, 'Education in parenthood offers, I submit, the main hope for the reduction of insanity.'[65] He was supported by Inspector-General of Mental Hospitals, Dr Frank Hay, who stated in one of his annual reports that 'a potential underlying cause of insanity must be sought in early malnutrition'.[66] Towards the end of his life Truby King told the London-based Mothercraft Training Society that in order to deal with insanity one had to start with the baby. Disputing that insanity was hereditary, he averred, 'Bring up a child healthy and normal, make him vigorous, give him a good body, and the probability is that he will never enter an asylum.'[67]

Well aware of developments in early twentieth-century Britain, Truby King also looked to the United States where paediatrics was firmly established as a medical discipline. By the 1870s a group of physicians practised as specialists in children's disorders and infant feeding. To mark the growing specialty, they founded professional organisations and journals. The American Medical Association on Diseases of Children was formed in 1880 and the American Pediatric Society in 1888. *Archives of Pediatrics* was published from 1884, the *Transactions of the American Pediatric Society* from 1889 and *Pediatrics* from 1896. During the 1880s and 1890s methods of artificial feeding became a major topic of discussion in American paediatric literature. This arose from attempts to reduce mortality among babies in asylums and hospitals. Two influential figures were Thomas Morgan Rotch, Assistant Professor of Diseases of Children at Harvard University from 1888 and full professor five years later, and Luther Emmett Holt, who succeeded Abraham Jacobi as Professor of Diseases of Children at Columbia University College of Physicians and Surgeons in 1901.[68]

Apart from children's diseases, infant feeding remained the principal focus of paediatric studies in the United States between 1900 and 1915: in that period some 90 papers on the subject were delivered by American Pediatric Society members at annual scientific meetings.[69] From the 1890s, paediatricians, led by Rotch, constructed an intricate technology for bottle-feeding babies known as the percentage method (also known as human-ised milk). It was based on the notion that artificial feeding of infants would be more successful if cows' milk were altered to approximate more closely the chemical composition of mothers' milk. This led to the creation of elaborate formulae for modifying cows' milk. Suggested procedures became increasingly complicated until, in the words of one physician, 'some of the articles seemed terrifyingly like treatises on mathematics or higher astronomy'.[70]

There was never unanimity among paediatricians about the percentage method. Jacobi and some other American paediatricians rejected it even at the height of its popularity. Nonetheless, percentage feeding had been widely adopted and was taught at leading medical schools in the early twentieth century. Holt was one of its proponents and the subject took up a large portion of his lecture course at the College of Physicians and Surgeons. Edwards A. Park, who became Chairman of Paediatrics at Yale and Johns Hopkins and who had studied under Holt, claimed that percentage feeding was 'an important factor in the development of pediatrics as a specialty'.[71] The technology added to the prestige of paediatricians by making their discipline appear more scientific. It also made them attractive to families who wished and could afford to give their babies the most modern scientific care. [72]

Truby King viewed Rotch's method as 'the first serious attempt to grapple with the whole problem of infant feeding in a thoroughly broad, methodical, scientific spirit'.[73] Alerted by Falconer to Holt's book, *The Care and Feeding of Children*, King then read Holt's more substantial work, *The Diseases of Infancy and Childhood*.[74] In 1907 Truby King wrote an article for the *New Zealand Medical Journal*, on 'Physiological Economy in the Nutrition of Infants', for which he 'borrowed freely' from Holt's work.[75] Truby King issued a set of instructions for mothers on artificial feeding in 1906, citing Rotch as an authority. He pointed out that, as breastfed babies did not obtain much food during the first 36 hours, neither should artificially fed babies. If the baby appeared restless and hungry, one or two teaspoonfuls of a solution of milk sugar (1 ounce to a pint of boiled water)[76] should be given at intervals of two to three hours. After a week the baby should be given equal portions of the milk sugar solution and a whey mixture ('humanised milk', for which the recipe was provided). The latter should be gradually increased, until finally given pure by the end of the first month and continued until the baby was nine months old. From that point, the modified milk could be mixed with whole milk gradually and, by the age of one year, whole milk only would be required. For the first three weeks, about ten feedings per 24 hours were recommended, with one at night. The number gradually declined, until it was six by six months, with night feeds stopping after two months. 'We can only give the average requirement,' he wrote, 'leaving it to the mother to make such slight modifications as may appear necessary or desirable from the appetite, condition, and weight of the child.'[77]

Scrupulous cleanliness of equipment, the use of fresh milk and sugar of milk and correct heating of the milk mixture were crucial. King recommended the use of a thermometer so that the milk would be heated only to 155°F, because boiling 'injures or destroys something essential to the perfect nutrition of babies'. In 1905 he wrote, 'If mothers resent the trouble of using a thermometer, and deliberately and knowingly choose that their offspring shall draw in with their milk active living organisms to fight against them and weaken or kill them, the matter is one for the maternal conscience; no law intervenes to prevent the maiming or killing of children.'[78] Despite the fact that no micro-organism had been isolated in the case of infant diarrhoea,[79] Truby King and his medical contemporaries were persuaded by the importance of germs in causing disease.[80] The goal was to create a germ-free environment, which involved environmental and behavioural change. Both seed and soil were important: 'It is necessary to be guided by the laws of nature' was his dictum, using the analogy of nurturing plants and animals.[81]

Truby King's particular contribution to the New Zealand infant welfare movement was the introduction of American formulae for infant feeding. Despite this, he never wavered in his belief that breast milk was best, a

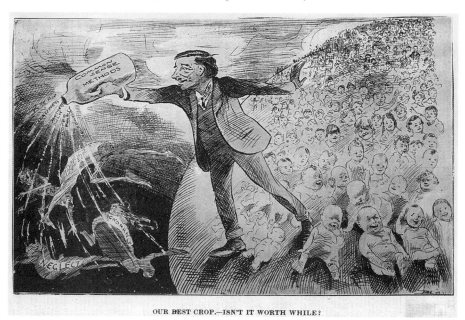

OUR BEST CROP.—ISN'T IT WORTH WHILE?

Dr Truby King's approach to infant welfare and his international fame are depicted, c. 1917.

view he claimed to have reached after observing, during a 1904 visit to Japan, the healthiness of breastfed Japanese infants. Some years later, he cited Dr John S. Fairbairn, consultant obstetrician of St Thomas's Hospital, London, and consulting physician to the Mothercraft Training Society. A staunch advocate of breastfeeding, Fairbairn claimed that the medical profession held some responsibility for the trend away from breastfeeding because they had excused and condoned rather than condemned the tendency to early bottle feeding.[82] King added that doctors had been 'deeply impressed by the conclusions of authorities such as Professor Holt, who asserted that among Society women in New York, three out of four mothers could not successfully suckle their babies, however much they might wish to do so'. King aimed to give mothers 'greater confidence in their power to breastfeed their offspring, and win them back to the natural expectation and desire to do so'.[83] He advocated breastfeeding to such an extent that following his death in 1938 the British journal *Mother and Child* maintained that he had 'hypnotise[d] thousands of mothers into the belief that breast feeding [was] *the* important factor in infant care'.[84]

Just as many doctors in the early twentieth century believed that 'civilised' women could not give birth naturally and required medical intervention,[85] so it was with breastfeeding. American paediatricians in particular, including Rotch, argued that although breast milk was the ideal food for infants, the conditions of modern life made its supply and quality unreliable.[86] These doctors increasingly viewed women, and especially 'nervous' upper- and middle-class women, as physiologically incapable of producing the quantity and quality of breast milk required to rear a healthy infant. Rotch maintained that the mammary gland 'could easily be adversely affected by nervous debility or other physiological problems'.[87] Truby King did not subscribe to the modern view that women could not give birth naturally; nor did he subscribe to the belief that modern women could not or should not breastfeed. 'It may be laid down as an axiom that Every Mother can nourish her offspring in the natural way. The exceptions are so rare and so striking as merely to prove the rule that, practically speaking, the breast-feeding of babies should be and could be universal.'[88] Yet, like Collins, he believed that hereditary patterns could be established unless checked. He argued that where the baby could not be breastfed, the best artificial feeding should be given to 'stem that progressive nutritional failure from generation to generation' – the well-fed, well-nourished bottle-fed baby girl would then grow up to be able to breastfeed her own children.[89]

With this in mind, he justified the time spent promoting a healthy system of artificial feeding. On the advice of Miss C. M. Beswick, the matron of Seacliff Mental Hospital, Truby King chose as his 'community nurse' a staff member of the hospital, Joanna McKinnon. While she was not a registered nurse, she was a 'bright, winsome' young Scottish woman[90] who learnt the formula and proceeded to teach mothers and caregivers how to modify cows' milk. McKinnon's obvious local success encouraged King to arrange for her to propagate his ideas more widely. Towards the end of 1905 she was boarded in Dunedin with the Murray family, and in 1908 she married their son. The *Evening Star* in December 1905 described McKinnon as 'the missionary in Dunedin of a rational system of feeding of infants'.[91] It was her personality and enthusiasm that attracted the interest of middle-class women, some of them wives of doctors who were sceptical about King's ideas.[92]

Together with an assistant, Miss A. M. O'Shea, who eventually became charge nurse at the Plunket Society's Dunedin headquarters, McKinnon supervised the setting up of a system of wholesale modification of cows' milk at the Taieri and Peninsula Milk Supply Company. The motives of Ambury, English and Company, Auckland's equivalent to Taieri, were later questioned by the *New Zealand Observer*, when it claimed in 1908 that 'the net result of the humanised milk movement so far has been to give a local milk firm an excellent free advertisement'.[93] McKinnon also continued to teach mothers to modify the milk in their own homes, and she drew King's attention to the plight of neglected infants (mostly illegitimate) who were boarded in licensed homes. This prompted him to use his seaside holiday home at Karitane to board two particularly malnourished babies whom he had found in a foster home, and marked the start of a hospital system for babies, at a time when infants were not normally admitted to general hospitals. It also led to the foundation of a training school for the new 'Plunket' nurses. By 1917 the Karitane-Harris Hospital, as it was then called, could accommodate about 19 mothers and their babies. The training course lasted three months for general trained nurses and six months for obstetric nurses, with a training fee of £15. 'Karitane' nurses, who were not registered nurses, were also trained there as nannies. Their training lasted for 12 months and cost £20. [94]

Maternalists take charge

With a wide public and political appreciation of the importance of 'infant life preservation', and an apparently clear solution to the problem, the responsibility for the infant welfare movement was soon picked up, in New Zealand as elsewhere, by middle-class women. In the United States, Molly Ladd-Taylor described how, by 1914, 'moved by the seemingly universal "pang of motherhood" and certain that they had a special role to play in the community by virtue of being mothers', thousands of middle-class women had taken up social service work; one of their special concerns was infant health.[95]

In New Zealand, at an enthusiastic public gathering at the Dunedin Town Hall on 14 May 1907, it was decided to form a society to continue the work done by Truby King and McKinnon. King declared that 'the Society's work might now be very well left to the ladies. It [is] a work for the women to attend to and not for me.'[96] A further meeting, two weeks later, was 'attended principally by ladies'.[97] The new organisation would be called the Society for Promoting the Health of Women and Children, following Truby King's advice that it was not possible to dissociate the health of the infant from that of the mother. Although the organisation was incorporated on 27 February 1908 as the Society for the Promotion of the Health of Women and Children, Lady Victoria Plunket, the wife of the Governor of New

Zealand, who was to become so intimately involved with the society, described it in January 1908 as the Society for the Protection of Infant Life, indicating where the emphasis lay.[98]

In Christchurch the Mothers' Union, an Anglican women's group formed in 1900, had invited Truby King early in 1907 to give a lecture to their monthly meeting on the 'Preservation of Infant Life'. In August the union formed a sub-committee to look into setting up a society similar to that in Dunedin, and, at a public meeting on 12 September, the Canterbury Society for the Preservation of Infant Life was launched. At another public meeting in the Wellington Town Hall on 21 October 1907, it was decided that the local Society for the Protection of Women and Children (set up in 1893) would undertake work in the capital like that done by the Dunedin organisation. In March 1908 the nucleus of an executive was elected from the committee of the Society for the Protection of Women and Children to establish a separate society and the Wellington branch of the Society for the Promotion of the Health of Women and Children was inaugurated at a meeting on 16 March 1908, convened by Lady Plunket.[99]

Lady Plunket first heard of Truby King's work at the October 1907 Wellington meeting. Already the president of the Mothers' Union, less than a month later she agreed to become the first patroness of the Dunedin society. She was, however, much more than a figurehead. Within a short time she had arranged a meeting in Auckland that led to the establishment of the Society for the Protection of Infant Life there.[100] She also helped to found societies in New Plymouth and Napier in March and June 1908 respectively. Her interest and social standing gave the new societies status. She also showed an interest in individual cases: in early 1908 she offered to pay for a sickly baby and his mother to travel from Auckland to the new Dunedin baby hospital. She was at the time employing a nurse to supervise the feeding and management of several babies in Auckland.[101]

As a prelude to setting up the Auckland society, Lady Plunket wrote a letter to the *New Zealand Herald* explaining the scheme. She pointed out that nurses, trained in Dunedin in 'the scientific and accurate feeding and management of infants', worked under a local committee, gave lectures and demonstrations by invitation, and personally visited and instructed any mother who asked them to do so, continuing such visits as long as they could be of assistance. She also noted that the society organised and supervised the supply of humanised milk, and concluded, 'The scheme which I have placed before your readers is not an untried novelty; it is working successfully at Home and abroad.'[102]

LEFT: Lady Victoria Plunket (1875–1968), c. 1905. S. P. Andrew Collection, ATL, G-14571-1/1

RIGHT: Joanna McKinnon receiving the first Lady Plunket nurse medal from Lady Plunket while Truby King looks on, 7 April 1908. Plunket Society Annual Report 1929–30

By mid-1908 there were six separate societies. In June, at Lady Plunket's suggestion, they became branches of the New Zealand Society for the Health of Women and Children, informally known as the Plunket Society. The Dunedin branch became the governing body of the society, because the baby hospital and nurse training centre were located there. Lady Plunket sought the advice of the Chief Health Officer, Dr James Mason, about a name for the nurses she intended to employ under the new society's aegis. Her suggestion of 'Dominion Nurses' was flatly rejected by Mason, who urged her to call them 'Plunket Nurses'. This name was publicly proposed at the meeting in Wellington in March 1908 by Dr William Collins,[103] and in April Joanna McKinnon was awarded the first Lady Plunket nurse medal.

The number of branches of the new society grew rapidly in the following years. In 1912 Health Minister Robert Heaton Rhodes, a Plunket Society supporter, released Truby King from official duties at Seacliff to undertake a national lecturing tour to help promote the society. By the end of the tour the number of branches reached 70.[104] As Gordon Parry has written of the tour, Truby King 'would electrify the audience, galvanising them into action on behalf of mother and child, and the following morning some worthy and hitherto unruffled housewife would wake and find herself the president of a local branch of the Society which would absorb every fleeting moment for the rest of her life'.[105] But it was more than King's persuasiveness that led to widespread involvement: the Plunket Society met a need among middle-class women in early twentieth-century New Zealand society.

From the beginning, many wealthy and prominent people were attracted to the cause, not just as philanthropists, but as participants. Much of the early planning in Dunedin was done at Olverston, the elegant home of Jewish businessman David Theomin and his wife, Marie, who became a committee member of the society and subsequently honorary treasurer. Their daughter, Dorothy, was also involved for many years, serving on the dominion executive from 1941 to 1955. Another member of the original Dunedin committee, and later vice-president, was the wife of Leslie Harris, whose father was the wealthy Jewish businessman Wolf Harris. It was possibly her influence that led to the offer of his house and estate at Andersons Bay for the society's hospital, relocated from its original site at Truby King's holiday home at Karitane, in 1910. The new hospital was called the Karitane-Harris Hospital. Wolf Harris, who had also displayed his interest in medicine by endowing the chair of physiology at Otago University in 1903, continued to support Plunket. In 1917 from London he acceded to Truby King's request to pay for an extension to the home.[106] Mrs Leslie Harris, having also moved to Britain, was on the executive of the Mothercraft Training Society for many years from its founding in 1918.[107]

The first president of the Dunedin Society was Kathleen Hosking, wife of a local magistrate. In 1922, after Sir John Hosking had been appointed a judge of the Supreme Court and moved to Wellington, Kathleen Hosking became president of the Wellington branch. The early Dunedin committee included the wives of other prominent local citizens, such as the wife of the current mayor of Dunedin, John Loudon, and the wife of the *Evening Star* editor and later Legislative Council member, Mark Cohen.

The recruitment of wealthy business interests was replicated elsewhere. In Auckland, it included both the wife and sister of Arthur Myers, a prominent Jewish businessman, mayor of Auckland 1905–9 and Liberal MP 1910–21 (later knighted for his services to Auckland). Cintra, the Myers' residence in Symonds Street, was the site of garden fetes for Plunket fundraising. Although they lived in London after the First World War, where Vera Myers also joined the executive of the Mothercraft Training Society, the couple retained an interest in Auckland Plunket. In 1923 Arthur Myers

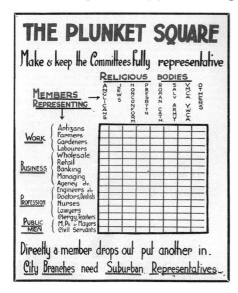

THE PLUNKET SQUARE

Make & keep the Committees fully representative

RELIGIOUS BODIES

MEMBERS REPRESENTING →

WORK { Artisans / Farmers / Gardeners / Labourers

BUSINESS { Wholesale / Retail / Banking / Managing Agency etc.

PROFESSION { Engineers etc. / Doctors, Dentists / Nurses / Lawyers

PUBLIC MEN { Clergy, Teachers / M.P.s & Mayors / Civil Servants

Directly a member drops out put another in.

City Branches need Suburban Representatives.

'The Plunket Square.' It was claimed that the first committee had followed these guidelines, and committees were encouraged to be fully representative, although there is no evidence that new members were selected on this basis. Note that Jews, who made up 0.2 per cent of the population, were listed second after Anglicans, who made up 41 per cent of the population in 1911. This was probably in recognition of the contributions of the Jewish business sector. The square was still being reproduced on conference reports as late as 1976.

donated £5,000 for the establishment of a Karitane Home in Auckland.[108] Others involved in the early Auckland Plunket committee included Emily Nathan, the wife of Alfred Nathan, another prominent member of the local Jewish community and director of a large merchant house, L. D. Nathan and Co. Ltd. His daughter-in-law Simone Nathan was also involved with Auckland Plunket for many years. Kate McCosh Clark, the widow of James McCosh Clark who had served as Mayor of Auckland from 1880 to 1883, succeeded Emily Nathan as president in 1909. Other committee members included the wife of Albert Devore, Mayor of Auckland 1886–9, and Eva Bagnall, the daughter of Lemuel Bagnall, Mayor of Auckland 1910–11.[109]

In Christchurch the new society's first major fund-raiser was a garden fete held in October 1907 at Elmwood, the home of lawyer and politician, Robert Heaton Rhodes and his wife Jessie. The Rhodes were well known for philanthropic efforts around Christchurch: in 1896 they had helped Nurse Sybilla Maude set up the first district nursing scheme in New Zealand. As Minister of Public Health (1912–15), Heaton Rhodes opened the fourth general conference of the society in Wellington in 1914. In 1917 he and his wife donated £1,000 for the Karitane hospital in Christchurch.[110]

It was not uncommon for the wives of politicians, from both the Reform and Liberal parties, to become involved in Plunket. These included, among others, the wives of Robert Stout, MP for Caversham 1875–9, Dunedin East 1884–7 and the City of Wellington, 1893–8; Joseph Ward, Prime Minister 1906–12; James Allen, MP from 1892 and acting Prime Minister 1916–18;

Thomas Sidey, MP for Caversham and South Dunedin 1901–28; Josiah Alfred Hanan, MP for Invercargill 1899–1925; George Fowlds, Minister of Health 1906–9; and William Massey, Prime Minister 1912–25.

Plunket committees also attracted the wives of local doctors. Bella Truby King was a prime example of this, serving on the Dunedin committee and as president from 1910 to 1914. Another was Truby King's niece Olive Allen, married to Dr Sydney Allen who had been assistant medical officer at Seacliff Asylum and was a surgeon at the Dunedin Hospital when his wife became involved with Plunket. One of the vice-presidents of the original Wellington branch committee was Margaret Fell, the wife of the editor of the *New Zealand Medical Journal,* Dr Walter Fell.[111] The wives of Drs William Young and James Mason were also on the original Wellington committee.[112] Young and his wife became lifelong friends of Truby King, and both husband and wife took on the role of patron of the Wellington branch.[113] In Auckland Maude Parkes, the wife of Dr William Parkes, was secretary and later president of the local Plunket branch. William Parkes eventually became chief medical officer of Auckland's Karitane Hospital from 1923 until his death in 1933. Truby King later commented that the establishment of Plunket in Auckland owed much to the Parkes.[114] This pattern was repeated around the country: the Westport branch committee boasted five doctors' wives in 1914.[115]

Another notable group were the wives of religious leaders. The president of the Dunedin Society from 1908 to 1910 was the wife of the Reverend Dr Thomas Nisbet, Presbyterian minister of the First Church, Dunedin, since 1904. Auckland's early committees included the wives of two Anglican bishops, Grace Crossley and Mary Averill, who joined the committee in 1915. (Bishop Alfred Averill himself was president of the local branch of the Society for the Protection of Women and Children.)

It would be misleading to see the appointment of these women solely in terms of their husbands' wealth, position and accomplishments. Rather, they tended to be active across a range of welfare organisations and participated in public life in their own right. For example, Christina Massey, president of Plunket's Wellington branch 1918–22, was involved with a range of organisations and was awarded the CBE in recognition of her services in 1918, and in 1926 the GBE, the first woman in New Zealand to receive the award. Susanna Hanan, a founder member of the Invercargill branch in 1910 and later active in the Wellington and Dunedin branches, was also involved with the New Zealand Free Kindergarten Union among other things. Helena Sidey was also active in a number of organisations, including the National Council of Women. A committee member of Plunket from 1912 and president 1936–7, Sidey probably had a special interest in health having almost completed a medical degree at Otago University herself. A fellow Plunket committee member was Margaret Ann Jackson, who was also involved with the local Society for the Protection of Women and Children. Lily Atkinson, on the original Wellington Plunket branch committee, was also active in the Kindergarten Schools Society, among other things, and was president of the New Zealand Society for the Protection of Women and Children, 1903–1911, and vice-president until her death in 1921.[116] Another member of the original Wellington committee was Anna Stout, who had helped to found the Wellington branch of the Society for the Protection of Women and Children in 1897.[117] Yet another was Mary Richmond who founded the free kindergarten movement in Wellington in 1905.[118]

Rachelina Hepburn Armitage, who set up the South Canterbury Plunket branch, was the sister of Reform Party politician and later Minister of Finance, William Downie Stewart. She was the first New Zealand woman to graduate with a BA from the University of Oxford, and while in England had become involved with leading British social reformers such as Octavia Hill. When she returned to New Zealand in 1899, she combined marriage and family with public activities, remaining active in the Plunket Society until 1953, by which time she was 80 years of age. Annie McVicar, who was the first secretary of the Wellington Plunket branch and a vice-president for many years, had a wide community involvement, for which she was awarded an MBE in 1938.[119] At that time she was still vice-president of the Wellington branch.[120]

Sisters of religious orders were also attracted to the cause. Probably the most famous was the Catholic nun, Mary Joseph Aubert, who was on the original Wellington branch committee.[121] Then aged 73, she was already famous for initiating district nursing work among the poor in Wellington, and was dubbed by Dr Agnes Bennett 'The Grand Old Woman of Wellington'.[122] The previous year she had opened Our Lady's Home of Compassion for young needy children, which became the first institution in Wellington to adopt Truby King's infant feeding advice.[123] She continued an active involvement for many years, later becoming a vice-president until her death in 1926.[124] In Dunedin the early committee included Sisters Ernestine and Evelyn. The Auckland committee included Anglican Superior Hannah Dawson, renowned for her social work around Auckland, and Sister Esther Charles, who ran a 'mission' from her home in Picton Street, which eventually formed the basis of the Presbyterian Social Services. She was awarded an MBE in 1919 and became one of the first women justices of the peace in 1926.

Some women with a nursing background were drawn to Plunket's voluntary structure. Alice Holford, matron of Dunedin's St Helens Hospital from 1905 to 1927, was on the original Plunket committee in 1907. She was also active in other organisations such as the National Council of Women. Another matron who served on a Plunket committee was Jessie Orr, lady superintendent of Auckland Hospital. The Auckland committee included Mrs Hutchinson, well known for her work as matron of the Door of Hope Home (a Methodist charitable institution for 'fallen' women and abandoned children). The first committee of the Wellington branch included the matrons of the local St Helens Hospital and the Salvation Army Maternity Home.[125]

Women doctors also became involved. They may have felt a particular affinity for this area of health because of their gender, or they may have been pressured by the social climate to consider this work appropriate.[126] One such doctor was Daisy Elizabeth Platts-Mills, who was Wellington Plunket's first president and was still an honorary physician to the society 30 years later.[127] She combined an active involvement in the Wellington branch of Plunket with private practice and with participation in other voluntary organisations such as the Mothers' Union.[128] Dr Eleanor Baker, a general practitioner in Te Kopuru and later a medical officer in the School Medical Service, wrote to the Auckland Plunket branch in 1912 asking for advice about forming a local Plunket Society.[129] New Zealand's first female medical graduate, Dr Emily Siedeberg, who was medical officer (and then superintendent) of St Helens Hospital, Dunedin, from 1905 to 1938, was sympathetic to Plunket and on the committee for the society's first year and continued to be a useful ally.[130] Siedeberg was not a Truby King supporter, but that did not stop her from backing Plunket. The same can be said of Dr Doris Gordon who served for a time as president of Plunket's Stratford branch.[131] One practitioner apparently found it hard to decide whether her role as woman or as doctor should take precedence: in 1919 Dr Hilda Northcroft joined the Auckland branch committee but the following year resigned from the 'Ladies Committee' to join the advisory board, which included local medical men.

Another professional woman attracted to Plunket was Winifred Lily Boys-Smith. As the first professor of home science and domestic arts at the University of Otago 1911–20, she sought to raise the status of domestic work by providing a strong scientific and technical training. She was a Plunket committee member in Dunedin from 1911 to 1917.[132]

Many wealthy and notable women of the early twentieth century followed the lead of Lady Plunket and took up the cause to 'help the mothers and save the babies'. While women found personal satisfaction in the involvement and forged friendships, they also took up the cause as an act of citizenship. In the view of a long-term Plunket Society committee member, Susanna Hanan, 'women should be interested in matters of public importance'.[133] As opposed to feminists, who fought for the rights of women in the workplace and equality with men, these formidable women were maternalists: they set out to promote the interests of women as mothers and the welfare of their children, and made the society their own.

CHAPTER 2

A Professional Organisation

A women's society

The Plunket Society soon adopted a formal framework. A 'constitution of rules' was drawn up when the Dunedin society was incorporated in 1908, and sanctioned at a conference with the Department of Health in 1913.[1] At the first annual conference in Wellington in 1909 it was decided to drop 'Promotion' from the title to avoid the risk of confusion with the Society for the Protection of Women and Children. In 1915 the society was granted royal patronage, becoming the Royal New Zealand Society for the Health of Women and Children. The central council established in 1917 comprised representatives from around the country but with an executive based in Dunedin, and a paid secretary. Gwen Hoddinott was appointed secretary to the council and the Dunedin branch, at a salary of £78 per annum, a post she was to retain until her death in 1941.[2] Initially the Dunedin branch paid a third of her salary.[3] On the advice of lawyer John Hosking the branches were separately incorporated, bound together by common rules yet controlling their own affairs, which was, he explained, akin to the British Empire.[4] In September 1917 the council wrote to the government, asking that Truby King be released from duties in order to respond to the request to render 'National and Patriotic service' in Britain. The council pointed out that the whole society was running so well and harmoniously that they had no anxiety that Truby King's absence would interfere with the efficiency and progress of the work.[5]

It has been noted that Plunket attracted a large number of middle-class women. There may have been certain social expectations that women become involved in local voluntary work: it probably enhanced their social status. Such work was clearly expected of the wives of doctors, as a socially aspiring professional group in the early twentieth century.[6] Some women undoubtedly joined Plunket to extend their social networks. For example, Simone Nathan, newly arrived from Paris, secured an invitation to the local Plunket committee as an entry into Auckland society.[7] For many years from 1911 Lady Sidey combined her involvement in voluntary welfare

Truby King with Plunket Society presidents outside Parliament buildings, Wellington, c. 1920. June Starke Collection, ATL, F-74992-1/2

organisations including Plunket with the presidency of the St Clair Ladies' Golf Club. Plunket's roll call of prominent citizens certainly meant chances to extend networks. An 'At Home' in relation to Plunket's Dominion Conference in Wellington in 1914 'afforded the opportunity to many fine women, working in a common cause, to make one another's acquaintance'. The local press report noted that Lady Liverpool was the guest of honour and that the Prime Minister's wife, Christina Massey, was also present. As was usual at the time, the reporter also described the dress of the most notable attendees.[8]

Joining voluntary organisations was a route into public life for middle-class women for whom paid employment was not an option.[9] It enabled them to extend their activities beyond the confines of the private sphere and to lead more purposeful lives. Sir James Allen, whose wife was heavily involved with Plunket, thought it was 'good for the women'. He commented in 1914 on the 'influence which the work had, not upon the mothers and children only, but also upon the ladies who were interested in the work'. If he 'might be permitted to say so with all humility', he had noticed over the previous six years 'the enormous change that was occurring over some of the women in this country because of the interest they took in this work'.[10] When Amy Carr, president of Plunket from 1914 to

Voluntary involve-
ment in Plunket
meant much more
than fundraising
and attending social
events. Here vol-
unteers are doing
Plunket washing
in Armagh Street,
Christchurch, during
the 1918 influenza
epidemic. *The Press*
(Christchurch)
Collection, PAColl-3031,
ATL, G-8615-1/1

1919, died in 1919 the Central Council said that she had 'devoted herself wholeheartedly to the cause of mothers and babies'.[11] Involvement in Plunket was more than a social activity: it meant a considerable investment in time, energy and even resources.

Some felt drawn to the work through their own experiences as mothers. Lady Plunket, mother of eight, pronounced on the many crimes she herself had unwittingly committed in the nursery.[12] As an annual report of the society explained, 'As women we all recognise the grave shortcomings of our own upbringing and education, and we are merely doing our best in a practical way to establish a better state of things for the present and future generations.'[13] Plunket was described as a mutual aid society: 'Mutual help of this kind – the giving of timely assistance, and the passing on of know-ledge from one mother to another – is undoubtedly one of the most potent and effective factors in the spread of enlightenment regarding health in the home, motherhood, and the rearing of strong capable children'.[14] Most of the committee members began their involvement once they had started a family, though there were some notable exceptions. Neither Jessie Rhodes nor Annie McVicar had children, yet both were long-serving Plunket committee members. Their roles could be described as 'public motherhood': as women they claimed an empathy with mothers. Although she never married, Mary Richmond, one of the vice-presidents of the original Wellington branch committee, declared at the age of 88 that 'you cannot find anywhere a more highly educated woman than an experienced and successful mother'.[15]

Plunket's committee members became personally involved with new mothers, especially in the early years when there were few trained nurses. The society's 1912 annual report proudly proclaimed that 'In every province of New Zealand there are women . . . who generously and gratuitously carry on the functions of local Plunket Nurses and do an inestimable service for the mothers and babies with whom they chance to come in contact or who seek their help'. One such mother in Otago had helped over 100 women. The 'incalculable amount of good' she had done was indicated by the 'grateful and appreciative acknowledgements' that had been sent to the society.[16] Delegates at the 1914 conference discussed the 'best means by which members of the Committees could get into personal touch with the mothers and babies'. It was agreed that if 'tactful, sympathetic' committee members could visit some of the homes, this would greatly increase its educational influence – and help the Plunket nurses.[17] At that time there were 27 Plunket nurses and 72 honorary secretaries.[18] The Wellington branch had noted at a meeting in 1915 an 'interesting' letter from a Mrs Barker who, living beyond the reach of a Plunket nurse, had saved the life of a neighbour's very delicate baby entirely through studying the Plunket Society's book and by writing to a Plunket nurse for further information.[19] The 1917 Plunket conference recommended that, where practicable, each branch should organise a band of volunteers to assist mothers with young families, either by taking the children out or by giving general assistance in the home.[20] In 1919, when the supply of nurses could not meet the demand, the Central Council advised branches that committee members should keep the Plunket clinics open, and, in urgent cases, communicate with the nearest Plunket nurse.[21] The women themselves were to dispense advice if no Plunket nurse were available. As a 1914 circular to branches stated, 'The Society will attain its highest aims to the fullest extent only when all its executive members [i.e. its volunteers] grasp thoroughly the meaning, scope and purpose of the Health Mission they have taken in hand.'[22]

Where nurses were employed, committee members oversaw their work. The Auckland branch honorary secretary, who was not herself a nurse, wrote in 1915, 'Of course our nurses always write full accounts of their work which they bring to me for perusal, and I then ask them to explain any unusual case which I see there. They also always read their reports to the meeting.'[23] In 1915 the Wellington branch decided that the nurses should have case books which were to be kept in the committee room so as to be accessible to committee members at any time.[24]

'Save the Babies Garden Party' at Cintra, the residence of Arthur and Vera Myers, Symonds Street, Auckland, 1917. *Auckland Weekly News*, 29 November 1917, ATL, N-P 313

One of the early concerns of the voluntary committees was the quality of milk supplies. In 1914 the society sent a deputation to the Prime Minister to press for municipal control of milk supplies.[25] Over the next few years the Auckland branch set up a sub-committee on milk supplies, sent a deputation to the Minister of Health, wrote to authorities in Paris and New York and invited to the annual general meeting a speaker who had experience of dairies in Denmark.[26] Milk was discussed at length at the 1917 general conference, and resolutions passed, 'that a closer inspection should be made of all cattle, in the hope of reducing tuberculosis, and that this Remit be placed before the Government for consideration'.[27]

In 1917 the new society adopted an idea current overseas: the holding of a Baby Saving Week, for publicity and fund-raising purposes. Shortly before the war Health Weeks had been held in Britain and Baby Weeks in the United States, France and Denmark. Britain set up a National Baby Week Council in 1917, with Lady Plunket among its members, and held a National Baby Week in July.[28] New Zealand followed suit. Christchurch raised £7,000 for its baby hospital through such an event.[29] Fund-raising was aimed primarily at the social élite, through the holding of garden parties and drama performances. The *New Zealand Observer* regretted the lack of any attempt to reach a wider public, commenting on the disappointing turnout for a Plunket dramatic evening and advising that the 'really charitable' should have been targeted rather than the 'butterflies of society who frequent Government House'.[30] Involvement in Plunket at this time appeared to be exclusive, which may in itself have helped to attract the rich and powerful.

The women of Plunket used their considerable contacts to their advantage. For instance, the politician and lawyer, Thomas (later Sir Thomas) Sidey, helped them to become an incorporated society.[31] The help of John Hosking, another lawyer and later a judge of the Supreme Court, was also solicited to draw up their constitution. This required branches to form an advisory board of three or more men (preferably including a doctor, solicitor and businessman). Women, however, made the decisions. Plunket's honorary secretary, Jean Glendinning, explained in 1916, 'Ours is essentially a woman's mission – a woman's society appealing to women. When men have helped us it has hitherto been in the capacity of advisers and friendly helpers whom we could turn to when in doubt – never as dictators of the policy and methods we were to pursue.'[32]

Relationship with the government

In 1914 Benjamin Broadbent, Mayor of Huddersfield in England, who had pioneered an infant welfare service there and who was, according to Truby King, 'a household word in England for everything bearing on the care of mother and child', commented that New Zealand's scheme 'should have the closest attention and study in the working out of a national system in Great Britain'. What impressed Broadbent was the 'the unification of State and voluntary effort': 'It is not co-operation merely; it is identity. The Society has the management of the whole work, and the State supports it both financially and morally.'[33]

Sir Joseph Ward, New Zealand's Prime Minister at the time Plunket was established, did indeed support it wholeheartedly. He attended the public meeting that led to the founding of the Auckland branch in February 1908; his wife Ada had attended the equivalent Wellington meeting some months earlier, and later became a branch vice-president.[34] In December 1907, before the society was even incorporated, the government pledged a pound for pound subsidy up to £100 to each of the four centres, and another £100 to the Karitane Home in Dunedin.[35] The following year this was increased to £200 for each centre and £500 to the Karitane Home. Following a deputation by society members to Ward in 1910, the subsidy was increased to £500 for the Karitane Home and £50 for each Plunket nurse, with a maximum of sixteen nurses in eight specified towns (Auckland, Wellington, Napier, New Plymouth, Christchurch, Dunedin, Timaru and Invercargill). This limit was lifted under a new agreement negotiated with the Minister of Health, Heaton Rhodes, in 1912. The subsidy was increased to £1 4s for each pound raised voluntarily to a maximum of £100 for each nurse.[36] The subsidy to the Karitane Home, now called the Karitane-Harris Hospital, was increased to £750 per annum.

Plunket also enjoyed the support of Ward's successor, William Massey, who headed the new Reform government elected in 1912 and remained in office until his death in 1925. Equally supportive was Defence Minister James Allen (he was knighted in 1917), who served as acting Prime Minister for extended periods during the First World War while Massey was overseas. As has been noted, both Massey's and Allen's wives were involved with Plunket. In 1917 Allen 'strongly eulogised the work of the Society and its worth to the Dominion'[37] and Massey declared that he was 'in full accord with the objects of the Plunket Society'.[38] The following year he formally opened the Mothercraft Training Centre in London and became a vice-president of the Mothercraft Training Society.[39]

Other politicians also backed Plunket. In 1911 a Plunket deputation convened by Liberal MP, Thomas Sidey, waited on the Prime Minister to ask that the usual subsidy be granted to the society. Addressing Plunket's fourth annual conference in July 1914, Health Minister Rhodes declared that 'the Government was quite in accord with the ideals of the Society, and was ever ready to give it substantial support'. A 1917 Plunket deputation to the Prime Minister was led by James Alexander Young, a Waikato dentist, who was a Reform MP and later Minister of Health.

The Department of Public Health had been set up in 1901 and the first Chief Health Officer, Dr James Mason, supported this new initiative in infant welfare. He held office until 1909 when the post of inspector-general of hospitals, occupied by Dr Thomas Valintine since 1907, was combined with that of chief health officer. The department had its own plans for infant welfare. Shortly after Plunket was established, Dr Agnes Bennett, medical officer to Wellington's St Helens Hospital, was sent to Sydney by the Health Department to investigate Dr William Armstrong's infant-welfare campaign and on her return a pamphlet was issued.[40] Yet Valintine felt that using the services of nurses solely for mothers and babies was a waste of resources; they should be combined with the work of district nurses generally. At the 1913 conference between Plunket and the Health Department it was agreed that, in 'the highest interest of the State', every woman in the country should be 'induced to avail herself of the services offered by the Society'. It was also agreed, however, that additional appointments of nurses had to be approved by the Health Department.[41] When Westport's Plunket committee applied to the department for a grant for a Plunket nurse the following year, it was told this would be forthcoming only if the Plunket work were combined with that of a district nurse. This was the beginning of a longstanding dispute. Plunket's president, Amy Carr, responded, 'emphatically protest[ing] against any such interference with the plan of the work of the Society'.[42] Valintine, a former country general practitioner, retorted that, 'If the Department pays the subsidy it naturally has a right to see that the money is well spent and it will certainly take up this attitude whatever your Society may think to the contrary . . . . and you will pardon me for saying that I do not regard you as being in a position to say how the Government subsidies can be best devoted and the Nurses' services best utilised. A certain amount of training and technical knowledge is required before anyone can give an opinion on that subject.'[43]

Plunket's volunteers were not to be cowed by a health-service male bureaucrat, however lofty his status. They resolutely believed that technical knowledge was not as important as a woman's instincts. They argued that they had a natural right as women to control a health service relating to women and children. The gendered nature of the dispute was spelled out in Jean Glendinning's 1916 letter that stressed the society's status as 'a woman's mission – a woman's society appealing to women', in which she postulated that 'any attempt to introduce bureaucratic formalism would be fatal to the further success and progress of the cause we have at heart'.[44]

Plunket leaders also felt it important to distinguish their scheme from the activities of the charitable aid boards, the colonial equivalent of the English Poor Law system.[45] The latter were associated in the public mind with 'charity', and 'we are most anxious to keep that element out of anything in connection with this work'. They considered it important to stress that, although the functions of the society were 'broadly humanitarian', they were 'not "patronising or charitable", or even in the ordinary sense "philanthropic", but essentially "patriotic and educational"'.[46]

Truby King responded to Valintine's suggestion that the work of Plunket

Branch locations, 1914. The network of nurses was already extensive but note the concentration around Dunedin and Southland. Report of Fourth General Conference 1914

and district nurses be combined, that the latter visited 'the sick poor of the indigent class, who receive it as a charity' and that 'the self-reliant class' would regard it as an 'absolute humiliation' to see a district nurse. As a mark of Plunket's difference, he noted that Plunket nurses were invited into the homes of the medical profession, which pointed to their acceptance among 'the higher professional classes'.[47] This was indeed to be a feature that distinguished Plunket from many overseas schemes and, in the long term, one of its strengths. Neville Mayman, commissioned by the New South Wales Legislative Assembly to conduct an inquiry into the welfare of mothers and babies in New Zealand, explained that the Plunket Society had 'taken the rather unusual course of appealing primarily to the better-to-do and more intelligent women of the community'. Also equating social status with intelligence, Truby King had told him that the society would have wider appeal by targeting the 'most intelligent' and 'most highly receptive members of the community' rather than restricting its activities 'to those of lesser intelligence'.[48]

Valintine did not get any support for his opposition to Plunket from Rhodes, but his successor, George Warren Russell, appointed in 1915, was sympathetic to the department's view. In 1916 Russell explained to Carr that from his brief spell as Minister of Health in 1912 he had tried to help the society, but now felt that it had not grown as he had hoped it would.

He pointed out that there were only three Plunket nurses for the whole of Auckland, which contained one-third of the country's population. The correspondence between Russell and the Plunket Society shows that the women who controlled Plunket could be patronising in their response to male criticism. 'We feel strongly that this remark is entirely uncalled for' was the response to one comment; 'we can find nothing to excuse your writing to us in this vein,' they scolded.[49] Carr affirmed that the Health Department itself was holding back the hiring of more nurses. She also took issue with Russell's statement that in districts where committees had been formed without Plunket nurses their work must be nominal, pointing out that many women had voluntarily assumed the role of Plunket nurse.[50]

With their emphasis on mutual aid, the women of Plunket felt united in a universal sisterly bond, with a shared experience of motherhood. Dissociating their movement from the work of district nurses also meant dissociating themselves from the new native health nurses, appointed under the Health Department's new Native Health Nursing Service in 1911, and consequently from the plight of Maori mothers and babies. This was left to the Health Department. The universal sisterhood did not extend to Maori.[51]

In September 1918 Russell wrote to the society that as six Plunket branches had sufficient money in hand to pay working expenses for the current year it had been decided to alter the basis of the subsidy: for the current year £3,000 would be paid instead of £4,400.[52] As a fixed sum was being allocated, he was happy for further branches to be set up and further nurses employed. The society objected strongly to being penalised for its successful fund-raising and made mileage out of the current 'national efficiency' concerns arising from the war, stressing that Plunket's work was of 'national importance, especially at the present time'.[53] Whether or not they were personally inspired by the cause of national efficiency, they certainly used it to their advantage. Asking for government assistance in 1915, they referred to 'the terrible sacrifice of life now going on', which gave 'additional urgency to the need for education in mothercraft'.[54] They also used their political influence and contacts in the fight against the Health Department. In 1917, noting that relations with the department were causing anxiety, Carr held that they needed to place their views before the government.[55] This had every chance of success since Plunket's vice-president was the wife of acting Prime Minister James Allen.

Plunket was also generally supported by the press. One local paper wrote that Russell's position was 'indefensible' and that it was 'surprising to find a progressive, open-hearted Liberal like Mr Russell dealing out what in other political days he himself would have called a real Tory trick'.[56] Russell backed down and paid a grant 'at same rate as last year viz. one hundred pounds for each Nurse employed or pro-rata if not for whole period and a grant of £750 for Karitane Hospital'.[57] His defeat in the 1919 general election has been attributed partly to his perceived failings as Minister of Public Health during the 1918 influenza epidemic,[58] but it is possible that his alienation of the Plunket Society played a significant part.

Plunket and the doctors

Dr Josephine Baker, head of the Child Hygiene Division of the New York City Department of Health, set up in 1908, recorded in her autobiography that in the early days of New York City's infant-health campaigns she was sent a petition by about 30 local physicians complaining that the local baby-welfare station was ruining their medical practices.[59] The United States Children's Bureau, established in 1912, reflected the views of its director, Julia Lathrop, who defined infant and maternal health in social rather than narrowly medical terms and hence alienated obstetricians and paedi-atricians.[60] The Plunket Society identified with the bureau and exchanged information with Lathrop.[61] She, in turn, applauded the work of Plunket and looked to New Zealand as an example of the system she hoped to establish in the United States.[62] After Lathrop's retirement in 1921, Plunket's Central Council sent a letter expressing appreciation of the valuable services she had rendered to the American child-welfare movement.[63]

Like the Children's Bureau, Plunket inspired mistrust among some members of the medical profession. The editor of the *New Zealand Medical Journal* at the time of the society's founding was Walter Fell, a prominent doctor whose wife, Margaret, took the minutes of the inaugural meeting of the Wellington Plunket branch.[64] Although he himself supported Plunket, he noted that the medical profession's general attitude was one of 'chilled indifference'.[65] The same year the *New Zealand Observer* asked: 'How Drs Bedford and Mackellar [who were on the Auckland Plunket Advisory Board] can brave the frowns of the BMA [British Medical Association] by championing the cause of the budding maternity nurses, to bring new competitors into the field?'[66] Two matters concerned the profession: the division of responsibilities between Plunket nurses and doctors, and whether the services should be free to all.

The battle over boundaries was fought by the medical profession through its association, the New Zealand Branch of the British Medical Association (NZBMA). Early in 1909 the association received a complaint from a doctor in Timaru that the local Plunket nurse, Alice Bowman (who had been matron of the Karitane Home in Dunedin from April 1908 to February 1909), had overstepped her authority in attending to his patients. Bowman replied that her relationship with the local doctors was generally good.[67]

Some of the early Plunket nurses were not registered nurses. In 1908, however, Hester Maclean, Assistant Inspector of Hospitals in the Department of Hospitals and Charitable Aid, wrote to Plunket's president, Kathleen Hosking, strongly urging the advisability of appointing only state registered nurses.[68] She explained that, in Britain, the district nursing societies that held high status in the profession, such as the Queen Victoria Jubilee Nurses and the Lady Dudley District Nurses, were staffed entirely by fully trained nurses. She thought it would be 'a very false step to associate the name of Lady Plunket with an inferior grade'.[69] In this she had the backing of the Trained Nurses' Association, of which she was president and which sent a deputation to the Plunket Society on the matter in 1908. This resulted in the drawing up of a set of rules specifying that Plunket nurses were to be qualified hospital or maternity nurses.[70]

These rules were clearly not immediately enforced. Two years later Dr Emily Siedeberg wrote to the *Otago Daily Times* about a baby who had died at the Karitane Home, blaming the nurses for delaying too long before summoning a doctor. Although she believed that Plunket nurses could be 'a real boon to the community', their most important function was to know when to send for a doctor. To her this was an argument for employing fully trained nurses only, as they would understand this duty.[71] During the First World War, some Karitane nurses, who were not required to be registered nurses, continued to act as Plunket nurses and sometimes even unpaid volunteers took up the post. From 1914, however, only registered nurses, midwives (or maternity nurses) were accepted for Plunket training.

The NZBMA sought to define the relationship between the new Plunket nurses and doctors. At its annual general meeting in February 1910 the association resolved to suggest that the Plunket Society should adopt the Model Rules for the District Nurses Associations, drawn up in Belfast, Ireland, in 1909. These rules would define the area in which the nurses could work and govern their relationship with the medical profession. At a meeting between Plunket and the NZBMA it was agreed that doctors were to be called 'in cases of serious illness only'. The words 'serious illness', it was explained, 'are not intended to include mere infantile ailments, eg simple diarrhoea, indigestion or colic, such as would ordinarily be dealt with by the mother or grandmother, without calling in a doctor'.[72] The Plunket nurse was thus defined by the medical profession as a surrogate grandmother rather than a health professional.

From the outset doctors sought to restrict the activities of the Plunket nurses to prevent intrusion on their own practices, and Plunket committees were generally sympathetic. As noted, the wives of many local doctors served on the committees and the society also realised the importance of co-operating with the medical profession to gain public respectability. In its early years the Wellington branch recorded 'with satisfaction' the support nurses had received from the local medical profession.[73] The Westport Plunket nurse's comment that she had the wholehearted support of the local doctors was considered worth repeating at the 1914 general conference.[74] The Auckland branch minutes boasted in 1915 of several cases to which Plunket nurses had been called by doctors: 'This is very satisfactory as the Committee is anxious to work hand in hand with the doctors'.[75] Following a 'misunderstanding' between a doctor and a nurse in Auckland the previous year, the committee had resolved that if a nurse were called in to look after a case which was also being attended by a doctor, the nurse must ring the doctor and ask if he was satisfied she should attend the case. Taking this to the general conference in 1914, Maude Parkes, the wife of Dr William Parkes, was informed that it was already covered in the rule book.[76] One Auckland doctor suggested that all cases should be diagnosed by a doctor and another that doctors should regularly attend at the Plunket clinics.[77] This led to the question of payment for services, the second factor about the new services that concerned the medical profession.

In June 1910 the Hawke's Bay division of the NZBMA put forward a resolution stating that a restriction should be placed on the 'unlimited use' of Plunket nurses. However, the South Canterbury division of the NZBMA objected that insisting on this would 'arouse hostility to the medical profession on the part of the public'.[78] Plunket's public image and support were already something to be reckoned with.

Most of the Auckland Plunket branch's 'Medical Men' thought that those who could pay should do so.[79] At its December 1910 meeting, 'the same old discussion arose regarding the advisability of patients who could afford it paying for the services of the Plunket nurses'. Dr Ernest Roberton framed a resolution on the subject for the next national conference.[80] The following

year, addressing the Auckland branch committee, Truby King emphatically vetoed the idea: 'the Society was an educative and patriotic one and
therefore payment was out of the question. Also . . . in five cases out of
eight the mothers in our own class know less than the poorer classes
regarding the proper rearing of children etc.'[81]

Truby King also wrote a long letter to Lily Atkinson, who had presided
at the founding meeting of the Wellington Plunket Branch and was a vice-
president at the time,[82] about the response of the local medical profession
to Plunket. He referred to the society as a 'health mission', and believed it
'a large order . . . for an association of Doctors (acting as they naively admit
"in the protection of their own interest") to demand the Society abandon
its original purpose and adopt a totally different and very limited function
prescribed by the doctors'. The doctors thought that, in future, the work of
Plunket 'must be limited . . . to the submerged and ignorant – or rather to
those who cannot pay'. Truby King claimed that the sole basis of distinc-
tion was 'money, not the need or otherwise of knowledge in the interest of
humanity and the race'. Some doctors said they wished to protect patients
from the ignorance of the Plunket nurses 'but the majority of objectors
have been frank enough to say that their ground of complaint was purely
pecuniary'. He pointed out that if the welfare of patients concerned them,
then they would not have promised such wholehearted support were the
society's work restricted to the poor: 'One would have to assume, that the
ignorant doing-to-death of the infants of the poor without benefit of clergy
(or rather doctors) would be a matter of little consequence – indeed a meritorious proceeding, one which commands the sympathy of the profession.'
Truby King saw the dispute not only as a professional one but also in
gendered terms. He wrote of the threats and intimidation by the medical
association to the Plunket Society, and responded to Atkinson's suggestion that 'tact and conciliation' were required.

> When an individual gentleman behaves very rudely to an individual lady,
> her first instinct is not, I think, to regard the case as one for the exercise of tact
> . . ., nor would such an attitude conduce to respect or consideration in future.
> Speaking as a man, I should say that the best way to treat the male beast
> when he becomes unreasonably exacting and overbearing is to be somewhat
> removed and distant towards him until he comes to his senses and behaves
> more decently.

He advised the women of Plunket to demand that the NZBMA place any objections before them in a businesslike way, as one society to another.[83]

Truby King was clearly not interested in advancing the interests of his medical colleagues. His loyalties lay with the society, and as such he was a useful ally to the women who ran Plunket. His own allies included Dunedin gynaecologist Dr Ferdinand Batchelor. When the latter died in 1915 the society recorded that it owed its foundation partly to the sympathy and encouragement Batchelor had given to King.[84] Another ally was Dr William Collins, who proposed the title 'Plunket nurses' in 1908, and was actively involved in the Wellington branch for many years, addressing annual meetings and acting as its honorary physician until his death in 1934. A respected member of the medical profession, Collins was president of the NZBMA 1904–5 and 1916–17.[85]

Their fanatical devotion to the 'cause' and their own recipe for saving infants did not endear Truby King and his wife Bella to doctors generally. For example, Bella King criticised the training of St Helens Hospital midwives, which provoked the ire of the medical officer to Dunedin's St Helens Hospital, Dr Emily Siedeberg. 'In trying to advertise the work of the Plunket Society,' she objected, 'Mrs. King is not called upon to condemn the teaching of thoroughly up-to-date training-schools.' She pointed out that there were non-Plunket methods of feeding infants which were recognised as successful by the medical profession throughout the world, and a thoroughly efficient nurse should be taught all methods.[86] Plunket's singular formula for feeding infants was to become central to disputes with other health professionals, though lying beneath the surface of the debates were the issues of professional status and control.

For the first ten years of the society's existence, Plunket nurses were, in effect, in competition with doctors. This is clear from their notes and reports to local committees. In 1913 the Auckland branch committee described babies as 'patients' who were brought to the rooms for 'treatment' and again when 'convalescent'.[87] In September 1910 Auckland's Nurse Brien claimed to be 'especially pleased' with her progress, 'as she had had some really bad cases'. In 1914 Nurse Macarthy, a Plunket nurse in Auckland from 1913 to 1920, mentioned one 'specially sick baby' that Dr Alice Horsley had rung her about. 'It was the most emaciated baby nurse had yet seen. It was too weak to suck from a bottle and an egg spoon had to be used.' In February 1915, 'Nurses reported a great deal of sickness among the babies, mostly diarrhoea . . . especially during the warm weather. Nurse Macarthy reported that one of the new cases she was called to was a case of pneumonia following on measles.' In April 1915, 'Five of the new cases were sent by Doctors . . . four of these babies were extremely ill with malnutrition and diarrhoea, two of them were not thought to live till morning, all required constant care and the most careful feeding, each one of these babies are making slow but good progress. There are four other cases of Diarrhoea also improving . . . the month has been a very strenuous one . . . .' In July 1916 Nurse Macarthy reported that she had received 'an urgent wire asking her to go to Putaruru [near Rotorua] at once to see a baby who had been ill with bronchitis, she wired advising the parents to call in a Doctor, this had been done, but wanted Nurse to go up . . . .' In December that year she reported that diarrhoea was 'very prevalent' – 'out of 13 babies 11 of them had it'. She told the committee in 1917 about a poor mother 'who was unable to buy milk for her sick baby', and the committee members contributed to the cost of the milk themselves. In February 1920 Macarthy again reported an unusual number of babies with gastric troubles, claiming the nurses had 'a strenuous time'. The report on 2 June 1921 read, 'Of the baby cases 40 were normal, 53 suffering from malnutrition, 4 diarrhoea, 7 other complaints.'[88]

New Zealand's infant mortality rate continued its downward trend, as the Plunket Society was not slow to point out.[89] In reality Plunket nurses were too few in number to have had any real impact on the rates. The society stressed, however, the reduction of the death rate was not the only issue: 'As a HEALTH Society we are more interested in firmly establishing the all-round fitness of the 24,000 or 25,000 annual new arrivals who will live, than we are in reducing the potential deaths from 2000 to 1000'.[90] Plunket nurses were only a small part of this; also important were personal contacts by volunteers, publications and correspondence. A weekly 'Our Babies' column was published in the *Otago Witness* from 1907, and the following year by fifteen other papers as well. In 1908 it was noted that hundreds of letters to the society had already resulted from that column.[91] By 1913, 200,000 copies were circulated weekly, and Plunket claimed that 'By one channel or another it now reaches practically every home in the Dominion'.[92] The patent infant-food company Glaxo certainly saw the potential of 'Our Babies' when it asked for its newspaper advertisement to be placed immediately after the column. But Plunket objected: it would not be associated with a patent baby-food product.[93]

Thousands of copies of the society's book, *The Feeding and Care of Baby*, were distributed. In 1912 it was noted that 'inquiries for the book were frequent and urgent'; the fifth edition of 5500 copies of *The Feeding and*

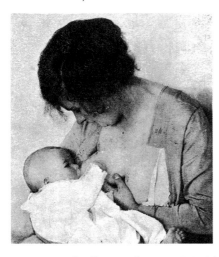

LEFT: Breastfeeding mother, c. 1923. The original caption read: 'Though the mother longed to nurse her baby it was contended that her milk was poisoning her child, and she was made to wean during the first ten days after birth, in spite of protests. A month later breast-feeding was quickly restored by treatment on "Plunket lines," at the New Zealand Mothercraft Training Centre, Earl's Court, London. The above happy snapshot was taken by the husband soon afterwards, when mother and child were flourishing (Published with consent of both parents.)'. *The Expectant Mother and Baby's First Month, For Parents and Nurses*

RIGHT: Clock-Face for Four-Hourly Feeding. Feeding by the clock was widely advocated in the Western world in the early twentieth century, though it became particularly associated with Truby King. *The Expectant Mother and Baby's First Month*

Care of Baby had sold out in little over a year,[94] and a new and expanded version with a print run of 10,000 was planned.

As a sign of its success, the society noticed that women who could not breastfeed 'become more and more apologetic', while others who could not breastfeed in the past could now do so with proper advice and encouragement, so that 'they are no longer subject to the humiliation of feeling themselves to be only "half mothers"'. Only five years before 'a large proportion' of young mothers did not even contemplate breastfeeding; now bottle-feeding was coming to be regarded as 'bad form'.[95] Along with 'strenuous advocacy' of breastfeeding, it noted, as 'special advances in baby-feeding', the widespread adoption of systematic clocklike regularity in the feeding of babies, the extension of intervals between feeds throughout the early months from two to three hours and the entire abandonment of night-feeding, i.e. between 10 or 11pm and 5 or 6 am. The latter was so 'refreshing and invigorating' to mother and baby that they

NEW ZEALAND'S POPULATION.

After close on 100 years of settlement New Zealand's population is just over one million. The birthrate diminished in 1918 to 23'45, while immigration has practically ceased.

The wastage of life endangers national survival and the greatest menace of all is the perennial wastage of infant life. New Zealand's future lies with her babies—we must save every life we can. To do this every care must be exercised in recommending a suitable food for infants.

In cases where a mother is unable to suckle her child there is no other food so closely resembling human milk as GLAXO. This is because GLAXO is simply the solids of the purest milk enriched with cream. The GLAXO process makes the milk germ-free, and breaks down the nourishing curd of the milk into minute easily-digestible particles, similar to the lact-albumen of breast milk.

GLAXO is a complete food in itself being instantly prepared by the addition of boiling water.

" The Food that Builds Bonnie Babies."

Samples together with Medical and Analytical reports sent free on application to :—

"GLAXO," Palmerston North, N.Z.

Glaxo 'human milk' formula was vehemently opposed by Truby King and the Plunket Society, though some Plunket supporters probably used it. Glaxo invoked some of the same concerns as did the Plunket Society. Glaxo advertisement, *New Zealand Medical Journal* (1921)

wondered why night-feeding had ever been contemplated.[96] Similar routines were promoted by the Children's Bureau in the United States.[97]

The impact of such teaching on individual mothers in this period remains unknown. An agent of the commercial baby food Glaxo told the Plunket Council that he personally knew 'a good many members of the Society – and prominent members at that – who are strongly in favour of Glaxo, who although they are helping the magnificent work it [i.e. Plunket] is doing, bring up their own children on Glaxo'.[98] Yet the members' commitment to Plunket cannot be doubted. Their sense of the importance of their 'health mission' was reinforced by the overseas interest the movement generated. Not only were they in contact with Julia Lathrop in the United States, but also with Dr Helen MacMurchy, medical adviser to the Canadian government on the health and well-being of children and from 1919 chief of the new Division of Child Welfare in the federal Department of Health.[99] Close contact was also maintained with neighbouring Australia. The Victorian Council of Women, for example, wrote to the Plunket Council for information, and subsequently set up the Lady Talbot Pure Milk Depots

Country and Year.	Infant Mortality Rate.	Country and Year.	Infant Mortality Rate.
Chile (1919) ..	306	Denmark (1919) ..	92
Hungary (1915) ..	264	England and Wales (1919)	89
Japan (1918) ..	189	Ireland (1919) ..	88
Spain (1918) ..	183	United States (birth-	
Germany (1919) ..	145	registration area) (1919)	87
Quebec (1919) ..	143	Netherlands (1919) ..	84
Italy (1917) ..	139	Switzerland (1919)	82
Finland (1919) ..	135	Sweden (1916) ..	70
France (1919) ..	119	Australia (1919) ..	69
Scotland (1919) ..	102	Norway (1917) ..	64
Uruguay (1919) ..	101	New Zealand (1919)	45
Ontario (1919) ..	96		

New Zealand was proud of its low infant death rate in the early twentieth century.
A. Balfour & H. H. Scott, *Health Problems of the Empire: A Survey in 12 Volumes*, ed. H. Gunn, 1924

in Melbourne.[100] Although the women of New South Wales had been involved in infant welfare for a decade, in 1918 the New South Wales Governor, Neville Mayman, studied the Plunket Society and argued that, 'There is a vital need in this State for an organisation of this character, and should one be formed I am convinced that the same beneficial results would attend it as have been obtained by the Plunket Society in New Zealand'. He had recently heard that the imperial government had started a movement to save the babies of Great Britain and the empire, and that British authorities, 'impressed evidently by the achievements of the Plunket Society', had invited Truby King to go to England to assist in launching the new organisation. Thus Plunket was sanctioned from the heart of the empire.[101]

In 1919–20 Robert Woodbury, Director of Statistical Research for the Children's Bureau in Washington DC, and his wife visited New Zealand, 'having been sent by his government to study Plunket methods'.[102] He presented his report to the annual meeting of the American Child Hygiene Association in October 1920. Discussing the reasons for the low the infant mortality rate for New Zealand, which in 1918 was 48.4 (excluding Maori) compared with 101 for the United States, he argued, 'Probably the most important of the preventive measures is the work of the Royal New Zealand Society for the Health of Women and Children.'[103]

CHAPTER 3

Plunket Becomes a Household Word: the Interwar Years

The Department of Child Welfare

At the conclusion of the First World War, concerns about infant welfare were high throughout the Western world. As historian Robyn Muncy has written, in the United States 'child welfare reform was one of the progressive beneficiaries of World War I'.[1] The result was the 1921 Maternity and Infancy Protection Act, also known as the Sheppard-Towner Act, which provided matching federal grants to the states for maternal and child health programmes. These included instruction on nutrition and hygiene, prenatal and child-health clinics, and visiting nurses for pregnant women and new mothers.[2] In Britain a Maternal and Child Welfare Act, passed in 1918, provided funding to local authorities for maternal and child welfare services, including salaried midwives, health visitors, infant-welfare centres, day nurseries and milk and food for needy mothers and infants.[3] Philippa Mein Smith dates 'the effective formation of the [Australian] infant welfare movement' to 1918 and the establishment of the Victorian Baby Health Centres Association in Melbourne and the Royal Society for the Welfare of Mothers and Babies in Sydney.[4] When the Canadian Federal Department of Health was set up in 1919, the Division of Child Welfare was the first to be formed, with Dr Helen MacMurchy as chief. The National Council on Child Welfare was also created in 1920 to co-ordinate child welfare voluntary activities in all provinces.[5]

In New Zealand the Minister of Health, C. J. (Sir James) Parr, outlined his plans for a reformed Health Department when he officially opened the sixth general conference of the Plunket Society in Wellington in 1920. He began by referring to the poor health status of British children and the dangers of creating a 'C3' population. To him Britain and New Zealand were one and the same. But he had 'the remedy of these evils': the creation of a Bureau or Department of Child Welfare. Parr explained that the work would be based on education, lectures and propaganda, and that Truby King was 'the man for this job'.[6]

This initiative was to be part of a restructured Health Department under

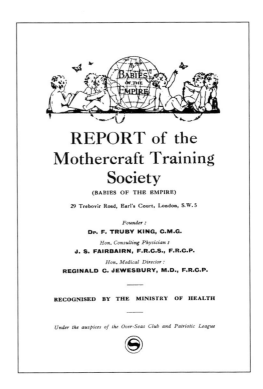

REPORT of the
Mothercraft Training
Society
(BABIES OF THE EMPIRE)

29 Trebovir Road, Earl's Court, London, S.W. 5

Founder :
Dr. F. TRUBY KING, C.M.G.

Hon. Consulting Physician :
J. S. FAIRBAIRN, F.R.C.S., F.R.C.P.

Hon. Medical Director :
REGINALD C. JEWESBURY, M.D., F.R.C.P.

RECOGNISED BY THE MINISTRY OF HEALTH

Under the auspices of the Over-Seas Club and Patriotic League

The 'Babies of the Empire' campaign was part of the widespread concern for infant welfare at the conclusion of the First World War. New Zealand was proud to be leading such an initiative, and Truby King became a national hero as a result. Report of the Mothercraft Training Society (Babies of the Empire) 1920–22

the 1920 Health Act. Dr Robert Makgill, then Acting Chief Health Officer and the official identified as 'the real author of the 1920 Health Act',[7] told Truby King that, in his opinion, the Plunket Society should be brought under the direct control of the Health Department.[8] It was perhaps with that goal in mind that Truby King was appointed to direct the new Division of Child Welfare. A recent departmental historian concluded he was an obvious choice, but that 'his independent and idiosyncratic nature did not sit easily within the new bureaucracy, where he regarded both dental hygiene and school hygiene as part of his fiefdom'.[9] Yet King had good reason for that belief. Parr described his plans for child welfare as 'the most important and far-reaching step' in relation to public health in the dominion. He intended to divide the Health Department into two sections, 'namely Public Health in general and Child Welfare'. Given the importance of child health, he wished to separate it from other health activities and make it a special department, with the approval of the Chief Health Officer, Thomas Valintine, who was to take up the new post of Director-General of Health. (In the written account of the meeting it was noted that Valintine nodded assent.) Parr pointed out that, as Director of Child Welfare, King would have to deal with maternity and child welfare, together with the extensive field covered by the Education Department from the hygienic and medical aspect, 'including the broad supervision of their medical and nursing staffs and advising the Minister on everything in this connexion'. He stressed that King would be expected to report directly to him and not through the general head of the Public Health Department.[10] This elevation of child welfare was testimony to its political importance in New Zealand at the end of the First World War. As Dr William Young, president of the NZBMA, declared, 'With a lowering birth rate, if our race is to survive, it is absolutely essential to take the greatest care in rearing the infants.'[11]

Truby King was offered a salary of £1,000. This was £50 less than Valintine's salary, which King interpreted as a sign of inferior status.[12] He was right. Reluctant to acknowledge Valintine's authority, in January 1921 King wrote to Parr reminding him of his original proposal: 'It is absolutely essential for the various Departmental Officers to recognise my advisory and supervisory position and status, and to know that I am responsible solely to yourself as Minister in Charge, and not to the head[s] of the Health and Education Departments'.[13]

A year later Truby King fell out with the minister himself over the distribution of his pamphlet *The Expectant Mother and Baby's First Month*. King clearly had an inflated view of the value of this publication. He claimed that the distribution of 50,000 copies would result in the saving of at least 100 lives in a very short time, each worth £10: 'looked at in a purely cold-blooded, commercial light, we can have so many sound healthy children for so many pamphlets, if we want them' and 'each young immigrant so saved [would be] given to us, as it were, in exchange for 500 sixpenny pamphlets'.[14] In 1922 Parr authorised the sending of the pamphlet to all married women under the age of 35,[15] but he was subsequently less convinced of its value, declaring that people merely 'chuck[ed] the pamphlet into the waste-paper basket'.[16] King took his mounting complaints about Parr's 'most disheartening and embarrassing obstruction, and lack of decent encouragement and support of any kind'[17] to Prime Minister Massey, whose wife Christina had been Wellington Plunket branch president for the previous four years. Parr, affronted, reminded Massey that he had been responsible for the creation of the Child Welfare Division and had strongly favoured the appointment of Truby King. He also complained that King had repeatedly clashed with other senior health officials, although 'I have invariably tried hard to adjust and smooth matters over'.[18]

King's responsibilities were initially wide-ranging. In 1921 Parr asked him to lead an inquiry into maternal mortality, at a time when this was very much in the public eye. In 1924 King, along with Valintine, repre-sented the Health Department at a public meeting in Palmerston North, held in connection with the annual meeting of the local Plunket branch, to launch a joint campaign to reduce maternal mortality.[19] Yet within a year the campaign to reduce maternal mortality was taken over by two new appointees to the department, Drs Tom Paget and Henry Jellett, and the ante-natal work was entrusted to Dr Elaine Gurr. King no longer headed a department concerned with all aspects of maternity and child welfare as originally intended by Parr.

King wrote his last report as the Health Department Director of Child Welfare in 1925.[20] His role within the department, and indeed the post itself, was short-lived. The division ceased to exist when its responsibilities were officially transferred to the Education Department. Under the Child Welfare Act of 1925, a new division was set up with John Beck as its first director. Its functions encompassed child welfare more generally, including delin-quency and not just health or 'the wastage of child life'. In her history of child welfare, Bronwyn Dalley described the 1925 act as something of a 'swansong' for child health and welfare.[21] From the Health Department's point of view, the transfer of child welfare to the Education Department also prevented any transfer of power and responsibility for child health from the Plunket Society to the Health Department. The latter continued to be responsible for maternity, the health of school children and for Maori infants, but not for the health of European infants and pre-school children; that remained firmly in the hands of Plunket. Ante-natal care was still shared between Plunket and the Health Department, though each act-ed independently, until the 1938 Social Security Act brought general practitioners into the picture. For the Health Department the demise of the Division of Child Welfare was a lost opportunity, but maybe it sensed that it could not gain access to Plunket through King. There is clearly a need to revise the common historical perceptions that King's appointment 'unit[ed] Government and Plunket policy on child health and childrearing'[22] and that, with King as Director of Child Welfare, 'the government was able, through the Plunket Society to effectively control how Pakeha babies were brought up'.[23]

Plunket and political support

The primary reason for the Health Department's failure to assume full con-trol of infant welfare was the continued and considerable political support enjoyed by the Plunket Society. As Dr Michael Watt, Director-General of Health 1930–47, wrote in his unpublished autobiography, 'I hope I will not be misunderstood if I say that Governments in their approach to the matter [Plunket] were in no sense deterred from proffering financial aid by knowledge of the fact that the Society had very wide membership and if so inclined could have exercised considerable political pressure.'[24]

Plunket had wide membership but also knew how to court political influence at the top. The 1920 general Plunket conference was presided over by Christina Massey; she also led a deputation of 50 women to the Prime Minister to ask for an increase in the government subsidy to the society. The deputation was introduced by Thomas Sidey, MP for Caversham, whose wife was later Plunket president (1936–7). Massey received the deputation sympathetically, replying that encouraging and assisting the Plunket Society had been one of his party's political platforms at the 1919 elections. He preferred to see the work done by a voluntary organisation than by a state department, which in his view would be less sympathetic.[25] In 1920 the government subsidy was raised from £100 to £125 for each of the 55 Plunket nurses employed, with additional subsidies of £1,000 to the Dunedin Karitane Hospital, £500 to the Christchurch hospital and £350 to Wanganui.[26]

It was William Downie Stewart, as Minister of Internal Affairs, who arranged that, from 1922, local registrars should send lists of births to all local branches of the society.[27] A lawyer by profession, Downie Stewart was a family friend of the Kings and acted as honorary solicitor to Plunket for many years.[28] As has been noted, his sister, Rachelina Hepburn Armitage, was responsible for establishing the headquarters for the South Canterbury branch of Plunket at Timaru, and was president of the Temuka branch from 1914 to 1928. His other sister, Mary, trained as a Plunket nurse.[29]

Massey's successor, Gordon Coates, was equally supportive and his wife was involved with the local Plunket committee.[30] Less than a month after becoming Prime Minister following Massey's death in 1925, Coates attended an appeal meeting to establish a new Karitane hospital in Wellington. He pronounced to loud applause that he himself knew little about babies though there were five of them at home and, implying an affinity between mothers and Plunket, he described his own wife as 'the best Plunket Nurse I know'.[31]

In 1926 J. A. (later Sir Alexander) Young, then Minister of Health, let the Wellington Plunket branch 'into a Cabinet secret' when he related how

Minister of Health, Sir Alexander Young, a long-time supporter of Plunket, at the Plunket Provincial Conference in Christchurch in 1933, flanked by Mesdames Cracroft Wilson (President, Christchurch Branch), Cecil Wood (Honorary Secretary, Christchurch), G. Gallaway (Vice-President), Jos (Kate) McGeorge (Acting President), and Miss G. Hoddinott (Administrative Secretary). Plunket Society Annual Report 1932–33

Coates had approved a Plunket grant of £15,000 without hesitation. He claimed that a further grant of £26,000 was also being considered. He told his audience that they had 'a very good friend in need in the Prime Minister, who would help them always to the utmost of his power'.[32] Young himself was a long-term supporter of Plunket, attending all the general conferences from 1917, when he represented the Hamilton branch and led a Plunket deputation to the Prime Minister, until 1936. His absence that year was noted in the conference proceedings.[33] From 1933 until his death in 1956 he was a member of the Plunket Society Advisory Board.

In the course of a 1928 Plunket deputation to the Prime Minister, Truby King complained about Jellett's recent publication, *Short Practice of Midwifery for Nurses*, and specifically the chapter on 'Infant Feeding'. Jellett had acknowledged Gurr as his dietetic authority. King, in his typically arrogant way, claimed the advice was 'in direct contrariety to the teachings of the Plunket Society, and, if followed, he was confident would be responsible for the losing of some hundreds more infant lives annually than at present throughout the Dominion'. Young, as Minister of Health, responded that the department had no control over the publication; Jellett was an advisory officer and not on the department's permanent staff.

Coates said the department should take steps to rectify the matter in any future editions of the book. He added that there was to be no friction between any department and the Plunket Society.[34] His loyalty lay with Plunket.

Some Ministers of Health were more supportive than others. King may have found Parr unsympathetic, but he had negotiated the higher government subsidy for Plunket nurses in 1920. Parr also took Director-General Valintine to task in 1921 over his department's lack of support for Plunket. He complained that certain health officials had, with Valintine's consent, deliberately made statements in their recent publications 'calculated to belittle and prejudice the valuable work of the Plunket Society in this country'. He pointed out that the Plunket executive had expressed 'grave objection' to the proposal by the secretary of the Health Department, E. A. Killick, that the society should come under, or be associated with, local hospital boards. He told Valintine, 'it is my desire (and yours I feel sure also) that your Department shall work not only in harmony with the Plunket Society but shall aid its work in every reasonable and possible manner'. Articles that tended 'to cast doubt upon the soundness of the Plunket Society's doctrines' were therefore not helpful. The present government, he concluded, was 'committed to extending and furthering the work of the Plunket Society'.[35]

One of the articles, in the departmental journal, was by Dr Michael Watt, the newly appointed Director of Public Hygiene and future Director-General of Health. Discussing infant mortality in New Zealand, it criticised the 'distinct tendency, in belauding the admittedly meritorious work of [Plunket], to ignore the achievements of the Health Department'. Watt concluded that the steady decline in infant mortality since 1900 was attributable, in the period 1900–06, to public health administration alone, and since 1907 to the efforts of Plunket and the Health Department.[36]

Arthur Stallworthy, Minister of Health from 1928 to 1931, was less supportive of Plunket than some of his predecessors. In 1930, in the light of the deepening economic recession, he suggested cutting the government grant to the society. This elicited an irate response from Plunket's secretary, Gwen Hoddinott, who proposed to place the matter before all MPs.[37] Stallworthy refused to bow to her 'unworthy political threats' and in this he had the support of the Health Department 'to a man'.[38] To Hoddinott he wrote, 'Does your Society seriously suggest that it has a right to demand of the Government an indeterminate amount of money over an indefinite period for unlimited expansion of your Society's activities without regard to Government direction or exigencies of Government finance?'[39] Valintine, who found an ally in Stallworthy, told him that government assistance to Plunket was 'on a too liberal scale', when they took into account the importance of Plunket in relation to other activities relating to health and social welfare. It was also too liberal considering that Plunket nurses did not work 'under the smallest supervision of nor in co-operation with the Department'.[40]

Before his retirement in 1930, Valintine treated Hoddinott to a lecture on infant mortality, prompted by Plunket's financial demands. He began by stating that no serious attempt had been made to question the society's claims about its contribution to the lowered infantile death rate. He believed that, 'stripping the question of the mere sentimentalism associated with [Plunket]', the work of its nurses was a small factor in the reduction. Re-iterating many of the points made by Watt in 1921, he noted that the decline had begun before the society's formation and long before its activities could have had any significant effect. He further pointed out that infant death rates had dropped even more rapidly in other countries, such as England. Moreover, New Zealand's birth rate was steadily declining and it was a well-known statistical fact that a lower birth rate produced a lower infant death rate. In relation to gastric and intestinal diseases, he argued, nurse supervision in the home and of the baby was no doubt important, but there had been just as great a reduction in the deaths of adults and older children from these causes, and better housing, cleaner food and milk supplies, improved water supplies and sanitation generally were also important. He did not wish to belittle the work of the society's nurses but rather to see it 'with due sense of proportion'. He maintained that even giving the same assistance as in the previous year would mean cutbacks in other areas of Health Department activity and 'a loss of efficiency'. He concluded that, as Plunket had 'on repeated occasions steadfastly opposed anything in the nature of Departmental oversight or supervision of its work I do not see that we can justify the grants asked for'.[41] In reply Hoddinott argued that credit for the reduced infant death rates could indeed go to Plunket. But in any case, she said, the society was less concerned with reducing the death rate than with improving the health of infants generally.[42]

As Plunket so often did when faced with an unsympathetic Minister of Health, it went to the top, sending a deputation to Prime Minister George Forbes in August 1930. Significantly the deputation was led by Labour MP Peter Fraser, later Minister of Health and Prime Minister under the first Labour government. Introducing the deputation, Fraser maintained that

Plunket 'had become a part of the life and history of New Zealand', that 'No one ever had anything but the highest commendation of the wonderful work done' and that 'New Zealand had led the way in a world movement'.[43] Although the reduced funding included in the Main Estimates was approved, the society was assured that the shortfall would be made good in the Supplementary Estimates, as indeed it was. A subsequent column in the *Dominion* noted how Stallworthy had changed his tune, quoting his view that no work done in New Zealand was comparable with that of the Plunket Society, and that the government's grant of £28,000 was 'probably the best investment the Government had made during the year'. The reporter noted cynically, 'In view of these fair words, it seems almost rude to recall that Mr Stallworthy's department cut down this year's grant to the society by £5315 and it was only reinstated in the Supplementary Estimates after pressure had been brought to bear on the Government.'[44]

Like other recipients of government money, Plunket suffered during the Depression. In April 1931 the government announced it was reducing all civil service salaries by 10 per cent. Recognising the universality of the cuts and the government's financial constraints, Plunket's Council reduced Plunket nurses' salaries accordingly.[45] A year later the government lowered civil service salaries by a further 10 per cent. Although Plunket subsidies were further cut, this was not passed on to nurses' salaries, in view of the fact that, even after the second cut, the Health Department's district nurses were better paid than Plunket nurses.[46] In 1932 the government appointed a National Expenditure Commission to review public expenditure and identify further savings. The commissioners recommended another cut in Plunket funding and argued that Plunket services should not be provided free of charge.[47] The defence of Plunket was led by Sir Alexander Young, once again Minister of Health, who vehemently opposed a user pays system. He was supported by the Plunket Society and the public.[48] In 1933 the government contribution remained at £22,615 (out of a total Plunket expenditure of £64,589) and the services remained free.[49]

November 1935 seemed to be the dawn of a new age: the first Labour government came to power promising social security 'from the cradle to the grave'. In 1936 a Cabinet committee was set up to prepare an outline for health and pensions legislation, and in July the subsidy of £125 per nurse for the 132 Plunket nurses was restored.[50] In 1937 Plunket's newly elected president, Daisy Begg, wrote to Health Minister Peter Fraser asking for a public statement of reassurance to refute the 'fairly widespread' idea that the government intended to take over the society's work under the

Plunket was held in high regard throughout the British Empire and beyond. This model of a typical Plunket room was displayed at the Canadian National Exhibition in the mid 1930s. Hocken Library, AG-7/7/28

new 'State National Heath Service'. This belief, she said, was having an adverse effect on fund-raising.[51] Fraser, whose wife Janet was involved with Plunket and many other women's organisations,[52] had no hesitation in providing that reassurance. He did so privately to Begg by letter, adding 'You are at liberty to give whatever publicity to this letter you think necessary', and publicly at the annual meeting of the Wellington Plunket branch a month later.[53] In his address he noted that Finance Minister Walter Nash had found that even doctors in Russia were familiar with the system.[54] He also wrote the foreword to the sixth edition of *The Expectant Mother and Baby's First Month*, which appeared in 1939, and took the opportunity to pay tribute to the work of the Plunket Society. Arnold Nordmeyer, Minister of Health once Fraser became prime minister, wrote the foreword to Plunket's 1945 official handbook, *Modern Mothercraft*, pointing out that the service had become indispensable and had no equal in the field of maternal and child welfare.[55]

Fraser had been unable to attend Plunket's 1936 general conference, which was opened instead by Sidney Holland, a new Opposition MP and future prime minister. Holland did not attempt to make political capital from this opportunity, claiming that it was 'a real tribute' that the society's work was regarded by MPs of all shades of political opinion as above party politics.[56] The 1938 conference was opened by Finance Minister Walter Nash, who was convinced that there was 'no society doing work of more value than the Plunket Society in New Zealand'.[57] He was at that time on Wellington Plunket's branch Advisory Board. Dr David McMillan, a Dunedin general practitioner before entering Parliament and the architect of Labour's 1935 blueprint for health, commented upon the 'great benefits which have accrued from our one health experiment along national lines'. Sceptical of Valintine's assessment of mortality trends, he described Plunket as having 'made New Zealand the doyen of the world in matters of infantile mortality'. He applauded the society as an example of collective responsibility. In his view, 'a national health service would utilise the Plunket Society, building and strengthening it by financial and administrative assistance, so developing a comprehensive infant welfare department'.[58]

Meanwhile the new Director-General of Health, Michael Watt, was even less supportive of Plunket than his predecessor. Like Valintine, he found the subsidies to Plunket 'liberal', given the limited government control.[59] He wished to combine the functions of departmental district nurses with Plunket staff.[60] Following his return from an overseas trip in 1939 Watt came out even more firmly in favour of the generalised public health nurse as opposed to the specialised Plunket nursing services, which he described as 'wasteful of time, money and effort'. He disapproved of Plunket's lack of adequate contact with the Health Department or adequate supervision by the medical profession. His bottom line was that 'infant-welfare work should be regarded as an integral part of the work of the Health Department'.[61] Yet the 'sentimentalism' of the women who ran Plunket and their political allies, identified by his predecessor, prevented this from happening.

An examination of the relationship between the government and Plunket in this period is revealing about public attitudes to state responsibility. Paradoxically, while the women of the Plunket Society insisted that Plunket, as a voluntary organisation, stood for self-help, they also believed in entitlement, i.e. that they had a right to support from the state. Yet such backing did not, in their view, imply state control over their activities. Robyn Muncy has argued that, in the United States, the power of the women's voluntary organisations in the infant-welfare movement was weakened in the 1920s when the Sheppard-Towner Act stipulated the setting up of local public agencies to oversee the services: 'though voluntary organisations were no less active during the 1920s, their authority distinctly diminished'.[62] The voluntary workers of the Plunket Society, by contrast, kept firm control over central and local policy- and decision-making.

By the 1920s and 1930s thousands of women were keeping Plunket functioning. They were still responsible for raising two-thirds of the society's running costs, though aided by grants from the Karitane Products Society.[63] An annual Plunket Day with street appeals began in the mid-1920s.

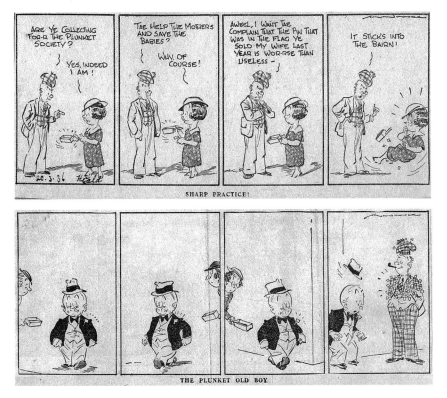

Two of a series of *New Zealand Herald* cartoons relating to the 'Plunket Day' annual street collections in the 1930s. *New Zealand Herald*, 20 March 1936, 24 March 1939

Volunteers were responsible for finding rooms for clinics, and from the late 1920s they were also involved in driving nurses around on a roster system. By 1931 there were more than 70 names on Auckland's list of volunteer drivers.[64] During the Depression local committees also set up special funds for expectant and nursing mothers.

Maternalists and their health professionals

Becoming president of the Plunket Society was no dilettante position for idle middle- or upper-class ladies: it attracted women of influence, confidence and commitment. The role was regarded as a considerable honour by the women themselves, and as the pinnacle of a long local association with Plunket. Until 1978, presidents were also required to live within easy reach of Dunedin, where they were expected to chair fortnightly meetings. They continued to be drawn from the wives of prominent men within the

Anne Pattrick, during her time as Matron of the London Mothercraft Training Society, 1919. *Anne Pattrick . . . A Memoir*

community. Margaret Johnstone, president from 1919 to 1933, was the wife of James Armour Johnstone, managing director of Wright, Stephenson and Co. Ltd, Dunedin director of the Commercial Union Assurance Company and owner of a world-renowned stud farm. He himself was a member of the Plunket Advisory Board, and their daughter later became involved.[65] Yet Margaret Johnstone brought her own skills to the job. She gave 'un-grudgingly of her time and energy . . . from designing patterns of baby clothes to the consideration of serious matters of policy'. [66] Kate McGeorge, who followed Johnstone as president from 1933 to 1935, was no less dy-namic and effective.[67]

Those who ran Plunket had a clear sense of the importance of their role and that of the Central Council. McGeorge, who had been associated with Plunket since 1912, commented in 1930 that council had a 'very definite duty both to the public and the government'.[68] Council members held an unshakeable belief in their ability to perform this function. McGeorge felt they were better acquainted with the nature of the work than health professionals, including the Director of Plunket Nursing, Anne Pattrick. She pointed out that she had been involved before Pattrick was appointed and knew 'quite as well as Miss Pattrick of the many difficulties connected with the carrying on of this department of the work'.[69] With this strong sense of their own centrality and importance, councillors were not about to allow control to devolve to paid health professionals. This attitude was tested in relation to both their nursing and medical directors.

In October 1920 Anne Pattrick was appointed Director of Plunket Nursing, in charge of nursing in the districts and Karitane hospitals. She held this position until 1934. Pattrick had trained as a nurse at Christchurch Hospital from 1911 to 1914, and subsequently as a Plunket nurse at the

Karitane-Harris Hospital. Marked by King for her outstanding qualities, she was immediately appointed to the staff.[70] While on active service in the First World War, she became engaged to an Australian soldier, but he died in England during the 1918 influenza epidemic.[71] During the war she was asked by King to help set up an infant-welfare centre in London along Plunket lines.[72] She was accordingly released from army service in January 1918 and appointed matron of the new Mothercraft Training Centre, a position she held until 1920.[73] A few weeks after Pattrick's return to New Zealand in 1920 her mother died and she threw herself 'heart and soul' into Plunket work.[74] Initially appointed matron of the Karitane-Harris Hospital in Dunedin, then nurse assistant to King when he was appointed Director of Child Welfare in the Health Department in 1920, she ultimately became Director of Plunket Nursing, a title specifically created for her.[75] King, who was largely responsible for the appointment, explained that 'Her wisdom, tact, devotion, and wide practical knowledge and experience – gained in New Zealand, at Home and in America' made her ideally suited for the job. He added that the London committee had done all in their power to induce Pattrick to remain there, and would have given her any reasonable salary, but, for family reasons, she would not entertain the idea.[76]

At the 1924 Plunket conference King expressed his view that the society was in safe hands as long as Pattrick was director. He had long regarded her as his virtual successor, explaining that the 'Plunket health mission was essentially women's work'. With women's committees, Karitane hospitals and Plunket nurses forming the backbone of the scheme, it was naturally the Director of Nursing who would fulfil the role of 'an ever welcome and trusted guide, counsellor and friend in all sorts of intimate and complex situations arising from time to time – situations in which a man would be more or less out of place'. King did envisage a role for men, as husbands and on the 'male Advisory Board for help in business matters'. He also anticipated a male Medical Director 'for the professional regulation and guidance of the whole organisation'. This, he explained, was needed 'to ensure that everything was kept on authoritative lines, abreast of the most advanced and reliable knowledge of the day'. It would give their work 'the highest medical status and sanction'.[77] He was correct to stress the importance of medical support to ensure the survival of Plunket, though limited in ascribing this role to men only.[78]

Pattrick was later described as the 'directing genius' of the expanding Plunket services in the 1920s.[79] She travelled the country, meeting, lecturing to and inspiring both nurses and local voluntary committees. Known to many of her Plunket friends as Nance, she was regarded as an excellent administrator and a model nurse.[80] According to her administrative assistant, Challis Hooper, she imbued the service with a 'high morale and sense of purpose'[81] as well as standardising and improving education in infant nursing. There was a further professionalising of Plunket nurses in 1928 when the council agreed to her suggestion that, wherever possible, the nurses appointed to permanent positions should hold general hospital, maternity and Plunket certificates.[82] It meant that Plunket nurses now had four years of training behind them.

In 1925 Pattrick took six months' leave to undertake midwifery training at St Helens Hospital, Gisborne.[83] Around that time her health began to decline, requiring several periods of extended leave. Hooper was appointed to ease her growing workload and retained the position until it was abolished as a cost-cutting measure in 1932. Pattrick was granted leave to go overseas in 1928, though her travels were delayed until June 1929 owing to ill health. She visited Canada, the United States and England, and while in Canada was one of the New Zealand delegates to an International Congress of Nurses in Toronto.

When she returned to New Zealand in October 1930, Pattrick found that her relationship with the executive of Plunket's Central Council had deteriorated. She faced claims of inefficiency in the service because of her constant illness, and her 'loyalty and obedience' to the council were questioned. This resulted in a power struggle between the voluntary members of the executive, the inner circle of the council and the salaried health professionals. In November 1930 Pattrick proposed that a nursing sub-committee be set up.[84] McGeorge clearly felt threatened by the development of the nursing side of the work, and reaffirmed the right – and ability – of the voluntary members to manage the Society. Her stance was 'emphatically endorsed by every member present'. She took exception to Pattrick's request for an additional council member who 'would understand matters from the nursing point of view'.[85]

In 1932 the council decided to change the instructions on Plunket writing paper. A directive that all letters were 'to be addressed to the Administrative Secretary' replaced the former instruction that 'All Central Council correspondence to be addressed to the Administrative Secretary, Medical and Nursing matters to the Medical Director and Director of Plunket Nursing'. When Pattrick queried why letters referring to professional matters should be addressed to the secretary, McGeorge reiterated that all matters relating to the society's work were the responsibility of the council. When Pattrick suggested this might undermine her position, McGeorge replied that the question of individual prestige did not enter into the society's work.[86]

In 1933 Pattrick made a further attempt to increase the power of the nursing profession within the decision-making process. She put forward seven recommendations to the council. She asked that the duties and responsibilities of the Director of Plunket Nursing be specifically defined as well as her relationship to the council and to the administrative secretary. She also sought the right to correspond directly with matrons of Karitane hospitals and district nurses and requested that she be consulted regarding staff appointments, all of which would be finalised by a 'nursing committee'. The latter body, intended to deal with all professional matters, was to include an approved representative of the Trained Nurses' Association. Finally, she proposed that the Director of Nursing visit various centres, with the charge nurse in each of the four main centres assuming the mantle of supervisory officer, to periodically visit the Plunket rooms in her area.[87]

The council responded that a schedule of duties had already been drawn up by the executive in 1930 and took strong exception to the suggestion of a nursing committee 'which would usurp the functions of the Executive'. Members also opposed the appointment of an 'outside representative' of the Trained Nurses' Association, pointing out that the association already had representation through the Director of Plunket Nursing and the matrons of the Karitane hospitals. They believed it to be impossible for charge nurses in the main centres to take on additional supervisory roles, and regarded it as the Director of Nursing's duty to visit branches.

At a council meeting on 2 November 1933 it was agreed that Pattrick's retirement was in the 'best interest of the work of the Society'. Judge Archibald Blair, a member of the Advisory Board, was asked to speak to Pattrick's brother in the hope that he would persuade her to resign. As nothing came of this, on 30 November Hoddinott wrote directly to Pattrick asking for her resignation by 2 December.[88] The Wellington branch committee, whose president, Anne Tythe Brown, had been a Plunket nurse and matron of Dunedin's Karitane hospital, sent an 'emphatically protesting' letter to the council, describing its action as 'arbitrary, unjust and utterly opposed to the best interest of the Plunket Society'. Together with Nelson and Lower Hutt, the Wellington branch called for a special conference to discuss the matter.[89] The capital had already shown some concern about the lack of nurses' influence on the council. In 1930, when new rules had been drawn up, Wellington had suggested that, as 'the most important salaried official', the Director of Plunket Nursing should be an ex officio member of the council. But there was no unanimity even within the Wellington committee: three months later the proposed amendment was withdrawn without explanation.[90] Before the special conference, Wellington delegates met at the house of Dr Thomas Corkill, honorary physician to Wellington's Karitane Hospital and a member of Plunket's newly appointed Medical Advisory Committee. Corkill deplored the fact that, since 1929, the council had denied Pattrick the opportunity of attending meetings when professional matters were being considered. All those present objected to the way in which Pattrick had not been given the opportunity to defend herself.[91]

The conference held in Dunedin on 22 February was tense: Pattrick was invited to attend only after a motion in favour was passed.[92] Sir Alexander Young began by expressing confidence in the council. 'To expect the executive of a corporate body to adapt itself to the dictates of its paid officers is unthinkable, and would lead inevitably to chaos.'[93] One of those who spoke in favour of Pattrick was Auckland branch president and council member Maude Parkes:

> We have heard eloquent speeches from several level-headed business men on the Dunedin Advisory Board, stating that no business or company would permit an employee to dictate to a manager, or a manager to a director. In this they are unquestionably right, but I would respectfully point out that the Plunket Society is not merely a business proposition, the most important side of our work is professional. I would also draw attention to the fact that, so far, we have heard no evidence whatever to prove that Miss Pattrick at any time dictated the terms to the Executive.[94]

Tythe Brown believed that many of the difficulties were a result of a lack of nursing representation on the council, 'and lack of frankness generally'. Walter Nash, delegate for the Lower Hutt branch and Labour MP, also supported Pattrick, claiming that the problem was that 'she was not acting as a servant should act'. Corkill described Pattrick as 'an inspiration and a leader', pointing out that her work had been invaluable, especially since King's health had declined, and that she had been the central professional figure of the society. He did not believe that she had exerted undue authority, but rather that her legitimate functions had been constantly curtailed. In her own statement Pattrick asked, 'Does the Council want the benefit of that officer's professional knowledge, experience and judgement in matters pertaining to the nursing work or does it simply want unquestioning acquiescence in decisions already arrived at by the executive irrespective of whether the Director of Nursing has had an opportunity of submitting her views on the matter?'[95]

A resolution was passed at the conference affirming confidence in her loyalty and professional capacity, and Pattrick agreed to remain in the service for six months to train her successor, Nora Fitzgibbon. A former matron of Auckland's Karitane Hospital, Fitzgibbon had been the first registered nurse to train at Dunedin's Karitane Hospital.[96] At the next general conference in August 1934, rule changes included changing the title of the head of the nursing services from Director of Plunket Nursing to Nursing Adviser to the Council, though she was now required to attend council meetings.[97] Although the setting up of a Medical Advisory Committee was sanctioned by the conference, the proposal to set up a Nursing Advisory Committee was dismissed without consideration. This was despite a deputation sent to the council by the Registered Nurses' Association before the conference 'to request that in common with other voluntary organisations employing nurses to include in the personnel of its Executive a nurse representative of the Registered Nurses' Association'.[98]

As one researcher has noted, the episode highlighted the Dunedin-based executive's dominance of the council and concern among some branches that important decisions were being made without a general conference mandate.[99] The 1931 constitution had given wider geographic representation on the council by increasing the non-Dunedin members from eight to twelve, though the seven executive members still came from the Dunedin branch.[100] Rule changes in 1934 specified that executive members came from branches within easily accessible distance of Dunedin rather than the Dunedin branch itself. Clerical and administrative staff of the council was also separated from the Dunedin branch (which had previously subsidised the secretary's salary). At one level the struggle was between Dunedin and the rest. Yet, most significantly, the Central Council ensured that decision-making remained in the hands of volunteers, not nurses. Indicative of the council's attitude to its paid employees, too, was the changed status of the Dominion Secretary under the 1934 rules, based on the belief that 'too much power had been given to a salaried officer': 'She should be there to answer but not to enter into free discussion'.[101]

Pattrick retired with a flourish in September 1934, overwhelmed by parting gifts and tributes from around the world.[102] The following year she was invited to lecture on infant welfare in Canada.[103] She also visited New York and attended the Congress of the International Council of Nurses in London in July 1937. She spent the last months of her life at Cromwell House and died at St Thomas's Hospital in London on 19 September 1937. After her death a memorial fund was established, supported by worldwide donations. A national memorial, in the form of a library for nurses specialising in infant health, was opened in 1941.[104] She was also commemorated by a stained glass window in the Christchurch Hospital Chapel where she had trained so many years before.

Pattrick had succeeded in professionalising the nursing side of Plunket, although the real power continued to reside with the Central Council (now known as the Dominion Council), which also wished to professionalise the medical side of the work. The stimulus here came from Truby King himself who had complained at the 1925 conference that the Otago Medical School did not take child health seriously. During the previous year he had attended an international Child Welfare Conference at Geneva, where a resolution was passed urging the establishment of chairs in infant welfare in medical schools throughout the world.[105]

Infant health was not entirely neglected at Otago. Dr Ernest Williams, who had undertaken postgraduate training at the Hospital for Sick Children,

Do they look at ease? An early twentieth-century group of medical students at the Truby King-Harris Hospital, Dunedin. Hocken Library, AG-7/1/1

Great Ormond Street, London, had been appointed lecturer in diseases of children in 1908. As honorary physician to the Karitane-Harris Hospital and the Plunket Society, he kept his students in close contact with the society's work.[106] In 1925 Dr Charles Hercus, Professor of Public Health and Bacteriology and later Dean of the Otago Medical School, explained that he dealt with the question of infant feeding and the Plunket Society in the Department of Preventive Medicine and that Williams stressed the importance of Plunket work when he lectured on childhood diseases.[107] That year Truby King was appointed lecturer in paediatrics at Otago. The following year, the Plunket Society enhanced the status of paediatrics at Otago by donating £3,000 to the university, 'to set up a fellowship in preventive work in regard to paediatrics and the well-being of mother and child in the antenatal, intra-natal and post-natal periods and the child up to school age'. It was also hoped that the fellowship, to be called the Lady King Scholarship, would materially aid in the selection of an understudy to King.[108]

As early as 1920 King had anticipated a time when his role in the Plunket Society would be made superfluous by the appointment of a 'highly capable doctor',[109] though it was not until the late 1920s that he began actively to reduce his involvement. On 15 January 1927 Truby King's loyal wife and supporter, Bella, died. King never recovered from her death; for him 'it was the beginning of the end'.[110] Among the accolades at her death was that from Dr Helen MacMurchy who described Bella as the very embodiment of the spirit of the child and maternal welfare movement. She felt sure that Truby King could never have done his great work without her aid.[111] Although Bella was described by her adopted daughter Mary as a 'meek little person', she and King clearly made a formidable team,[112] and he began to go downhill mentally after her death.[113] Over the next few years he made several trips to Australia, where he and Mary set up a Karitane Products Society factory, to Britain, where he spoke at the National Conferences on Maternity and Infant Welfare in London in 1928 and 1930, and to continental Europe. Now in his early seventies, he was becoming cantankerous and aggressive, and inclined to emotional outbursts. According to Mary, he was 'old and tired'; his powers of concentration were failing and his 1930 address at the National Conference in London did his reputation 'untold harm'.[114] He was increasingly unpopular in Australia where he stirred up controversy on infant feeding, and the Karitane Products factory failed owing to lack of support.[115]

The 1928 Plunket conference resolved that the society would pay the salary and travelling expenses of a medical director. Dr Thomas Derrick,

The main waiting area, Plunket rooms, Thames. Note the homely environment, including a portrait of Truby King above the mantelpiece. Plunket's first paid medical director, Dr Thomas Derrick, and his wife helped found the Thames Plunket Society. Plunket Society Annual Report 1933–34

an Auckland general practitioner, was appointed in October 1928 on the advice of King. A graduate of Edinburgh University, Derrick had come to New Zealand in 1913 and set up in general practice in Thames. He and his wife had been founding members of the Thames branch of the Plunket Society.[116] Less than two years later, in May 1930, he tendered his resignation on account of 'indifferent health' and his contract with the society, which provided him with an annual salary of £500, terminated at the end of October 1930. Because all discussion of his resignation was conducted 'in committee', it is uncertain if he left voluntarily or if he was pushed, though Pattrick seemed surprised at the stated reason for his resignation.[117]

In November 1930 Dr Martin Tweed was appointed to act as honorary medical adviser during Truby King's absence from New Zealand, again on the advice of King. Tweed was born in Ashburton in 1890 and studied medicine at Guy's Hospital, London. Following active service in the First World War he returned to New Zealand and began practice in Carterton. He first expressed an interest in the Plunket Society in 1921 when he wrote to the Central Council enclosing a newspaper clipping about the opening of a branch in Carterton.[118] The following year he attended the Plunket Society's general conference as a representative from the Wairarapa town. When the Karitane Products Society was set up in 1927, Truby King chose Tweed as one of the directors. After nine months working for the Plunket Society in an honorary capacity, Tweed told the council that he found it impossible to combine the work with his private practice.[119] With the approval of Truby King, it was decided in November 1931 to offer Tweed a contract of £400 per annum plus travel expenses.

In 1932, without consulting the council, Truby King publicly announced a new scheme to establish maternity wards at Karitane hospitals. President Margaret Johnstone countered the announcement, describing the proposal as impractical. The council then asked newspaper editors not to publish anything by Truby King as the society's General President, without its permission.[120] Aware of King's failing powers, in July 1932 the council recommended that 'for his own sake and for the welfare of the Society [King should] give earnest consideration to the question of resigning from active participation in the affairs of the Society'.[121] The resolution was approved by the Advisory Board and two of its members, Judge Archibald Blair and Sir William Hunt, were asked to convey the decision to King. Although his response is not recorded, he further embarrassed the council three months later when he came out publicly in support of the National Expenditure Commission's recommendation that Plunket should begin charging mothers for its services. He argued that free services were demoralising, that 'people got into the bad habits of taking everything as a right and giving nothing in return'.[122] This was considered an 'extraordinary change of front on the question of the Society's principles'. As Blair pointed out, 'Ever since its foundation more than a quarter of a century ago the policy of the Society has been to make its service free whether these services are given to the poor or to the rich.'[123] King's statement was attributed to his 'mental condition due to advancing years', but it was no temporary aberration. He again broached the subject of payment for service with Tweed in 1933.[124]

The society's relationship with its founder continued to deteriorate. In 1933 Hoddinott reported that King had made a 'violent, personal attack upon me as secretary', an attack, she claimed, which embraced the executive.[125] When King died on 10 February 1938, however, his recent relations with Plunket were quickly buried and he was heralded as one of New Zealand's icons, the originator of the world-famous Plunket Society.[126] His daughter received a telegram from the Queen.[127]

In November 1933 the executive decided that it required a full-time medical officer, mainly because of the growing medical and public criticism directed towards Plunket.[128] It was agreed that Tweed be asked to become full-time medical adviser, with a salary of £1,200 and a five-year contract.[129] Three-quarters of his salary was met by the Karitane Products Society.[130] A year later the council expressed misgivings about what Tweed had achieved for Plunket, and asked him to present a research plan for the following two years. They did not, however, allow him to attend a BMA conference in Melbourne in 1935 in order to upgrade his knowledge of international trends.[131] This decision contrasted with the council's willingness to release Nursing Adviser Nora Fitzgibbon for a nine-month study trip of infant-welfare organisations in the United States, Canada, England and continental Europe in 1936–7, funded by the Karitane Products Society. Over the next two years Tweed constantly annoyed the executive by his failure to provide the promised monthly reports or details of his travel expenses. In 1937 he was directed to use train and service cars for journeys exceeding 50 miles, 'unless cases of emergency should arise where suitable trains and service cars would not fit in'.[132]

At the end of 1936 President Helena Sidey complained to Hunt, as chairman of the Karitane Products Society, about Tweed's shortcomings. She referred to his 'indecision, procrastination and weakness generally' when an opinion was required. He apparently turned up to address meetings unprepared, and lacked initiative. 'The position will become intolerable if we have to "drive" him all the time and this would appear to be the only chance we have of getting him to do constructive work for the Society.'[133] The council felt more than capable of passing comment on the competence of a health professional. In March 1937 the executive told Tweed that he lacked 'the personality, initiative and driving force to gain and hold the confidence of the Executive, and Council members' and that his term of office would not be extended.[134] The council's attitude was made clear in 1937 when Tweed asked if he might be permitted to make a statement. Sidey took exception to having the agenda interrupted but it was agreed that a statement would be received after the luncheon adjournment. That afternoon a discussion between the council and Tweed took place 'in committee'.[135] He was advised that it would be in his own interest to announce that he had no intention of applying for a renewal of his contract.[136] Later that year the council declined the Medical Advisory Committee's request that Tweed be sent abroad to study modern methods in the feeding and management of children.[137] At the same March 1938 meeting at which the passing of Sir Frederic Truby King was recorded, Tweed's resignation on the grounds of ill health was accepted 'with regret', with effect from 31 May.[138]

It has often been assumed that King and Plunket were one and the same. As Olssen put it, 'The Society aped the prophet.'[139] Yet the dispute with Tweed was not because he criticised Truby King and his ideas; indeed Tweed showed great loyalty to King.[140] Rather it was the Central Council –

Funeral procession for Sir Frederic Truby King, the first private citizen to be honoured by a state funeral, 1938. *Evening Post*, 12 February 1938, ATL, G-48805-1/4, PAColl-0614

the women who ran Plunket – who were not impressed by his attitude towards his employers and his inability to command the respect of the growing number of New Zealand paediatricians. Council members turned to doctors and businessmen for medical and financial advice but were determined to retain control of Plunket services. It was this determination that shaped their relationships with Pattrick, Tweed and King himself in this period.

Plunket services and their reception

In 1920 the Plunket Society employed 55 nurses; by 1939 the figure had risen to 131, giving each nurse a new baby caseload of around 160 per annum.[141] From 1922 registrars notified Plunket of all non-Maori births and the society invited new mothers to make an appointment for the Plunket nurse to call. After three months, the mothers were invited to bring their babies to the local Plunket clinic for regular check-ups and advice. Reviewing this pre-Second World War period, historians from the 1970s placed new interpretations on the relationship between infant nurses and their clients. They argued that infant-welfare services, in New Zealand and elsewhere in the Western world, were forced upon women by the new scientific experts, who denigrated women's skills and undermined their confidence as mothers. As Kathleen Jones explained in 1998, the assumption was that 'Advice handed down was advice received, uncritically accepted, and debilitating for the average mother'.[142] For Australia, Claudia

The Royal New Zealand Society for
the Health of Women and Children

(Plunket Society)

Dear Mrs...
*   We were delighted to hear of your baby's birth and trust
you will call on the services of the Plunket Society if you wish
advice or help.*

The Plunket nurse visits your district on.............................
*If you wish her to call please fill in and return the accompanying
card or telephone*..................*between*..............*and*..........

This card was sent to all new non-Maori mothers inviting them to use Plunket services.

Knapman noted the tendency to conceptualise infant-welfare clinics in terms of maternal surveillance and middle-class experts tyrannising their clients.[143] The overall impression was one of unwanted, unwarranted, 'scientific' ideas imposed on a passively receptive female audience.[144]

In New Zealand the most influential exponent of this view was Erik Olssen. Describing how Truby King's doctrines were based on establishing routines and the production of self-regulated citizens, he maintained 'it is beyond doubt that the new prescriptions became the orthodoxy'. He stated that by 1930 some 65 per cent of all non-Maori infants were under the 'control' and care of Plunket, and by 1947 the figure had risen to 85 per cent. After 1921, Olssen claimed, the government and the Plunket Society worked together to 'impose' King's views on most Pakeha, and Plunket's 'fast-growing cadre of nurses helped impose the conception of ideal character'.[145]

Others expanded on this. Helen May argued that one result of Truby King's campaign was 'several generations of anxious mothers' who passed down their Plunket books from one generation to the next. She held that kindergartens did not contradict King's regimen but were based on 'kindly order', thus implying that the mothers' regimen at home was unkind.[146] In her 1987 MA thesis Belinda Hitchman, too, drew on Olssen as the basis for her analysis. She concluded that King's 'influence on his colleagues and the wider society through the Plunket Society, cannot be underestimated . . . Generations of New Zealand mothers, from the Society's inception to recent years, have attempted to regulate their lives and the lives of their infants to King's dictates.' Hitchman claimed that

Plunket nurses'
uniforms, indoor
and outdoor. The
outdoor version
was described as
'military grey with
green facings'.
Plunket Society
Annual Report
1927–28

Indoor.   Outdoor.

'anecdotal evidence collected from friends and relatives indicates that
many mothers felt tyrannised by King's regimes for good infant care'.
The imposition of 'expert' advice meant 'a further erosion of their self-
confidence and knowledge about themselves and how to raise children'.[147]

Matters to be addressed here include the extent to which nurses propa-
gated the 'Truby King precepts', their relationship with mothers, the
degree to which mothers followed advice offered and the impact this
had on their maternal confidence. Some doctors certainly described Plunket
nurses as doctrinaire. For example, when Dr Sydney Morris, Director of
Maternal and Baby Welfare in New South Wales from 1925 to 1934, visited
New Zealand in 1924 he asserted, 'The average Plunket nurse of his experience was so rigid and dogmatic about infant feeding that she regarded
Truby King's rules as a ritual, in which the "slightest deviation [became]
magnified . . . into almost a heinous offence".'[148] During the 1938 dispute
over infant feeding (see Chapter 4), some doctors commented on the
nurses' dogmatism.[149] Yet other doctors acknowledged variation among
the nurses. A 1938 Medical Research Council survey based on the responses
of medical practitioners revealed that services 'varied to some extent with
the type of Plunket nurse in their particular district',[150] suggesting that
they were not all of a batch. Dr Basil Quin, honorary medical officer to

Auckland's Karitane Hospital, complained in the 1940s that some of the older Plunket nurses used only their own recipes for infant feeding.[151] They had considerable independence, and very little supervision. One Plunket historian found that nurses who disagreed with their director were sometimes brought to task by their local lay committee, indicating the nurses had independent views.[152] Plunket's own archives reveal that in the 1920s at least one nurse wrote one thing in the Plunket book and another on a piece of paper given to the mother.[153] A 1945 survey discovered that 'the great majority of nurses' advised a more liberal diet for infants than that written in Plunket schedules.[154]

Did the nurses tyrannise their clients and undermine women's self-confidence? It is hard to reconcile this image with the nurses who hopped on and off public transport in the burgeoning towns and cities and walked for miles in the new suburbs, or those who travelled long distances in the country by bicycle or, from the late 1930s, sometimes by car. On her retirement in 1950, Auckland Plunket nurse Mary Carmichael, who joined the service in 1923, looked back at her experiences. She had affectionate memories of the tramwaymen who never passed her by even if the chains were up. 'They recognised the grey uniform of the Plunket nurse and always stopped,' she said. 'In fact they often recognised me personally for I had been to the homes of many of them to care for their babies.' She reflected 'with rather a shudder' on the hours she worked: 'There was no limit to the time given. The nurse had her "round" to do and then had to be prepared to go out at call'.[155] Another Auckland Plunket nurse, Ivy Margaret Johnson, who worked from 1925 to 1946, 'had made herself available to mothers and their babies during the day, at night and during holidays'.[156] One nurse in 1921 described a very serious case of mastitis which the doctor had left entirely in her hands; she reflected that morning and evening visits greatly increased her workload but were clearly appreciated by the mother.[157]

The *Auckland Star* reported that, despite salary cuts, in the 1930s nurses sometimes dipped into their own pockets to prevent mothers from going short.[158] During the Depression charge nurse Helen Chapman visited the market regularly on Thursday mornings to buy food which would be distributed by the nurses to mothers in need in Auckland. Wellington's charge nurse also found that, in the 1930s, she was spending up to two days a week organising charitable relief.[159] Nurses recognised that many mothers required more than education. When Marion ('Maisie') Shepherd described her experiences as Plunket nurse in Rangiora from 1929 to 1939 she recalled how she and a Plunket committee member helped a Maori family in extreme poverty who were new to the area and had no contacts.[160] Shepherd later explained how Plunket nurses dispensed food and baby clothes in the Depression. Her impression that 'mothers were glad to see me' suggests the building of a personal relationship.[161] The general appreciation of Shepherd's services was indicated by the way in which she was overwhelmed by presents when she left in 1939.[162]

The nurses and mothers often seem to have developed such relationships. Local committee reports commented on how the nurses gained the love and esteem of the mothers.[163] In her history of motherhood Sue Kedgley claimed that 'For thousands of mothers in the 1920s and 30s, the Plunket nurse was a pillar of support. Plunket was a household name by now, and the Plunket nurse was looked upon almost as a surrogate mother to thousands of "Plunket babies".' 'Surrogate grandmother' is possibly a more accurate description. The nurses were, after all, occasional visitors to the home; the relationship did not involve constant supervision or any usurping of the mother's role. Kedgley also cited the nervousness of one mother about an impending Plunket nurse visit because she felt she was being inspected; much depended on the personalities of the nurse and mother.[164]

Jane Lewis has argued that, in England, clinics were probably the most successful part of the infant-welfare services, since women could choose whether or not to attend.[165] Descriptions of Plunket clinics, where mothers brought their babies after three months, suggests that they, too, were well patronised. The Wellington branch committee described the local Plunket rooms in 1915 as 'very crowded during the times the nurses attend'.[166] In the Auckland suburb of Onehunga one nurse expressed concern in 1926 at the number of women who, having seen the crowds waiting, left the clinic before the nurse had a chance to see them (an appointment system was not generally used until after the Second World War).[167] When new central rooms were opened in Auckland in 1927, the secretary wondered how they had managed in their old quarters, 'where, on busy days, it was impossible to find seating accommodation for the many waiting mothers, babies and their friends'.[168] A 1936 press report noted the enormous popularity of the system as indicated by 84,000 visits to Auckland's Plunket rooms that year, with nurses seeing as many as 60 or 70 babies in an afternoon.[169]

Mothers could choose not to attend if they did not like the nurse. This happened at one clinic in 1919; the local Plunket committee, which had received numerous complaints from mothers about that nurse, replaced

Plunket had a tangible presence in almost every small town in New Zealand. Plunket rooms, Gore, c. 1935. Plunket Society Annual Report 1935–36

Central Plunket rooms, Christchurch. Plunket Society Annual Report 1930–31

her and attendance went up immediately.[170] In 1932 the Lower Hutt branch sacked a nurse, after receiving complaints regarding her 'manner and approach to mothers'.[171] From early on, it was recognised that the nurse's personality was all-important. As the report of Wellington branch's first annual general meeting in 1908 noted, 'The Society was to be congratulated on the personality of the nurse who did not only good to the babies but to other members of the families by the interest she took.'[172] Not all reports were favourable. In 1919 Dr Hilda Northcroft, then on the Auckland Plunket committee, received complaints from mothers about nurses. The committee seconded Mrs W. R. Wilson to 'speak to the nurses about being more tactful with parents'.[173] Two 'country women' complained, when consulted in 1934, that though educated, 'the Plunket nurse would not credit them with an ounce of brain between them, so they ceased calling on her'.[174]

For some their relationship with the nurse was not the prime factor in clinic attendance. As Mein Smith found in Australia, a visit to the clinic offered a chance for the mother to 'display her pride and joy'.[175] Another attraction might have been the chance of a weekly outing, and meeting

An hour and a half was allocated for the first 'confidential chat' between the nurse and the expectant mother. Plunket rooms, Cambridge Terrace, Wellington, January 1949. Archives New Zealand Te Whare Tohu Tuhituhinga O Aotearoa: National Publicity Studios Photographic Collection, ATL, F-33848-1/2 (A 10, 065)

other mothers.[176] For others it was simply 'curiosity', to see whether their baby had gained weight.[177]

In the 1920s and 1930s women increasingly availed themselves of ante-natal services provided. The Auckland clinic reported in 1932 that 'the greater percentage of expectant mothers who come to us are advised to do so by mothers who have previously attended the Clinic'.[178] Dr Vera Scantlebury Brown, who visited New Zealand in 1924 before taking up the post of Director of Infant Welfare in Victoria, Australia, maintained that one of the attractions of the ante-natal care was that at the clinics they were examined by women only.[179] This medical attention was free (an added attraction), mothers were given practical advice (about types of cots, for example) and patterns for baby clothes could be purchased at minimal cost, which proved very popular.

The enthusiasm with which women of the 1920s and 1930s embraced the new child-rearing literature suggests they were not reluctant recipients of advice but rather actively sought and evaluated information for themselves. This was a generation who could read, respected the written word and had been educated in scientific values. Compulsory primary education was rigorously enforced after 1900, and access to secondary education improved. Science held a new status in society. Although home science, introduced into schools as a subject in the matriculation examination, did not attract a lot of support from pupils, by the 1920s science (natural and physical) was a core subject in most secondary schools.[180] Later it was noted that the 'ability to think for herself' was an important asset for motherhood, so that 'it would appear that office girls and businesswomen constitute a high proportion of the good mothers with happy thriving families'.[181]

If paediatrician Professor Emmett Holt was the United States' early twentieth-century Benjamin Spock,[182] then Truby King was New Zealand's in terms of his publication, *The Expectant Mother and Baby's First Month*. It went through six editions and became both the Health Department and the Plunket text for mothercraft.[183] Later editions were expanded in length, and two editions were published in Britain in 1924 and 1933. The Plunket Council recorded in 1924 that it had countrywide assurances from husbands and wives, and from registrars who had been instructed to issue it with marriage licences, as to the general appreciation of the publication.[184] At Plunket's annual conference in 1922 Kathleen Hosking, president of the Wellington branch, queried Health Minister Parr's idea that the *Expectant Mother* was 'flung into the waste-paper basket'. It was her experience that when there had been a shortage of copies, those available had been passed from one woman to another. Mrs Buchanan of Nelson stated that since the distribution of the book, their nurse had had a considerable increase in visits from expectant mothers. The Christchurch branch was unable to keep pace with the demand. Auckland delegates said that during the shortage they had a 'desperate time': many people left the office indignant because the nurse could not supply the book. Tweed claimed that the reply he usually got on asking a woman if she had the book was, 'Yes, but it is lent.'[185]

What about the content of the advice? As with child-rearing guidelines in other countries, the emphasis was on establishing routines in feeding, sleeping and bowel movements. This approach was believed to produce a well-balanced adult, who could exercise self-control and cope with deferred gratification. In the less child-centred world before the Second World War it was also regarded as convenient for the parents. The response of one London mother to the advice given by Plunket's London-based Mothercraft Training Society would have appalled post-1945 child psychologists: 'Your methods are so easy to use at home, that although I have to run the house and cook mid-day dinner, I hardly know I have a baby'.[186]

In 1953 the British *Family Doctor* published an article on modern child care. This cited the 'Truby King precept that the baby should be kept away from his mother almost entirely, except when it was to be fed. Fondling and cuddling were forbidden, and rocking or dandling the baby was positively to be avoided.'[187] Olssen reiterated this interpretation of King's philosophy: 'mothers should not rock, tickle, or play with their babies'.[188] However, a closer reading of Truby King's manual, *Feeding and Care of Baby*, suggests that this was a distortion. King claimed that 'Babies who are allowed to lie passively in their cots and who do not get sufficient mothering tend to be pale, torpid, flabby and inert'. Babies were to be moved, picked up and carried about at regular intervals. King maintained that the absence of such 'mothering' could lead to rickets or 'wasting away with marasmus' (in modern parlance, 'failure to thrive'). Foreshadowing Dr John Bowlby, author of the maternal deprivation thesis (see Chapter 5), he explained that 'This has been a common fate of babies boarded in institutions or licensed homes, and physicians have remarked how much rarer are such diseases where the baby, though placed under otherwise similar conditions, gets a good deal of handling through the presence of older children'. This was beneficial; it was 'excessive and meddlesome interference and undue stimulation' that was supposedly harmful. By 'undue stimulation' he meant that the baby was not to lead 'the life of an infant prodigy in a side show, decked out for exhibition half its time and always at hand for special performances before special visitors'. This did not mean, however, 'that babies are not to be allowed to play or to be judiciously played with. Play is the natural, joyous overflowing expression of child life and activity, and as such should be encouraged; but the baby's earliest play should be mainly with its first playmate – itself – its own feet.' He added that parents should 'Never play with and excite a baby just before bedtime'. To King, 'injudicious handling' meant 'jolting, swinging, rocking, or concussion' which might indirectly upset the stomach through the nervous system. He explained, 'If a woman's whole aim were to induce vomiting, she could not set about it more scientifically than when, picking up her baby and deftly balancing it face downwards with the belly and chest supported on her open palm, she proceeds to rapidly pat the back with the other hand, thus subjecting the stomach to a series of direct concussions and squeezings while the head dangles over her wrist.'

For the treatment of colic, however, he recommended applying warmth to the feet and abdomen, massaging the belly with fingers dipped in warm oil or 'handling baby as shown in Figure 49 opposite'. This was a picture of a nurse giving the baby a big cuddle, with an accompanying caption: 'Nurse gently but firmly pats, rubs, or squeezes left side of back with right palm, while left arm and hand keep body upright, with belly pressed against nurse's chest'. Breastfeeding, which he strenuously promoted, also afforded an opportunity for closeness, as stressed by psychologists from the 1950s.[189] King himself claimed that breastfeeding 'foster[ed] the highest development of maternal love and devotion'.[190] Intervals between feeding were designed primarily to strengthen the digestive system, a major concern at a time when the primary cause of death was related to gastric upsets.

Fear of gastric upsets leading to fatal disease also determined King's advice on bowel movements. Mein Smith noted his instruction not to 'let 10 o'clock in the morning pass without getting [baby's] bowels to move'.[191] The full quote, however, was 'Don't let 10 o'clock in the morning pass without getting the bowels to move if there has not been a motion in the previous 24 hours'.[192] According to contemporary medical belief, 'A constipated child should always be regarded as on the verge of diarrhoea: babies readily pass from one extreme to the other.'[193] So how did King recommend making them move? He advised against all purgatives. He cited American paediatrician Holt on enemas but warned that 'Much harm is done by the habit of giving ordinary enemas to babies'. He suggested a gentle massage of the abdomen with a warmed hand, using warm oil. 'Persistent constipation is a serious affliction, needing careful treatment under medical supervision.'[194]

The pre-Second World War era was undoubtedly less child-centred than

"It won't trouble you at night, madam. It's had a Truby King training."

Cartoon depicting the 'Truby King methods'. The caption reads, 'It won't trouble you at night, madam. It's had a Truby King training'.
New Zealand Herald, 29 January 1941

the post-1945 period, and Truby King's psychology did involve instilling discipline for the sake of future character formation, but the strictness of the time had its limits. In 1936 'Hygeia' penned an 'Our Babies' column entitled, 'Is Smacking a baby a satisfactory method of teaching him self-control?' The writer maintained that the Plunket Society would never countenance 'smacking' as a remedy for the correcting a baby's apparent naughtiness. Such an approach would have the 'effect of subduing, or frightening the helpless little creature into submission'.[195] Self-control from the mother as well as the baby was expected in this period. Nor did the society itself follow King's dictum, cited by Olssen, that babies should be 'ignored at night'.[196] The 1922 guidelines for mothers employing Karitane nurses specified that if the baby was fretful at night the nurse should be given additional rest during the day.[197]

Olssen claimed that Truby King's advice became more authoritarian as time went on, and Mein Smith elaborated on this when she wrote that 'in 1937, disciples updated his schedules to feeding 5-hourly from birth'.[198] Whoever these 'disciples' were, they were not Plunket employees, whose official line was spelled out by 'Hygeia' in 1938: 'Most babies do well with five feeds a day, at intervals of four hours. Should baby be small or weak he may need six feeds, at intervals of three hours.'[199]

Plunket advice stressed parent-directed child care. It was said to be a mistake to pick up the baby whenever it cried. 'Hygeia' also asked, 'Should Babies Cry?' The writer maintained that if the baby were fed at regular intervals, with the right quantity of suitable food (however that was measured), there should be no crying or discomfort between times. If the baby cried, it was the mother's duty to find out and treat the cause, not merely to stop the cry by giving food. She suggested some possible causes and responses. Most significantly,

If he wants attention, of which from an early age every baby is very fond, he will cry as soon as his mother goes out of sight . . . Often his cries cease as soon as he sees or hears his mother coming to him – in other words, he is rapidly becoming a spoiled baby. In this connection one cannot begin too early to train a baby. If a mother waits a few months before commencing, she is lost. She should begin when baby is born to make him understand that she means what she says – it is for the child's good. We now come to the treatment of a baby who cries simply because he wants attention, which is – baby must cry it out. One of the hardest trials of a young mother is to hear her baby cry and not give into him.[200]

It may have been convenient to believe this was for the good of the child. Established routines, rather than a more relaxed and child-centred method of infant care, helped women to better organise their own daily lives, especially if there were other children to look after as well. Kindergartens and crèches were not widely used, despite the founding of the free kindergarten movement in the early twentieth century. Women living in the new urban and suburban settings could not so easily turn to their extended family or husbands for child care assistance. Yet standards of housekeeping in the new bungalows of the 1920s were high. In the pre-antibiotic era but following the discovery of the bacterial causes of major infectious diseases around the turn of the century, there was an increased focus on maintaining a germ-free environment.[201] Both advertisements and child-rearing guidelines encouraged this. With such expectations, the ordered routines may have assisted with the maintenance of breastfeeding, which continued to be central to Plunket advice. From 1930 Plunket changed its logo to include a breastfeeding mother and child. Although routines came under fire from the new child psychology of the 1950s, as will be discussed later, many of those who had borne children in the 1920s and 1930s were staunch supporters of the older methods. In response to criticism of routines by Timaru MP the Reverend Clyde Carr in 1952, five out of six mothers selected at random from the current telephone book dismissed the criticisms as 'ridiculous': 'Mrs Skelton of Auckland said she had brought

". . . And, remember,—not an interjection out of any of you!"

In the more liberal post-Second World War climate, the Revd Clyde Carr MP criticised Plunket methods as disciplinarian. The 'babies' depicted here include leading politicians, Sidney Holland, Arnold Nordmeyer and Walter Nash. *New Zealand Herald*, 2 October 1952

up her three children as Plunket babies . . . If babies were fed at any old time mothers would never have a free moment,' she said.[202]

Writing of infant welfare clinics in Australia, Kereen Reiger noted a complex process of resistance, negotiation and acceptance by mothers in relation to child-care advice.[203] Plunket routines undoubtedly found favour with many mothers who nevertheless made only selective use of the advice given. In a series of letters to the *New Zealand Herald* in 1934, E. N. Reid responded to 'Anti-Plunket' who complained 'with an exclamation of horror' that the Plunket nurse was 'let loose on her district!', without medical supervision of her work. Reid wrote, 'I cannot see that she is more "let loose" than any citizen who puts up a sign offering services or goods for sale to the community. The public takes them or leaves them at its own discretion.'[204] A 1934 report of interviews with country mothers noted that while one was a 'strict Plunket mother, and her bairns were bonny', two were 'not strictly Plunket'. The reporter noted, 'They used that amusing qualifying sentence, "But, of course, we use our own judgment."'[205] A 1936 medical researcher noted that one woman visited the Plunket clinic simply to have her baby weighed and ignored all feeding advice.[206] Another said of a woman he interviewed about Plunket, 'She used the Plunket Sister but did not necessarily follow her advice.'[207] Dr Marie Buchler told Dr Montgomery Spencer during the infant-feeding disputes in 1938 (see Chapter 4) that, 'At a sherry party on Friday, nearly every married woman came . . . and told how they used to go to the Plunket nurse and then add on ounces to what she had suggested and pretend they were doing what she said!'[208] The *New Zealand Medical Journal* editor claimed in 1938 it was a 'common experience to hear an intelligent mother say, "I had the baby on the Plunket system, but I saw he wasn't getting enough, so I gave him more – but I didn't tell the nurse"'.[209] These 'intelligent' mothers still, however, consulted the nurse.

The successful expansion of the Plunket Society in the 1920s and 1930s was not accomplished just because it was centrally run by a group of highly skilled women who had secured political support. Nor were the identification of infant health as a matter of state importance at the end of the First World War and King's appointment with the Department of Health the determining factors. Plunket thrived because it met a need. Philippa Mein Smith has commented that the infant welfare movement was not responsible for the decline in death rates, but took off once they had decreased.[210] With raised expectations of survival and smaller families by the 1920s, mothers invested more time and energy in child-rearing. They were 'modern' women who wanted 'modern' advice, and turned to the nurses for guidance, as well as for support and reassurance. Yet this process did not undermine their confidence as mothers. A 1938 *New Zealand Observer* writer reminded her readers that, 'Being a conscientious mother is an anxious business. The individual problems may be small, but they loom large after a few wakeful nights with a fretful child. The Plunket nurse has met with the same problem a thousand times and she deals with it with calm efficiency.'[211]

CHAPTER 4

Complementary or Competing Services: Plunket and the Medical Profession in the Interwar Period

Doctors and nurses

During the interwar period, the voluntary sector of Plunket remained in control of the society, relinquishing power neither to its own health professionals nor to the Health Department. The most significant challenge to Plunket came from private medical practitioners, specifically those with an interest in child health. As stated earlier, a similar system to Plunket was instituted in the United States under the Sheppard-Towner Act of 1921. By the end of the decade, however, the American maternalists had lost control of infant welfare to the medical profession. As Sheila Rothman has written, 'By 1929, the medical profession had mounted a highly effective campaign that eliminated the program and made obsolete its assumptions about the proper methods of delivering health care.'[1] Unlike their American counterparts, Plunket survived the paediatric challenge. At the end of the interwar period, Director-General of Health Michael Watt complained that Plunket still operated without 'adequate supervision of its work by the medical profession'.[2]

As in the United States under Sheppard-Towner, the infant-welfare services and the medical profession were intended to work in harmony, providing complementary services. Plunket nurses were engaged in preventive medicine, general practitioners in treating patients. Yet there is evidence from the beginning that Plunket nurses treated sick babies, sometimes with the backing of doctors. Plunket's Medical Director, Dr Martin Tweed, thought this was probably still the case in the 1930s:

> Though it is no part of a Plunket nurse's duty to 'call in a Doctor' yet she must be ever ready to advise it at the earliest possible moment and she can always ring up the doctor and discuss the case with him and so put herself 'on side'. Nine doctors out of ten will be so flattered by the Nurse's action that they will generally leave the . . . case to her after the first consultation and then back her emphatically in all that she advises the mother to do.[3]

Plunket nurses were explicitly instructed to delete references to babies' ailments (other than dietetic) and to deaths in their annual reports. As Plunket's secretary Gwen Hoddinott explained in 1934, 'it is not considered advisable, in view of the criticism sometimes made by the medical profession in regard to the treatment of disease by Plunket nurses, for such references to be published in the reports of Plunket Nurses presented to the public by Committees.' Nurses were advised that they were only to include references to deaths in their confidential reports to the committees.[4]

In many cases cordial relations were maintained between Plunket nurses and doctors. In 1920, as part of a fund-raising campaign, Auckland Plunket sought testimonials from local doctors. These were forthcoming and enthusiastic. Not surprisingly, Dr Sydney Allen, married to Truby King's niece and practising medicine in Auckland, responded positively: 'I have great pleasure in testifying to the excellence of the work done by the Plunket nurses. They have at all times been of the greatest assistance to me in my professional work – always reliable and always ready to assist in the care and feeding of babies requiring aid. They are invariably tactful in their dealings with the mothers and with the medical man.'[5] He was not alone in this assessment. Plunket files contain letters in a similar vein from ten other local doctors, including C. H. (later Sir Carrick) Robertson. Dr Julius Delepine, who graduated from Edinburgh University the year before Truby King and had been practising medicine in New Zealand since 1913, wrote, 'I cannot speak too highly of the work done by the Plunket Society in Auckland . . . As a medical man, I . . . much appreciate the help given cheerfully by the nurses, who are always ready to come to the rescue, to help to save the babies and guide the mothers.'[6]

Not all doctors agreed. In 1926 Dr Vera Scantlebury Brown assessed the work of the nurses as 'generally good', though there was 'a tendency for them to overestimate their responsibilities, and to underrate the knowledge of the medical profession'.[7] Two years earlier Truby King had received a letter from Dr MacCormick of Auckland complaining about the attitude of a Plunket nurse and enclosing a letter he had received from her. King had been sympathetic to the nurse until he read her letter. He fumed, 'She manifestly appreciates neither the right attitude of the Nursing Profession towards the Medical Profession, nor the fact that it is utterly preposterous and contrary to all the rules of the Society for any of our Nurses to become the sponsors and advocates of any patent food.' (She supported Benger's Food.) King pointed out that one of the important points impressed upon nurses in training at the Karitane-Harris Hospital was never to criticise a doctor or his treatment, 'Yet here is one of our Nurses actually writing on the Society's paper a most impertinent and familiar note – informal, ignorant and inappropriate, from its lack of date at the top to its "Yours Teruely" at the bottom. No doubt the letter has been written hastily, but that is no excuse for writing illegibly, with utter informality, without stops, or with stops of the wrong kind!' He concluded that her attitude of assuming higher knowledge than the doctor was 'utterly unwarrantable'.[8]

That same year Plunket's Oamaru branch president dismissed the local nurse because of a doctor's complaint that she was not 'working in conjunction with the medical men'. It took a deputation, led by the Reverend Dr Hunter, which protested against the dismissal and testified to her 'unremitting care and attention to the mothers and babies and to her loyalty to the medical profession', to persuade the president and committee to reinstate the nurse.[9] It was neither the first nor last time that members of the public were to intervene on the side of Plunket nurses against the medical profession.

Auckland Plunket's most unremitting opponent in the early years was Dr Geoffrey Bruton Sweet, described as New Zealand's first specialist paediatrician.[10] Born in Devonshire, England, in 1870, Sweet had emigrated to Australia with his parents at the age of twelve. He graduated in medicine at Sydney University in 1893, moved to New Zealand in 1896 and, as was common practice at the time, did a stint in Britain to enhance his training. From 1905 until 1910 he was resident medical officer at the Great Ormond Street Hospital for Sick Children, London, where he developed his knowledge and skills in paediatrics. After that he set up a private practice in Auckland, was for many years consultant to the children's wards at Auckland hospital and published widely on infant health.[11]

Sweet and Truby King constantly challenged each other in print.[12] Their disagreement revolved around the level of protein to be added to infant feeding formulae, with both claiming endorsement from paediatric research. They also differed as to whether infant feeding required medical supervision, and whether Plunket services should be confined to the poor; much more than medical research was at stake. Sweet believed that medical supervision was essential: 'the medical man who allows the entire supervision of the feeding of his infant patients to pass into the hands of nurses is not doing his duty or giving the babies a square deal and a fighting chance of survival'. Nor could mothers be trusted. He argued that even with his 'simple' mixtures 'ludicrous mistakes are sometimes made by mothers whom Nature has gifted with little intelligence'. [13]

Sweet argued that Plunket catered for only a fraction of New Zealand's infant population, since the elaborate methods by which humanised milk was prepared, and its cost, prohibited its use by the poor. In fact the preparation of humanised milk was simplified by the production of 'emulsion', an additive available at Plunket clinics, often free of charge to poor mothers.[14] Sweet argued that the well-to-do had every chance of surviving in any case owing to their better conditions of hygiene and environment. The focus of the infant welfare campaign should be on 'saving the babies of the poor and thriftless' if they were to reduce mortality and assist 'in increasing the fighting population of the British Empire'.[15]

Sweet's fight was not just with Truby King but with the Plunket Society itself. In 1922, the Auckland branch secretary, Eileen Partridge, held that it would be 'fatal' to move a 'weaker' nurse to the Remuera or Epsom districts: 'These mothers would be away to Dr Sweet at once,' she said, suggesting they were in direct competition.[16] Sweet complained to the Auckland committee about the nurses' interference with treatment of babies under his care. He discovered that his feeding advice had been frequently criticised, and that mothers were being warned that their infants would be injured if they followed it.[17] In her response Partridge asked for the names of the nurses involved, and told him that the society was anxious for its nurses to be of the greatest possible assistance to doctors and to work harmoniously with them.[18] Sweet then threatened to sue for libel unless Plunket guaranteed that it was making a serious attempt 'to check this reprehensible conduct', but as he provided no names nothing further happened.[19]

By 1930 Sweet was running his own clinic in competition with Plunket. Mothers paid 2 guineas a year and could receive advice twice a month for that sum.[20] Auckland Plunket's head nurse, Beatrice Goulstone, noted, 'Dr Sweet is working very strenuously with his clinic. Still we march along.'[21] The following year it was recorded that they were losing a few babies to Dr Sweet, but since attendances for the month of June were 1000 up on the previous June, 'I think we are still holding our own!!' the new head nurse, Helen Chapman, boasted.[22] In the early 1930s Auckland Plunket was overseeing 76 per cent of all local babies as shown by birth notifications.[23] In 1931 Pattrick attributed the growing 'criticism and misunderstanding' from Auckland doctors to Sweet, pointing out that he often addressed medical groups.[24] Problems were occurring in particular with medical staff at the Karitane hospitals.

Karitane hospitals

By the end of the 1920s New Zealand had six Karitane hospitals. Fund-raisers had no difficulty locating potential benefactors for such a visible venture, especially when local pride was at stake. The first, operating from 1907, had been located at Truby King's holiday home at Karitane, and in 1910 was moved to Wolf Harris's house and estate, which he had donated to the society. In 1917 the purpose-built Lady King Karitane Hospital opened at Cashmere, Christchurch, following a Baby Week fund-raising effort. Wanganui's Truby King-Stewart Karitane Hospital was opened in 1919 by the wife of the Governor-General, Lady Liverpool. It was located at the former residence of John Stewart and his wife, who had bequeathed their house to the society following their deaths in 1913 and 1916 respectively. In 1924 a Karitane Hospital and Mothercraft Home was established in Auckland. It was gifted by A. C. Caughey, joint founder of the trading firm Smith and Caughey, with assistance from Sir Arthur Myers. From 1935 it was known as the Truby King-Karitane Hospital. In 1926 the Truby King-Hunt Karitane Hospital was opened in Invercargill, owing to the

The opening ceremony of the Plunket Society's Karitane Home in Mt Albert, Auckland, 16 October 1924. The property was donated by A. C. Caughey, founder of Smith and Caughey's upmarket department store. More than a thousand people attended. *Auckland Weekly News*, 19 October 1924

munificence of Sir William Hunt. Chairman of a farm merchant company, Wright, Stephenson and Co., Hunt was a successful businessman who received a knighthood in 1932 for his services to agriculture and business. In Wellington a combined Mothercraft Home and Central Plunket Office had been opened in 1923 as a result of fund-raising by the Men's Committee of the local Plunket branch.[25] In 1927 the Sir Truby King and Lady King Karitane Hospital and Mothercraft Home in Wellington was officially opened by the Duchess of York, wife of the future King George VI. It was sited on Truby King's property at Melrose.[26]

These hospitals, each of which accommodated about 30 babies and ten mothers, were staffed by matrons, nurses and honorary visiting paediatricians. In addition to the small complement of trained staff, each hospital had a number of Karitane nurse trainees, who paid for their training in the care of young babies and their mothers over a sixteen-month period, during which time they carried out the bulk of the nursing work. Only Dunedin's hospital trained Plunket nurses before the 1960s.

The care of premature babies ($5^1/_2$ pounds/2.5 kilograms or under at birth)[27] was one of the primary functions of the hospitals. In a public appeal on behalf of Auckland's Karitane Hospital in 1931 the *New Zealand Observer* claimed that fathers were the proudest of all when their babies began to gain weight. The writer added, 'Many of them are most attached to their delicate children, but simply don't know what to do with them. An extremely worried and frightened father arrived at the Karitane Home, not long ago, carrying his tiny son and heir in a cardboard shoebox.'[28] Other babies were admitted with nutritional problems or because of failure to thrive. Dr William Parkes, Chief Medical Officer of the Auckland Karitane Hospital, found it necessary to state in his first report that the hospital was not a 'foundling home where babies may be dumped to suit the convenience of the parents',[29] a warning he reiterated over the next few years. Nor did the hospitals admit babies suffering from infectious diseases or problems other than dietetic; these were treated in public hospitals. Because the Karitane hospitals took in weak and small babies, there was a prevailing belief in the 1920s and 1930s that the hospitals kept alive the 'better dead' babies. Staff were at pains to point out that this was a myth, including in their annual reports photos of ex-patients who had grown up to be 'bonny' children.[30] The teaching of 'mothercraft' was an additional function, which usually involved helping mothers to establish or re-establish breastfeeding, and to give them 'a sensible and confident outlook'.[31]

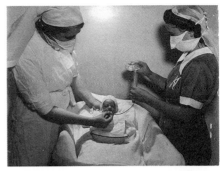

Much of the work at the Karitane Hospitals was increasingly focused on treating premature babies. These four images from the 1940s show: 1. Babies being transported to the hospital in a specially designed and heated carrier. 2. A baby too small to feed being nourished by the nurses through a tube (in the early days an eye-drop had been used). 3. Triplets and quadruplets were often admitted. Here are the 'East Tamaki Triplets', daughters of Mr and Mrs N. L. Koller, 1944. 4. Plunket was proud of its successes and kept in touch. Here are the triplets 'off to school'. Auckland Branch Annual Report 1948–49

In 1931 a dispute broke out in Auckland's Karitane Hospital between the acting matron, Joan Carmichael, and one of the consulting doctors, Dr Samuel Ludbrook. After qualifying in medicine at Otago University in 1919, from 1922 to 1926 Ludbrook worked in London, for a time as resident medical officer at Shadwell Children's Hospital. In 1926 he was appointed visiting physician to the children's ward at Auckland Hospital and to the city's Karitane hospital.[32] The dispute started when Ludbrook complained that, although he was an honorary physician to the Karitane Hospital, he had never been asked to see any babies. Carmichael showed him two cases, in one of which Ludbrook advised changing the diet. She tried the diet for

24 hours, but as the infant began to vomit again, she phoned Ludbrook and told him that the baby was back on the previous diet. Carmichael clearly did not like Ludbrook; she described him as supercilious and claimed he had been prejudiced against them by Sweet.[33] Ludbrook discussed her refusal to carry out his instructions at a meeting of the honorary physicians. As a result, Carmichael submitted her resignation in April 1931, because she felt strongly that the Plunket Society 'would be discredited in the sight of an already hostile medical profession and the world in general, if the services of a Matron who had refused to carry out a doctor's order were to be retained on the staff of a Karitane Hospital'.[34] Ludbrook also handed in his resignation in June 1931, explaining to the secretary, 'I find myself in disagreement with certain aspects of the Policy of the Society and of the Medical Control of the Karitane Home and as the authorities are not inclined to consider my suggestions it is impossible for me to retain my position on the staff.'[35]

As Ludbrook was aware, the dispute was not about a particular case but rather about control and authority. Karitane hospitals appeared to be relatively unusual in the degree of control exercised by the matron. A 1931 circular letter to all Karitane medical staff stressed that 'the direction of the work must be very largely left to the Matron, with the Medical staff as advisors, who are prepared to loyally co-operate, even if, on occasion, it means subordinating their own views to the general practice and teaching of the Society and the Hospital'.[36]

In 1933 the wording of the contract for new honorary medical staff was discussed by Auckland branch secretary Eileen Partridge and Dominion Secretary Gwen Hoddinott. Partridge claimed to be aware of the complaints by Auckland doctors, led by Sweet, that matrons had too much power and independence. As a result, she did not think it advisable to state that a doctor should subordinate his views to that of a nurse. Rather, she suggested specifying that a doctor on the honorary medical staff must be prepared to 'loyally support Matron'. In her opinion, 'These men . . . are always seeking for something new . . . that will give them some advantage over their colleagues in practice'; she suggested adding that the doctor always had the general hospital where 'he can practise any other form of dietetics he chooses'.[37]

The wording of the contract caused an outcry among medical staff. It stated that the honorary medical staff should undertake all medical treatment 'apart from dietetics', which had been underlined by Hoddinott.[38] Dr William Parkes, chairman of the Auckland honorary medical staff, replied

that the regulation had obviously not been drafted by a medical practitioner, 'who would never dream of placing a confrere in such a humiliating
position'. He continued indignantly that to insist upon a medical officer
having no say in the feeding of his patient was an insult which no doctor
'with a shred of self-respect would tolerate for one moment'; it was 'an
absurd and irksome restriction', and if it became more widely known 'the
whole profession would be up in arms and demand an inquiry'.[39]

Although he admitted that this requirement was no different from that
laid out in the 1931 circular, Tweed backtracked and apologised for the
'unfortunate mistake', claiming that he had always been careful to insist
that medical authority in the Karitane hospitals be supreme in all matters
of treatment, including diet which was, after all, 'the most important part
of all treatment in these Hospitals'.[40] Hoddinott told Tweed that 'emphasis
was placed upon the offending passage on the advice of Miss Partridge'.[41]
She had apparently been more than prepared to accept the advice of a
non-medical voluntary worker. It was not until 1936, however, that the
Dominion Council revised the by-law which had specified that honorary
medical staffs should attend the hospitals from time to time 'as requested
by the matron'.[42]

Another resignation occurred in 1934, this time at Wellington's Karitane
Hospital. Dr Thomas Corkill, who had been on the honorary medical staff
since the Mothercraft Home had opened in 1923 and whose wife had been
on the Plunket committee, resigned in 1934 because 'with certain aspects
of the present policy I am in complete disagreement'.[43] He had been patently
shocked by the way in which Pattrick had been dismissed the previous
year, and by her exclusion from any council discussion of professional
matters since 1929.[44] Tweed recounted a 'stormy interview' with Corkill

The Karitane Hospital,
Melrose, Wellington,
overlooking Lyall Bay.
ATL, G-21673-1/1

in March 1934 (or, he added, 'at least he was stormy and I was quiet') in which Corkill complained about the council running the professional side of the society's work.[45] Again in July, when the society's rules were being reviewed, he complained that the council's power was 'too far reaching'.[46] Ethel Cameron, a council member from Wellington, explained that Corkill had also taken exception to the fact that he had not been permitted to speak at the conference in Wellington in August 1934 when the appointment of the full-time medical adviser was being discussed.[47] Tweed later expressed his view that Corkill had left the hospital board for the same reason that he left the Plunket Society, 'i.e. lack of courtesy towards Medical Opinion, and too much lay interference in purely professional matters'.[48]

Plunket feeding practices and malnutrition

By the 1930s medical attention had shifted from the declining problem of infant diarrhoea to malnutrition.[49] An orthopaedic surgeon, Dr James Renfrew White, held that 80 per cent of young New Zealand children showed signs of rickets and Dr Edward Gunson asserted that a full '74 per cent of our school children who show physical defects are victims of faulty nutrition'.[50] Some paediatricians argued that it was faulty feeding in infancy rather than the economic depression that was responsible for the malnutrition of school children.[51] They specifically attributed it to Plunket feeding advice, both artificial and natural.

Plunket's artificial feeding practices relied on two products, Kariol and Karilac, which were intended to give artificially fed infants the nutritional value that they would get from breastfeeding. They were devised by Truby King, building on theories of early twentieth-century American paediatricians. In discussing the percentage feeding system advocated in the United States at this time, Richard Meckel pointed out that these theories were losing favour by the second decade of the twentieth century and that they had led down dead ends.[52] In New Zealand, however, these theories had brought about the development of an extremely successful manufacturing company which that helped substantially to underwrite the Plunket Society.

It was at Seacliff that Truby King experimented with the making of 'humanised milk' and developed the synthesised artificial cream which became known as 'New Zealand cream' or 'New Zealand emulsion', and eventually as Kariol. Consisting of a vegetable oil, cod liver oil and dextrose, it was given to the baby by teaspoon, and was described as the best, simplest and safest means of supplying the fat element of the milk, much safer than using cream or top milk. It was particularly useful in hot weather, and was soon exported widely. Karilac was a sugar mixture, consisting of sugar-of-milk (lactose), dextrose (or glucose) and gelatine. It was dissolved in boiling water and added to milk, sweetening it to resemble human milk.

Truby King assembled the machinery to make the emulsion at Seacliff, and paid for it himself. In 1921 he offered the plant to the Health Department, pointing out that it could supply ten to twenty times as much emulsion as could be used in New Zealand. The offer was not taken up.[53] The factory at Seacliff continued operating until the mid-1920s when a new factory was opened on King's Melrose property. The factory was unprofitable under King's management, and in order to prevent him from going bankrupt a group of businessmen and friends formed the Karitane Products Society (KPS) in 1927.[54] The original directorate consisted of Truby King and his daughter Mary, Dr Theodore Gray (the Director-General of Mental Hospitals) and his wife, Dr Thomas Derrick (Plunket's Medical Director, 1928–30) and his wife, Dr Martin Tweed (Plunket's Medical Adviser, 1933–8), Anne Pattrick (Director of Plunket Nursing, 1920–33) and her brother P. E. Pattrick (a Wellington accountant), Helene Hall (president of the Wellington branch of Plunket), Archibald Blair and Sir William Hunt, who was nominated chairman.

Profits from the KPS were used to subsidise the Plunket Society and its officers' salaries. In 1928 the KPS approved a grant of £200 towards the

The Karitane Products Society factory was built on Truby King's Melrose property in Wellington. Staff are shown packing Karilac or 'Plunket Emulsion', destined for Capetown, London and elsewhere. The Karitane Products Society Ltd and Plunket Society Annual Report 1927–28

salary of a tutor sister at the Karitane-Harris Hospital. The following year it met £500 of the medical director's £850 salary.[55] By 1934, when the medical director's salary was £1200, it provided £900.[56] In 1934 the KPS, having accumulated a surplus of £7,000–8,000, also granted a bonus of £10 to each member of the society's permanent staff, and gave £1,000 to each of the six Karitane hospitals. In 1935, £7,000 was donated as an endowment fund for nurse training, and £4,000 towards the rebuilding of the Dunedin hospital the following year. Plunket was careful to play down this association, but its critics exploited the connection. Ludbrook remarked in 1931 that Plunket nurses used Karilac only to swell the profits of the KPS.[57] Dr Sydney Morris, Director of Maternal and Baby Welfare in New South Wales, claimed that Plunket nurses were 'merely sales representatives for his [i.e. King's] emulsion and his sugar'.[58]

Plunket nurses were not permitted to prescribe patent medicines or promote commercial products, other than Kariol, Karilac and a later variant, Karil. When Scantlebury Brown visited Auckland's Plunket rooms in 1924, she noted that 'jars were encouraged' in distributing the emulsion 'so that they could be boiled and the mothers did not go away with the idea that they were having a patent food of any kind'.[59] At first these products were available only at Plunket rooms, but by the 1930s they were also sold in chemists and grocery shops. When an alternative infant feeding product, Anchoria, came on the market in the 1930s, its producers claimed that, 'the Plunket Society is definitely antagonistic towards ANCHORIA, but they have no grounds for this attitude beyond the fact they are getting no profit from our product, as is the case with Karilac and Kariol'. This commentator claimed to know of an incident where the Plunket nurse told a mother that as a result of using Anchoria the baby would 'probably develop knock knees and cross eyes!'[60]

In 1933 the matron of Auckland's Karitane hospital said that ' many of the Doctors in Auckland . . . think we tend to underfeed the babies with sugar'.[61] It was Kariol, however, that aroused most medical opposition. In 1931 Ludbrook claimed that the prevalence of rickets and scurvy among school children in New Zealand was much greater than in England and he attributed this to the use of Kariol for infant feeding. Long-term results of Plunket's low-protein feeding formula, according to New Zealand paediatricians Elspeth Fitzgerald and F. Montgomery Spencer, included 'poor [weight] gain, flabby muscles, poor resistance to disease, secondary anaemia, defective calcification of teeth and possibly rickets'.[62] Fitzgerald and Spencer presented papers to a well-attended Modern Infant Feeding session at the 1935 NZBMA annual meeting, in which they opposed Plunket's feeding schedules.[63] They were supported by the majority of their medical colleagues: as the *New Zealand Medical Journal* editor commented, 'when the only remarks directly adverse to the Plunket Society were made, there was applause all round the room'.[64]

Some doctors defended Plunket. They included Dr William Parkes, who claimed in 1931 to have been astonished when Drs Northcroft and Ludbrook diagnosed rickets in a ten-month-old baby supervised by Plunket. He 'asked for any grounds for stating that a child who was robust, active and apparently in the pink of health and condition without the trace of a suggestion of anaemia could possibly be called rickety, simply because it had cut no teeth'. Parkes added that the baby's diet was not changed, and in the course of a few weeks the teeth began to be cut quite naturally and normally – 'to the great satisfaction of the mother and Plunket nurse', he added smugly.[65] Dr Ernest Williams, honorary medical officer to the Karitane-Harris Hospital from 1908 to 1949 and lecturer in paediatrics at the Otago Medical School, also argued that there was more flexibility and simplicity in Plunket feeding systems than allowed for by critics.[66]

Mounting medical criticism prompted Plunket to appoint a Medical Advisory Committee in 1933. In the light of 'apparent growing criticism by the medical profession of the Society's teachings, particularly in regard to methods of artificial feeding',[67] the council asked the committee to 'make recommendations . . . in regard to any modification of or departure from the present teaching of the Society'. Its members included Drs Harold Pettit, Helen Deem, Thomas Corkill, Hugh Widdowson, Ernest Williams, Stanley Brown and Martin Tweed. The committee held its first meeting in 1934.[68]

Fully aware of the intended discussions of infant feeding at the 1935 NZBMA meeting, Tweed suggested the previous year that Dr B. Wyn Irwin be engaged for three months at 10 guineas a week to collect data on infant nutrition.[69] Irwin, the first graduate of a new Bachelor of Medical Science at Otago University in 1928, held a Lady King Scholarship at the time. He was asked to investigate 500 cases of naturally fed infants and 500 artificially fed by Plunket means, though in the event he examined only 548 babies in total.[70] Tweed presented Irwin's findings as 'the first authoritative data procured in regard to the results of the Society's system'. Irwin concluded:

One is not justified in taking such a pessimistic outlook as to the health of the coming generation as many from general practice, orthopaedic, and public health adult and school surveys, would opine . . . I found not only *one* perfect specimen but *scores* of them . . . I feel that, given good Mother and good stock, the Plunket Society through its Nurses produces good babies and by systematic following up, good older children, and they cannot be made responsible for the many who depart from this mean through maternal carelessness and ignorance.[71]

In other words, Plunket could take the credit but not the blame. Spencer later pointed out disparagingly that Irwin had 'never specialised in children's diseases, nor studied the subject outside New Zealand'.[72]

Fitzgerald believed it 'very significant that the majority of New Zealand graduates who have gone overseas to study have returned to New Zealand profoundly dissatisfied with the Plunket system'. She thought New Zealand was 'hopelessly behind the times in this respect'.[73] The new paediatricians had all studied overseas. They appear to have been particularly influenced by Dr McKim Marriott, Professor of Pediatrics at Washington University and author of *Infant Nutrition*, who argued that a 'moderate excess of protein . . . apparently does no harm: it is well digested and absorbed and causes no general disturbances'.[74] He concentrated on developing simple, digestible and affordable infant feeding methods rather than on trying to imitate human breast milk. Dr Edward Cronin, whose own children were 'Plunket fed' (presumably with no ill effect), spent four years working in London, visited continental Europe and then went to the United States where he worked under Marriott. He claimed to have been surprised to be converted to Marriott's methods, 'loyal New Zealander as I was', but never used Kariol once he returned to New Zealand.[75] It was pointed out in a press article in 1934 that the latest English textbook by Parsons and Barling described Plunket's the method of feeding as both 'complex and unnecessary'.[76]

The most strident criticism of Plunket, or at least the most public, came from Montgomery Spencer, a Wellington paediatrician and a member of the honorary medical staff of Wellington's Karitane Hospital from 1934.[77] In 1937 Spencer drew the attention of the Plunket Council to an 'extreme case of malnutrition' of a child under constant care and attention from the society, claiming to have seen 'many such cases' during the past few years. Spencer drew on his overseas experience in paediatrics to support his conviction that New Zealand lagged behind other countries in the appreciation of the 'normal' baby.[78] After graduating in medicine at Otago University in 1918, Spencer had done two years postgraduate training in

Britain and for one year was a Rockefeller Fellow at the Children's Hospital, Boston. He returned to New Zealand and practised in Hamilton from 1922 to 1928, after which he studied diseases of children at Harvard University and returned to practise paediatrics in Wellington. Spencer pointed out in 1938 that 'other countries had been through the percentage feeding era, but had grown out of it 15 to 20 years ago in favour of simpler methods giving better nutritional results'.[79]

Spencer castigated the Plunket nurses' use of the weight chart. He pointed out the error in adopting a standard weight curve established from averages taken from clinics serving slum populations overseas, and complained that Plunket nurses endeavoured to keep the infants' weights down to this level. He was confident from his case notes that many New Zealand babies were 'literally being starved', and attributed the high incidence of malnutrition among primary school children to starvation during infancy.[80] He pointed out that 'the curve on our weight charts, as used in the Plunket books, is LOWER than that used in cities such as New York. This should hardly be a matter for national pride when one contrasts our heredity, homogeneous stock, climate etc. with those of a downtown section of that city.'[81]

Although, in his view, Plunket nurses may have tried to keep weight down to match the weight chart, he also knew of a case of force feeding (admittedly by a Karitane and not a Plunket nurse), which he equally deprecated. This baby had been breastfed for five months. At nine months

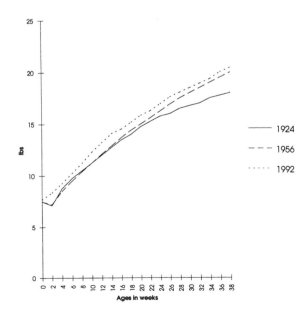

The weight charts printed in the 'Plunket Baby Books' have varied only slightly over seventy years. *Plunket Nurse's Advice to Mothers: Baby Record Book*, 1924, 1956; *Health and Development Record*, Department of Health, 1992.

when his weight was falling slightly, the parents employed a Karitane nurse. As he explained,

> the parents were banished from the room at meal hours, the baby was wrapped tightly in a sheet so that he couldn't move a limb, and then proceeded twenty minutes of forced feeding, during which time the baby was screaming the whole time. During that twenty minutes the nurse managed to get down the full complement of food, and then for the next half-hour she would hold up the lower jaw so that he couldn't eject it. Owing to the forced feeding the baby put on weight, not very satisfactorily, from the ninth to twelfth month. All right. They couldn't, or they didn't want to, keep the Karitane nurse any longer . . .[82]

Spencer's criticisms went far beyond the use of a particular formula in feeding, to Plunket practices more generally. He complained in his initial letter to the Plunket executive in 1937 that it was 'not at all uncommon for mothers to be told by Plunket nurses that my methods of feeding will prove harmful to their babies'.[83] The society's president, Daisy Begg, responded that nurses were instructed about the appropriate attitude to the medical profession during their training, and in their rules and guidelines. She sought Spencer's advice on how to make the requirements more effective.[84] Like Sweet, he did not provide any individual names. Indeed he claimed to know the names of only two Plunket nurses in Wellington.[85] This indicates his inability to work with and understand Plunket nurses, and also the latter's failure to carry out the part of their contract which specified that 'Whenever a Plunket nurse takes up duty with a Branch, she should establish personal contact with all local Medical Practitioners without delay'.[86] Not only was Spencer a consultant at Wellington's Karitane hospital, he was one of two practising paediatricians in Wellington.[87]

On 20 May 1938 an article appeared in the 'Health Supplement' of the *Dominion* entitled 'The Value of Proper Nutrition for the Young', about children who were suffering from being 'under, or wrongly, nourished'. The author gave details of one particular child, apparently his own.[88] The child's mother, on the advice of the Plunket nurse but 'against her own wishes', had refrained from weaning the child at three months old, 'when that seemed the obvious course'. She attended the child welfare centre weekly, had her baby weighed meticulously and was advised about feeding and treatment. Although the little girl appeared bright and healthy, the mother was greatly worried at her failure to put on weight as she should, and at

her increasing distaste for food. At fifteen months she decided, on her own
initiative, although the nurse did not seem perturbed by the baby's condition, to take her to a specialist. The specialist told her, from examining
her weight chart, that the child had been badly undernourished since three
months, when she should have been weaned. Her weight chart suggested
that she should have been placed before a doctor many months before. As
a result, she was on the verge of rickets. Yet a few weeks under the care of
the specialist, the article explained, served to create in her a real appetite
for food, and instead of putting on weight at the rate of only an ounce or
two a week, and sometimes even slipping back, in the second week after
consulting the doctor she gained 13 ounces.[89] Although no names were
given, many people probably guessed the specialist was Spencer since, as
noted, there were only two paediatricians practising in Wellington.[90]

The article also stated that, 'in encouraging the mother to feed her baby
up till the last possible moment, *even to the ninth month after its birth*,
malnutrition sometimes starts through the quality of the milk deteriorating,
although its quantity may be maintained'.[91] This concern for the 'quality'
of breast milk had long had currency among some paediatricians. In 1921
Dr Henry Washbourn, who graduated at Edinburgh University in 1908, had
argued that some babies thrived better on artificial food than mother's milk.
He commented, 'This is not to be wondered at when we look at the mothers
and at the lives they lead.'[92] Many American paediatricians also favoured
scientifically based infant formulae over breastfeeding.[93] Spencer later com-

'A normal breast-fed baby.' This baby was weaned
at nine months and then given a 'normal diet for
age'. In the 1930s the Society felt the need to point
out that babies breastfed until nine months did
thrive. Auckland Branch Annual Report 1938–39

mented on the 'fetish of giving the baby its natural food for as long as possible'.[94]

Five days after this article appeared Ernest Williams was asked to call a meeting of the honorary medical advisory committee 'to advise the Society in reference to recent medical criticisms'.[95] Responding to an invitation to participate, Corkill, who had encouraged the Plunket Society to appoint Spencer to the Wellington hospital's honorary medical staff in 1933,[96] advised Begg to invite Spencer because 'there is no man in New Zealand who has given these matters more thoughtful consideration or whose views are more widely respected among the medical profession in New Zealand'.[97] The committee met on 17 June in Wellington to 're-examine Plunket feeding'. Spencer was asked to speak, but was then 'thanked and dismissed'; he was not invited to partake in the discussions. One of the doctors present, Ian Ewart, senior medical officer at Wellington's Karitane Hospital, held that this had further antagonised him and led him to go to the press.[98]

Spencer told a *Dominion* reporter that 'It is the opinion of specialists throughout New Zealand that the Plunket system of feeding does not supply even the bare minimum of food values required for a baby's perfect development and health'.[99] Spencer listed six other specialists in New Zealand who had made a special study of the subject, and who disagreed with Plunket's methods. They were Samuel Ludbrook, Elspeth Fitzgerald, Edward Cronin, Marie Stringer Buchler, Roy Howells and Thomas Corkill. Buchler, who had been a Lady King Scholar 1934–6, agreed completely with Spencer.[100] She congratulated him privately for raising the issue, commenting that the 'Plunks' were 'getting touchy'.[101] Fitzgerald told him

New Zealand Herald, 25 June 1938

that she had issued a short statement in support, but that '*The Press* in Christchurch refused publication – it is practically owned by very powerful Plunket sympathisers'.[102]

At the June 1938 meeting some doctors argued in favour of abandoning Kariol for the cheaper cod-liver oil. Williams was concerned about the effect this would have on the KPS and possibly Plunket subsidies. He claimed from a 'scientific' point of view that the Karitane Products factory was an 'amazingly fine' institution and Kariol the best emulsion available. He believed that the objections to Kariol were usually on account of its smell. He urged the committee to consider very carefully before recommending to the council that the emulsion produced 'at such enormous expenditure and by such amazingly up-to-date machinery should be scrapped just because we want to simplify things'.[103]

The June 1938 meeting passed a motion proposed by Corkill which explained that the percentage system of feeding had come under criticism during the past six or seven years and that a simpler system of diluted milk with added sugar, 'based on certain scientific principles', had been devised. 'This meeting after full deliberation is of the opinion that it is in the interests of the work of the Plunket Society amongst the infants of New Zealand that a change to this method should be made.' Further, 'Pending the appointment of your new Medical Adviser, we recommend the immediate increase in the protein content of the milk mixture, and the commencement of mixed feeding [e.g. eggs and vegetables] at six months.'[104]

The motion was favourably received by the Dominion Council, which resolved that nurses should be taught alternative methods of infant feeding so that they would be able 'intelligently to cooperate with a medical man'.[105] The council did not have a problem with incorporating new ideas into Plunket training and sought to reassure the medical profession on that score, though, if possible, they wished to wait until the appointment of a medical adviser before doing so.[106] The KPS also thought medical leadership important. Its board told the council that Plunket should obtain the services of a world-renowned dietician as its new medical adviser, adding that it would be prepared to find the necessary salary for such an appointment.[107] The society, however, decided it would not be prudent to have its medical director or adviser funded by the KPS. Although it continued to accept donations from the KPS, the latter no longer paid a significant part of the director's salary.[108] Some in the society had already become aware of the danger of being seen to have vested commercial interests if the KPS paid the director's salary.[109]

For different reasons, Plunket and the KPS were not keen to become embroiled in a medical dispute, but rather wanted to ensure the smooth running of the services they offered. Around this time Mary King forwarded a letter to Fitzgibbon, written by Truby King in 1928, which she thought might be helpful. In it King had stated that it was never his intention or desire that the Plunket Society should be 'restricted in any way to the carrying out of my own personal opinions and convictions or conclusions (professional or otherwise) but simply that it should continue to carry out the original aims and objects of the Society'. He had always intended that those who ran Plunket would constantly seek further knowledge and disseminate it, irrespective of its source. He himself had always been ready to scrap any opinions or advice he had published 'in favour of simplifications, modifications or other changes justified and made expedient or desirable by the advance of practical knowledge'.[110]

Divisions of responsibility

As letters of support to Spencer indicated, some doctors and parents agreed that Plunket's weak milk dilutions had led to underfeeding and that the delay in introducing solids until the ninth month led to some under-nourished and unsettled babies. Spencer was congratulated for bringing it to public attention.[111] But the extent and duration of the problem were clearly exaggerated. Keen to restore public confidence in Plunket, Williams issued his own press statement. He worried that the press articles might encourage people to think that Plunket was 'deliberately and adversely under-feeding infants': 'Not only was such a suggestion contrary to fact, but an examination of many thousands of normal infants supervised by Plunket nurses would at once nullify such criticism'.[112] One survey on child nutrition in the Depression, by Hugh Somerset, came out in support of Plunket: 'There is every indication that the Plunket system is effective in improving nutrition of children who are found to be underweight'.[113] A May 1935 *Dominion* article commented that the cold weather and the difficulty mothers had in finding imported overcoats long enough for their children 'has drawn attention to the fact that the New Zealand environment, food and habits are evolving a race of taller people'. This finding was corroborated by school medical officers.[114]

Yet the dispute between the doctors and Plunket was about more than feeding advice; it was, as Spencer pointed out, about 'status and responsibilities'.[115] The new paediatricians were attempting to stake out their territory. Buchler told Spencer how keen she was to set up her own clinic.[116] Hilary Marland has written of The Netherlands that the development of infant-welfare services there between 1901 and 1930 related primarily to 'job creation, career consolidation and the carving out of a new specialist field of endeavour in the medical profession'.[117] In 1930s New Zealand the desire for more involvement by doctors led to suggestions that nurses were not equipped to administer child-health services. It was not just the specialist paediatricians who were affected, it was also the old story of general practitioners losing patients to Plunket.

Following Parkes's death in 1933, Dr Russell Tracy Inglis became chairman of the honorary medical staff at Auckland's Karitane Hospital.[118] Tracy Inglis was also medical superintendent of Auckland's St Helens Hospital, 1906–36, and the first president of the New Zealand Obstetrical and Gynaecological Society set up in 1927.[119] At the 1934 annual general meeting of Auckland Plunket, Tracy Inglis described Plunket nurses as 'laymen' in their profession. This sparked a flurry of correspondence in the local press.[120] The letters included one from 'M.B., Ch.B.', who argued that a newly qualified doctor, straight out of medical school, knew as much about infant dietetics as the average Plunket nurse. He claimed that many sick babies were being treated by Plunket nurses instead of being referred to 'a man who has been trained for the job'.[121] 'Plunket father' responded, however, that it was well known that 'honoured members of the profession found the Plunket nurse a valuable ally'.[122]

Speaking at the medical advisory committee meeting in June 1938, Dr Edward Cronin admitted that the Plunket nurse 'who knew her job could manage an infant feeding case much better than the average practitioner'.[123] Despite this, he advocated a scheme whereby doctors would be paid to take charge of the clinics. He thought these doctors would be better able to keep contact with the general practitioners than would the nurse. Williams also admitted that Plunket nurses could justifiably be criticised for remaining in contact with sick children 'for an unnecessarily long time'. He believed that was at the heart of Spencer's criticisms. Dr Herbert Robertson from Wanganui added that 'the biggest grouse in the profession is that they are not getting the cases referred back to them, and are losing pounds, shillings and pence'.[124]

The meeting passed another resolution that Plunket's council consider establishing a limited number of clinics in the larger centres under the supervision of a doctor interested in baby feeding. The intention was that he or she would see cases referred by Plunket nurses, with the object of referring them, when necessary, to their own private practitioner.[125] Responding to the motion, Fitzgibbon thought the proposal was an excellent one provided the right doctors were available. C. B. Barrowclough, the society's lawyer and an executive member, believed that the matter was essentially one for the consideration of the medical profession. He pointed out that Plunket had no funds to finance such a scheme, and that it was up to the medical profession to submit its recommendations on how it could be carried into effect. Williams thought the proposal should be held in abeyance until it were ascertained whether it had NZBMA approval.

In the late 1930s the NZBMA and the Labour government were in the process of negotiating new health services. How would paediatric services fit into the picture? Would the government and the NZBMA act upon the paediatricians' suggestion of clinics run by paediatricians? The latter were still few in number, had no professional organisation and remained largely dependent on Plunket for consultancies in their chosen specialty.

With regard to Spencer, within a week of the *Dominion* article the Wellington Plunket committee moved that the council be asked to consider the question of Spencer's position on the staff of the hospital.[126] They discussed it again at the following meeting, and considered it 'not equitable' that he should hold a position given his views.[127] The council left the decision to the Wellington branch, expressing full confidence in the ability of branch president Vida Jowett to deal with the situation tactfully.[128] It was not Spencer who resigned immediately but Ewart, leaving Spencer as next senior honorary physician.[129] In handing in his resignation Ewart 'took the trouble' to tell Jowett that 'New Zealand was the only country where nurses prescribed for babies'.[130] Although the council left the decision on Spencer's appointment to the Wellington branch, Begg told Jowett that the executive considered that it would be 'extremely undesirable' to have Spencer as senior honorary physician to the hospital.[131] Spencer himself had no qualms about continuing his services, explaining to Jowett that he was satisfied that 'Plunket [feeding] schedules [had] been altered so as to go a good way towards satisfying . . . [medical] recommendations'.[132] The executive, however, again informed Jowett that it was 'most strongly of the opinion that in view of Dr Spencer's recent public criticism of the Society it is inadvisable for Dr Spencer to be on the staff of the Wellington Karitane Hospital'.[133] In March 1939 Drs Reay Mackay and Morvyn Williams were appointed to replace Ewart and Spencer.[134] It appears that in the end Spencer the paediatrician needed Plunket more than Plunket needed Spencer.

The debate surrounding Plunket diets and nutrition was used to critique the Labour Government's 'socialist diet'. This shows the extent to which the nutrition debates had reached public consciousness. *New Zealand Herald*, 28 June 1938

Begg received a letter from Dr Fred Bowerbank, chairman of the council of the NZBMA, expressing the association's regret about the society's adverse publicity. The NZBMA had suggested to the Minister of Health that infant nutrition be studied by the newly formed Medical Research Council but Bowerbank informed her that this was not intended as a 'reflection upon the methods of the Society'.[135] Health Minister Peter Fraser was sympathetic to an investigation of child nutrition, but at the same time reassured Plunket that he thought it would be 'regrettable if anything were done or said to detract from its services to the Dominion'.[136] Correspondence between Director-General of Health Michael Watt and John Malcolm, Professor of Physiology at Otago (1904–43), however, suggests that the criticism of Plunket was the reason for the investigation. Watt wrote to Malcolm about Plunket's change of feeding formulae, 'Apparently they were satisfied that they could not stand the test of a scientific investigation. I do not know how to advise you about our proposed investigation. As you say it seems rather futile to inquire into a system of infant feeding which is no longer in force.' He suggested continuing with a more general survey.[137]

It is clear that publicly Plunket continued to enjoy the confidence of government and the NZBMA hierarchy.[138] Responding to an overseas inquiry, Mary Lambie, the Health Department's Director of Nursing, explained that

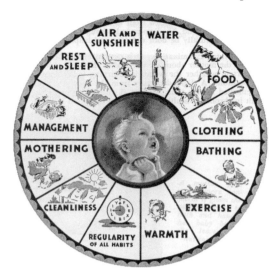

Some commentators stressed that diet was only one of the twelve essentials for baby care taught by the Plunket Society and that the debates around diet did not invalidate its overall teaching. *Modern Mothercraft*

the only points of criticism had been that the protein percentage in the infant feeding formula should be higher, and that mixed feeding should be introduced earlier, and that these had been rectified by altering the feeding tables. She pointed out that Truby King himself had made alterations from time to time, adding that, 'The Society is so well grounded into the life of New Zealand that it is very unlikely that it will ever be hurt in this country', though much depended on the appointment of a new medical adviser.[139]

One writer for the *New Zealand Observer*, a self-proclaimed 'member of the great dumb sisterhood', came out in support of Plunket:

> without the great, free service of the Plunket Society one would either muddle along, with guess work and grandmothers' tales as a guide, or constantly seek expensive advice from medical specialists. Even the most fanatical worshipper at the shrine of the BMA will admit that the medical gentlemen are not averse to pocketing all the stray guineas that come along. . . . A few possibly wish that the Plunket Society were not quite so free with its advice.

She cited Margaret Hitchcock, matron of Wellington's Karitane Hospital, who pointed out that Plunket promoted twelve essential rules for infant health, only one of which had been attacked. Plunket nurses, she added, were the first to admit that no 'system' was 100 per cent efficient. But they constantly added to their knowledge, utilising a wealth of experience that was unlikely ever to come the way of any one medical practitioner.[140]

Ante-natal care

Ante-natal care was another area where Plunket came into direct conflict with the medical profession. Although there was some pressure for Plunket to extend its involvement into this area, its goal of maintaining good relations with the medical profession meant that it was eventually surrendered to the doctors. As Philippa Mein Smith noted, pregnancy, like childbirth, was pathologised in the interwar period.[141]

Ante-natal care was a twentieth-century invention. Its British origins are usually traced to the work of an Edinburgh physician, John William Ballantyne, who developed the concept of a 'pre-maternity' hospital where 'morbid pregnancies could be brought under observation and suitably treated'.[142] The aim was to protect the foetus and to reduce infant mortality.[143] The world's first ante-natal clinic is said to have opened in Adelaide, Australia, in 1910. Sydney and Melbourne followed, in 1912 and 1917 respectively.[144] In the United States, the Boston Lying-In Hospital set up a clinic in 1911.[145] Many of Britain's infant-welfare centres established ante-natal clinics during the First World War. Truby King was fully cognisant of the overseas developments and hoped that Plunket nurses would contribute to this area in New Zealand.[146]

This was also the hope of Health Minister Sir James Parr, who announced a new initiative to reduce maternal mortality at the 1921 Plunket conference and appealed to the society to help in providing ante-natal care. The Wellington branch president, Kathleen Hosking, replied that Plunket nurses were already providing ante-natal care and advice.[147] Three years later, an official safe maternity campaign was launched at a special meeting in conjunction with the annual general meeting of the Palmerston North branch of Plunket, attended by Drs Thomas Valintine, Tom Paget, Truby King, David Wylie (representing the NZBMA) and Maui Pomare (Minister of Health).[148] This campaign aimed to bring down the rate of maternal mortality, as well as the death rate among infants, especially in their first month. Pomare was sure that the Plunket Society, which had been so successful in child welfare, would be equally successful in co-operating with the Health Department in its work of reducing maternal mortality. Valintine, too, claimed to be confident that joint efforts of the NZBMA, the Health Department and the Plunket Society would go far towards achieving this end.[149]

The Health Department had already attempted to undertake ante-natal work in relation to the St Helens hospitals, with limited success.[150] It now saw an opportunity to reach a far greater number of women through

Plunket's extensive network and at the same time recoup some of the health budget spent on the society. The departmental officer placed in charge of setting up ante-natal clinics was Dr Elaine Gurr. The first six clinics were established in October 1924 in the Wellington Health District, at the St Helens Hospital, the Alexandra Home for Unmarried Mothers, the Salvation Army Maternity Hospital and at the Plunket rooms in Kent Terrace, Lower Hutt and Petone. In February 1925 Gurr opened five ante-natal clinics in Christchurch, again using the St Helens Hospital, charitable institutions and Plunket rooms. Auckland Plunket set up an ante-natal clinic in 1926, run by a Health Department nurse for the first year, and thereafter by a Plunket nurse. By 1928 there were 21 free ante-natal clinics in New Zealand, seven attached to St Helens hospitals, eight attached to other maternity hospitals and six run by Plunket.[151] A decade later Plunket had set up eleven ante-natal clinics, and the clinics in Auckland, Wellington and Christchurch each employed a nurse to work full time on ante-natal care. There were also five clinics attached to St Helens hospitals, and 24 at other hospitals.

Much of the early ante-natal care involved giving advice. For example, the Auckland branch set aside a room in 1922 where pregnant women could have a 'quiet confidential chat with the nurse'.[152] Yet nurses also conducted medical examinations. Dr Agnes Bennett introduced the sphygmomanometer to measure blood pressure at Wellington's St Helens clinic in 1925, and this equipment was subsequently installed at Plunket clinics.[153]

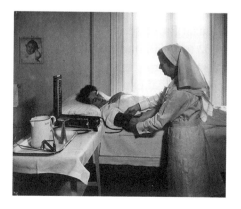 

Plunket's ante-natal clinics were medically equipped. As Timaru's Plunket nurse, Miss Barnett, commented in 1937: 'We have been more or less requested not to do these tests by the doctors. We have instruments for taking measurements but do not do it'.
Plunket Society, Auckland Branch photograph album

CHAPTER 5

Helen Deem and Paediatrics, 1939–56

Plunket's new medical adviser

In 1939 the Plunket Society, already under pressure from an expanding paediatric profession, was about to experience a different kind of challenge as new theories and methods of child-rearing became popular. Plunket was fortunate in its choice of Dr Helen Deem as its new medical adviser. She managed to win the support of the paediatricians and their society (formed in 1947), as well as Plunket's lay hierarchy. Although supportive of the new theories relating to infant feeding, birthing and parenting, largely promoted by lay groups, she was careful not to alienate the medical profession. Politically astute, she recognised that loss of medical backing could do irreparable damage to Plunket's public image and provide the Health Department with the means to take control of infant welfare services. At her death in November 1955, the Plunket president, Lady Elizabeth Bodkin, rightly noted that she had 'enlisted the support of the medical profession and immeasurably raised the prestige of the Plunket Society'.[1]

Truby King died at Mount Melrose, Wellington, on 10 February 1938. He had been little more than a figurehead for some time and was certainly not, as has sometimes been claimed, a controlling influence in Plunket. He played a very limited role during the 1930s dispute between the society and paediatricians. Yet in the late 1930s the women who ran Plunket believed that, in order for Plunket to retain public respectability, survive and prosper, it required a strong authoritative medical leader. This attitude reflected the high cultural authority enjoyed by the medical profession in the mid-twentieth century. Some also thought it advisable to have a male figure of authority. When the appointment of a new medical adviser was discussed in November 1938, Dr Ernest Williams reassured the council that a woman would be just as acceptable to the medical profession as a man. He clearly had Deem in mind, and after much deliberation it was resolved to offer her the post with the approval of the Medical Advisory Committee.[2] Even then, some council members, such as Auckland branch president Irene Allan, had misgivings about appointing a woman. Allan was also

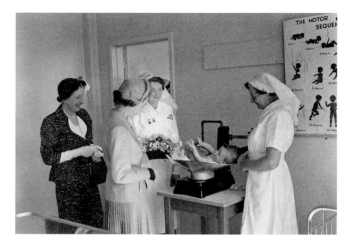

Dr Helen Deem (far left) with Queen Elizabeth II during the royal visit to the Truby King-Harris Hospital, 27 January 1954. Also in the photograph are Dorothy Batt (Matron of Otago Plunket–Karitane Hospital, 1944–67) and Sister D. Drayton. They were not alone: 360 Plunket committee members turned up to greet the monarch in the hospital grounds. Archives New Zealand Te Whare Tohu Tuhituhinga O Aotearoa: National Publicity Studios Photographic Collection, ATL, F-42942-1/2 (36/P/1)

concerned that, as Deem had the support of the NZBMA, and more particularly the Health Department, her appointment might bring them 'very near Government control, just what we don't want'.[3] Deem came, after all, with testimonials from Drs Watt and Turbott of the Health Department, as well as Professor Carmalt Jones and Dr Corkill (the latter among Plunket's critics in the late 1930s).[4] Allan's concerns were to prove unfounded.

Helen Deem (*née* Muriel Helen Easterfield) was born in Wellington on 26 February 1900 to Thomas and Anna Maria Kunigunda Easterfield. Her mother came from Bavaria. Her father (later Sir Thomas) was from Doncaster, England. He was foundation Professor of Chemistry at Victoria University of Wellington and, from 1919 to 1933, Director of Nelson's Cawthron Institute, the first privately endowed research institute in the Southern Hemisphere with a special interest in agricultural science. Dr Herbert Robertson, who had known Deem all her life, supported her application to be Plunket's Medical Adviser, claiming that she had a mind 'somewhat like her father, which was adapted to investigation, and to research matters'. He considered this to be 'a most necessary factor now that the teachings of the Society are under discussion so much'.[5]

Deem had been educated at Wellington Girls' College and Otago University. After graduating in medicine in 1925, she spent a year as house surgeon at Wanganui Hospital and seven months as Oamaru Hospital's sole resident medical officer. With a growing interest in infant health, she followed an unusual path for a doctor by taking the Plunket nurse training course at the Karitane-Harris Hospital. In 1928 she was the first recipient of the Plunket Society's Lady King Scholarship. This gave her the opportunity to research breastfeeding, the basis of her MD thesis, which she completed in 1928. It was later published in *Archives of Disease in Childhood* in 1931.[6]

In 1929 Helen married John Stanley Longton Deem, a civil engineer, and moved to his home town of Wanganui where two years later she gave birth to their daughter, Philippa. While practising medicine in Wanganui, she was appointed lecturer and honorary physician to the Truby King-Stewart Karitane Hospital, and in 1933 became a member of the Plunket Society's newly formed Medical Advisory Committee. Following the tragic death of her husband at the age of 38 while holidaying at Mount Ruapehu in 1933, Helen moved to Wellington and became senior resident at Wellington Public Hospital, working in the women's and children's wards. After seven months in Wellington, she decided to further her studies in England and worked her passage as ship's doctor on board the *Port Melbourne* in May 1934.[7] In England she worked at the British Hospital for Mothers and Babies in Woolwich and London's Great Ormond Street Hospital for Sick Children. In 1935 she gained the Diploma of the Royal College of Obstetricians and Gynaecologists.

Returning to New Zealand in 1936, she was appointed school medical officer to the South Auckland Health District and assistant to Dr Harold Turbott, Hamilton's Medical Officer of Health. During her time with the Health Department she studied nutritional and public health problems among the pre-school and school children of the Taupo-Tokaanu district. She pioneered a dried milk scheme for Maori schools and a diphtheria immunisation campaign in the Waikato.[8]

Dr Robertson suggested to Plunket president Daisy Begg that Deem be asked to participate in the discussions on the future of Plunket in June 1938. Begg did not act on the suggestion, possibly because Deem was employed by the Health Department. In the event this proved to be fortuitous for Deem as she came to Plunket without having alienated either the paediatricians or the society. Had she been involved in the debates, it is clear Deem would have supported the paediatricians in their demand for more paediatric control of Plunket. Nevertheless, Deem was a strong supporter of the society throughout her time as Medical Adviser.

Importantly for the future of the Plunket Society, Deem had the confidence and support of Dr ('Sammy') Ludbrook, whom she described as 'New Zealand's pediatric [*sic*] prime mover'.[9] Ludbrook founded the Paediatric Society of New Zealand in 1947 and was its first president.[10] The nature of their relationship was revealed in Ludbrook's appraisal of her proposed paper on infant health to an NZBMA conference in 1946. Reassuring her that the subject she had chosen was a good one, he said, 'I know that you have the material and will present it in your usual brilliant fashion', and added, ' I will be at hand to protect you from your assailants.'[11] Two years later, he wrote supportively, 'We are looking forward to seeing you in September. In the meantime do not try to achieve too much. I can see great changes coming shortly and remember you will have the backing of the more informed members of the profession if you are in need of it.' [12] Deem thanked him for his reassurance.[13] Dr Basil Quin, Auckland paediatrician and medical officer at the local Karitane hospital, told Deem in 1950, 'It is not flattery to say that you are the life blood of the Plunket Society as it is now, and if you disappeared from us the Society would assuredly founder. Such would be a disaster from every angle.'[14] Deem also enjoyed a longstanding friendship with another paediatrician, Dr Alice Bush. When the latter congratulated her on her OBE in 1952 Deem replied thanking Bush for her co-operation, support and friendship over the years.[15]

Upon taking up the post of medical adviser, Deem quickly gained the confidence of the Plunket executive and council. They had none of the qualms they had with Tweed when it came to approving an overseas trip for Deem, though when she first suggested it in 1943 they did not think the time was right.[16] Three years later Deem was awarded a grant from the Carnegie Corporation of New York to study international advances in paediatrics. Plunket's executive resolved that the society would be responsible for any expenses over and above the Carnegie grant and that Deem be urged to go as soon as possible.[17]

In her early years with Plunket Deem carried out some important work. In 1940, together with the society's Nursing Adviser, Nora Fitzgibbon, she undertook a height/weight survey involving almost 9000 New Zealand infants, the first of its kind in New Zealand. Although this was not controversial, the executive insisted on seeing the results before publication.[18] Together with Fitzgibbon, she wrote a new handbook for Plunket, *Modern Mothercraft. A Guide to Parents* (1945); a second edition appeared in 1953. In 1946 she was appointed lecturer in preventive paediatrics at the Otago Medical School. The Carnegie grant enabled her to spend four months in

The Plunket Society's Medical Adviser,
Dr Helen Deem, and Nursing Adviser
Nora Fitzgibbon updated Plunket's official
handbook in 1945. After eight reprints, it
was revised in 1953, and went through nine
further reprints.

the United States in 1947, where she represented New Zealand at the fifth
International Paediatric Congress before visiting Britain and Scandinavia.

When Deem proposed changes to Plunket's feeding schedules in 1950
she had the support of the council, which fully endorsed her submission
to the Paediatric Society.[19] The following year she was authorised to
implement changes in Plunket's methods of infant feeding. At the same
meeting members 'spoke in appreciation of Dr Deem's work for the society
and her interest of the mothers and babies of New Zealand'.[20]

Deem and the paediatricians

Helen Deem made it clear from the beginning that she wished to have more
paediatricians involved in Plunket services. In her annual report for 1942–3
she pointed out that it would be ideal to have paediatricians attached to
all clinics, though she admitted that there were not enough specialists
available.[21] In August 1943 she told the executive that in Auckland at least
the full-time services of a paediatrician would be desirable, to supervise
the work of the nurses.[22] She outlined her views on paediatric involvement
in Plunket services in her annual report for 1947–8: she wished to see
attached to the clinics specially trained doctors who were really interested
in normal infants and pre-school children as well as in sick children. These

doctors would be responsible for giving every child a periodic check-up, and would advise on special measures for those who were not making normal progress or were exhibiting behaviour problems. The paediatric consultant would not only take unnecessary responsibility off the nurses' shoulders but would also extend general practitioners' knowledge of paediatrics, by working with them.[23]

As part of her promotion of paediatric involvement in Plunket, Deem planned to have medical students taught at Plunket clinics by paediatricians. In pursuit of this, she looked to a report of an Inter-Departmental Committee set up jointly by the British Ministry of Health and the Department of Health for Scotland (known as the Goodenough Report, 1944) on the future training of medical students in Britain. Its recommendations included paediatric training of medical practitioners, with an emphasis as much on nutrition and the development of normal healthy children as on the treatment of sick children. In New Zealand, fifth-year medical students already attended ante-natal and post-natal sessions at the Queen Mary Maternity Hospital, and from 1945 they visited Plunket rooms in Dunedin to observe the nurses' work, hear 'the mothers' problems and viewpoints' and view 'normal' babies and pre-school children.[24] They also attended the Karitane Hospital. 'Irene', a Plunket nurse trainee in 1947, remembered that part of her job at the hospital was to show medical students how to feed, bath and care for babies. 'When I was there they were all men and I remember they weren't very interested. It was part of their training. They had to do it whether they liked it or not.'[25]

Deem's determination to strengthen medical training in child health was reinforced by her overseas trip in 1947. She stressed that her plans were

Garry Carr has his chest measurements taken by Sister A. Rountree at Plunket's Auckland branch headquarters, 1957. Watching are his mother, Mrs S. Carr (on right) and a group of medical students. This was a new scheme to introduce medical students to well baby care. Plunket Society, Auckland Branch photograph album

'largely based on the training medical students were receiving elsewhere'. Her models were Newcastle-on-Tyne, Edinburgh, and Toronto, each of which had a professor of child health. She hinted at a dual purpose of having paediatricians teach at the clinics when she wrote, 'I think this would be good way of introducing pediatricians [*sic*] to the Plunket Clinics.'[26] The council, predictably, was wary. Mrs Gilmour (Lyttelton) thought it revived the 'old problem' as to whether the society's work was to be under the control of local medical men. Deem retorted that if Plunket did not adopt the suggested scheme, the doctors would open their own clinics, attached to maternity hospitals. The council agreed that in the event of the scheme being adopted, the university should be asked to pay the paediatricians.[27] Teaching sessions started in Dunedin and Auckland. In Dunedin the clinics were conducted by Deem herself and Dr Murray McGeorge, then a senior lecturer in paediatrics. In Auckland Dr Alice Bush was proposed by Ludbrook to take the classes.[28] Bush, better known for her involvement in the family planning movement,[29] had been a visiting paediatric consultant at Auckland's Karitane Hospital since 1940. Deem described her as 'a tower of strength to Plunket affairs in Auckland'.[30]

Deem's response to a draft memorandum by Ludbrook in 1950 to the Director-General of Health reveals her underlying concerns. Ludbrook advocated the appointment of a director of child health, because of the 'absence of adequate supervision of the technical side' of infant health care. Deem thought this memorandum had 'most dangerous possibilities as far as the future of the Plunket Society and its relations with the Health Department are concerned'. She reminded him that certain 'high-powered' officials in the Department wanted the Plunket Society to be taken over by the government and she held that the sentiments expressed in the draft letter would strengthen the government's hand in this direction. While Deem reminded him that she also wanted to see paediatricians attached to Plunket clinics, she added,

> In kindness to the medical profession I did not state that my overseas observations of the conduct of infant welfare clinics by paediatricians convinced me that much more than their presence was required to make the sessions wholly successful in so far as the interests of the mothers and babies were concerned.[31]

She was probably referring to her impressions of some American clinics which she found 'more office-like than . . . our Plunket rooms', with the sessions 'conducted in a business-like manner'.[32] She told Ludbrook that Plunket services were appreciated by the great majority of mothers and that voluntary effort in terms of finance raised and services rendered was 'magnificent'. In her view, any official pronouncement that tended to undermine public confidence in the society and its work might have 'most unfortunate repercussions'.[33]

Ludbrook continued nevertheless to express to Deem his 'grave concerns' about the supervision of Plunket nurses: 'What goes on between Plunket nurse and her patients, for example in St Heliers [a suburb of Auckland] – only because of ignorance or inexperience or excessive belief in Plunket dogma and in some cases just stupidity – could be avoided if experienced pediatricians were working with them'.[34] He was supported by Dr Basil Quin, who told Deem that many of the older Plunket nurses used no system but their own, and that no attempt was made to keep them up-to-date. Although he complained that some nurses used 'astonishing mixtures bred from their own fancy', it could equally be argued that their advice was the culmination of experience. Yet there was little medical supervision, and in Auckland eight or nine doctors had set themselves up in competition with Plunket.[35] Deem claimed to be disappointed by these criticisms of older Plunket nurses, and pointed out that since 1942 nurses in training and in practice had been taught the American Marriott system of feeding, along with their own.[36] But she, too, thought the time was right to consider a simplification of the society's guidelines on infant feeding. She reassured Quin that 'No one is more keen than I am to secure co-operation between the medical profession and the Plunket Society'.[37]

A new feeding schedule for infants was presented at Plunket's Medical Advisory Committee meeting in November 1950, and agreed to by the Paediatric Society in 1951.[38] The source cited for the new schedule was Frederick Clements, Senior Medical Officer in the Australian Commonwealth Department of Health, and Chief of the Nutrition Section of the World Health Organization (WHO).[39] Adopting the paediatricians' feeding practices was a strategy Dr Ian Ewart had proposed in 1938 in order to diffuse medical criticism of the society and undermine paediatric opposition.[40] This was finally achieved; paediatricians could no longer criticise Plunket for its outmoded feeding practices.

Advice relating to breastfeeding was also changing. Paediatricians believed that breastfed infants should have their diets supplemented,[41] and this is what Deem now recommended. Opposition came from Dr Ernest Williams, who assured Deem that he was not swayed in his opinions by the 'Teachings of Sir Truby King'. He realised that the understanding of nutrition had increased dramatically since King's day and admitted that he was 'perhaps old fashioned'. He nevertheless expressed surprise that it was considered necessary to fortify the milk of healthy mothers for apparently healthy babies. He went on to point out that it was important to create a placid unworried atmosphere for breastfeeding, and that supplements might militate against this. But, he conceded, 'the evidence you give of decisions arrived at by British and American paediatricians is very conclusive and amply supports your contention in respect of additional Vitamin D'.[42]

Although Deem met the Paediatric Society criticisms of Plunket's feeding schedules, she did not pursue her plan to incorporate paediatricians into Plunket clinics. In 1952 she told Ludbrook, 'I have toyed with the idea of using paediatricians or paediatrically minded general practitioners at the Plunket rooms, but after weighing the pros and cons have thrown the idea overboard.' Instead she persuaded the council to strengthen the nursing service by appointing district nurse supervisors, something Pattrick had advocated in the 1920s.[43]

New child psychology and breastfeeding

The post-Second World War period saw the emergence of a new child-rearing doctrine that rejected routines and discipline in favour of a more permissive approach. This was based on the growing belief in psychology that an adult's emotional stability was based on emotional needs in infant having been met. Dr Maurice Bevan-Brown, a Christchurch psychiatrist, explained to Deem in 1945 that his work relating to psychological medicine and mental hygiene had led him to take an interest in child welfare and particularly the activities of the Plunket Society. Deem replied that she, too, was interested in practical psychology and realised its importance in any scheme of child welfare, but that she considered the amateur child psychologist 'a blight on the community'.[44] Presumably she numbered herself among the amateurs, for when she was asked to review Bevan-Brown's book, *The Sources of Love and Fear*, in 1950, she replied that she was not a psychologist and did not pretend to understand the science of psychoanalysis, and suggested that Dr Geoffrey Palmer, a Dunedin psychiatrist, be asked. Perhaps more significantly, she added that, after making a careful study of the contents, she had come to the conclusion that it would not be in the interests of the Plunket Society for her, as its medical adviser, to review the book. She acknowledged it as an important contribution to the subject of child care, but thought that some of its contentions, based on psycho-analysis, were 'highly controversial'.[45] It cannot have helped that a contributor to Bevan-Brown's book commented that some of the advice of Plunket nurses 'filled me with horror . . . dismay and despair'.[46]

Charles Maurice Bevan-Brown had completed a BA at Canterbury College, University of New Zealand, in 1909. He gained an MA at Cambridge University in England in 1912, and taught at Wanganui Collegiate for a time. He subsequently graduated in medicine at Otago University in 1921. Two years later he returned to Britain, set up a private practice in psychotherapy in Harley Street and practised psychiatry at London's Tavistock Clinic. In 1940 he came back to New Zealand and began work in Christchurch. He was a pioneer of analytical psychotherapy, and first president of the New Zealand Association of Psychotherapists.[47] Applauded by Ernest Beaglehole, Professor of Psychology at Victoria University of Wellington and head of the Mental Health Association,[48] he was also a 'potent influence' on Parents' Centre, a lay group formed to encourage natural childbirth and more relaxed parenting.[49] According to one of the founders of Parents' Centre, his book 'spread like a forest fire, and was quickly out of print'.[50] Truby King and Bevan-Brown shared an interest in child psychology and, according to Sue Kedgley, towards the end of his life King asked Bevan-Brown to take over the Plunket Society. As she commented, 'Had he done so, the Plunket Society would undoubtedly have taken a very different course.'[51] King, however, had no authority to make such an offer and it is unlikely that the council would have acquiesced. Bevan-Brown was an outsider who had resigned from the NZBMA,[52] and any formal association with the Plunket Society would have lost it the all-important support of the medical establishment.

Bevan-Brown was influenced by Sigmund Freud. In *Sources of Love and Fear*, he pointed out that Freud's work had led to the recognition that an individual's mental health or ill health depended largely on the type of nurture received during the first five years, and in particular during the first year. Bevan-Brown believed that breastfeeding (or the deprivation thereof) was of long-term psychological importance. As Freud had put it in the early 1900s, 'No one who has seen a baby sinking back satiated from the breast and falling asleep with flushed cheeks and a blissful smile can escape the reflection that this picture persists as a prototype of sexual satisfaction in later life.'[53] Bevan-Brown similarly saw a 'close similarity between breast-feeding and adult coitus', suggesting that both were orgasmic. For girls, he believed there was a connection between oral deprivation in the first year and vaginal frigidity 20 or more years later. He confidently claimed that if the female baby was adequately breastfed and thus achieved 'a complete and satisfactory sensuous relationship with her mother', she would not be frigid as a wife, provided she did not marry a man she disliked. Breastfeeding in itself was not enough; it was the experience of the breastfeeding that was important – 'unless this breast-feeding process is a true human copulation, that is to say, unless it is a mutual reciprocal and personal act as well as a mechanical process, the baby may not thrive'. He explained that Freud used the word 'sexual' to describe feelings experienced by mother and infant in this 'copulative breast-feeding process'.[54]

Helen Deem's thinking was more in line with a 1944 British Ministry of Health Advisory Committee report on breastfeeding, which she had consulted. The committee believed in the importance of breastfeeding, and that the physical well-being it promoted was conducive to sounder psychological well-being, 'but further than this in the direction of psychological argument, we are not prepared to go'.[55] It noted that there was no unanimity among psychologists on the psychological effects of breastfeeding.

Yet Deem was a staunch advocate of breastfeeding as the best and safest form of infant feeding, which remained central to Plunket teaching.[56] She carried out three national surveys of the extent and duration of breastfeeding, in 1939, 1945, and 1952 (involving 9000, 7700 and 12,000 babies respectively).[57] In 1939, 91.5 per cent of mothers were breastfeeding when first seen by the Plunket nurse. By 1945 this had dropped to 82.1 per cent

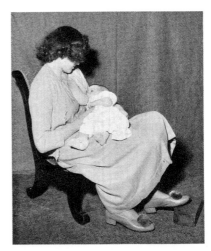

RIGHT: The Plunket Society and its Medical Adviser, Helen Deem, continued to be strong advocates of breastfeeding in the postwar era. *Modern Mothercraft*

OPPOSITE: Plunket nurses often visited new mothers in maternity hospitals, introducing them to Plunket services. *The Work of the Plunket Society in New Zealand*, 1945

and by 1952 to 74.4 per cent. The studies confirmed the general impression that breastfeeding was declining in the post-war years, a trend New Zealand shared with Britain. Duration of breastfeeding was also declining. In 1938, over 80 per cent were breastfed for the first three months, and over 60 per cent for six months.[58] A decade later only 21 per cent were breastfeeding for more than six months.[59] In the 1950s Plunket continued to advocate breastfeeding for six to nine months, though it was realised that breast-feeding for nine months was becoming exceptional.[60]

In 1953 Deem wrote to 33 nurses in areas with above average breast-feeding rates. Their replies indicated that with supportive staff at the local maternity home or hospital and a supportive Plunket nurse, the chances of successful breastfeeding were high. A nurse from Takapuna said they had two very co-operative nursing homes that 'do all they can to establish breast feeding'.[61] Another replied that the local hospitals gave the mothers 'a good training . . . Our Doctors are keen on Breastfeeding. We ourselves are keen.'[62] The nurse from Matamata replied, 'the local hospital is an excellent one and as all the doctors and Sister Ferguson, the Matron, are very keen on breastfeeding, the number of babies fully breastfed on discharge is very high (82%)'.[63] The nurse from Morrinsville reported upon a co-operative staff at the local hospital where she spent one and a half hours one morn-ing a week. She sometimes persuaded women to breastfeed who had not planned to do so.[64] Enthusiasm for breastfeeding shines through the let-ters: 'I myself am very keen on babies being breastfed for as long as possible so perhaps my enthusiasm may be infectious and have some effect on the

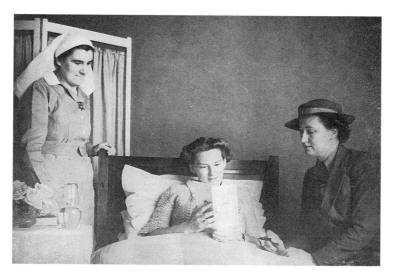

mothers. I always endeavour to visit the mothers as soon as possible after they leave hospital, because I think that is the usual time when they wean off their own bat, or grandma's advice . . .'.[65] 'Also I think that being able to meet the mothers in Hospital makes a big difference. I find that the mothers I have met and talked to in Hospital usually ring me for advice if they are worried about the baby before my first visit . . . Why they keep on breastfeeding longer than others I just don't know, but I'm sure most of them wouldn't without supervision.'[66] Another replied, 'Above all I think a calm confident approach that they can breastfeed successfully without too much fuss goes a long way with them.'[67]

Not all doctors were supportive, however, and this may have influenced some women.[68] Other factors apart from attitudes of health professionals were thought to help determine breastfeeding rates. Deem believed that some form of home help would promote breastfeeding; the government had briefly toyed with the idea of home helps in the post-war period, but the concept had been largely abandoned by 1950.[69] The return of mothers to the paid workforce during and after the war was also considered important, though later studies questioned the primacy of this factor.[70] Mothers were possibly influenced by fashion magazines, advertisements for milk formulae and American films; it might have been part of the Americanisation of post-war New Zealand society.[71] Deem noted that breastfeeding in the United States had been the exception rather than the rule for many years – it was estimated in 1953 that 5 per cent of American babies were breastfed at three months.[72] Nor did the famous American child-rearing guru of the 1950s, Dr Benjamin Spock, strongly support breastfeeding; he devoted only four pages to breastfeeding in his 1946 bestselling manual, *Baby and Child Care*, compared to 24 pages given to artificial feeding.[73]

As elsewhere in the Western world, Spock's book was greeted with great enthusiasm in New Zealand. A psychiatrist by training, Spock promulgated new theories of child psychology based on flexibility in infant feeding, toilet training and general child management.[74] While he was no enthusiast for breastfeeding, he did promote a more relaxed style of feeding that was not to be governed by the clock and was incorporated into the new psychology of breastfeeding. As Bevan-Brown explained, feeding the infant whenever he or she wanted it would lead to an 'intimate personal relationship'. He cited the work of Dr C. Anderson Aldrich, Director of the Child Health Institute at Rochester in the United States.[75] In 1938 Anderson and Mary Aldrich had published another landmark in American child care literature,

Babies are Human Beings, which promoted a more relaxed approach to child-rearing, with cuddling being considered not only acceptable but essential.[76] Beaglehole also believed in 'frequent feeding periods, not limited in time, nor artificially interrupted, not governed in frequency by the clock', and explained the psychological advantages. Increased feeding meant less likelihood of frustrating the infant, less hatred and 'personality distortion' as the child grew up. The child was more likely to be happy and co-operative.[77]

Although Deem did not advocate strict adherence to 'feeding by the clock', she claimed to believe firmly that the average New Zealand mother, who had no help in the home, should work to some kind of plan, otherwise her house management would be chaotic. Her encounters with the

Suggested Routine Day for the Nursing Mother and her Baby.

5-6 a.m.—Mother wakes and takes a glass of hot water, a cup of weak tea, or orange or grapefruit juice. Baby is changed, fed and put back in his cot to sleep. If there is no help in the house, father might prepare the morning drink, change baby and bring him to his mother.

7.15 a.m.—Mother rises.

8 a.m.—Breakfast.

9 a.m.—Sun bath for baby when old enough and weather suitable. Kicking exercise in cot.

9.30-10 a.m.—Bath and dress baby.

10 a.m.—Give fish liver oil, feed, hold out for bowel action. Put in cot to sleep in the open air or on a balcony or verandah.

10.30 a.m.—Morning drink for mother, followed by domestic duties.

12-12.30 p.m.—Lunch, or dinner to suit household.

1.30-2 p.m.—Change baby, feed and put outside in cot or pram.

2-3 p.m.—Rest for mother with feet up while baby sleeps.

3 p.m.—Afternoon tea. As baby grows older, outing in pram.

4.30-5 p.m.—Give orange juice, kicking period in crib or in play pen.

5-5.30 p.m.—Afternoon toilet—sponge face, hands and buttocks. " Social hour " with parents.

5.30 p.m.—Fish liver oil, feed baby, and toilet. Put to bed in well ventilated room.

6-6.30 p.m.—Evening meal. Father assists with clearing the table and washing dishes.

7-9 p.m.—Relaxation and recreation — sewing, reading, writing, listening to radio programme, etc.

9 p.m.—Prepare for bed, warm bath, etc.

9.30 p.m.—Hot milk drink. Feed baby, change and tuck down for the night.

The mother may prefer to go to bed early, in which case the baby should be brought to her for the last feed. This offers another opportunity for father to help. If baby is too sleepy at 9 p.m. his mother may find it a good idea while he is very young, to leave his feed until he wakes about midnight. The above schedule can be adjusted to suit individual needs and to fit into any household.

When baby is five months old or alternatively weighs 15 lbs. instructions will be given for introducing solid foods.

'Suggested Routine Day for the Nursing Mother and her Baby.' *Modern Mothercraft*

'unhappy offspring of many psychologists' had persuaded her that their hypotheses did not always work. She herself favoured a 'middle of the road course', with mothers relying on their maternal instincts and innate common sense, provided they understood the rudiments of infant care.[78] In 1951 she advised Dr Henry Roberton from Christchurch, who was preparing a paper on breastfeeding, that mothers should be told about 'sane planning' with regard to the baby's daily routine, with feeding times adjusted according to circumstances. She had met a few mothers, whom she described as 'intellectuals', who had tried self-demand feeding with the first baby, but for the second worked to a plan that they modified appropriately; all were of the opinion that the second method was better, particularly with first babies.[79] Deem believed there were other benefits. As she explained to Alice Bush, 'Good food, rest, planning the day to simplify the household chores as much as possible, and last but not least, encouragement and friendship, all contribute to extending the period of breast feeding.'[80]

It has been argued that routine feeding broke the crucial rule that the more the baby fed, the more the breast produced.[81] Yet Deem and others who promoted routine feeding were well aware of the importance of emptying the breasts at each feed.[82] Many women successfully breastfed on a routine system. The decline in breastfeeding coincided with the growing popularity of demand feeding. Although the latter did not in itself did not undermine breastfeeding, its demanding nature might have deterred some women. As one report noted, it made feeding a full-time occupation.[83] Bottle feeding could be done by anyone, including the father, who was to have a greater role in child-rearing under the new child psychology (see below). Ironically, the greater stress on meeting the baby's emotional needs might have contributed to a decline in breastfeeding.

Deem's concerns to ease the burdens of child-rearing for mothers also coloured her approach to smoking. She hated to think of breastfeeding mothers as 'inveterate smokers', and was aware of evidence from the Karitane hospitals that some mothers who had difficulties with breast-feeding had been heavy smokers. However, she believed in moderation and considered that, if a mother who had been used to smoking was harassed by looking after the home and baby, she should be allowed to have a cigarette. She felt that more co-operation would be obtained by meeting the mothers halfway than by being too rigid.[84]

Theoretical underpinnings to the new permissive methods of child-rearing were provided by a British contemporary of Spock, the Freudian psychoanalyst Dr John Bowlby. In April 1948 the Social Commission of the United Nations set out to study war orphans and institutionalised children. As one historian wrote, 'Few people can have thought that an investigation into such a subject would be central to a social revolution.'[85] Bowlby was commissioned by the WHO to write a report on the mental health aspects of the problem. He had already been conducting research at the Child Guidance Department of the Tavistock Clinic into the effects on young children of temporary separation from their mothers. From his studies he concluded that infants and young children required for their mental health a warm, intimate and continuous relationship with their mother (or permanent mother-substitute) in which both found satisfaction and enjoyment. He labelled the absence of this relationship 'maternal deprivation'.[86] The popular version of his monograph, *Child Care and the Growth of Love*, became a bestseller immediately after it was published in 1953.[87] His theory was picked up by child psychologists throughout the Western world and widely used to argue for the importance of mother–child bonding, achieving the 'status of essential truth'.[88] It reinforced views that had already become predominant among many child psychologists and paediatricians.[89]

In 1947 Deem visited the Department of Child Health at the University of Durham, England, directed by Professor James Spence.[90] The following year Spence visited New Zealand at the instigation of the Otago Medical School, and attended a four-day conference of the Paediatric Society. He gave a public address on child health needs in which he emphasised the importance of emotional well-being.[91] Commenting on 'modern trends in paediatrics' in 1950, Deem also noted contributions made by the Gesell Clinic of Child Development, New Haven, to knowledge of the mental and physical growth of babies and young children, and to the understanding of a normal child's expected behaviour at different ages.[92] Paediatrician Dr Arnold Gesell, a major influence on Spock and his followers, had set up a guidance nursery at the Yale School of Medicine, where professionals studied children's behaviour as they played in rooms containing one-way mirrors.[93] Gesell's performance tests were now demonstrated to medical students and Plunket trainees to enable them to appreciate an infant's stages of development, and were being used in Plunket clinics. The aims of the tests were to identify problems. Deem believed that if psychological problems and psychosomatic disorders, which were 'unfortunately seen all too frequently to-day', could be prevented by a better understanding of a child's emotional needs, then it was important to include this in the teaching curriculum for doctors and nurses.[94] Yet she also thought that some doctors went too far in diagnosing behavioural problems. In 1955 she wrote to Professor Alan Moncrieff of Great Ormond Street Children's Hospital, London that much advice given by doctors at clinics was 'extremely poor on the management of simple behaviour problems which in many instances are merely phases of development'.[95] Despite her comment to Bevan-Brown about amateur psychologists, Deem was drawn into child psychology.[96]

Preparation for parenthood

Once ante-natal care had been taken over by the medical profession under Social Security, Plunket turned its attention to 'Group Mothercraft Classes for Expectant Mothers'. In 1949, for instance, the Wellington branch's charge nurse noted that the amount of personal ante-natal supervision was declining as more people were going to doctors but that the increase in mothercraft instruction meant that 'the work of the antenatal clinic was very steady'.[97] In addition to individual talks to expectant mothers, 'group instruction' had been started in October 1948.[98] After Deem returned from her overseas trip in 1948 she initiated ante-natal classes based on those she had attended in New York and Toronto. Their immediate popularity indicated that they met a need.[99]

Some of the new classes involved exercises to music, to be carried out during labour and after the birth to help the mother regain her figure. These were known as Margaret Morris exercises. Interested in eurythmics and posture, Morris had developed her pre-natal exercises in England in the 1930s to assist in natural childbirth. By 1933 she was demonstrating exercises at ante-natal clinics in England.[100] In 1936 Dr Sylvia Chapman, Medical Superintendent of Wellington's St Helens Hospital, taught the exercises to Wellington's Plunket nurses, who then introduced classes.[101] At Christchurch Plunket's ante-natal clinic the exercises were introduced in 1938 by a trained masseuse and ran for many years.[102] In Auckland's central Plunket rooms, the classes, conducted from 1941 to 1943 by a Health Department officer Dr Isabel Houghton, were well attended. Auckland Plunket's head nurse enthused that the medical profession in all English-speaking countries advocated the use of Margaret Morris exercises, and that the classes in Auckland were supported by doctors.[103] They were discontinued in 1943 without explanation, but when Chapman introduced similar classes at Wellington's St Helens Hospital, she found that some doctors disapproved, as they linked the exercises with the teachings of natural childbirth. Through its ante-natal classes Plunket became caught up in the debates surrounding the natural childbirth movement.[104]

In 1950 Dr Thomas Corkill, now senior obstetrician at Wellington Hospital, a member of the Nurses and Midwives Registration Board and author of a textbook for midwives,[105] was invited to speak at a conference for Plunket nurses on 'Group Mothercraft teaching to expectant mothers'. He argued that much damage had been done through linking ante-natal exercises with the psychological side of labour. It had become almost a cult with some enthusiasts and many mothers had believed that a painless labour would assuredly follow. He considered teaching on childbirth could be 'fraught with great dangers unless the instruction given was completely factual'. He referred to the teachings of Dr Grantly Dick Read, a British doctor who published *Revelation of Childbirth: the Principles and Practice of Natural Childbirth* in 1942, which was reprinted annually until 1953 (latterly as *Childbirth Without Fear*).[106] An advocate of natural childbirth, Read believed that women suffered pain in childbirth largely because they were afraid and unprepared. If women could be taught to relax during labour, they would not require pain relief. The concern was not just for the mother but also for the baby. Bevan-Brown, strongly influenced by Read,[107] explained that for the future mother–child relationship it was vitally important that the mother be conscious at the time of birth and also aware of the child as a person immediately afterwards: 'it would be difficult to deny that the *conscious* act of producing a living child must be the crowning experience in the fulfilment of womanhood'.[108] Like Read, he held a romanticised view of motherhood, where woman's reproductive role was celebrated as the epitome of her existence.[109] When asked by New Zealand women for the names of local doctors practising his methods, Read could name only one – Bevan-Brown.[110]

Corkill told Plunket nurses in 1950 that if Read's teachings were followed, the patient's medical adviser should give all the instruction, and that no nurse should ever mention the word 'fear' to the class. The conference report noted, 'The Sisters were all adamant that they fostered the confidence of their clientele in their own medical adviser. All denied that they dabbled in the psychology of childbirth, talked of avoidance of fear, or tried to teach "relaxation".'[111] Sydney Lusk, Plunket's Nursing Adviser, thanked Corkill for his 'straightforward and constructive talk' and assured him of the society's wish to co-operate with the obstetricians in every possible way.[112]

The movement for natural childbirth was gaining public support in New Zealand around 1950 as a response to what some considered excessive medical intervention in childbirth. The Natural Childbirth Association was formed in Wellington in 1951, changing its name to Parents' Centre in 1952. Among its stated aims was the promotion of 'those practices which have beneficial effects upon early parent-child relationships such as education for childbirth, rooming-in, breastfeeding, home confinement and permissive methods of child care'.[113] Corkill dismissed Parents' Centre members as 'a bunch of Communists',[114] while Flora Cameron, the Health Department's Director of Nursing, described them somewhat disparagingly as 'the jump for joy people'.[115]

Once Wellington Parents' Centre was incorporated as a society in 1952, its organisers, Helen Brew (president) and Christine Cole (later Christine Cole Catley, vice-president), made contact with Plunket as a kindred organisation. Brew pointed to their common membership, maintaining that nearly all the women in their association were 'Plunket mothers', and that many of them had worked, or were working, on Plunket committees. She also noted they shared a commitment to the health of women and children.[116] One Wellington Plunket nurse, Nancy (Nan) Clayton, had been involved in the initial planning of the Natural Childbirth Association.[117] She was later described as 'a motherly presence at Wellington Kent Terrace Plunket ante-natal clinic, with a mind intuitively tuned to new ideas'.[118] Her lectures, according to Cole and Brew, closely resembled the ideas in a book the Parents' Centre had been sent by the Maternity Center Association of New York, which in turn were based on the teachings of Read and British physiotherapist Helen Heardman.[119] Cole and Brew claimed that those who had attended Clayton's lectures found them exceptionally helpful.[120] Wellington's charge nurse, P. E. Clifford (Mrs Simpson from 1952), had also reported in 1949 that Clayton's services had been 'in much and increasing demand'.[121] In her annual reports she continued to comment favourably on the classes; in 1952 she wrote, 'The value of this service is evidenced by the many expressions of thanks and appreciation that reach us from time to time'.[122] Privately to Deem she gave a very patronising and much less sympathetic account of Clayton's success.

> Clayton's rather sentimental attitude towards birth and motherhood, etc. would make a tremendous appeal, of course, and I think this is what has been responsible for it all. Most of the young things expecting their first baby, just think the world of her, and she certainly is very good to them, and has that

kind understanding manner that they simply fall for in their rather emotional and uplifted state. You know how it is.[123]

Deem personally supported the Parents' Centre movement. A Parents' Centre historian described her as a 'fairminded woman' who had announced that she would be the first to enrol in their classes if she again fell pregnant.[124] Deem also agreed with Simpson that Brew was 'quite sincere' in her wish to give as many women as possible the chance to enjoy natural childbirth as she had.[125] Yet publicly Deem remained cautious since Clayton's approach had met with much criticism from obstetricians. In response to an enquiry from Deem, Corkill confided his belief that Clayton was harming the Plunket Society by advocating natural childbirth. He thought there was definite conflict between the obstetricians and the Parents' Centre; he would not allow his patients to attend the courses. As a result Deem and Lusk asked Clayton to discontinue her talks on childbirth. They explained that certain doctors were not allowing their patients to attend the society's talks on account of her alleged advocacy of natural childbirth. Without the support of the medical profession, Deem predicted, 'our Group Mothercraft classes will soon become a thing of the past'. Clayton was also asked to cease her involvement with the Parents' Centre classes at the YWCA.[126] Simpson feared a public outburst when the decision became known.[127]

Helen Brew was not about to give up. She wrote to Deem that she had the assurance of Clayton and Gisa Taglicht, the director of the YWCA's classes in rhythmical gymnastics, that natural childbirth was never discussed in the classes. She herself insisted that women should attempt a natural childbirth only with the active support of their doctors. Brew explained that most doctors were not interested in the psychosomatic approach to childbirth and the classes led to easier confinements and enabled mothers to co-operate better with their doctors and nurses. She thought it would be unfortunate, in view of the demand, if such courses were discontinued because of a misunderstanding about their purpose.[128] She further pointed out that fifteen doctors' names appeared on the consent forms filed at the Centre, indicating that not all doctors shared Corkill's views. The secretary of the Obstetrical and Gynaecological Society, Dr Patrick Skinner, verified Brew's claims, informing Deem that no mothers attended classes without their doctor's written consent.[129] Simpson told Deem that the movement for natural childbirth was 'rather bigger than we imagined, and more of the doctors sympathetic than would appear, though how they would react at an actual show-down, is difficult to say'.[130]

A remit to the 1952 Plunket Dominion conference, asking that the birth talk for mothers be reinstated and that additional lectures be given as required, proved that there was indeed an affinity between Plunket's lay membership and the Parents' Centre. Deem again stressed the importance of retaining doctors' support for Plunket to ensure its survival, and the motion was defeated.[131] As she told Brew and Cole, she did not wish to see Plunket part company with doctors as had happened in Canada. The Canadian Mothercraft Society had been established in Toronto in 1931 on the lines of Plunket by a New Zealander, Mrs Irving Robertson, but its strong advocacy of natural childbirth had lost it the support of the medical profession.[132] Deem felt Corkill's support was particularly important to Plunket because he was a member of the Nurses and Midwives Registration Board, which had links with the Nursing Division of the Health Department. She was not prepared to furnish the department with ammunition to usurp the role of Plunket.

Deem was also concerned about the appropriateness of a single woman giving the birth lecture and lamented the failure to obtain the service of a married Plunket nurse for the Wellington Parents' Centre.[133] When Deem discussed reinstating Clayton's lectures the following year, she vetoed any future combined classes for husbands and wives, and specified that birth be excluded from the talk to fathers, along with any reference to sex. With regard to the talk given to mothers she said,

> You must exercise the utmost discretion throughout the course to avoid all intimate emotional or sexual details with no references to natural or painless childbirth. In answering questions on this latter you must state that all advice on this must be sought from the patient's own medical practitioner and you must in no way indicate that you consider it favourably.

Within these limitations she hoped that the classes would once again become popular with the medical profession.[134]

Nan Clayton continued to ally herself strongly though unofficially with Parents' Centre, and in 1954 was granted life membership.[135] Parents' Centre personnel gave talks to Plunket mothers' groups, which from the 1940s were being set up throughout the country.[136] By 1956 Lusk expressed the 'general opinion . . . that [Parents' Centre] have modified their views considerably in the last year or two', adding that they had been very 'psycho' to begin with.[137] Corkill also told Dick Read, who had written to him in 1956, that if there had been any extension of natural childbirth in New Zealand, it was because Parents' Centre had modified its views. He explained that medical opposition had been related to 'the exaggerated emphasis which has been given to certain debatable psychological opinions', and also to the tendency of Parents' Centre 'to undermine the confidence of patients in the guidance of their own doctors'.[138] That year Auckland Plunket allowed Parents' Centre classes to be held in its rooms.[139] Once Parents' Centre gained medical support, the association was no longer seen to jeopardise the status of Plunket. The episode shows how health services, in this case ante-natal classes, were dependent on the politics of the relationship between various health providers.

Fathercraft

The writings of advocates of natural childbirth help to explain why the exclusion of the birth lecture to fathers made the classes more acceptable to obstetricians. Bevan-Brown believed that the husband should be knowledgeable about the birth process in order to help his wife, specifically to protect her from peremptory doctors and nurses. He regretted the convention whereby doctors regarded husbands as superfluous and even a nuisance during childbirth, and tried to keep them out of the way. For the conscious or 'non-narcotized' childbirth which he advocated, the close presence and support of the husband was most desirable.[140] Christine Cole

Parenting at this time was considered to be primarily a female domain.

LEFT: Here a group of homecraft teachers and the Director of Education, Dr C. E. Beeby, inspect a Plunket Society Mothercraft Demonstration in 1951. Plunket Society Annual Report 1951–52

RIGHT: A Plunket nurse instructs schoolgirls on bathing a baby, 1950. Note the embroidered names on their caps. Plunket Society, Auckland Branch photograph album

confirmed that the exclusion of husbands was routine in 1950; when she asked an eminent obstetrician if her husband could be present at the birth, she was told, 'Indeed not – never heard anything so extraordinary!'[141] It was agreed at the 1950 Plunket nurses' conference on ante-natal teaching that the lecture on the birth of the baby should be omitted from the 'fathercraft' classes.[142]

The Parents' Centre's name reflected its conviction that both parents should be involved in parenting.[143] In 1944 Plunket's council also preferred 'parentcraft' to 'mothercraft', explaining that the implications of the latter were too narrow. Parentcraft included traditional female activities of cooking, home management and budgeting and child care, but also gardening and woodwork, and 'knowledge of civic and public affairs'. Both parents had a role to play in promoting home life and the family. It cited a recent report on post-war education published in *National Education*, which stated that parentcraft was designed to create a sense of social responsibility both for private and public affairs; it was an education in citizenship.[144]

By stressing parenting as opposed to mothering, Parents' Centre meant something different and more specific – drawing men into the sphere of infant and child care. Yet had they previously been excluded? When Plunket instructions were given in the home, fathers were not totally ignored. When she retired in 1957, Joan Carmichael reminisced about her 34 years as a Plunket nurse in Auckland. Although she had found the 'grannies' the hardest to persuade about Plunket's usefulness, many fathers, too, had not been very co-operative at first. She usually found that the best method was to visit the home when the father was there for a meal and gain his interest by explaining the reasoning behind Plunket advice.[145] One man writing to the *New Zealand Herald* in 1934 described himself as a 'Plunket Father'.[146] The expectation that fathers should become involved in child care is clear from a 1944 letter to the paper: 'The position of the young mother is a desperate one, as at the present time many of the fathers are overseas, and no outside help is obtainable'.[147] Lusk's impression was that 'a great many husbands did a lot in the morning and evening'.[148]

From 1939, when the Labour government introduced fourteen days free stay in hospital for mothers who had just given birth, fathers were often forced to take sole charge of the household. Yet husbands' domestic abilities were not rated very highly by some female commentators, whose condescending attitude reinforced stereotypes and marginalised men in child care. In 1940 'Hygeia' wrote an article about a father's responsibilities when a new mother came home from the maternity hospital. In the scenario she depicted, the mother's absence had led to a neglected home, as his 'masculine attempts at the "chores" had resulted in chaos'. The husband had also failed to feed himself adequately, so that the wife, on her return, 'lovingly tries to make up for her absence by giving him the best cooking she can contrive'. Then he proceeded to unload all his business worries on her, which he had been 'keeping especially for her sympathetic ear'. The result was unnecessary stress for the mother, and the failure of breast-feeding. The young father was advised that, to avoid this, he was to secure help in the home for at least two weeks after her return. If this were not possible then, not only did he have to do the 'chores' himself, but he had to do them cheerfully, 'as if it was his greatest desire in life', for his wife's sake who had after all borne his child.[149]

In 1945–6 Karitane bureaux were set up in the main centres to co-ordinate the employment of Karitane nurses.[150] The expectation was that the nurses, who were in short supply and great demand at the time, would stay with a new mother for three or four weeks at most. Nancy Fannin, head of the Auckland bureau, claimed the calls for help usually came from harassed fathers. 'Most fathers set to; they cope with the housework as well as they can and do the washing.' Many took their annual holidays to be on hand. She concluded, with a smile, that, 'When it's all over, they usually come in and tell us how good they were.'[151]

Fathers in the 1950s were expected to help with child-rearing. In 1953 Deem told Clayton that talks to fathers 'must be kept simple and practical so that they may effectively help their wives'. The section in *Modern Mothercraft* on 'Suggested Routine Day for the Nursing Mother and her Baby' indicated when fathers could offer help. The daily routine started at 5–6am and finished at 9.30pm. Fathers had no involvement until 5pm, when it was specified that the baby was to have a 'social hour' with parents. From 6 to 6.30pm was the parents' evening meal time and the father was expected to 'assist' with clearing the table and washing dishes. At the end of the schedule, it was noted that if the mother preferred to retire early, the baby could be brought to her in bed for a feed. This gave 'another opportunity for father to help'.[152] In stressing the supportive role, Plunket was not so different from Parents' Centre in the early 1950s. Bevan-Brown explained that the place of the father after the birth was to offer support, material and moral, and that his role was subordinate to that of the mother for the first year at least.[153]

Once ante-natal classes started for women there was pressure to extend them to include men.[154] In 1949 Auckland Plunket's head nurse reported

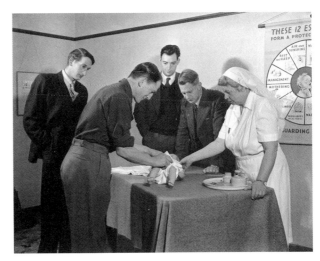

Prospective fathers receiving instruction in the art of changing infants' nappies under the direction of the Sister-in-Charge at the Plunket Society's rooms in Dunedin, June 1952.
Archives New Zealand Te Whare Tohu Tuhituhinga O Aotearoa: National Publicity Studios Photographic Collection, ATL, F-33861-1/2 (A 27268)

that it was 'becoming the rule rather than the exception for expectant mothers to ask whether some of these Mothercraft talks could be extended to the prospective fathers'.[155] She hoped to include 'Fathercraft Talks' in their schedule in the near future, though Auckland did not in fact introduce classes until 1957. The first classes were those run by Nan Clayton in Wellington, starting in 1948. Each class included about fourteen 'young prospective fathers, a few accompanied by wives for moral support'. The head nurse explained, 'Because many of the men are shy Miss Clayton tries to make her talk as natural as possible.'[156] The class was held on a Saturday morning, at the end of a six-week course for the mother. In 1950 Christchurch held its first fathercraft class, reported in the local press. There were seven pupils, two accompanied by their wives who, the reporter of the event suspected, came along to ensure their husbands did not 'play the wag'. The reporter maintained that many husbands showed 'cunning' by pleading ignorance of infant care so they would not have to attend to the baby during the night. Yet there was also great enthusiasm among the men, in the 'flush of expectant fatherhood'.[157] In 1950 Christchurch's classes attracted 27 men; the following year an attendance of 60 was recorded, and 77 by 1955. This did not increase at the same rate as female attendances at ante-natal classes which rose from 1401 in 1952 to 2371 in 1955.[158]

Fathercraft classes, as outlined at the 1950 conference on ante-natal teaching, included instructions on 'bathing, making up milk mixtures, signs of commencing labour' and also 'making nursery furniture [and] safety first on the home front'.[159] In the 'do-it-yourself' climate of the post-

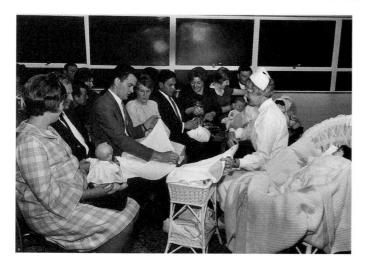

By the 1960s 'parentcraft' had replaced 'fathercraft' and both partners attended together. Plunket Society, Auckland Branch photograph album

war years, fathercraft appeared to be largely about making nursery furniture and safety in the home.[160] In 1946, Auckland's head nurse commented that 'quite a number of fathers come to measure the demonstration cot with a view to making the cots themselves'.[161] The same year Nora Fitzgibbon wrote an article on Plunket nursing for New Zealand's nursing journal, *Kai Tiaki*, in which she discussed the role of fathers in infant care. She maintained that the Plunket nurse usually found the father just as interested as the mother in child care, and that he could be taught 'to handle the baby, to help in the home, and to make things such as a kicking pen and strong toys which will be required for the child as it grows older'. She went on to say that if the nurse took an interest in his garden, the father would be encouraged to grow vegetables and small fruits, which were 'so valuable in the dietary'.[162] In 1949, referring to the 1500 children in the one- to five-year age group who were admitted to public hospitals in New Zealand the previous year with accident injuries, Deem spoke of the importance of guards for heaters. If these could not be bought, fathers could make them from common household equipment.[163] At the 1946 Plunket conference it was suggested that fathers could construct moveable ramps for the new state houses to avoid mothers with prams having to cart them up and down stairs.[164]

As a result of a 1953 conference remit, the revision of the *Baby Record Book* in the mid-1950s included a short section on 'Advice to Fathers'.[165] One delegate had suggested that mothers needed to be re-educated to co-operate with fathers, who were often not 'given permission' to do things.[166] Others had also pressed for more active male involvement. Quentin Brew

This cartoon suggests that fathers did indeed have some input into child care in the 1950s. The caption refers to the Plunket telephone fundraising appeal of 14 May 1957. Plunket Society, Auckland Branch press cuttings

"NO—this is NOT a Plunket Appeal number!"

(Helen Brew's husband and an educational psychologist) argued at a 1957 Parents' Centre conference that most men were capable of much of that subtle, non-verbal communication through which mothers understood and enjoyed their babies.[167] The same year, Nurse R. D. Watson, who was in charge of Auckland Plunket's ante-natal classes, claimed that many New Zealand fathers refused to touch babies until they were a year old. She thought this was a pity, because they missed so much. Her classes aimed to give both parents an interest and confidence in handling the new baby.[168]

Deem, herself a widow who had brought up her child without the support of a husband, nevertheless envisaged a crucial role for fathers. She believed it important for them to establish a bond of friendship with their children: 'The building up of family ties is one of the aims of all social services, because nothing much goes wrong with a family which works and plays together'.[169] In the new child psychology and its emphasis on environment and family, fathers had a role to play.[170] Katherine Arnup noted that post-war Canadian child-guidance authors began to point out that bottle-feeding had the added advantage of enabling the new father to assume responsibility for feeding the baby.[171] The rate of breastfeeding did drop in New Zealand in this period, as has been noted, and fathers were being taught how to make up milk formulae in the ante-natal classes started in the 1950s. Yet the inclusion of a fathers' section in the *Baby Record Book* aimed to help promote breastfeeding by easing some of the strain on the new mothers; Plunket continued to stress the importance of breast-feeding.[172]

Pre-school children

By the late 1930s professionals began to identify a gap in health services for those between infancy and school age.[173] The neglect of pre-school children in New Zealand's health system was commented on by Dr David McMillan in his blueprint for health under the new Labour government in 1935.[174] He advocated the setting up of 'Post-Plunket clinics' for this age group. Commenting that so many beautiful babies 'went off' in this period,[175] Deem envisaged a role for Plunket. Noting that there were about 100,000 children in this group in New Zealand, she pointed out in 1940 that the 'pre-school problem' was exercising child welfare organisations throughout the world.[176] New Zealand's response to the 'world emphasis on the young child' was not as different from Australia as Philippa Mein Smith has suggested.[177] Indeed the links with Australia were strong. In 1938 Deem had visited Dr Vera Scantlebury Brown, Director of Child and Maternal Welfare in Melbourne, and was clearly influenced by developments there.[178] Inspired in turn by a visit from British psychiatrist Dr Susan Isaacs, Brown had proposed setting up a model nursery kindergarten. Such pre-schools were subsequently set up in most of Australia's capital cities, starting with Melbourne in 1939. These Lady Gowrie Child Centres ran pre-school educational programmes, and observed the health of groups of up to 90 pre-school children.[179] Significantly they were health centres first, with a doctor and infant welfare nurse to inspect the children, and model pre-schools second.[180]

Deem began to plan her own pre-school centre in 1939. It was finally

The Helen Deem Pre-school Centre in Dunedin was considered innovative, though at the time of its opening safety features were not as important as they were later to become. Plunket Society, Auckland Branch photograph album

set up in 1941 in the grounds of the Truby King-Harris Hospital, assisted by the Dunedin Branch of the Free Kindergarten Association.[181] The aim was to give practical instruction to Plunket and kindergarten trainees on the management and behavioural problems of the toddler.[182] Before the centre was established, Miss E. S. Hamilton, its first Educational Director, spent several weeks working in the Melbourne Gowrie Centre. Deem was Medical Director of the new centre. After four years, the pre-school moved to new accommodation where it catered for up to 60 'normal' children between the ages of three and five years. By 1947 the local press had declared the 'experiment' a great success.[183] New premises, opened in 1955, included observation booths that enabled observers to watch the children without being seen.[184] Deem reported that the centre provided 'a wealth of material for child study, illustrating individual differences in children of the same age, normal growth and development, and the emotional and physical health progress of the individual children'.[185] She hoped that, with their training and experience at the centre, the nurses would be able to pass on valuable advice 'designed to foster self-reliance, independence, initiative, confidence and good social behaviour' in the child.[186] One of the centre's most important benefits, according to one public health dissertation, was that it gave 'a busy mother respite from all day care of her children'.[187] This fitted the prevailing belief that the two most important factors in rearing healthy children were 'healthy mental attitude of the mothers' and 'happy home surroundings'.[188] Both, though, depended on full-time motherhood, the dominant ideology of the 1950s.[189]

Like Scantlebury Brown in Melbourne, Deem wished infant health clinics to incorporate sections for pre-schoolers, made attractive by wooden toys and sandpits.[190] Christchurch and Wellington both possessed pre-school clinics by 1940, run by a full-time nurse, and Wellington had set up an area in its grounds with outdoor playing equipment for children. In 1941 Auckland also set up a pre-school section. Such involvement was interpreted by the Health Department, however, as encroachment on its patch (see Chapter 6).

Deem may have considered herself an amateur psychologist, but like other paediatricians of the time she was drawn into child psychology. She agreed that human relationships were very important, commenting on the increasing evidence supporting the view that many nervous disorders seen in adolescents and young adults could be traced to unfortunate incidents in early childhood. This reinforced the view that parents needed guidance and encouragement to bring up their families to be emotionally stable.[191]

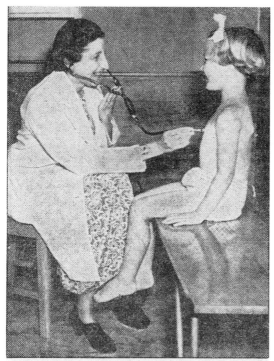

IT'S FUN, ISN'T IT? The late Dr. Helen Deem had a happy knack of dispelling the fears of the most nervous child. Here she had obviously established friendly relations.

New Zealand Free Lance,
9 November 1955, ATL, N-P 856-10

Her philosophy was simple: 'If only people in general could learn to understand little children and each other too, I feel sure that the World could be a much happier place to live in'.[192]

Helen Deem was highly regarded by those with whom she came into contact through her professional work. Not only did she enlist the support of the Plunket hierarchy and paediatricians, she was also loved and respected by nurses and mothers. Plunket nurse Eleanor Alden later described her as 'outstanding'; she was 'full of vim, she could lecture and you could hear a pin drop . . . People trusted her.' Alden always felt she could ring Deem about any problems and advice would be willingly given. Another Plunket nurse, Val Jones, described her as 'absolutely marvellous', pointing out that she 'had a nice sense of humour and an asymmetrical smile' and that importantly she 'never spoke down to the mothers'.[193] In 1952 Helen Deem was awarded the OBE for services to child health. She died in Dunedin on 26 October 1955, eight months after learning she had lymphatic leukaemia. She spent her last few months ensuring the smooth transition of the society's medical administration to her successor. When Frederick Clements was consulted by Deem on a possible successor, he replied that it should be someone of experience, who was as 'well orientated to the whole child as you are'.[194] She also consulted Howard Williams, a New Zealander who was then Director of Clinical Medicine at the Royal Children's Hospital, Melbourne. He told Deem that the person would have to have 'character', sensitivity to social needs, and the right balance between clinical and social paediatrics. 'To these essential ingredients medical and administrative ability, and intelligence must be added. What an order! Yet you have more than a good measure of all these combinations and that is why you have achieved so much.'[195]

CHAPTER 6

Plunket and the Government, 1939–60

Promoting motherhood

The Second World War, like the First, gave Plunket political ammunition: in looking after the welfare of mothers and babies they were performing an essential national service. Opening Plunket's general conference in 1944, Mrs W. Appleton, the Mayoress of Wellington, identified herself as a mother of 'five Plunket children'. She considered there was no more important work than Plunket, 'from a woman's point of view'. She described the help she had received with one of her sons who had been 'most difficult in the baby stage', but had made good progress under the supervision of a Plunket nurse, and was now 'doing a great job in the Air Force'.[1] Plunket was given formal recognition when Britain's National Baby Welfare Council awarded it the British Commonwealth Challenge Shield for the best record of child welfare work in the British Commonwealth during 1939–44.[2]

The Labour government needed little encouragement to continue supporting Plunket. Already in 1936 the subsidy of £125 per Plunket nurse per

Plunket Aid volunteers were trained in the Second World War to help out in the event of an emergency. Here they practise evacuation from Auckland's Plunket Headquarters, 1942. Plunket Society, Auckland Branch photograph album

Plunket Society conference, 11 August 1939. The President, Daisy Begg, is seated in the front row, centre, and on her right is the Administrative Secretary, Gwen Hoddinott. ATL, C-22529-1/2

annum had been restored, and by 1946 the rate had increased to £177 10s. From 1947 the subsidy was altered from a flat rate to 60 per cent of the nurse's salary; a decade later this amounted to £387 for each Plunket nurse per annum. From 1939, the subsidy for Karitane hospitals was transferred from the Health Department budget to the Social Security Fund. The new subsidies for Plunket meant that government contributions more than trebled from £25,132 in 1938–9 to £87,095 in 1949.[3]

As Plunket's president from 1937 to 1950, Daisy Begg led Plunket over most of Labour's term. Like her predecessors she had a strong sense of women's rights and responsibilities to become involved in public affairs that concerned them. She kept the society in the government's eye. During the 1944 Plunket conference, for example, she led a deputation consisting of all the delegates to the Ministers of Health and Agriculture concerning tuberculosis in milk. She negotiated with the Director of Housing regarding the design of the Labour government's new state houses.[4] A member of numerous women's organisations apart from Plunket, she saw herself as representing the women's point of view. At the 1946 conference, speaking about the condition of maternity hospitals, she expressed her conviction that 'it was time women took a hand in this matter and made known what service they wanted and where. Hospital Boards were composed almost entirely of men, and it should not all be left to men.'[5]

At the end of the Second World War Plunket ideology was in tune with the government's desire to promote the stay-at-home mother. Delegates at the 1944 conference passed a remit stating that 'this meeting is unanimously of the opinion that no mother of young children should be given opportunity and encouragement to leave the upbringing of her children to others while she engages in industry'.[6] Yet women felt increasingly let down by Labour in promoting this ideal, and made their views known through

Plunket, along with other women's groups such as the Housewives' Association (formed in 1939).

One disappointment to women was the government's home aid scheme. Shortly before and during the Second World War, Plunket had been at the forefront of promoting such a scheme, which attracted much interest and support among women's groups generally.[7] As two public health researchers declared in 1941, 'It is our opinion that this lack of domestic help constitutes the most urgent Public Health problem in New Zealand today.'[8] In 1942 Begg argued that 'The mother must be given the most honoured place in the community and be given practical help'.[9] The government's maternity benefits, introduced in 1939, giving new mothers a fortnight's free rest in hospital, were a positive step. In the context of Labour's social security and the prevailing belief in entitlement, the *Listener* in 1944 reported a conversation between two mothers in a Plunket waiting room, who believed that every mother should be '*entitled* to some domestic help', and that if the government wanted women to have more children, as they had signalled, 'they will have to give us more monetary assistance'.[10] The government's Home Aid Service, set up in December 1945 under the Employment Act, aimed to provide home aids to housewives in need, regardless of their ability to pay. By 1948, however, only 64 domestic aids were available.[11] After studying a similar scheme in Sweden, Helen Deem believed that the New Zealand equivalent failed because those involved were not given adequate status through training and the awarding of a diploma.[12]

Even more significant in the loss of support for the government were the continued shortages of goods after 1945. The difficulty of obtaining

Mothers waiting to see the Plunket nurse had plenty of opportunity to exchange views. Plunket Society rooms, Papanui, Christchurch, 1944. *The Work of the Plunket Society in New Zealand*, 1945

This 1946 National Party election poster encouraged housewives to vote against the 'shortage government'. Courtesy Professor Barry Gustafson

layettes during the war exercised mothers. In 1944 Plunket carried out a survey of available resources in Auckland, only to find that 'all articles asked for [materials, blankets, wool etc] gave a nil result'.[13] But what was acceptable under war conditions became less acceptable when it continued following the war, and resignation turned to indignation.[14] As Auckland Plunket's head nurse, Helen Chapman, reported in 1947, 'We have made repeated appeals for better distribution of fine wool, flannel and blankets without any noticeable results. Mothers still have to walk many miles and make many visits to shops, and then return home tired and depressed after a hopeless search for these things'.[15] The shortage of materials was compounded by the petrol restrictions which prevented home deliveries of groceries, and the 1946 introduction of Saturday closing of shops added to housewives' burdens. Mrs J. A. Harris (Lower Hutt) argued at the 1946 Plunket conference that the stress caused by the non-delivery of household goods was one of the reasons for the decline in breastfeeding. She had weighed bundles being carried by women, and had found that they were carrying 'incredibly heavy' parcels, along with babies and small children. She maintained that 'strenuous efforts had been made to keep the matter away from politics, but women had a big weapon, and could mould public opinion, and this was the only thing left to do'.[16] It was the National Party which 'mobilised the shopping vote, backing a consumerism dedicated to home-makers'.[17] Labour's 'shortage government' was losing support among mothers and this undoubtedly contributed to its defeat at the polls in 1949.

Plunket's access to the corridors of power in the 1950s was undoubtedly aided by the fact that the society's president from 1950 to 1957, Elizabeth Bodkin, was the wife of the Minister of Internal Affairs 1949–54, William Bodkin (knighted in 1954). When she was elected, however, Bodkin upheld the tradition of the supposedly apolitical maternalists: she maintained that, although she was the wife of a Cabinet minister, 'as President of the Plunket Society she had no politics'.[18]

Plunket services received a further boost under National. In 1950 an additional subsidy over and above that from the Social Security Fund was granted to Karitane hospitals – a pound for pound subsidy on building costs. Voluntary contributions to the hospitals were subsidised on the same basis from 1952. The previous year Cabinet had approved a special grant of £10,000 to cover the increased cost of maintaining Plunket's District

LOOK PLEASANT, PLEASE

Plunket was such a recognisable icon in the 1940s that it was used in political cartoons.

VISIONS OF THE NEXT GENERAL ELECTION

ABOVE: The 'Compulsory loan' associated with socialist Paddy Webb was not successful in making the baby smile for the camera, October 1940.
LEFT: Plunket's attempts to educate both Labour (Walter Nash) and National (Sidney Holland) during the 1951 snap election was captured in this cartoon which suggested the babies were not overly impressed by either party's promises. Plunket Society, Auckland Branch press cuttings

Nursing Services. In 1952 a further special grant of £5,000 was approved to establish a fund to help struggling Plunket branches. This became known as the Plunket Security Fund, and from 1954 the government subsidised it on a pound for pound basis. It did not, however, accede to the request to raise the subsidy on nurses' salaries from 60 to 70 per cent. By 1955 government contributions included a 50 per cent mileage allowance toward the running expenses of cars, the actual costs of rail and road services fares, and a 20 per cent subsidy on the purchase price of motor vehicles. The government was now meeting £159,909 of Plunket's annual running costs.[19] Two years later Treasury noted in a report that Plunket was regarded 'almost as part of the New Zealand way of life'. Discussing the possibility of curtailing subsidies, the report stated,

> the basic fact remains that for over forty years the State has paid increasingly heavy subsidies for this purpose. On each occasion in the past when the matter has been considered, the Government of the day has decided to provide increased subsidies rather than face the upheaval that a change of policy, such as withdrawal or curtailment of State financial aid, would inevitably bring in its train.[20]

LEFT: As Treasury was well aware, the Plunket Society was part of the 'fabric of New Zealand society' and was featured in the Christchurch Centennial Celebrations in 1950. Plunket Society Annual Report 1950–51

RIGHT: This beautiful baby on Plunket's 1957 appeal poster touched the hearts of New Zealanders and the appeal raised £143,641. However the Society still depended on substantial government support. *Auckland Star*, 13 May 1957

The Plunket Society enjoyed wide public and political support, but the Health Department continued to oppose this trend of ever-increasing state funding being diverted to Plunket. The result was an official inquiry in 1959.

Plunket and the Health Department

In the post-war era there was a territorial dispute between Plunket and the Health Department over pre-school health services. In 1940 the two bodies had introduced a joint scheme for examining pre-school children, using Plunket rooms and Departmental School Medical Officers.[21] By 1943, 80 clinics had been equipped for the purpose at Plunket rooms and kindergartens, and 5628 children were examined that year. This revealed, according to the Director of School Hygiene, Dr Harold Turbott, 'minor structural deformities of bones and joints, and [too high] malnutrition'. His remark that 'Dietary errors are very obvious in the home control of these children'[22] may have been a veiled criticism of Plunket's dietary advice.

In 1948, to reflect this involvement, the Health Department's Division of School Hygiene was renamed the Division of Child Hygiene and when Turbott was appointed Deputy Director-General of Health, Dr Lyell Davis replaced him as director of the division. In 1950 Davis reported favourably on the collaboration between Plunket and the department, noting that 'many medical officers of health spoke highly of the relationship'.[23] Turbott, however, was not so convinced. He had already upset Plunket in 1947 by announcing that the society was giving up its involvement in pre-school health supervision;[24] three years later he complained of 'Plunket infiltration into pre-school care work', which he saw as unnecessary and mere 'empire

Helen Deem argued that there was plenty of work for both Plunket and the Health Department in supervising the health of pre-school children.
Plunket Society, Auckland Branch photograph album

Some Plunket pre-school work pre-dated the collaborative efforts with the Health Department.
Plunket Society Annual Report 1935–36

building'.[25] He admitted that it was the department's aim to undertake the entire pre-school medical service for New Zealand.[26]

Dr Gordon McLeod, division director from 1951 to 1955, stated in his first annual report that 'the departmental policy of achieving as great a cover of the pre-school child as possible will be continued'.[27] Auckland's Medical Officer of Health, Dr A. W. S. Thompson, had appointed a part-time paediatrician and set up a Child Health Clinic, where the department held its own pre-school clinics.[28] Plunket noted, however, that by 1953, according to the department's annual report, only about 30 per cent of pre-school children were being examined. [29] Arguing that there was plenty of work for both bodies to do in respect of pre-school children, Deem emphasised the need for greater co-operation. She told Health Minister Jack Marshall that the society had approached the Health Department to set up a conference of interested parties, only to be told by Turbott that 'no good purpose would be served' by such a gathering.[30] Unlike Turbott, she believed that Plunket nurses, 'with their great deal of experience' were able to do the 'culling', and referred to an article in *The Lancet* based on a survey carried out in England to support her argument.[31]

Even more fundamental territorial disputes occurred in relation to district nursing services. Michael Watt, Director-General of Health 1930–47, believed a specialised infant health service was 'wasteful of time, effort and money'.[32] In 1940, since the department did not have a nurse stationed in Taihape, he suggested to the Plunket Society that the Plunket nurse there should undertake departmental duties, including school and tuberculosis work, 'as an experiment', and that financial adjustments should be made between the society and the department. The council agreed, provided the

A Plunket nurse visiting a rural mother, December 1949.
Archives New Zealand Te Whare Tohu Tuhituhinga O Aotearoa: National Publicity Studios Photographic Collection, ATL, F-33856-1/2 (A16, 507)

society's medical and nursing advisers and the local branch approved. Watt clearly saw this as the first step. Deem was well aware of his belief in the advantages of a combined service, particularly in country districts.[33]

By 1950 Plunket nurses undertook general public health nursing in Taihape, West Otago, Central Otago, Palmerston, Kaikoura, Maniototo, Banks Peninsula and South Westland. In other areas the work of the district nurse was extended to include Plunket duties. By 1950 this included Porangahau, Queenstown, Hanmer Springs, the National Park, Mangakino, Granity and Reefton. From Plunket's viewpoint, 'combined areas', where district nurses undertook Plunket work, were not a success. Under the arrangement, the Plunket branch or sub-branch reimbursed the Health Department at the same rate for which the part-time services of a Plunket nurse could be obtained. However, the department made no charge for any areas where a Plunket committee did not function.[34] Not surprisingly, Plunket committee members began to question the purpose of their work, if the services were provided regardless. By 1957, the Health Department was refusing to accept contributions from voluntary committees for the work carried out by district nurses. This was demoralising for the committees and in some places led to their disbanding.[35] As Plunket's president, Jocelyn Ryburn, explained to Prime Minister Walter Nash in 1958, 'Strangely enough the . . . problem which is seriously exercising us is not caused by our not receiving money from the Government, but by our being unable to find a way of paying money to the Government.' Committees had no incentive to continue: 'Thus we lose not only a committee that voluntarily raises funds, but also an invaluable local agent of preventive medicine education.'[36]

Plunket formed an important part of the social life of women in small communities. The Titahi Bay Plunket Committee was formed by eight young mothers, who between them had thirty children. Plunket Society Annual Report 1955–56

Nor would the Health Department allow the Plunket Society to supervise infant work carried out by district nurses. Turbott considered that Plunket supervision of all nurses in infant welfare work was 'in line with their usual technique of infiltration'.

> They were allowed the 'privilege' of visiting and advising our nurses in combined areas because without this concession they would never have agreed to the idea and we would have had Plunket and district nurse in the area instead of one nurse. They now blithely argue they have supervisory control of our nurses in infant welfare work. This is nonsense. We do not need their visit at all except for diplomatic reasons.[37]

When one district nurse undertaking Plunket work complained about inspection by the Plunket provincial nursing supervisor, she was supported by Turbott, who reiterated that district nurses were supervised by the Health Department only.[38] Mary Lambie, Director of the Health Department's Nursing Division, also noted that some departmental nurses felt local Plunket committees were interfering unduly in their work.[39]

Plunket and Maori

Many women in rural areas and small towns wanted a Plunket nurse as opposed to a district nurse. In one place, Meremere, the mothers called a public meeting and set up a Plunket sub-branch without the knowledge of either the Health Department or the Plunket Society, though their request for a Plunket nurse was subsequently turned down by the department.[40] Although it is unknown whether the drive for a Plunket nurse in Meremere, a small settlement in the Waikato which included Maori residents, came from the European population only, in other areas there is evidence of resistance to 'combined schemes' covering both races. In 1949 Plunket's Nursing Adviser, Sydney Lusk, received a letter from the white population of Tolaga Bay on the East Cape of the North Island, a predominantly Maori area. This set out 'in no uncertain terms the determination of the district to fight against any service given to them by a District Nurse who is also attending the Maoris . . . The letter is so definite [wrote Lusk] that I feel it would be quite useless to pursue the matter further.'[41]

The local Plunket Committee explained its grounds for opposition. It asked pointedly if, under a 'combined scheme', Maori mothers would be attending the rooms at the same time as European mothers. It expressed the belief that the nurse would be 'snowed under' by Maori, since Europeans were in the minority. The letter alleged that about half the Maori children suffered from tuberculosis or venereal disease, and expressed fears about their contact with European children. Lusk concluded, 'They feel that Head Office [in Dunedin], in fact no one in the South Island understands what the white people have to tolerate, living in a Maori district . . . and confidentially we were told that the whites would not use the services of the District Nurse.'[42] In short, the local European population felt the nurses were contaminated by their association with Maori, and that all Maori were potential sources of infection.

A similar response came from Kaitaia in Northland, another predominantly Maori area, where the whole population was served by two district nurses. An investigation of the nurses' work revealed that they were not welcomed in European homes. The nurses suggested that one of the reasons for this was that mothers did not like them calling after they had been visiting Maori homes.[43] A remit from Northland was sent to Plunket's 1949 Provincial conference, asking 'that more publicity be given to the fact that Maori babies may receive attention from the Plunket nurse'. Dr Jeanie Fougere, a local GP, mother of two and a member of the Plunket Dominion Council, explained at the conference that the remit had been sent in by a

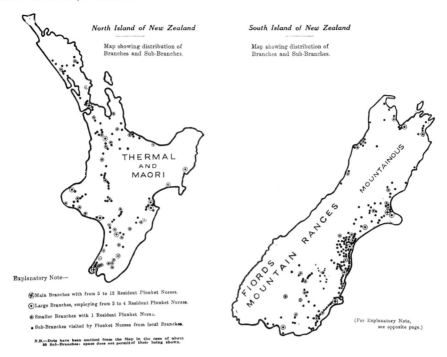

North Island of New Zealand

Map showing distribution of
Branches and Sub-Branches.

THERMAL
AND
MAORI

Explanatory Note—

Main Branches with from 5 to 12 Resident Plunket Nurses.

Large Branches, employing from 2 to 4 Resident Plunket Nurses.

Smaller Branches with 1 Resident Plunket Nurse.

Sub-Branches visited by Plunket Nurses from local Branches.

N.B.—Dots have been omitted from the Map in the case of about 50 Sub-Branches: space does not permit of their being shown.

South Island of New Zealand

Map showing distribution of
Branches and Sub-Branches.

MOUNTAINOUS

FIORDS MOUNTAIN RANGES

(For Explanatory Note,
see opposite page.)

Plunket's coverage had expanded greatly by 1931 but there was still a huge unattended area marked 'Thermal and Maori'. Plunket Society Annual Report 1930–31

sub-branch committee without reference to the branch committee and that when it had been discussed there had been a division of opinion.[44] The following year the European population of Kaitaia asked Health Minister Jack Watts to help them obtain a Plunket nurse for the area, since local women refused to use the district nurse because she was regarded as a 'Maori' nurse. The deputation wanted their own nurse for European work only, and they wanted a Plunket nurse. They subsequently withdrew their opposition to sharing a nurse with local Maori, following a baby show held to raise funds for the Plunket nurse, at which the prize-winner was a Maori baby. Racial barriers seem to have been broken down on that occasion, and Maori mothers were then encouraged to bring their babies to the Plunket clinic at Kaitaia.[45] In 1955 the Health Department and Plunket agreed to a segregated service at Whangarei, the main population centre in Northland. It was decided that the district nurse would do all the infant welfare work in one isolated area where there was at that time only one Pakeha baby. With that sole exception, the district nurse would see Maori babies and the Plunket nurse Pakeha babies.[46]

Plunket remained very much a European organisation, sending its mobile van into the burgeoning suburbs of the 1940s and 1950s.
Plunket Society, Auckland Branch photograph album

This segregated system had been the norm since the Health Department had introduced its own Native Health Nursing Service in 1911.[47] Maori mothers were permitted to visit Plunket clinics, but Plunket nurses were not to go into Maori homes. Maori infant health was the responsibility of district nurses. At the 1945 general Plunket conference one delegate moved that the work of the society be extended to Maori. Deem spoke of the work of district nurses, pointing out that it was wasteful for both to visit homes. The amended motion, 'That the work of the Society be extended to include the Maori people within our city and town boundaries', was carried.[48]

In 1953 Turbott pointed out that 'Maori infant welfare has for many years been recognised as the responsibility of this Department although there has been an increasing tendency for the Plunket Society to edge its way, it is contended unnecessarily, into this field'.[49] Two years later the Health Department refused to allow the Plunket Society to locate a nurse in Auckland's Howick and Panmure–Mount Wellington district, because it suspected that the births listed in Plunket's application included Maori babies.[50]

Turbott need not have worried about this 'infiltration'. Regardless of Health Department restrictions, Plunket had never had much success in attracting urban Maori. Dr Wilton Henley, a Lady King Scholar who conducted a research project into the health of over 1000 babies in 1939–40, claimed the study to be representative of a cross-section of infants in Auckland at that time. The subjects, he explained, were determined solely by the infants' attendance at the Plunket rooms. Yet the study included only one Maori and one Chinese; the rest were European.[51] There were then about 2000 Maori living in the Auckland urban area, and almost 2000 others defined as 'alien'.[52] There was little change in the 1940s. Of the 202 mothers of Maori babies born in Auckland in 1950 who were sent the society's routine letter offering the services of the Plunket nurses, only 24 responded.[53] This 12 per cent response rate was in sharp contrast to that of over 80 per cent for their European counterparts.

The racial antipathy of some mothers may have inhibited Maori from attending. Then there was the attitude of the nurses. Stella Petersen, president of the Palmerston North branch of Plunket, claimed in 1945 that, in her area, Plunket nurses were refusing to see Maori babies who had been brought to the rooms, stating that they were acting under instructions from head office.[54] After receiving statements from some branches that Plunket nurses would not attend Maori mothers, Lusk sent out a questionnaire to all Plunket nurses in the North Island and some in the South Island. The nurses denied all suggestions of racism. 'In most cases,' Lusk reported, 'it had been found that Maori mothers had not the idea of continuous supervision of their babies, and that as soon as her baby was well the average Maori mother ceased to attend the rooms.'[55]

Some Plunket nurses were probably more sensitive or more receptive to cultural differences than others. At least one teacher in a Native school did not rate the chances of a Plunket nurse staying long in a Maori area. She claimed that any Plunket nurse sent to her particular settlement 'would be reduced to the gibbers in a week'.[56] From 1942 grants from the J. R. McKenzie Trust provided bursaries to train Maori Karitane and Plunket nurses.[57] A decade later Deem reported that they had trained 'several' Maori women.[58] In 1952 it was noted that those who had been assisted by the McKenzie Trust had 'proved very satisfactory', though no further detail was provided.[59]

The fact that Plunket nurses did not visit Maori in their homes meant that they did not build up the same relationship with the Maori mothers as they did with their European counterparts. Lusk and Deem told nurses that they should visit the homes of Maori 'living in European style'. In 1945, however, Lusk repeated the a council member's account of a nurse making a first call: 'The door was opened by a Maori mother – thereupon nurse is supposed to have said, "Oh, I'm not allowed to call on you" and to have left'.[60]

Such insensitivity at the local level did not preclude some concern about the state of Maori infant health. In 1945 Petersen suggested to the council that Plunket investigate the problem of high Maori infant mortality rates,

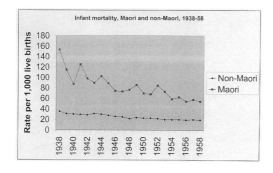

Infant mortality, Maori and non-Maori, 1938–58.

which were then four times higher than those for non-Maori.[61] She put the motion to the council again in 1946. Deem had observed Maori living conditions when she was Assistant Medical Officer of Health for the Waikato in the late 1930s. In her opinion Maori housing conditions and sanitation would have to be vastly improved before any spectacular results could be expected. She agreed that there was urgent need for an investigation into all factors contributing to the high infantile mortality and that Plunket should offer to co-operate with such an undertaking in a designated area. Petersen's motion, 'That the Plunket Society approach the Health Department with a view to organising a survey commencing with one Maori district, to try to discover the factors contributing to the high Maori infant mortality and to consider ways and means of meeting the existing unsatisfactory position', was carried.[62] Nothing, however, came of this before the 1960s.[63]

The 1959 Consultative Committee on Infant and Pre-school Health Services

In 1948 the Health Department attempted closer co-operation, or control, of Plunket when it suggested that Deem be appointed to a departmental position, much as Truby King had been in the early 1920s. Plunket's executive resolved not to consider this until an assistant to Deem was appointed, and the suggestion did not resurface. The following year the Health Department asked for representation on the society's Dominion Executive and Council. While claiming to be 'deeply appreciative' of the friendly relations that had always existed between the two organisations, Plunket did not accede to this request.[64]

Turbott, who emerges as the arch enemy of Plunket, appeared to be more conciliatory in 1953 when he and Flora Cameron, Director of the Nursing

Distinguished visitors
to Plunket included the
Director-General of the
United Nations World
Health Organization, Dr
George Brock Chisholm
(third from left), with
Dr Helen Deem, Dr
H. B. Turbott and
Matron Janet Mackay
at the Truby King-Harris
Hospital, Dunedin.
Plunket Society Annual
Report 1949–50

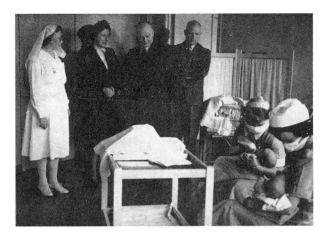

Division, were invited to a Plunket council meeting. When Plunket president Elizabeth Bodkin complained that the Health Department did not give adequate recognition to Plunket – there was, for instance, no mention of its work in the department's last annual report – Turbott replied that he had nothing to do with the report,[65] but as there were a number of voluntary societies in the dominion, they could not be included. He expressed surprise at the suggestion that the department did not adequately recognise Plunket's work, and added that it directed interested overseas visitors to the society. In thanking Turbott and Cameron for attending the meeting, Mrs W. T. Simmons said she felt that the two bodies had a great opportunity to show overseas visitors what could be done by co-operation between the state and a voluntary organisation. Turbott replied that he had been a friend of the society for many years. He considered that someone was poisoning the minds of the council about him. He also thought that the discussions between Health Department and Plunket officers were not fully reported to the council.[66]

The council was clearly not persuaded by his tone. At the same meeting it was resolved

> That a statement be prepared setting out all the matters at issue between the Society and the Department of Health and forwarded to the Minister of Health with a request for a meeting with him, and that if after the meeting it is deemed advisable we ask for a Cabinet sub-committee to investigate the whole matter of relationships between the Plunket Society and the Health Department.[67]

It would take four years for the government to agree, and the stimulus came from a crisis in Karitane hospital finances. In 1957 the new Labour government had been elected to office on a platform of 'family welfare'. Plunket again asked for an increase in the government's subsidy of Plunket nurses, from 60 to 70 per cent of their salaries, but this was declined.[68] It was the cost of maintaining its institutions, the Karitane hospitals, that was the real drain on Plunket funds. Although they accepted donations, they were classified as public hospitals under the Social Security system and were not allowed to receive payments for their services. Income did not match outgoings; for example, in the 1940s, expenditure at Auckland's Karitane Hospital increased by 72 per cent while income increased by 45 per cent. The situation continued to deteriorate in the 1950s, despite further government assistance, which amounted to 68 per cent of the hospitals' income by 1958.[69] At that time the six hospitals had an overdraft in excess of £20,000.[70]

Plunket's mounting debts prompted it to approach individual MPs in search of additional government support. The Minister of Health, Rex Mason, received letters from members of both major political parties, including John (Jock) Mathison, Gordon Grieve, Brian Talboys and Norman Kirk, a future prime minister. The latter, having been approached by the Christchurch branch concerning its Karitane hospital, wrote to the minister, 'I am sure I do not need to remind you of the valuable and important part the work of this hospital plays in the life of the community.'[71]

In November 1958 Mason was invited to attend a Plunket council meeting to discuss finances. He announced that the government would provide an emergency grant of £23,000 to tide the Karitane hospitals over the coming year, but that any further financial assistance would be determined after a more complete investigation of the society's finances. President Jocelyn Ryburn pointed out that when Plunket applied to the government for grants or subsidies, it did not see the Health Department report on which Cabinet's decision was based. She asked for an inquiry, under an independent chairman, to hear the submissions of both the society and the department, a suggestion that was received sympathetically by Mason.[72] In December he presented a paper to the Cabinet Committee on Social Services, in which he outlined the proposed inquiry, suggesting that it be conducted by the Board of Health. But for 'political and other considerations' the committee thought this would be unwise. It favoured a public inquiry.[73]

According to the *New Zealand Herald*, the government ignored Plunket at its peril: 'For a country that has come to regard the Plunket Society as a national institution, the possibility that several of the long-established

The Auckland Karitane Hospital might have to close unless the Government raised its subsidy, Mrs I. Horton, president of the Auckland branch of the Plunket Society, said in Wellington today.

WILL HIS NEXT BOTTLE BE FULL?

Imagery involving infants had a powerful public and political appeal, reflected in this cartoon drawing attention to the financial plight of the Karitane hospitals. *Auckland Star*, 6 November 1958

Karitane hospitals may have to close down through lack of funds ranks as an emergency'. The editor was critical of the Labour government's response to appeals over the past year, and noted that no such procrastination was involved when Prime Minister Walter Nash received calls to assist overseas charities. 'As matters stand, generosity abroad is ill-matched by apparent parsimony at home.'[74]

By March 1959, the terms of reference of the committee of inquiry had been broadened. It was now to investigate all infant and pre-school health services, though Mason assured the Plunket executive that the society's affairs would be given priority.[75] The consultative committee was headed by a retired Supreme Court judge, Sir George Finlay. Its members included Dr James (Jim) Watt, a Wellington paediatrician and the son of the former Director-General of Health, Mary Dowse, Mayoress of Lower Hutt, and Malcolm Mason, a public accountant and young father.[76] It received evidence in mid-1959 and reported in November 1959. Both Watt and Mason later sat on the Plunket Council's Advisory Board.[77] Either they were already sympathetic to Plunket or their experiences during this inquiry persuaded them of the society's value.

Health Department officials who gave evidence included Turbott, Flora Cameron and Dr Gerald Lennane, Director of Child Hygiene. The departmental representatives pointed out that a major function of the Karitane hospitals, the care of premature babies, was gradually being transferred to public hospitals. In 1957 only 23 per cent of New Zealand's 2363 premature babies were admitted to Karitane hospitals. They also questioned the

Wanganui Karitane
Hospital. *The Work
of the Plunket Society
in New Zealand*,
1945

hospitals' training scheme since Karitane nurses were costly to employ and
therefore not available to many members of the community.[78] Lennane recommended that Karitane hospitals be phased out. Turbott also commented
on pre-school health services. Overlooking the fact that pre-school medical
inspections had started only a decade before, as a collaborative effort
between Plunket and the Health Department, Turbott told the committee
that, 'The Department had always maintained that it was its duty to
provide health supervision for the pre-school child, the incursion of the
Plunket Society into this field being considered unnecessary and a dupli-
cation of State-provided services'. He added that Plunket could not provide
supervision by medical personnel and referred to the lack of control over
standards of training of Plunket and Karitane nurses by the Nurses and
Midwives Registration Board. Cameron recommended the establishment
of polyclinics in place of Plunket and other clinics, to integrate all child
health work. In the *New Zealand Herald*'s view, the Health Department
submissions and the questioning of Dr Alice Bush and others by its legal
representative at the Auckland hearing 'can leave little doubt about these
officials' objectives' – the closing of Karitane hospitals and the assumption of other Plunket Society activities by state-run polyclinics.[79]

Plunket's major submission was written by its new Medical Director, Dr
Neil Begg, who had taken up the post in 1956.[80] Begg, born in 1915, came
from a well-known Dunedin family, his paternal grandparents having been
among the early Scottish settlers of Otago. His aunt was former Plunket
president Daisy Begg. His father, a physician and surgeon, was Director of

Medical Services to the New Zealand Defence Forces during the First World War, and died in London in 1919 during the influenza pandemic. Begg graduated MB ChB from Otago in 1941. The following year he married Margot, a librarian and granddaughter of one of the original professors at the University of Otago, in Dunedin. They were to have two daughters and two sons. During the Second World War Begg served with the medical corps of the Second New Zealand Expeditionary Force in the Middle East, Italy and Britain, reaching the rank of major. After the war he decided to specialise in paediatrics and trained in London, Edinburgh and Stockholm from 1946 to 1948. In 1947 he gained the Diploma in Child Health. The following year he attained membership of the Royal Colleges of Physicians of Edinburgh and London (later elevated to the fellowship, in 1957 and 1977 respectively). In 1949 he returned as a paediatrician to Dunedin Hospital, the Truby King-Harris Hospital and Queen Mary Maternity Hospital, and was appointed a lecturer in paediatrics at the medical school. He also set up a private paediatric practice, which he sold in 1956 to become full-time director of Plunket. He was initially appointed as medical adviser, but in 1957 the council changed his title to director of medical services because the original title caused confusion in New Zealand and overseas. At the same time the title nursing adviser was altered to director of nursing services.[81] It appears that the council no longer felt threatened by its health professionals.

Begg's first challenge was to respond to the 1959 inquiry. With the help of his wife, he wrote an extensive submission, in which he analysed child health services internationally.[82] His recommendations included setting up an independent Children's Advisory Council. In his view it was 'undesirable that the centre of gravity of a learned profession should be in a Government department'.[83] His submission promoted not just Plunket but a specialised and independent paediatric service. The society was now fully supported by a medical profession that remained highly suspicious of state control. Dr Herbert Green, acting Medical Director of Auckland's new National Women's Hospital, was a staunch supporter. As the *New Zealand Herald* noted, 'Departmental officials may have received a shock last week when in . . . Green, they found a formidable advocate for the Karitane hospitals.'[84] Green was clearly concerned about the encroaching powers of the department, in his case through the Nurses and Midwives Registration Board, which he saw as dictating to the medical profession.[85] A senior paediatrician at National Women's Hospital, Dr Jack Dilworth Matthews, was another who strongly endorsed the Karitane hospitals as 'an essential

Plunket Headquarters Staff, 1959.
Front row (left to right): Kathleen
Rapps (Secretary of the Society,
1945–63), Neil Begg (Medical
Director, 1956–76), and Janet
Mackay (Director of Nursing
Services, 1958–65). Hocken Library,
AG-7/7/16

complementary service' to that provided by his unit at the National
Women's Hospital. He believed it was important, given the prevalence of
hospital staphylococcal infections, not to concentrate all premature babies
in one big unit. He did, however, urge more doctor participation in Plunket
clinics and the appointment of regional medical supervisors, preferably
paediatricians, to supervise Plunket nurses.[86] The *Evening Post* announced
that 'the BMA sides with Plunket Society [and] opposes the Health Department' on the subject of pre-school health.[87]

The consultative committee's final report was very supportive of Plunket. 'The Plunket Society is a manifestation of self-help in possibly its
highest form. It would, we think, be calamitous to destroy it (for destruc-
tion is involved) in favour of further dependence upon the State.'[88] A
Plunket executive member, Peter Smellie, commented that the society had
been 'greatly cheered and encouraged' by the volume of public sympathy
and support.[89] The editor of the *New Zealand Herald* claimed the community was united under the slogan 'Hands off the Plunket Society and its
work'.[90] In 1959 Plunket was indeed widely regarded as 'part of the fabric
of the New Zealand way of life'.[91] As the committee's report enthused,
'there can be no doubt that the reputation enjoyed by the society, the
qualifications and attributes of its nurses and the widespread public need
that it fills, have combined to create for it a degree of public favour and

public approbation which have gone far to secure the cooperation of almost all mothers in the country'.[92]

Concerning the claim that the society reached 'almost all mothers', the report noted that it had supervised 88.6 per cent of all European babies born in New Zealand in 1958. It did not, however, reach Maori mothers and babies. Begg had tried to pre-empt criticism here by including a section in his submission on 'Infant Welfare Services to the Maori Race'. In this he regretted that Plunket services were currently 'denied' to Maori. Foreshadowing later concerns about self-determination, he averred, 'It would do something to restore dignity to the race to be permitted to participate in the planning and management of its own health service. There is no reason to doubt that the young Maori mother would not be willing to play her part.' Maori, he asserted, should be granted the same right to choose their infant health advisers as other New Zealanders.[93] The committee sought the opinion of the Department of Maori Affairs, which suggested that Maori were happy with the present arrangement.[94] The committee did add, however, that specialised help from Plunket nurses should be as available to Maori mothers and children on the same basis as it was for Europeans, and that Maori mothers should have the choice.[95]

At a time when consensus about the value of welfare and the classic welfare state was at its height in New Zealand, the public response to the committee demonstrated that belief in the virtues of voluntarism was alive and well. According to the *New Zealand Herald*, the committee 'attuned itself to the present-day mood of New Zealand', with self-help, self-reliance and voluntary work recognised as attributes to be fostered. It perceived the public to be reacting against 'excessive regimentation and dependence on the State'.[96] The *Napier Daily Telegraph* described the report as a 'Salutary Victory of Voluntary Service', praising the stand taken against departmental ambitions as a major victory by a body that was 'etched deeply into community life'.[97] Yet it might not have been the principles of voluntarism per se that ensured Plunket's continued popularity. Many women simply appreciated the free and individual services provided by the Plunket nurses and the other opportunities the organisational framework gave them for coming together.

There were some criticisms of Plunket from women of other voluntary organisations, notably Parents' Centre and Nursery Play Centre. As Parents' Centre historian Mary Dobbie explained, 'Everyone was conscious of the Plunket Society's deficiencies but wary of providing ammunition for the Health Department to shoot it down. Rather an attempt was made to suggest ways in which Plunket might be improved.'[98] Begg had been aware of the importance of Parents' Centre to Plunket since becoming Plunket's Director of Medical Services. In 1956 he reassured Mrs A. Rose, the newly appointed president of Plunket's Christchurch branch and a council member, that Parents' Centre was not a threat to Plunket. He told her that he believed Plunket was 'big enough' to help other groups interested in infant welfare. Rather than regarding Parents' Centre as a competitor, Plunket should co-operate with it and, in so doing, perhaps influence it.[99] He also courted Parents' Centre itself, as is clear from a letter he wrote to it in 1956. He set out to show that he shared the centre's beliefs, claiming to see in its publications the 'excellent influence' of Dr Benjamin Spock with his 'sensible preventive psychiatry'. He explained that he had been lucky enough to meet Spock during a visit to the United States the previous year, and approved of his philosophy on the relationship between mother and child. Begg hoped that Parents' Centre would consider including a paediatrician on its advisory committee, since paediatric training was nowadays 'angled towards the pattern of growth, physical, intellectual and emotional, and deviations from this pattern', with prevention playing a larger part in the speciality than in any other branch of medicine. He concluded, 'Please accept my best wishes and assurance that the co-operation you have offered is gratefully received. We will, of course, be pleased to work with you in any field which will be of benefit to the mother and child.'[100]

Dr Alice Bush, a key figure in persuading the NZBMA to approve the Family Planning Association and its work in providing contraceptive advice,[101] also supported Parents' Centre. She told Begg that the centre was 'honestly attempting to produce better parents'. This was 'a most worthy objective' and merited assistance from Plunket. She also warned that 'crankiness thrives on opposition'.[102] Begg agreed that Parents' Centre was 'doing a valuable work in kicking the profession along' and told her that he was trying to forge a closer relationship.[103] In mid-1959, at the time of the Consultative Committee hearings, an article on 'Plunket and Parents' Centres' appeared in the *Parents' Centre Bulletin*. It noted that many mothers served on both Plunket and Parents' Centre committees, and that every possible avenue for further co-operation should be explored.[104] Both sides saw an advantage in co-operation. The gap between the supposedly conservative Plunket Society and progressive Parents' Centre was not as great as sometimes assumed.[105] The centre itself had achieved medical respectability by the end of the 1950s. In January 1958 Professor Harvey Carey organised a pivotal conference on ante-natal instruction at National

Women's Hospital, to which he invited representatives from the Obstetrical and Gynaecological Society, Parents' Centre and Plunket. In early 1959 the work of Parents' Centre was approved by the Medical Association. This was accompanied by the establishment of a medical directorate. Chaired by Jim Watt, its members included Neil Begg.[106]

The consultative committee rejected Parents' Centre criticisms of Plunket, concluding that

> The suggestion by the parents' centres that some of the less adaptable Plunket Nurses have firmly adhered to antiquated routines, if it is well founded (as to which we have no information except their assertion), is not likely to remain valid in the light of the policy already being introduced by the society's Director of Medical Services and by those collaborating with him.[107]

Playcentres had also accused Plunket of being too 'mechanistic' in its child care advice. The committee's response to this was that future methods of child care would be determined by 'an authoritative body', comprising trained paediatricians.[108] Other committee recommendations included the formation of a Child Health Council and the instigation of a chair of child health at the Otago Medical School.

The committee's report was considered a great victory for Plunket. Begg's autobiography described its publication in late 1959 as the 'best Christmas present the Society could have received'.[109] However, he added, 'in the event we overestimated the advantages the Report would bring us'. The reality, in his view, was an increased bitterness between the Health Department and Plunket. The department later commented that only one of the four members of the committee was a medical practitioner, 'which made difficult the deciding of problems concerning the provision and organisation of medical services'.[110]

In May 1960 Plunket's council called an emergency meeting when it discovered that the Health Minister Rex Mason did not intend to implement the committee's recommendations.[111] He was quoted in April as having said that 'Public health nurses – provided they are in sufficient number – are perfectly able to carry out the health supervision of all infants and children whether in town or rural areas'.[112] This provocative statement was later contradicted when he announced that 'the department has no desire to curtail the activities of the [Plunket] society in country areas'.[113] The Plunket council did not trust him. When it learned from Begg that Mason intended to form a Board of Health sub-committee on child health, on

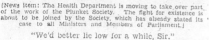

[News item: The Health Department is moving to take over part of the work of the Plunket Society. The fight for existence is about to be joined by the Society, which has already stated its case to all Ministers and Members of Parliament.]

"We'd better lie low for a while, Sir."

"There are times when I think it would've been a good idea, if the Government had insisted on nationalising 'em!"

During the 1959–60 dispute the Health Department was depicted as empire building, as indicated in this cartoon, 3 July 1960. Four days later it was reported that 'full agreement' between the Health Department and Plunket had been reached, which apparently did not delight all parents. (Note the involvement of the father in infant care, and the baby bottle by bedside.) *Marlborough Express*, 3 July 1960; *Evening Post*, 7 July 1960

which six of the eight professional voices would be departmental officers, the council decided to launch a 'publicity and fighting campaign'.[114] The NZBMA wrote to the Deputy Prime Minister, C. F. (Jerry) Skinner, explaining that a recent executive meeting had resolved to inform government that 'medical opinion throughout New Zealand supports the Plunket Society in its desire to have a child health council established separately from the Board of Health'.[115]

The Plunket council sent a cable to Prime Minister Walter Nash in England stating that it was gravely disturbed by Mason's recent decisions 'which threaten the Society's existence', and demanding the implementation of the consultative committee report.[116] On Nash's return, the council sent a deputation to inform him that Plunket would under no circumstances agree to governance by a sub-committee of the Board of Health.[117] After meeting the delegates Nash released a press statement in support of Plunket.[118] A Child Health Council, of which two of the ten members were Plunket representatives, was established as an advisory body.[119] Begg later claimed that 'the Department and the Society had a few superficial discussions and formed a Child Health Council with the Director-General of Health as chairman. It gradually died of inanition.'[120]

The Committee's report had recommended that Karitane hospitals be classified as Class B (private registered hospitals) under the Hospitals Act of 1957 in order to increase funding, with benefits payable at the Class B rate. Such a move would also allow various government subsidies on voluntary contributions for maintenance and alterations. This secured the immediate future of the hospitals. When Nash agreed to a government grant of £160,000, Auckland Plunket proceeded with its plans to build a new hospital, which opened in 1962. Other Karitane hospitals also received funding for renovations or new buildings. In 1963 a new hospital opened in Christchurch, along with a new nurses' home at Wellington's Karitane Hospital.

The National Party was not slow to see the potential voting power of Plunket. With a general election pending, Plunket's council received a letter from the leader of the Opposition, Keith Holyoake, asking for more information on points of difference between the society and the Health Department.[121] A further letter from Holyoake, setting out the National Party's attitude to the Plunket Society, was circulated to the press. The council thanked Holyoake for his support during the society's negotiations with the government over the Finlay report.[122] On 30 November 1960 the council resolved that 'a letter of good wishes be sent to the Hon K. J. Holyoake, as Leader of the National Party and Prime Minister elect'.[123] Nash's response to Plunket had been supportive, but possibly too little too late.

CHAPTER 7

Neil Begg and Social Paediatrics, 1960–78

The Health Department and the Salmond Report

Don (later Sir Donald) McKay, Minister of Health, Social Security and Child Welfare from 1962 to 1972, was sympathetic to Plunket. He came from a small country town area where the Plunket committee was very active, and his wife had served as secretary and president: 'I know one of the great joys she has had, has been her contact with the Plunket Society'.[1] The year he became minister, Cabinet approved an increased subsidy on Plunket nurse salaries from 60 to 66.6 per cent, to take effect in 1963. That year Turbott, now the Director-General of Health, surprised Plunket by announcing at an NZBMA meeting that in future 'the care of the baby and pre-school child will be in the hands of the general practitioner and the Plunket Society'.[2] Yet, the tensions between Plunket and the Health Department continued unabated, particularly in relation to demarcation between Plunket and district nurses, now called public health nurses. In 1962 Begg asked Turbott for a ruling on the coverage of Maori babies, since 'recently, voices have been raised saying that the Plunket Society will not care for Maori babies. This carries the stigma of racialism and we would like to deny it.'[3] This request must be seen in the light of growing Maori urbanisation, which made it difficult to retain the traditional distinctions

How to 'solicit' Maori mothers? The winning baby of the Dannevirke Baby Photograph Contest (out of 134 babies) 'was a beautiful Maori child, whose proud parents were Mr and Mrs Hape, a well-known Dannevirke family'. *Plunket News* 1965

undertake the survey, which was conducted mainly by telephone. Interviewees were told that the Health Department and the Plunket Society were conducting a survey into the nursing services for mothers with new babies.[18] Begg later remarked, 'We were therefore very heavily involved. Somewhere along the line, however, the whole plan was altered.' He believed that the survey had gone far beyond the agenda set out by the committee, and bore little resemblance to the report that had been commissioned by the Survey Committee.[19]

The survey was published in November 1974 under the authorship of Dr George Salmond, now Director of the Management Services and Research Unit in the Health Department. He explained that the object was to determine whether mothers and infants in the Wellington area had access to medical and nursing services that met their needs. He began by citing the Labour Party manifesto of 1972: 'Everyone is entitled to the best possible health service. The only acceptable criterion of a person's right to medical care ought to be a person's medical need. All people who need medical care should receive it as of right.'[20] Salmond was influenced by 'the inverse care law', a theory developed by Julian Tudor Hart, a left-wing general practitioner in Wales, which postulated that in the market distribution of medical care, the availability of health care and resources stood in inverse ratio to the estimate of that population's need.[21]

The Wellington survey encompassed 520 mothers, each with a five-month-old baby. They came from five areas, two classified as low socio-economic status areas, a city core area centred on the suburb of Newtown, and Porirua City, a satellite working-class area. Over 40 per cent of mothers living in these areas were either Maori or Pacific Islanders, with roughly equal proportions of each. In the other areas less than 10 per cent of mothers were Maori or Polynesian. It was found that at five months there was a clear difference in health status between Porirua infants and those in other parts of the Wellington area.[22] Salmond's analysis of health services demonstrated that practically all mothers in the middle and high socio-economic areas received care from a Plunket nurse. In Newtown 73 per cent of the care was given exclusively by Plunket and 16 per cent by public health nurses; the remaining 10 per cent used both caregivers. In Porirua, 50 per cent of care was provided by the Plunket Society, 30 per cent by the public health nursing service and 5 per cent by both. Fifteen per cent of Porirua mothers did not receive care from either agency. Salmond concluded that Tudor Hart's 'inverse care law' applied to Wellington.[23] He claimed that Plunket's activities were 'best suited to the needs and expectations of relatively well educated and economically secure mothers with small planned families, living in established residential areas and usually with private transport'. He wrote that, 'Many traditionally trained Plunket nurses must find if difficult to communicate with and to relate to the needs of working-class mothers'; he believed this was borne out by the fact that 29 per cent of Plunket supervised mothers in Porirua stated that the nurse had been unable to help them.[24] An epilogue gave a Porirua Cook Island mother of eight's impression of a nurse who was, by implication, a Plunket nurse.[25] The quotation, which was very critical of the nurse, accusing her of unfriendliness,[26] was repeated in full in the *New Zealand Medical Journal* and in the daily press.[27] Salmond could have chosen to highlight a different kind of response, as a range of comments was included in the report, and more than two-thirds of Porirua mothers had commented on the nurse's helpfulness.[28]

Neil Begg believed that the report was a deliberate assault on Plunket.[29] He was concerned by the implication that Plunket had no interest in disadvantaged areas, which he claimed was untrue. He pointed out that the society had been trying to get extra government funding for new housing areas since 1962. Begg's argument was that Plunket's services in such areas needed to be subsidised by the government, 'until such time as they settled down into a normal cohesive community existence'. In his view, the report, with its comparison between the city group and the new housing area, highlighted the differences between people who were in similar economic circumstances but were socially disadvantaged by their housing conditions. He asserted that it was not possible to study medical services

A Plunket mobile van in the new Auckland suburb of Mt Roskill in the 1950s. According to Neil Begg, these 'instant suburbs' of the post-war era lacked adequate social amenities and abounded with social problems. Archives New Zealand Te Whare Tohu Tuhituhinga O Aotearoa: National Publicity Studios Photographic Collection, ATL, F-33855-1/2 (A6780)

without studying the milieu in which they operated.[30] It was also important to consider 'the quality of parents and their informal support systems'
and the 'ill-advised and ill-planned housing policies of successive governments'.[31] He drew attention to the section of the report that described these
artificial 'instant' communities, where state houses were built on rural land
for families judged to be in special need, who were separated from their
friends and relatives. The report noted that social problems abounded
under these conditions.[32]

Salmond challenged Begg's response. There was no evidence, he felt, to
support Begg's contention that Porirua mothers lacked friends and kinship
support: 'In many ways the latter is the more stable community'. It was
hardly surprising that he and Begg differed in their interpretation of the
findings 'given our official positions and fundamental differences in what
we respectively hoped to achieve as a result of participation in this
research'.[33] The following year, Salmond wrote,

> In retrospect I now appreciate that the Plunket Society did not want a proper
> evaluative study to be done. All they wanted was conjunction of preconceived
> ideas . . . . I certainly was not going to be told what my research must show by
> Dr Begg or anyone else . . . . Apart from lending their name to this Joint Study
> the Society contributed nothing to the project apart from carping criticism.
> This study clearly illustrates the very considerable difficulty research workers
> have when working in fields, where objectivity and rational decision making
> are the last thing that major protagonists want.[34]

In retaliation, Begg argued that the report was part of the Health
Department's long-term strategy to undermine Plunket. The report revealed
continuities with earlier departmental views. Pointing out that 70 per cent
of Plunket's funding now came from the state, Salmond wrote, 'Any organisation which accepts a large measure of financial support from the State
must make a proportional sacrifice of its independence.'[35] In the report he
promoted the concept of health centres in place of specialised clinics like
those run by Plunket.[36]

As far back as 1970 Begg had claimed there was no point in continuing
the joint study, following the appearance of a report from a Board of Health
committee set up in 1966 under the chairmanship of Cyril Dixon, Professor of Preventive and Social Medicine at the University of Otago. This
reaffirmed the statement made by Watt almost 30 years earlier that it was
'wasteful of time, money and effort to have specialised nursing services

in rural areas'.[37] Plunket suffered a further blow in 1970 when the Health Department extended its own nurse training programme to include infant health instead of sending its nurses to undertake the three-month post-graduate Plunket course at the Dunedin or Auckland Karitane Hospitals. Until 1970, a third of the places at the Karitane training schools had been reserved for public health nurses. Now the Plunket Society had lost its monopoly on the training of nurses in infant care. Ryburn sent a circular letter to all MPs claiming that recent Health Department policies were threatening Plunket's existence.[38] There was an immediate press reaction. A *New Zealand Truth* headline claimed, 'Health Department rocks the Cradle . . . Our Plunket Services are threatened by a Health Department takeover.'[39] Two weeks later another article appeared: 'Danger ahead for Plunket. The Plunket Society in peril? It's scarcely credible! But the danger is very real.'[40] Dunedin's *Evening Star* ran an editorial entitled 'Plunket Society is treasured'.[41] The matter was also raised in Parliament by the MP for Dunedin North, Ethel McMillan. She claimed that it was 'inconceivable that the Government should even consider the disbanding of the system', an outcome which she regarded as implicit in the withdrawal from specialised Plunket nurse training. 'I am sure that the mothers of the past, the mothers of the present, and the mothers of the future would all associate themselves with my remarks, because they know that the work of this society has meant so much to the present generation and will mean a great deal to generations yet to come.'[42] The Health Department itself was not impressed by the publicity. At the August meeting of the Joint Steering Committee, Heggie argued that the Plunket memo sent to all MPs shortly after their last meeting cast doubt on the feasibility of co-operation. Other Health Department representatives were equally unhappy. Joan Mackay declared that she was 'very bewildered' and 'rather offended' by Plunket's lack of trust in the department. Hiddlestone suggested that in future the Plunket Society should 'aim for the right target'.[43]

This meeting was the last held by the committee for the next two years, and it was finally disbanded in February 1974. Of an April 1973 meeting Begg commented that 'talking to the Health Department . . . is like butting at a locked door'.[44] Nor was the National Co-ordinating Committee, which replaced the Joint Steering Committee, any more effective, according to Joy Reid.[45] Following a meeting in December 1976, Begg claimed that Plunket's services had been 'mired down and diminished not by lack of money, but by the constant bickering on matters of little importance, with a Department which sets up barriers rather than aiming to help us in our work'. He believed that any future discussions should be conducted directly with politicians and not the Health Department.[46]

The White Paper on Health and voluntarism

Throughout the 1960s, despite poor relations between the Health Department and Plunket, the Minister of Health and the government continued to support Plunket. In its 1969 election manifesto the National Party promised to 'continue its policy of generous grants and assistance to the Plunket Society' and affirmed that the society 'should be maintained as one of the important voluntary health organisations in the community'.[47] With National back in power, Prime Minister Keith Holyoake declared in 1970 that Plunket was 'so much a part of our New Zealand way of life that to me any threat to its future is quite unthinkable and would never be condoned'.[48] He noted that government grants to the society, excluding hospital benefits for patients in the Karitane hospitals, had increased since 1965 from about $430,000 a year to nearly $600,000.[49] In reply to a question in Parliament, Don McKay reiterated that it was his government's policy to continue the generous grants and assistance to the Plunket Society.[50] The following year he announced a new financial arrangement. This replaced the existing percentage method by a subsidy equal to the actual expenditure on Plunket nurse salaries and head office salaries, as well as a nurses' uniform allowance and a contribution to nurses' superannuation.[51] Private hospital benefits were also increased. This offered some relief to the Karitane hospitals, though they continued to struggle (see below).

The Labour Party also appeared to support Plunket. During the 1970 parliamentary debate in which Holyoake had declared his support, Lyttelton MP Tom McGuigan spoke out in favour of the society, and wondered if members opposite had 'any real appreciation of the value of voluntary organisations'. Referring to the threat of the Plunket Society being 'swallowed up by a department of the Government', he maintained that a specialised nurse with skills in the area was more valuable than an all-purpose public health nurse. He spoke at length about the advantages of Plunket, not least of which were the 700 branches and sub-branches which 'mobilise tens of thousands of our citizens and convert them into non-professional health workers'. He concluded that the Labour Party supported the aims and objectives of Plunket and lauded its public work. 'Its history of voluntary services and its outstanding record of continuity in the supply of trained nursing personnel cannot be overvalued. We recognise this experience of child care, and we would assist the society to expand rather than make any move to restrict its activities.'[52]

Labour became the government in 1972. Like most New Zealanders, the new Minister of Health, Bob Tizard, had personal experience of Plunket: 'My mother took me through the hands of a Plunket nurse and my own four children have also been through the very sympathetic hands of a Plunket nurse'.[53] Yet the Labour government felt strongly that, to realise the 'laudable aims of the Thirties',[54] health services required reform and a caucus sub-committee was set up for that purpose. Concerned about the implications for Plunket, the council was not reassured by Tizard's words: 'I am sure that you realise the inherent limitations upon the independence of any organisation which receives so much of its funds from taxation receipts'.[55]

The Labour government's deliberations resulted in the 1974 White Paper on Health, which proposed fourteen regional health authorities to organise all aspects of health care. When Tom McGuigan, who had replaced Tizard as Minister of Health in September 1974, released a preview of the White Paper to the press on 23 November, he backtracked on his earlier support for Plunket. He now claimed that the society, along with other voluntary agencies, was a hindrance to New Zealand's health service. As a result Plunket's council called an emergency meeting on 3 December, believing Plunket's future to be 'definitely in jeopardy'. In response to Reid's inquiry, however, acting Health Minister Norman King denied that the government intended to destroy Plunket.[56]

Reid had already expounded on the value of Plunket to Tizard. She contrasted medical services that were firmly in the hands of professionals and could be 'supplied, or provided, or delivered by a benign authority', with the preventive medicine in which the Plunket Society engaged and which was in the hands of 'non-professional health workers' mobilised by Plunket. The latter was an example of 'citizen participation', but to be successful those citizens had to be able to make decisions and exercise control.[57] These views clearly emanated from Neil Begg who frequently aired his views on 'citizen participation'. He argued that the White Paper's focus on health professionals and administrative efficiency was 'out of touch with preventive medicine'. It fostered the belief that increased numbers of health professionals and more administrative efficiency would secure a healthier population. Like Reid he claimed that 'preventive medicine needs citizen participation. . . . and citizen participation is stimulated if local people are asked to accept real responsibility. If you take

Community involvement and 'citizen participation' created a sense of ownership of the Society. LEFT: 'The whole community sets to work to build a Plunket Clinic' at Tokoroa in 1961. RIGHT: By the late 1960s the women were doing the maintenance themselves. *The Plunket Society of New Zealand*, 1961; *Plunket News*, October 1967

autonomy from the Plunket Society you take away also its motivation.'[58] In 1976 Plunket sponsored Begg's trip to China where he saw 'the living embodiment of principles well known to the Plunket society'. In his opinion, the Chinese system succeeded because it had 'informed and motivated ordinary citizens to do their own preventive medicine' and because that power had been decentralised.[59] Begg's 'army of non-professional health workers' had to be involved in policy-making 'in a meaningful way'. Only then would they be stimulated by feelings of pride and responsibility: 'They are the ones who will be setting the patterns of child health in each community'.[60] Parents would not only be involved in decision-making, but would also be agents of health reform by example: people would be more likely to be influenced by a neighbour than by a health professional. If community leaders were persuaded to act in a certain way, this would become fashionable and 'gradually percolate to all strata of society'.[61] He gave the example of a local Plunket Mothers' Club and its 'good neighbour' policy which welcomed all newcomers and provided support and assistance to those in need. 'Concern for each other, a will to learn, a desire to help, self respect and a sense of responsibility – these are the currencies of preventive medicine.'[62] Paediatricians were merely advisers, and their advice 'must be broad, general, practical and understandable to the average person'.[63] Truby King had made a similar point when he expressed his aim to make 'every woman the competent executive in her own home . . . . Doctors and nurses can only be casual visitors.'[64]

Begg also took his views to the United States. When he addressed an American medical audience in 1968, the chairman answered all the questions from the floor himself, preventing Begg from further comment. Afterwards his host, Dr Burns Dobbins,

> apologised for the chairman's rudeness and explained that he probably thought that I was a socialist spreading socialist propaganda. It had never occurred to me that the 'people involvement' concept had any political implications but perhaps my east-west comparisons had evoked the ghost of McCarthyism. I remembered this episode at a later date when an invitation to speak at Princeton University was cancelled because of my supposed socialist leanings.[65]

Not all American medical audiences were hostile. The American Medical Association invited Begg to another important meeting at which a Coordinating Council for Maternal and Child Health was set up. Begg was appointed an honorary member. He was also invited to visit a number of state health departments and several medical schools.[66] Commenting on an American Medical Association project called Operation Reach Out, he noted that governments were beginning to see that voluntary citizen action was not only effective but also economic, 'and President Nixon made a plea for more voluntary effort in many walks of life'.[67]

Within New Zealand, the Labour government remained unconvinced. Reid was invited by Director-General of Health Dr John Hiddlestone to serve on a Consultative Committee on Voluntary Agencies to consider the White Paper. The fact that the committee was dominated by personnel from the Departments of Health, Education and Social Welfare seemed to confirm Reid's fears that the government wished to destroy Plunket.[68]

Although Plunket always claimed to be apolitical, its uncertain future under Labour possibly inspired some of its members to reject Labour in the 1975 elections. Michael Bassett has argued that Plunket was politically motivated and that its Council was made up of key National Party supporters:

> In an emotional outburst, their President claimed that Government was planning to abolish Plunket. Like a particularly ill-disciplined firework, Mrs J. Reid exploded frequently during the next few months, usually with assertions about Government intentions long since disavowed by the Minister. Branches of the Society were stoked up with highly misleading versions of the White Paper and expected to supplement Dunedin's attack. With varying degrees of willingness they obliged.[69]

There certainly appeared to be a sense of relief that, after the 1975 election, Labour and the White Paper were off the agenda. In its annual report for the year 1975–6, Plunket's Auckland branch noted widespread concern about the threat the White Paper posed for voluntary organisations such as Plunket, and hoped that the change in government would ensure the society's future as an essential family health care service.[70] Plunket's attack on the White Paper was not politically motivated, though some of its members might have been; it was driven by fear for the society's survival.

'Citizen participation'

In 1970 Labour MP Ronald Bailey described how Plunket encouraged mothers to become 'ambassadors for public health'.[71] This was clearly the way in which Begg viewed Plunket, a view strengthened in his mind by the society's involvement in various preventive health campaigns, such as those directed at bovine tuberculosis, hydatids, water fluoridation and immunisation.

Along with the promotion of breastfeeding, the provision of clean milk supplies had been one of the society's earliest concerns, though it was not until 1936 that it directed its attention specifically to the eradication of bovine tuberculosis. That year the disease, the major form of tuberculosis in children, was made a topic for Plunket's general conference. It was revealed to delegates that, of New Zealand's two million cows, approximately 180,000 suffered from tuberculosis, and that each year between 250 and 400 people, mainly children, were hospitalised with tuberculosis acquired through drinking infected milk.[72] A crusade was launched to create a demand for milk from tuberculin-tested cows, and to lobby the government to make such testing compulsory. In the meantime mothers were instructed to boil all milk, even that supposedly pasteurised. When a bill for compulsory testing came before Parliament in 1944 the Society sent submissions. Compulsory testing was enacted but not implemented, it was discovered, because of a failure to agree on the level of compensation to be offered farmers who had to have infected cows destroyed. The society repeatedly urged the government to implement the act and finally congratulated the Minister of Agriculture in 1950 when the compensation problem was settled. The society kept up pressure to ensure that the legislation was enforced, pressing for the elimination of tuberculosis from all cattle in New Zealand.[73] In 1955 a submission was sent to the Commission of Inquiry into the Tuberculin Testing of Town Milk Supplies.[74] Some individual women took up the cause as their own, and Plunket provided the institutional framework for this. When Stella Petersen retired from the council in 1959 she was thanked for the work she had done over the years on the elimination of tuberculosis from milk supplies. 'The enormous amount of research she did, the data she collected, the departmental officers she interviewed, and presentation of the case she made at different conferences and deputations over the years, were vital factors in the eventual success of this important movement for the protection of our children.'[75]

It had been common knowledge since the 1880s that hydatids could be prevented by stopping dogs, the carriers, from eating raw offal.[76] However, little action had been taken before the 1950s. In that decade the Departments of Agriculture and Health took up the cause to eradicate hydatids.[77] At its 1957 general conference, Begg persuaded Plunket to help. His own 'very considerable personal activity' in the campaign arose from seeing children in hospital with hydatid disease of the brain in the 1950s.[78] As well as becoming secretary of the Otago Federated Farmers' Hydatids Committee in February 1957 and later secretary of the South Island Hydatids Committee, Begg engaged in an energetic educational campaign, giving some 60 talks to groups of farmers around the country in 1957, and 23 in 1958. His success in enlisting Plunket meant that the society, according to an historian of the hydatids eradication campaign, 'made available its extensive organisation to assist in the educational drive on hydatid disease and [was] undoubtedly influential in interesting farmers' wives in the preventive measures that should be adopted by each farmer'.[79] In 1958 Begg enthused about the campaign: 'It gives assurance of the tremendous power the Plunket Society has in preventive medicine . . . The spade-work put in, all over the country, by our branches and sub-branches and mothers' clubs has been invaluable. It is a tremendous advantage in preventive medicine to have a toe-hold into every community . . . .' He asked, 'What more effective machinery for the dissemination of medical knowledge, that can produce an essential climate of public opinion, could there be than the widespread and enthusiastic workers of the Plunket Society?'[80] By 1959, when the Hydatids Act was passed and the National Hydatids Council was established, there were some 500 voluntary committees of farmers and others fighting the disease. Once Federated Farmers took over, Begg noted 'a very happy and effective co-operation between the Plunket Society, which initially carried all the administration and secretarial burden, and Federated Farmers and the other great rural organisations'.[81] Throughout the 1960s Begg continued to bring the disease to the attention of the Plunket Society, commenting that wives and mothers still had an important part to play in helping to prevent dogs from eating raw offal, even after the introduction of DDT, which killed the parasite in dogs.[82]

Begg also claimed success for Plunket's policy of citizen participation in relation to fluoridation. In 1957 Plunket's council issued a statement in favour of fluoridating public water supplies. As Begg commented, 'This problem has been debated hotly everywhere, and it is to be hoped that the cold logic of the benefits that could accrue from this well-tried method will prevail over less-informed opinions.'[83] The Health Department had carried out its own water fluoridation trials in Hastings from 1953, and by 1957 a Royal Commission reported favourably on the experiment.[84] By the early

Prospective victim
. . . or farmer of the future?

Hydatids develop in children who live in rural areas and cause long illness and sometimes death.

Half-hearted, sceptical attitudes towards making offal safe for feeding to work-dogs is keeping hydatids active.

The key to hydatids control is to boil all offal you feed dogs. Pluck cut up and boiled for 30 minutes, is safe food.

You can dose and clear your dog of worms but it will quickly be re-

infested unless its food is cleared of infection by *boiling*.

Never throw raw lungs, livers, hearts or spleen to your dogs. They become infected by eating hydatid cysts in those organs.

Burn or bury carcasses lying on your property, or at least remove and heat-treat or bury the pluck.

The best attack in hydatids is the breaking of the disease cycle by feeding only sound material to dogs. Reinforce this attack by dosing your dogs regularly with arecoline.

PROTECT YOUR CHILDREN from hydatids
● Insist on strict hand-washing after handling dogs and always before eating.
● Wash vegetables and fruit you eat raw.

Condemned children . . . condemned livers . . . this is the price of apathetic hydatids control.

10.7

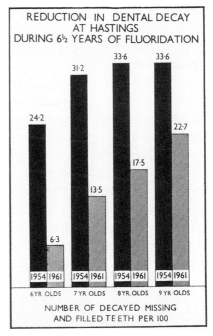

REDUCTION IN DENTAL DECAY AT HASTINGS DURING 6½ YEARS OF FLUORIDATION

NUMBER OF DECAYED MISSING AND FILLED TEETH PER 100

ABOVE: A graphic illustration of the reduction in dental decay at Hastings after six and a half years of fluoridation. *Plunket News*, 1962

LEFT: A Health Department hydatids poster – in some preventive campaigns the Health Department and Plunket were firm allies.

1960s there was widespread support for fluoridation; one press report on the Hastings trial declared it had led to a 'spectacular reduction in dental decay among children'.[85] Likewise a 1962 report by the British Ministry of Health supported fluoridation of water as bringing substantial improvement in the teeth of children and as a safe and practical procedure.[86] Not all agreed, however. Auckland Mayor, Dove-Myer Robinson, who was also president of New Zealand Anti-Fluoridation Association, was vehemently opposed to fluoridation on the grounds that it was anti-democratic: 'Who would want to be 100 per cent healthy but not have his liberty?' He maintained that the association was not fighting fluoridation, but rather the 'pride and status of the Health Department, the medical and dental professions'.[87]

In this instance Plunket and the Health Department were firm allies. The society began recommending fluoride tablets to mothers from the early 1960s. By 1963 nearly half New Zealand's infants were participating in the scheme. Begg noted, 'This is a practical and tangible way of showing people that fluoride tablets do encourage beautiful teeth, and the process is satisfactorily safe.'[88] The following year he announced that there was a quiet revolution occurring in the dental health of New Zealand children,[89] and claimed that there would be less opposition now that local authorities saw which way the wind was blowing.[90] This view was shared by Sir John Walsh, Dean of the University of Otago Dental School, who declared in 1964 that 'the greatest contribution to dental health in recent years was the work of the Plunket Society'.[91]

Immunisation was another form of preventive medicine supported by both Plunket volunteers and health professionals. Plunket nurses were directed to encourage immunisation, though they did not do the immunising themselves. Immunisation record cards were issued to all babies under Plunket supervision from 1958 for doctors who wished to make use of them.[92]

In 1956, the year the Salk vaccine against poliomyelitis was introduced, there were around 1400 reported cases of polio in New Zealand. In 1957 the Plunket Society assisted the Health Department in its vaccination campaign against polio by making its rooms and facilities available to departmental officers.[93] In 1961 the Salk vaccine, which had to be administered by injection, was replaced by the Sabin oral vaccine. In April 1962, when the Health Department launched a campaign to immunise all pre-school children, Plunket nurses, public health nurses and chemists' shops were called upon to distribute forms. Begg enthused in his 1962 annual

report that, 'By far the most exciting venture in the field of preventive medicine was the Sabin Vaccination project': over two million people had been
vaccinated. He believed the efforts of Plunket's professional and voluntary
workers had ensured that 97 per cent of an estimated 780,000 pre-school
population had been vaccinated. This had been achieved first because most
pre-school children were known to the Plunket nurse, second because
Plunket branches and mothers' club members personally visited thousands
of homes asking for co-operation, and third because voluntary workers
willingly undertook clerical and transport duties. 'It is impossible to overestimate the contribution made by these good citizens,' claimed Begg, who
described the campaign as 'a blue print for future endeavours'.[94] Director-
General of Health Dr Douglas Kennedy thought the first round of the oral
polio vaccination campaign went 'wonderfully well'; 'As to commending
your voluntary workers,' he told Begg, 'that is the least they deserve'.[95] Here
was one instance in which the Health Department saw value in the Plunket
Society. Concerned about the number who did not complete their immunisations, Reid commented in 1966 that, 'to those who remembered the
almost annual epidemics of polio, it seemed inconceivable that any
mother could neglect the means of protecting her children'.[96]

Begg also ensured that the Plunket Society lent its support to the triple
vaccine (DTP) which protected against diphtheria, tetanus, whooping
cough (pertussis)), introduced in 1960. He came out publicly in favour
of DTP when it was attacked by Dr Stanley Hickling, a former Health

ANTI-TETANUS EFFORT

Hats off to the Te Horo
Plunket Mothers' Club! Recently it organised a tetanus
vaccination   c a m p a i g n.
Everyone in the district was
visited, 144 people were vaccinated in the School Dental
Clinic and six weeks later
received a booster dose. Only
one person failed to turn up
for the second time. In February a third and final dose
will be arranged—and booster doses are planned for
five years hence.

An account of the anti-tetanus endeavours of
the Te Horo Plunket Mothers' Club. *Plunket
News*, 1966

Department officer who was now attached to the University of Otago's Department of Preventive and Social Medicine. Hickling argued in 1966 that New Zealand children were being overimmunised against diphtheria, tetanus and whooping cough.[97] He was against giving boosters, arguing that, given the low incidence of diphtheria in New Zealand, only tetanus toxoid should be routinely given beyond five years of age. By contrast, Begg called for complete triple immunisation for all young children.[98]

When measles and rubella vaccines were introduced around 1970, Plunket promoted these. In the early 1970s Plunket's Director of Nursing Services Margaret Nicholls noted the continued prevalence of these diseases and that some doctors opposed immunisation.[99] Instructed to ask mothers about immunisation, nurses reported that opposition was mainly on religious grounds, though some cited transport problems. One nurse declared in 1972 that she herself frequently took children to doctors' surgeries to be immunised.[100] Other nurses did this too, according to Nicholls.[101] There also appeared to be some ignorance regarding immunisation. When questioned in 1973, only one-third of Wainuiomata mothers knew what their babies had been immunised against.[102] The number of deaths from measles did drop in the 1970s, from 24 deaths in 1970–3 to nine during the period 1974–7. Begg remained confident that it was a matter of time and education, and that good sense would prevail.

Begg also hoped that 'citizen participation' and education by example would apply to breastfeeding, which had been declining in popularity since the 1950s. Begg was confident that 'a new fashion would be set by intelligent and well-informed young mothers'.[103] Others were not so sure. Agreeing that fashions were important, Janet Mackay, Plunket's Director of Nursing Services 1958–65, stated that at the present time women 'just don't want it'.[104] In this instance it appears that 'intelligent' women were not promoting preventive medicine. The Auckland branch charge nurse, Phyllis Hilkie, pointed to the increase of married women in the paid workforce as a possible deterrent to breast-feeding.[105] In 1945 married women made up 17.2 per cent of the total female paid workforce, and 41.5 per cent by 1966.[106] However, one public health researcher, who interviewed 20 mothers from Christchurch in 1963, did not find that the wish to return to work influenced the decision to breastfeed; rather she thought it was the influence of neighbours and friends.[107] Similarly a study of a group of women who gave birth in 1972 found that only 1 per cent of mothers stopped breastfeeding in order to return to work.[108]

Begg was highly impressed by the activities of La Leche League, a voluntary organisation promoting breastfeeding, which had been set up in Chicago in 1956 and which he encountered during a visit to the United States in 1968.[109] He applauded these young volunteers for their involvement in maternal and child health and for bringing 'fresh air and a new dimension to the issues'.[110] He regarded the league as a prime example of a 'citizen's health movement', which had done more for child health than 'most of the government-funded, international, professionally-led institutions'.[111] Begg and Plunket supported the activities of La Leche League when it became established in New Zealand during the second half of the 1960s.[112]

Breastfeeding did become more fashionable in New Zealand in the 1970s.[113] A Wellington study found that the proportion of all mothers breastfeeding rose from 62 per cent in 1972 to 82 per cent in 1978, and the median length of time of breastfeeding also increased from five weeks in 1972 to seventeen weeks in 1978.[114] The women's liberation movement of the 1970s contributed to this trend: as women sought to reclaim their bodies from the medical profession, natural childbirth and breastfeeding again became popular.[115]

With his conviction that education was an important part of preventive medicine, Begg persuaded Plunket to appoint Dr Margaret Liley as Assistant Director of Medical Services. Liley, who qualified in medicine in 1953, attracted Begg's attention in the early 1960s when she was teaching antenatal classes for women at Auckland's National Women's Hospital. He encouraged her to give talks to Plunket Mothers' Clubs. When she took up the Plunket job in 1966, Begg extolled her virtues: 'Any-one who has heard Dr Liley speak and seen the enthusiasm for her subject, would not doubt that [her health education classes] will increase further . . . .We are very fortunate to have her with the Society.'[116]

Liley wrote *The Plunket Schoolbook of Childcraft*, which was used for the School Certificate home science curriculum from 1972.[117] She also became involved in providing sex education classes. This was an area in which other women doctors had become involved, such as Dr Alice Bush during the Second World War, and Dr Elsie Davidge of the Health Department in the 1950s.[118] Sex education classes were recommended by a 1954 committee of inquiry set up to investigate alleged sexual activities among adolescents in Lower Hutt. The resulting Mazengarb Report suggested that mothers accompany their daughters to the classes, and fathers their sons.[119] Bush ran such classes through the New Zealand Family Planning Association.[120] Margaret Liley also held mother-and-daughter evening lectures on sex education for intermediate school children from 1968, and her husband William delivered some of the father-and-son lectures.[121] Despite their labels, the classes did not insist that the child be accompanied by the same-sex parent, though a parent had to be present. The charge sister of Plunket's Auckland branch, Iris Christoffersen, who helped Liley to run the classes, claimed, 'We don't moralize at all. We give them the facts.'[122] Yet Begg described the classes as an introduction to the adult sexual and reproductive functions and hoped that they might open the door to an expansion of talks on 'ethics, growth and the art of living' for secondary school children. He understood the classes to be about 'family living and the wider philosophies . . . with details of reproduction, parenthood and the importance and rewards of family life'.[123] Contraception was not discussed.

New Zealand's ethnic minorities

Plunket could not afford to ignore the growing number of people from different ethnic groups if it wished to provide health care for all children under five. Post-Second World War prosperity had led to growing employment opportunities in the cities and consequently to urbanisation of Maori and migration from the neighbouring Pacific Islands. The percentage of Maori living in urban areas rose from 38.4 per cent in 1961 to 78.2 per cent by 1981.[124] The total number of New Zealand residents of Polynesian origin or descent increased from 2159 in 1945 to 65,694 by 1976.[125] Most had come in the 1960s, attracted by full employment, industrial development and affluence. The 1970s, however, saw an economic downturn, and because they were mainly in unskilled jobs, Maori and Pacific Islanders were the first to be hit by the recession, becoming New Zealand's 'brown proletariat'.[126] Poor health status was one indicator of their socio-economic deprivation.

The attention given to Porirua in the early 1970s was paralleled by the investigation of infant health problems in South Auckland. In 1967 Dr Morag Hardy, later a visiting physician to Auckland's Karitane Hospital, was funded by the Auckland Medical Research Foundation to study child malnutrition in Auckland. In 1971 the *New Zealand Weekly News* proclaimed, 'Many New Zealanders were shocked recently to hear that, in spite of this country's much vaunted child health programme, problems of malnutrition and diseases like anaemia and rickets were increasing alarmingly among children up to four years of age.'[127] Hardy had conducted a study of 600 cases of child malnutrition, and finding that Maori and

Pacific Islanders were vastly over-represented among these cases, she followed up over 100 Pacific Island cases in their homes.[128] Her research, published in the *New Zealand Medical Journal* in 1972, concluded that a reshaping of health services was urgently required.[129] The *New Zealand Herald* editor proclaimed that the survey demanded '[more] research, a vigorous education programme for families and future mothers and, above all, an expanded Plunket service'.[130] The *New Zealand Medical Journal* editor agreed that an expansion of Plunket services was needed to combat child malnutrition in Auckland.[131] Liley maintained that Health Department restrictions on the number of nurses Plunket could employ (243 at that time) were hampering the society's efforts to combat infant malnutrition in Auckland.[132]

One initiative taken by Plunket in 1971 to assist Pacific Islanders was the appointment of Dr Dennis McCarthy as the society's adviser to Pacific Islanders.[133] Begg described McCarthy as 'a gift from the gods'.[134] Seventy-two at the time of his appointment, McCarthy had spent most of his working life in the African colonial service. From 1952 he was a New Zealand Medical Research Council research officer in the south-west Pacific, attached to the Otago Medical School. He had several times been seconded by the WHO as a consultant and for a time acted as medical officer to the Cook Islands. In 1978 he was awarded an OBE. When he retired to New Zealand in 1970 his daughter, who was involved with Plunket, suggested that the society might usefully employ him among Pacific Islanders. His function was to visit their homes, have a chat and a 'cuppa' and discuss such matters as the Social Security system and diet. He appeared to be very well received; a *Weekly News* feature writer in August 1971 said that Islanders 'call him poppa, because they have known him for so long'.[135] He also lectured to Plunket nurse trainees. In 1973 Plunket also funded the publication of a book, *The Care of Babies and Small Children*, designed especially for Pacific Island parents in New Zealand, and written by Jacqueline Baker, a registered nurse and mother who had lived for some years in the Pacific Islands.[136]

In 1976 Joy Reid accompanied an Auckland Plunket nurse, Miss Bradley, on home visits in a Pacific Island neighbourhood. Reid reported that language problems meant the nurse had to spend much time on explanations, 'but more than this, the nurses are the only contact which these mothers have'. She noted that the nurse was spending up to three hours with one mother. Commenting on their heavy workload and responsibilities, Reid concluded that more nurses were needed in this area.[137] At the 1976 Plunket

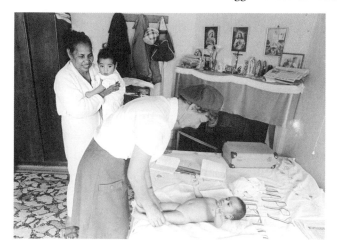

A Plunket nurse
visiting an Island
mother in the 1970s.
Auckland War Memorial
Museum, N5.5, 376

conference Mrs L. Hafoka, former president of Auckland's Oranga sub-branch, suggested that Pacific Island nurses be appointed to assist Plunket nurses. During the discussion, Christoffersen explained that Plunket already attempted to work through the churches which helped with language problems and employed 'one or two' Pacific Island nurses and one Maori nurse married to a Pacific Islander.[138]

Public concern about the health of Maori and Pacific Islanders provided fuel for Plunket to further expand its services, and led to a five-year contract signed by Reid and Health Minister Frank Gill in December 1977. Plunket was provided with $1 million to take total responsibility for health surveillance of all babies and pre-school infants in South Auckland, an area where a third of the population were Maori or Pacific Islanders. Dr Ian Hassall, a young paediatrician who had graduated in 1965, was appointed Deputy Director of Medical Services to take charge of the South Auckland project, assisted by Mona Clements, newly appointed Deputy Director of Nursing Services in Auckland. Under the contract, government funding paid for Plunket nurses' salaries, their cars and equipment, and the rent of their rooms.[139] At the opening of the administrative centre and training school in Otahuhu in May 1978, a local paper announced a 'new chapter in child health'. [140] The goal was to increase the number of Plunket nurses in the area from the existing 20 to 120 within two years. By November 1978 52 nurses were employed in South Auckland.[141]

The Salmond report did not appear to have done Plunket long-term damage: dealing with a diverse ethnic community was now entrusted to the society.[142] Hiddlestone himself appeared conciliatory in 1978 when he told Plunket conference delegates that he believed in an expanding role for voluntary organisations like Plunket in future health services: 'Looking to the future I sincerely believe we can confidently expect increased collaboration – not a takeover, not progressive dominance, but rather increased respect for our mutual and complementary roles'.[143] It appears that in the mid-1970s the Health Department was encouraging mothers to use Plunket, and that the regional co-ordinating committees were showing some signs of successful collaboration between the nurses of the two agencies.[144]

In 1977 a group of Plunket nurses from Wellington, Hutt Valley and Porirua Basin formed an unofficial working party to initiate a survey replicating the 1972 Wellington study. To avoid any impression of bias, this survey was not conducted by the Health Department but contracted to a private organisation, Urban Research Associates of Wellington. The report concluded that the mothers in Porirua were more satisfied with the services they received from Plunket nurses in 1978 than they had been in 1972, and that this reflected improved nursing services.[145] These changes included new emphases on psychological, educational and social aspects of child development in Plunket training, reorientation courses for practising Plunket nurses, and extra efforts by nurses to re-establish contact with mothers who did not keep clinic appointments.[146]

The results of the survey would not have surprised Mrs A. J. Hamer, Plunket's Deputy Director of Nursing Services, who visited Porirua in July 1975. She reported that 'the warmth and enthusiasm of those visited have convinced me completely that the Plunket Society is far from "dead" in Porirua'. She recommended the setting up of a mobile clinic with a 'specialist nurse' to deal entirely with Island and Maori people in the area. The council paid for the caravan out of head office funds, to be repaid some time in the future.[147] Porirua, the subject of so much controversy in the mid-1970s, was also the first area to have a Plunket Karitane Family Support Unit once the Karitane hospitals were closed in 1978.

The end of the Karitane hospitals

Karitane hospitals had been set up to accommodate babies with feeding problems and their mothers as well as premature babies, and to train Plunket and Karitane nurses in infant care. By the 1970s infant diarrhoea was no longer the problem it had been, the learning of 'mothercraft' in an institutional setting was not popular,[148] and maternity hospitals increasingly set up their own premature units. Paediatrics had changed its focus from nutritional to developmental problems, and the changes were reflected in the type of cases referred to the Karitane hospitals. Despite this new focus, the hospitals were seldom full; although Plunket's six hospitals could accommodate 45 mothers and 210 infants up to the age of three, they were on average using only half of those beds. By the 1970s justifying the growing expense of the hospitals became a serious concern for the Plunket Society.[149]

One of the traditional functions of the hospitals was the training of Karitane nurses. These women, generally not registered nurses, learned skills in baby care and went on to become nannies in private homes. As late as 1973 at least one paediatrician, John Landreth, believed that the training was valuable to the trainees 'and their friends' when they subsequently married and had children of their own.[150]

The training also enjoyed an international reputation, and was valuable to those who wished to travel and work overseas. Many travelled abroad, mainly to Australia or Britain.[151] In 1936 the Auckland Karitane Nurses' Club recorded that two members had started general nurse training, three had married and seven had gone to England that year.[152] This tendency to travel increased after the Second World War, and particularly in the 1960s. It was noted in 1964 that many girls went overseas and wrote back to say how popular Karitane nurses were.[153] Four years later complaints were registered in England that not enough Karitane nurses were available. According to the Brighton and Hove Mothercraft Clinic, which acted as a clearing house for the New Zealanders, 'Many applicants who have

The training of Karitane nurses was an important function of the Karitane hospitals. Little changed between the 1940 and the 1960s, except the length of the skirts. LEFT: Karitane nurses in training at Wanganui, c. 1945. RIGHT: Karitane nurses, late 1960s. *The Work of the Plunket Society in New Zealand*; Auckland Branch photograph album

previously had a Karitane Nurse are so disappointed that we cannot help them: they speak so highly of these girls.'[154] Marylyn Kavanagh, a Karitane nurse trained in Christchurch, reported in 1964 on her experiences in Britain, where she had spent sixteen months. The rates of pay were practically double those in New Zealand, and the nurses were responsible only for the children: 'Here you do everything, including housework and laundry if a mother is away,' Kavanagh said. Caring for the two young children of Lord Freyberg (son of Sir Bernard Freyberg) at their home in Godalming, Surrey, and for a patient in a flat in St James' Palace were just two of the many jobs that came her way. She was also employed by a colonel in the Life Guards, the brother of actor Sir Michael Redgrave and looked after the baby of a naval commander and his wife, Lord and Lady Bailey.[155] In 1973 the Auckland branch reported that one of their nurses had obtained a position with the Freyberg family and was 'enjoying the experience'.[156] However, not every Karitane nurse's career prospects were quite so glamorous.

Training to be a Karitane nurse before the 1950s was an expensive proposition. Until 1956 they paid a tuition fee of £40 as well as a linen fee of 30s and a uniform fee of £15. This meant that the sixteen-month training, allowing for £1 per week for personal expenses, cost £120. It was noted in the 1940s that although there was no shortage of applicants for training, the expense precluded young women without private means from taking the course.[157] Few of the trainees thought of it as a permanent career option. In 1952, the Auckland branch reported that of 20 who trained in 1949 only four were still working as Karitane nurses locally.[158] That year, Plunket's Nursing Adviser, Sydney Lusk, estimated that a Karitane nurse's average length of service was two years.[159] This was partly because many did not need the work, and partly because of the nature of the work itself. Deem noted the low wages compared with those paid generally, and the lack of freedom compared with other occupations.[160] She referred to a salary of £2 per week plus board, though elsewhere a salary of £4 4s was indicated at a time when a labourer's weekly wage was £7–£8.[161] Still, it was noted that there was no 40-hour week for Karitane nurses.[162] In 1956 an ex-Karitane nurse gave examples of the ways in which her two daughters were being exploited as Karitane nurses. In one instance her daughter worked fifteen hours a day and had no days off. When she relaxed between 8 and 10pm she was asked to 'do the mending etc.'. In addition to caring for two lively boys she was expected to be nurse to the granny. She gave six other examples of gross exploitation of Karitane nurses.[163]

In the post-war period Karitane nurses were in great demand. Already in 1944 it was noted that only about one-tenth of requests could be met.[164] Karitane bureaux were set up in 1945 to co-ordinate the supply of Karitane nurses. The nurses were instructed to stay with each mother for a maximum of four weeks. Some took babies into their own homes rather than live in. Despite an increase in minimum salary to £3 10s set by the Stabilisation Commission in 1947, demand continued to far exceed the supply. The problem with moving in quick succession from one family with a new baby to another was that the nurse had consecutive disturbed nights.[165] Among those desperate for a Karitane nurse was a woman doctor, Christobel Dickie, who was supplied with Karitane nurses until her twins were two years of age and then told that nurses were preoccupied with new babies. She wrote directly to Deem, who was very sympathetic, commenting that Dickie, as an obstetrician and gynaecologist, was doing an excellent job for women of Auckland and it would be a shame if she had to stop working. It is not known whether Deem was able to help her.[166] Paediatrician Dr Alice Bush employed four Karitane nurses over the first year of her daughter's life, 1943–4, and took a Karitane nurse to London with her in 1946 to care for her new-born son.[167]

In 1950 a bursary system for Karitane nurses was introduced: the McKenzie Trust gave £100 to eight selected girls.[168] Thanking Sir John

Karitane nurses at the Society's golden jubilee film premiere in the Regent Theatre, Dunedin, 1958. Portraying the nurses as glamorous and fun-loving was an attempt to combat a worrying shortfall in the number of recruits. Plunket Society Annual Report 1958–59

McKenzie, who was a member of Plunket's Advisory Board, Elizabeth Bodkin claimed that the funding for Karitane nurse training was helping 'the most important section of New Zealand society, the mother who is bringing up a young family'.[169] Bursaries did not, however, improve the recruitment rate. Whereas it was claimed in 1944 that there was a four-year waiting list for training, and that before the war some had applied six years ahead, by 1951 all Karitane hospitals with the exception of Christchurch were 'distressingly short of applicants for Karitane training'.[170] In an attempt to recruit more trainees, the training fee was dropped from 1956, and the minimum age of entry lowered from 20 to seventeen years of age.[171] In 1961 the minimum age was lowered to sixteen.[172] The shortage of recruits continued into the 1960s and 1970s. In 1972 Dunedin's Karitane Hospital could take 32 trainees but was down to eleven. The maximum for Invercargill's hospital was 30 but they only had eight. In an attempt to increase enrolments and also, they said, to discourage young women from seeking abortion, Begg and Liley announced in 1974 that solo mothers could now keep their babies with them when they trained as Karitane nurses.[173] Previously they had been taken on as domestics. The new policy did not, however, have any impact on recruitment. There was also a shortage of domestic workers. This was at least partly related to the introduction of the domestic purposes benefit in 1973: as the Plunket Council pointed out, 'previously many girls found independence for themselves, a home for their babies and a job situation where they could care for and maintain contact with their babies'.[174] The children of the domestics had been a useful addition to the hospitals, providing the trainees with experience of 'normal' babies.

In 1973 Plunket attempted to make Karitane nurse education more appealing by introducing a community component into the training. The students spent twelve months in the hospital and six months in the community, visiting kindergartens and playcentres and working with Plunket nurses. Their time was no longer taken up solely with supplying unpaid labour for the hospitals. In 1977, however, the Director of Nursing Services, Joy McMillan, pointed out that this unpaid labour performed the overwhelming bulk of the hospitals' nursing and domestic work. The exploitation of nurses was also referred to by the New Zealand Nurses' Union in 1977, and from time to time in the newspapers. McMillan calculated that, with approximately 230 Karitane trainees in the six hospitals, it would cost an additional $760,000 per annum if they were to be paid. Three of the hospitals maintained and financed a Karitane nurse bureau. McMillan found it hard to justify this as a hospital responsibility. She wrote that at one hospital, a considerable part of the bureau's focus revolved around the skiing season and the service that the Karitanes could provide in allowing families to carry out this activity.[175] This was not considered appropriate. The Health Department had for some time considered that, because Karitane nurse employment was restricted to the well-off, it was not appropriate to spend public money on training costs.[176] Karitane nursing had been described back in 1944 as 'one of the relics of social snobbery in our democratic society'.[177] In the 1970s the newly established Department of Social Welfare did employ some Karitane nurses to help mothers in need,[178] but training these women did not justify the expense of running a baby hospital.

Without the tuition fees of Karitane nurses from 1956, and with the declining number of beds occupied in the 1960s, Karitane hospitals found it increasingly difficult to pay their way. To help the Karitane hospitals' financial problems, the National government gave a special grant of $59,000 for the year ending March 1972 and $80,000 for the following year.[179] The incoming Labour government kept up these special grants, providing $181,000 for 1973–4.[180] The following year it provided $220,000, but told Plunket that future financial assistance would be determined by the Caucus Committee on Health.[181]

Plunket made a submission to the committee with supportive letters from seven paediatricians and the Medical Superintendent of National Women's Hospital, Algar Warren. In his letter, paediatrician Basil Quin claimed it would be a bold politician who interfered in the running and control of the Karitane hospitals: 'By the number of its members and its nationwide character I believe the Plunket Society could exert a very powerful effect on Government'.[182]

The Labour government's caucus committee put forward a new funding scheme for the Karitane hospitals, which involved contracting half the beds to local hospital boards, which would pay for these whether they were used or not. Begg opposed the suggestion, fearing that the hospitals would become a repository of chronic cases. He pointed out that the society's work was preventive medicine, not treatment, and that many of the hospital cases were there for educational or social reasons.[183] He spoke of the changing role of Karitane hospitals from infant hospitals to 'a real extension of the community family support systems'.[184] Neil MacKenzie, visiting physician to the Wanganui Karitane Hospital from 1973, also thought the contract system would be a retrograde step. As physical sickness became less important and social and psychological health more important in paediatrics, the Wanganui Karitane Hospital would be the focus of child health and care in the community.[185]

This new focus in paediatrics was an international trend. In 1975 the *British Medical Journal* featured an account of a mother-baby unit in Oxford that had opened a decade earlier. With a theoretical standpoint of 'developmental medicine' and a concern with 'disturbed family dynamics', the unit had as its main purpose the 'urgent containment of potentially disastrous family situations'. More than three-quarters of the mothers complained of distressing anxiety or depressive symptoms. The service aimed to prevent baby battering and enable parents of children with developmental disorders to make a realistic adjustment to them. 'Our aim is to contain the whole range of paediatric, psychiatric, social and legal problems within the scope of one closely integrated team.'[186]

In the 1960s Begg declared that his travels had taught him that the facilities of the Karitane hospitals were 'the envy of paediatricians in other parts of the world'.[187] A 1971 public health thesis claimed that Karitane hospitals had led the world for many years in their 'heavy accent on mother and baby being admitted together'.[188] From 1968 the University of Otago's Department of Psychological Medicine conducted research into infant–maternal relationships in collaboration with the Plunket Society at Dunedin's Karitane Hospital, led by Professor Peter Lewis and Professor Wallace Ironside, head of the university department and subsequently Director of the Department of Psychological Medicine at Monash University, Melbourne. The results of their research, known as the Karitane Project, were published in the *New Zealand Medical Journal* in 1974. They coined the term IDDS, infant development distress syndrome, or the screaming baby–weeping mother syndrome, in which stress and anxiety caused a breakdown in the mother–child relationship. Begg maintained that Lewis and Ironside had shown that the admission of mother and child to the Karitane hospital could cure the condition in about eight to ten days.[189]

In April 1975 a meeting representative of all Karitane hospitals decided unanimously that the government's proposed contract beds scheme was totally unacceptable to the Plunket Society and that negotiations be reopened as soon as possible.[190] A pilot scheme in Southland had lapsed because it was acceptable to neither the local Karitane Hospital Board nor the Southland Hospital Board. As Begg pointed out, the latter had previously had use of the beds free of charge.[191]

In 1975 Plunket looked into the possibility of aligning itself to the new

Department of Social Welfare, set up in 1972, rather than the Health Department. Pointing out that the hospitals' main contribution to the nation's health was going to be in the province of the mother–child relationship rather than in nutritional or infectious diseases, Begg and other senior paediatricians thought this realignment appropriate.[192] However, the suggestion was firmly rejected by Plunket's Director of Nursing Services, Iris Christoffersen, for professional reasons. She reminded the council that the training of Plunket nurses was very highly regarded as a community health programme in nursing and that it would not be acceptable for it to become part of social welfare training.[193] Furthermore, the Department of Social Welfare did not wish to be encumbered by the hospitals. It argued that care could be provided in less costly smaller units, and that the hospitals were not located in areas of greatest need.[194]

It has been argued that the move to 'developmental paediatrics' in the United States was led by academic paediatricians in an attempt to create a niche at a time of declining infant mortality rates.[195] Yet, to some extent at least, paediatricians in New Zealand were responding to the changing clientele within Karitane hospitals, largely referred by Plunket nurses or general practitioners. In 1971 seven of the 25 babies and three of the mothers at Dunedin's Karitane hospital were 'more social problems than feeding problems'. Their 'problems' included separated mothers and unmarried mothers, babies whose mothers had been hospitalised and babies for adoption; many came from 'some sort of disturbed home or background'.[196] In 1972 Joyce Andrews, Plunket president from 1978 to 1981, spoke of the changing role of Wellington's Plunket Karitane Hospital: 'We seem to get more of the social and economic problems, the battered baby, the psychiatric mother, the illegitimate baby. We do on occasion take in some boarder babies [babies for adoption].'[197] Four years later, when bed occupancy was the highest in four years, it was reported that 'the type of patient has changed. Many are disturbed mothers, requiring psychiatric care, which is rather sad'.[198] A similar pattern was noted in Auckland: 'most of our admissions of mothers showed a distressing predominance of emotional disturbance . . . and this tends to upset normal mothers coming into the Hospital to establish breast feeding'.[199] In 1973 Christchurch's Plunket Karitane Hospital matron referred to the growing number of 'Child Welfare babies in our hospital awaiting adoption'.[200]

Given this perception of the role of Karitane hospitals, some argued in favour of setting up more hospitals. Auckland Plunket Karitane Hospital's Chief Medical Officer, Alison Hunter, pointed out that 25 per cent of

Auckland's infant admissions that year had been at the request of public hospitals, Health Department medical officers and the Social Welfare Department: 'Karitane is providing a community service which is not catered for by any other source'. Patients included 'babies whose mothers were deserted or unsupported, those of failed or unstable de facto relationships and those of very young parents who were ill-equipped or unwilling for the demands of parenthood'.[201]

As early as 1972 Joy Reid had warned of the necessity to take a close look at the future functions of the hospitals. She did not doubt their usefulness, and believed the council should do all it could to keep the hospitals open. She pointed out that the hospitals did not belong to the executive or the council; they belonged to the branches and their surrounding areas: 'At no stage will the Dominion Executive or Council say their hospital must close. This is a decision which can only be made by the hospital and branches.'[202] In 1975 she told the council that it was important to continue the fight to keep the hospitals open, though Begg warned that 'the position is more desperate than I have ever known it'.[203] In 1976 it was reported that unless a better system of funding were developed, the hospitals would have to be closed during the coming year as the debt to head office was growing monthly and could not be met.[204] Reid admitted that the executive might have to consider whether the society could afford to continue to maintain the hospitals or whether it would be wiser to divert all its efforts to the district work.[205] At the time of Begg's retirement in mid-1977 the hospitals were definitely in trouble.

Dr David Geddis took up office in April 1977 as Plunket's new Medical Director. The same month Iris Christoffersen retired as Director of Nursing Services, but continued as acting Deputy Director in Auckland until January 1978. Joy McMillan took up the post of Director of Nursing Services. As Gordon Parry wrote, 'the new directors were thrown in at the deep end. Within a week of taking up their appointments they were instructed to begin one of the most important surveys in the Society's history. Over the next few months they visited all six hospitals and consulted widely.'[206]

Geddis was very much in the 'psycho-social' school of paediatrics. Born in Ireland, he qualified at Queen's University, Belfast, in 1970. He was then appointed house officer at the Royal Victoria Hospital, Belfast, and later worked as senior house officer at the Royal Belfast Hospital for Sick Children. After a year in Canada as a resident at the Toronto Hospital for Sick Children, Geddis moved to New Zealand in 1973 to become a registrar and assistant lecturer at the Department of Paediatrics, Dunedin

Hospital. He was later appointed senior registrar and from January 1975, spent six months overseas studying child abuse at centres in Tasmania, the United States and England. Before returning to New Zealand in 1976, he spent a further year in Belfast as a lecturer in child health at Queen's University. When he took up the appointment as Plunket's Medical Director he was 30 years old, and married with three children. He was described as a specialist in the problems of child abuse.[207]

Geddis produced a confidential report on the Karitane hospitals in November 1977. Although he considered the hospitals played an important role in catering for babies from disturbed backgrounds and abuse situations, he did not believe that they offered any meaningful long-term benefits to these infants. He favoured replacing the larger hospitals with smaller, more easily managed neighbourhood units. The new focus in paediatrics, which had been used in the early 1970s to argue for the usefulness of the Karitane hospitals, was now being used to justify their closure.[208]

McMillan wrote a more detailed report on the state of the hospitals. The number of premature babies admitted had dropped from 637 in 1958 to 88 in 1976; they were now being catered for in maternity hospitals. During her inspections, it became clear that the overwhelming majority of infant admissions were of a 'welfare' nature. Some were awaiting adoption; others had permanent physical defects. She was disturbed to hear several matrons explain that these babies would 'eventually die here'. McMillan summed up the functions of the hospital as primarily a baby-sitting service or an orphanage, though she noted there were also some mothers with 'stress' problems.[209] The new Deputy Director, Ian Hassall, also believed that the hospitals had almost turned into a baby-sitting service. He thought it was 'good to be able to do this sort of thing, but that it did not justify the expense of a hospital'.[210]

The evolution of the hospitals into a baby-sitting service affected staffing. McMillan pointed out that the situation in all six hospitals had been 'desperate' for some time. Good qualified staff was almost impossible to obtain, she claimed, owing to lack of job satisfaction: 'Conscientious, qualified girls may see little profit in baby-sitting and changing napkins'. Staff appeared to display no interest or experience in handling 'stressed' mothers. Neither did there appear to be any current guidance or direction in treating them.[211]

On 1 February 1977 Peter K. Cressey (B. Com, ACA) began work as Director of Administration, a post replacing that of the secretary of the society.[212] His assessment of the situation reinforced the conclusions of the other reports. He pointed out that the six Karitane hospitals owed headquarters over $200,000 with little hope of paying it back. On his visit to Wanganui in August 1977 only one mother and three babies were in residence. The treasurer of Wellington Karitane Hospital told him that the hospital was 'staggering from crisis to crisis', that there was no hope of paying back the $70,000 owed to headquarters, a debt which was affecting local branches, and that the property would sell very well. A senior Wellington councillor told Cressey bluntly that the hospitals should be closed: 'they are a financial disaster and serving no worthwhile function. Plunket nurse training does not require a hospital. Karitane nurse training is useless anyway'. The Wellington Karitane Hospital chairman also described the situation as a 'crisis', with a shortage of trained staff. At Invercargill Cressey met five paediatricians and a representative of the Social Welfare Department who told him, 'There is no medical superintendent as such. We never meet and discuss direction or policy. Qualified nursing staff are very difficult to get . . . we have reached the end of the line.' The paediatricians described a nearly completed obstetrics hospital that had been planned 20 years earlier on the assumption of an increasing birth rate. 'It will be big and it will be empty . . . . There is not room for both.' Cressey concluded, 'This report presents a woeful and totally depressing state of affairs.'[213]

In December 1977 Plunket's finance committee recommended replacing the hospitals with smaller facilities. Joy Reid outlined the financial crisis at a special meeting of the council in March 1978. Running costs had more than trebled since 1971, and the hospitals accounted for 37 per cent of the society's costs but handled only 4 per cent of its cases. There was an average occupancy rate of just 54 per cent when the break-even point for private hospitals was about 70 per cent. Reid also pointed out that the Minister of Health had shown interest in the proposed alternative scheme, which was in line with current government policy of taking health care into the community. The executive moved that, 'The recommendations of Dr D. C. Geddis for the establishment of Family Support Units should become the policy of the Society and it is accepted that this will probably involve the closure of the existing six Plunket Karitane Hospitals'.[214]

The council agreed, with two dissenting voices, those of Mrs J. E. Jennings of Southland and Mrs I. Stewart of Wanganui. A week later the Karitane Hospitals boards were formally advised of the decision and told that the society would hold a special conference on 2 May to consider the council's recommendations. Gordon Parry described the subsequent reaction: 'The letters which poured in were couched in emotional terms, the telephone calls received by President Joy Reid were not all friendly'. In Invercargill, the council decision was rejected as 'arbitrary, high-handed and unreasonable'.[215] The press picked up on the news before the special conference was held: on 3 April the *Auckland Star* announced that the hospitals were to be replaced by a network of family support units.[216]

'Save the Hospital' lobby groups were busy before the special conference. In Invercargill a petition of 10,882 signatures was presented in support of the local hospital, and 7000 Aucklanders opposed closure there. In Southland, Pauline Rout later explained, 'Everyone wanted to sign', though when the petition was then taken to the conference, 'Plunket didn't even want to look at it.'[217] Reid emphasised the decision was a matter of finance, asking delegates: 'Did we really want government to take over completely, or were we going to face facts and make some firm decision of our own on future policy?'[218]

John Russell from Invercargill said that Southland people were proud of their Karitane hospital. He spoke of tremendous local support, which was the whole essence of the Plunket Society. Closing the hospitals endangered the society. Reid, however, rejected a Southland delegation amendment to delay closure until the family support units had been operated for a trial period. The resolution in favour of closing the hospitals was passed by 316 votes to 44.[219]

As Parry wrote, 'To many in the Society the news came as a shock. It had all the appearances of a crude coup, a highhanded decision reached without proper consultation with the thousands of willing volunteers who had toiled so long and so hard to make the hospital system viable.'[220] In a 1980 *Listener* article, journalist Lynley Hood claimed that the Southland delegation returned home bewildered and angry. No one north of the Clutha had appreciated what their Karitane hospital meant to them. Each bedroom carried a plaque bearing the name of the sub-branch or Plunket mothers' club responsible for its renovation. Not only did they raise money: the women painted and papered, curtained windows and laid carpet, and added matching bedspreads and lampshades, and pictures on the walls. Other community groups had also been involved, including Lions, Rotary, Rotaract, Jaycee wives, Masonic Charitable Trusts and the Invercargill Licensing Trust. The result was 'the embodiment of Southland community concern and pride'.[221] In 1976 it had been reported to the council that the Invercargill hospital had powerful support from Plunket committees, service organisations and individuals: 'when we require a new piece of equipment for the Hospital, there always seems to be someone around willing to help'.[222]

The Wellington and Dunedin Karitane hospitals closed in July 1978. Auckland followed in October and Christchurch in December. But Invercargill was not going to give up without a fight. From April to December 1977 locals raised $45,000 to keep the hospital operating. The Invercargill branch of the Plunket Society sought a Supreme Court injunction challenging the president's refusal to accept the Southland amendment at the May conference. The injunction was granted and the decision to close the hospitals was declared void.

Both Invercargill and Wanganui had support from their local hospital boards to keep their hospitals open. Although the West Otago branch did not strive to keep the local hospital open, it too served an injunction on the society in December 1978, declaring that the resolutions of the May conference were invalid. The West Otago people were concerned about the use of the funds from the sale of the Dunedin Karitane Hospital: they wanted an assurance that the area in which a hospital was located had some priority in the future distribution of funds. The council affirmed that this assurance had already been given.[223]

On 31 January 1980 a special conference formally amended the rules of the Plunket Society to delete all reference to hospitals. This change ensured that no Plunket branch could legally own, operate or support a Karitane hospital.[224] Invercargill closed its doors on 28 March 1980, and all six hospitals were now on the market. The following day the Invercargill branch held a closing gala day, reminiscing about the Karitane golden jubilee in 1976, when they had spent the proceedings on furnishings. Hood concluded her story of Invercargill Karitane hospital with the local perception of Plunket bureaucracy,

> A Karitane board member stops to admire the jubilee furniture, and to tell a story: 'We had some people from Plunket executive through here the other day. Do you know what they said about this table and chairs? They said, "These will look nice in our Wellington office."'[225]

Hood's article began with a description of a massive holly hedge, backed by a cluster of tall trees. which surrounded the hospital. She compared this to the Grimm Brothers' description of the wood surrounding the enchanted Sleeping Beauty and the castle whose occupants froze in time for

Invercargill's Truby King-Hunt Karitane Hospital, c. 1945. In 1978 Lynley Hood compared the hospital to the castle in the Sleeping Beauty, 'frozen in time for a hundred years'.

a hundred years. The Karitane hospital, too, she wrote, was 'standing in a time-warp'.[226]

Paediatrics was changing, but so was the Society. Sheila Horton commented that with the closing of the hospitals, the old fighting spirit had gone.[227] The council congratulated Reid, who had overseen the moves to close the hospitals and had retired in 1978, for the way in which her 'arguments had always been handled in a lady-like way'.[228] Was Reid to be among the last of the traditional maternalists?

CHAPTER 8

Community Paediatrics, 1980s and 1990s

Paediatricians as children's advocates

In 1977 Health Minister Frank Gill set up a Board of Health Committee on Child Health, with Plunket's medical and nursing directors, David Geddis and Joy McMillan, among its 23 members. The committee's 1982 report noted that New Zealand was often considered an ideal place in which to bring up children. The climate and environment, the committee asserted, made it a fine place for children, 'but health and safety wise, it will only become the ideal place if we work to make it so'. Indeed, New Zealand had slipped from a position of worldwide pre-eminence in child health to one of distinctly second order.[1]

In 1951 New Zealand proudly boasted the second lowest infantile mortality rate in the world, surpassed only by Sweden. Commenting on the Health Department's claim in the late 1960s that New Zealand was falling behind other countries in infant mortality rates, Neil Begg obstinately held that 'Generally speaking . . . New Zealand remains one of the world's leaders in this field'.[2] The following year he pursued this theme, arguing that most of the countries New Zealand was being compared with – European countries, Britain, the United States and Australia – had much higher abortion rates, thus skimming off the high-risk layers of 'unwanted babies'. These bigger abortion rates 'underline the fact that international comparisons are not valid and that it is surprising that New Zealand has maintained such a satisfactory position'.[3]

Despite Begg's attempts to explain it away, New Zealand did appear to be slipping in the international scale in the 1960s,[4] and by the early 1970s his confidence could no longer be sustained. New Zealand now ranked tenth in death rates for the one- to twelve-month age group, and twenty-sixth for the one- to four-year-olds.[5] This had changed little by 1982 when the Board of Health issued its report, which noted that the rate for infective and parasitic disease was eight times higher than among Swedish children. The incidence of respiratory disease was seven times higher, motor accidents were almost four times higher, and all other accidents were double

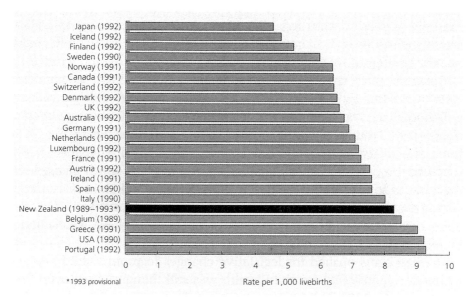

Japan (1992)
Iceland (1992)
Finland (1992)
Sweden (1990)
Norway (1991)
Canada (1991)
Switzerland (1992)
Denmark (1992)
UK (1992)
Australia (1992)
Germany (1991)
Netherlands (1990)
Luxembourg (1992)
France (1991)
Austria (1992)
Ireland (1991)
Spain (1990)
Italy (1990)
New Zealand (1989–1993*)
Belgium (1989)
Greece (1991)
USA (1990)
Portugal (1992)

0   1   2   3   4   5   6   7   8   9   10

*1993 provisional   Rate per 1,000 livebirths

New Zealand's poor international standing in infant mortality rates, evident in the 1970s, continued into the 1990s when it ranked nineteenth among 23 OECD countries. *Our Health, Our Future*, 1994

the Swedish rate. The mortality rate for one- to twelve-month-old babies in New Zealand was 6.4 per 1000 births, while the rate for Sweden was 2.3. Other countries with rates of three or less included Denmark, Norway and the Netherlands, while Australia, England and Wales and the United States all had rates below five.[6] Maori and Pacific Islanders' infant mortality rates were significantly higher than for the rest of New Zealand's population, but the committee refuted this as a cause of New Zealand's poor international ranking since Maori and Pacific Island births together comprised less than 20 per cent of the total. New Zealand would have improved its infant mortality rate position by only two places if these were omitted.[7]

Community paediatrics in the 1980s and 1990s involved two approaches. The first identified and targeted at-risk groups, the second was concerned with environmental hazards and community safety. These strategies reflected a more general paradigm shift in public health practice. Virginia Berridge has argued that in Britain from the 1970s biomedical notions of direct causation gave way to epidemiological concepts of relative risk and statistical correlation. The new approach involved education, but also led to the concept of the 'environmental citizen', 'a rational consumer protecting him or herself from environmental risks' (Berridge gave the

baby" and its parents, and what New Zealand can do to help and prevent them'.[25] A 1969 Health Department review of child health confirmed that battered baby syndrome had recently come to prominence.[26]

It was not until the early 1970s, however, that the issue achieved heightened publicity, possibly assisted by Kempe's visit to New Zealand in 1973. Plunket nurses were more likely than most to encounter battered children during their home visits. Plunket's acting Director of Nursing, Val Jones, stated in 1973 that nurses were 'alert to possible baby battering where tensions are too great for mothers to cope'.[27] District reports, recorded in Plunket's executive minutes in the 1970s, began to refer to battered babies. In October 1973, for example, the nurses' reports included three cases of battered babies, in Auckland, Wellington and Rotorua, two of whom died.[28] The following year, cases included one in Helensville: 'Child aged 10 months with cigarette burns inflicted by the mother, now being cared for by grandparents', and in Invercargill: '3-year-old admitted to Hospital, deprivation and child abuse – multiple bruises and cigarette burns on hands'.[29] In the 1970s mothers of battered babies were singled out as a category for admission to Karitane hospitals. Auckland's Karitane Hospital report for 1977–8 stated that some mothers and babies were admitted 'for relief in tense domestic situations where danger of abuse was imminent'.[30] In 1976 the *New Zealand Herald* noted that 95 of the 636 babies admitted to the hospital that year had been abandoned or rescued from abuse situations.[31]

In 1975 a *Herald* article on 'baby-bashing' pronounced that 'Child beatings that result in death may be much more prevalent in New Zealand than is generally supposed'. The paper cited Auckland Plunket's Nursing Adviser, Mrs J. M. Adams, who said that sometimes the nurses suspected abuse but had to have good evidence to bring it up in court. When asked, she could not say whether baby-bashing was increasing, but 'people are more aware of it now'. Children of solo parents were particularly at risk, she thought.[32] The identification of child abuse with solo parenthood could be seen partly as a reaction to the new social trend, disapproved of by many, of women keeping children born out of wedlock. The number of single-parent families in New Zealand was growing, aided from 1973 by the introduction of the domestic purposes benefit, which offered state financial support for single parents.

Because it was perceived as a 'medico-social' problem, in the 1970s paediatricians became involved in researching and dealing with child abuse. A 1978 *New Zealand Listener* article cited a Department of Social

Welfare report, *Child Abuse in New Zealand* (1972), in which the preface by the Minister of Social Welfare, Lance Adams-Schneider, stated, 'It is pleasing to note that . . . child abuse is not a problem of major social importance in New Zealand.'[33] This provoked the ire of Geddis, who had just returned from the second International Conference on Child Abuse and Neglect held in London. He held that the minister was 'talking off the top of his head': child abuse was 'a major problem' in New Zealand. Auckland Hospital's Deputy Medical Superintendent, Dr Roger Greenhough, stated that child abuse was a 'recognisable disease'. Dr Fraser McDonald, Superintendent of Auckland's psychiatric hospital, and vice-chairman of the Mental Health Foundation, was also cited in the article. He claimed to have noticed a lack of 'mothering' knowledge among abusive mothers.[34]

Child abuse was one of the themes chosen by the 1978 IYC Child and Health Committee. Geddis was asked to create a 'think tank' on child abuse, sponsored by the National Child Health Research Foundation.[35] As a result, New Zealand's first national conference on the subject was held in September 1979 in Dunedin, convened by the foundation and chaired by Geddis.[36] In 1981 a National Advisory Committee on the Prevention of Child Abuse was set up by the Minister of Social Welfare, again with Geddis as chairman and with Hassall as a member. Hassall had also been involved with the issue as chairman of the Child Abuse Prevention Society, set up in 1977, which ran a phone service (Parent Help) for parents afraid they might harm their children.[37]

Geddis noted approvingly that Plunket's concern about child abuse was reflected in the way he was permitted, as the society's Medical Director, to devote time to the work of the national committee.[38] To mark the seventy-fifth jubilee of the Plunket Society in 1982, Associate Professor Barton Schmitt from the University of Colorado, was invited to New Zealand, funded by the KPS. He spoke with Plunket nurses throughout the country, gave the Peter Lewis Memorial Lecture at the society's general conference and delivered a keynote address at the second National Child Abuse Prevention Conference in Palmerston North. This conference was hosted by the Mental Health Foundation, after an approach from Geddis and Hassall.[39] In September 1984 Geddis attended an International Congress on Child Abuse in Montreal, and in August 1986 he led a New Zealand delegation to the International Congress on Child Abuse and Neglect in Sydney. He also visited England that year to investigate a Health Surveillance Programme mounted for at-risk babies in Sheffield, and consulted community paediatricians in Newcastle, Nottingham and Oxford. In 1984 Geddis wrote that the medical profession would 'soon be asked to play an even greater role than hitherto in attempts to alleviate one of the tragic paediatric problems of our time'.[40]

The paediatric focus was on prevention and early detection. In particular there was an attempt to identify at-risk families. A 1970 British report claimed it would be ideal if a first battering could be anticipated, but regretted that this was rarely possible. It declared, however, that all those professionally concerned should be aware of the syndrome 'and of the characteristics of the parents'.[41] This was later described as an attempt to create 'a prism through which we anticipate possibilities, imagine outcomes of present actions and thus attempt to control or colonize the future'.[42]

From 1974 to 1976 a project based in Dunedin supported nearly 300 at-risk mothers with psychiatric treatment and home visits involving Plunket nurses and community groups. As a result of the intervention, according to Geddis, 'the situation of 75 per cent of the mothers improved'.[43] In 1977 Geddis and his Dunedin paediatric team (a psychiatrist, a senior Plunket nurse and a medical social worker) investigated whether abuse could be predicted before birth. They interviewed 150 mothers who had been referred to them and classified them as 'high risk', 'moderate risk' or 'low risk'.[44] A decade later this was described as a 'psychosocial risk scoring system for antenatal and perinatal use . . . to predict future parenting problems'.[45] Although one commentator wondered whether the identification of an at-risk parent might heighten the potential danger by adding to existing family stress,[46] the general trend in paediatrics was in favour of such classification.

In his talk to the 1982 conference, Schmitt stated categorically that child abuse could be prevented. Families 'with a high potential for abnormal child rearing practices, of which child abuse is an extreme' could be labelled 'dysfunctional families, multiproblem families, multi-risk factor families, precarious families, socially disorganised families or families in need of extra services'. He explained that no screening had been able to predict those parents at specific high risk for abusing their children since the prevalence of child abuse (1–2 per cent) was low compared with the prevalence of dysfunctional families (15 per cent). Nevertheless, he optimistically believed that high-risk families could be identified and that hospital and community programmes could help them to become adequate parents. The Denver Parenting Checklist could identify 'the most commonly described antecedents of abuse, such as serious psychiatric illness or aggressive tendencies in the parent, drug addiction, deprivation or abuse of the parent as a child, inadequate support systems, intolerance of children's behaviours, an unwanted pregnancy or previous abuse of a sibling'. He claimed that scores of over 70 per cent were seen in dangerous people who should never be left alone with children.[47]

A decade after it had first featured the topic, in 1989 the *New Zealand Listener* ran another article on 'The row over child abuse'.[48] 'Drastic legislative changes to the management of violence against children will come too late for Baby C,' it announced, 'beaten to death by her mother well over a year after a Plunket nurse first noticed evidence of abuse.' The article, inspired by the introduction of a new Children's and Young Persons' Bill, asked 'who should protect our children, and how much power should those protectors have?'

Through his involvement with the National Advisory Committee on the Prevention of Child Abuse, Geddis had helped to draft the new bill, and was optimistic about the proposed changes. In 1984 he returned from the International Congress in Montreal, convinced that the planned legislation would propel New Zealand to the forefront in terms of enlightened social legislation.[49] His plan included compulsory reporting of suspected child abuse, and child protection teams operating around the country.[50] The setting up of multidisciplinary child protection teams had been advocated at the 1979 child abuse conference, and the first was set up in Dunedin in 1980, with financial support from the 1980 Telethon fundraising effort. Others were formed in Hamilton and South Auckland, the latter with Hassall as chairman.[51] By 1987, there were about 31 teams in existence.[52] However, a working party from the Social Welfare Department subsequently overturned the pre-eminence of child protection teams. As Bronwyn Dalley explained, for many the proposals had swung too far in the direction of children's rights and the role of professionals, and isolated children within their family networks.[53] The 1989 *Listener* article supported the turnaround: 'There seems little point in pumping resources into high-powered think-tanks when there are too few front line workers to bring information to the teams'. It estimated that Geddis's scheme would cost $10 million in its first year. The article supported increased funding for 'existing well-structured charitable organisations – such as the Plunket Society', though there was no evidence of this happening as an alternative.[54] Geddis believed that the redrafted legislation was 'too weighted in the direction of family control' and would not ensure adequate protection for the abused child.[55] He thought the Act was 'based on the simple philosophy that since it is within families that abuse occurs, it is to those families that we must look for solutions. Such an approach is naïve. It ignores reality. It is to be hoped that the fate of the children who will be subjected to this experiment will be better than many of us anticipate.'[56]

Harry Hendrick noted that the silence of the 'abused' children them-selves 'engulfs us with its enormity' in the debates surrounding child abuse from the 1960s.[57] Geddis and Hassall advocated a 'voice for children'; in 1978 Geddis called for the setting up of a Children's Bureau or a Children's Commission.[58] He hoped the IYC would force the issue into the public arena, and made personal submissions to the Royal Commission on the Courts, attempting to show how the abused child was often failed by the law. He believed that society required a fundamental change of attitude to 'one that allows children to be thought of as people'.[59] The IYC Committee on the Child and Health recommended the appointment of a child com-missioner.[60] This was eventually built into the legislation a decade later, as a last-minute addition according to Geddis.[61] Hassall was appointed to the new position of Commissioner for Children. Although his appointment was not a result of his paediatric qualifications, his own work in the area had led him down the path of child advocacy. Along with other professionals in law, politics and social work, he had come to view children as disad-vantaged by certain political and economic developments and powerless to defend themselves against those policies.

In Britain in the 1980s 'child sexual abuse' had overtaken child abuse as a dominant public issue.[62] Delegates at New Zealand's 1982 National Conference on Child Abuse Prevention were concerned that child sexual abuse was inadequately dealt with here.[63] On his return from the Sydney congress in 1986, Geddis maintained it was clear that 'while our proposals for the physically abused child are amongst the most advanced anywhere, we have a lot of work to do with respect to the problem of sexual abuse of children'.[64] The 1989 *Listener* article described the 'Cleveland crisis' in England as 'a mistake of mammoth proportions', when an epidemic of sex-ual abuse had been falsely diagnosed. The article warned that Cleveland could happen in New Zealand where 'a belief that incest is rampant has become an in-group pastime of numerous middle-class Pakeha women'. The article warned against allowing the agendas of certain interest groups such as feminists to dictate the work of the proposed child protection teams. Geddis was concerned, on the other hand, that Cleveland might provoke a backlash, in New Zealand as well as Britain, and deter people from listen-ing to child abuse victims.[65] New Zealand followed the overseas trend. Its own local epidemic of suspected child sexual abuse culminated in the 1993 conviction of Peter Ellis in the Christchurch Civic Crèche case, a verdict upon which Lynley Hood convincingly cast doubts in *A City Possessed* (2001).[66]

Paediatricians played a major role in rediscovering child abuse from the 1960s. By the 1990s, however, the issue had become a 'socio-legal' one, with the agencies of law (courts, police, lawyers) playing a crucial role in determining the problem and solutions.[67] In New Zealand this changing emphasis saw John Spencer, lecturer in family law at Selwyn College, Cambridge, invited to deliver the keynote Truby King lecture at the 1993 Plunket conference.[68] Yet paediatricians continued to be involved. In 1998 New Plymouth's Dr Robin Fancourt headed the organising committee for the Twelfth International Congress on Child Abuse and Neglect, held in Auckland.[69] Fancourt was also involved in both Children's Agenda and an organisation called Doctors for Sexual Abuse Care, and set up the Brainwave Trust, which was concerned with neglect of children's developmental needs.[70]

Efforts to identify at-risk parents also continued. One apparently successful American programme, the 'Hawaiian Healthy Start programme', was 'designed to identify at-risk families' and to provide home visits as a preventative measure. Labour Party justice spokesman Phil Goff claimed in 1996 that the scheme had averted abuse and neglect in most of the families involved.[71] He also referred to a long-term research study headed by Dr Phil Silva, an educational psychologist at the University of Otago, involving 2000 children studied from birth to the age of 20.[72] He noted the study's findings that children from dysfunctional families were 100 times more likely to be serious criminals, welfare dependants and educational failures as those from stable homes. This had lasting implications for the nation: 'The children we fail to support today will cost the country dearly in policing imprisonment, welfare and health spending . . . Early intervention for at-risk families from the time a child is born is the most cost-effective investment that New Zealand can make in the longterm reduction of the welfare bill.'[73]

In 1996, the United Nations Children's Fund ranked New Zealand as having the sixth highest rate of infant abuse of 23 industrialised countries.[74] New Zealand's worsening economic position in the 1990s was believed to be a contributory factor, but personal responsibility was still held to be paramount. Plunket's Director of Nursing Services, Anne Cressey, had referred to economic circumstances with attendant social problems 'leading to suspected or actual child abuse' in 1988.[75] In an 1992 editorial on

SIDS continued to be disguised under the medical classification of disease. It was not recognised as a discrete category in the New Zealand Department of Health's 1964 report on infant mortality.[91] In his 1971 annual report, Begg included a section on 'Sudden Unexpected Deaths' or 'SUDs', pointing out that little was known about this mysterious condition but that intensive research was going on in the United States and Britain.[92] Two years later he noted that cot deaths, which might be as high as one in ten infant deaths, were concealed somewhere in the infant mortality figures. He reported that the National Health Statistics Centre was planning to separate this category from others – such as respiratory infection – to form a clearer picture of these 'mysterious and tragic deaths'.[93] Soon after becoming medical director in 1977, Geddis commented when discussing post-neonatal mortality (one to twelve months) that the main cause of death was viral pneumonia, though he thought this was a misleading diagnosis and that most were probably cot deaths.[94]

In 1984 a 165,000-signature petition to Parliament led to the setting up of a workshop on the problem of cot death.[95] From that emerged a National Steering Committee on Cot Death, with Professor John Dower as chair, which issued a report the following year.[96] Meanwhile the Plunket Society also became involved, inviting Professor John Emery to New Zealand in 1986 because of his international standing in the field of cot death research. Emery was Emeritus Professor in Paediatric Pathology for the Sheffield Health Authority. Without being more specific, Emery claimed that post-neonatal deaths, of which 62 per cent were cot deaths, had 'social/community origins'.[97]

Although SIDS was labelled 'non-preventable' in 1982, it was not long before at-risk groups and factors were identified. The Health Department's 1984 publication, *Recording Child Health and Development*, stated that 'cot death cannot yet be predicted with any useful accuracy, but the *risk* of the baby dying in this way can be estimated. Similar risk factors apply to both post-neonatal death and cot death.' The reader was referred to a table outlining the key indicators:

age of baby – 1–4 months; birthweight – under 2500 grams; age of mother – under 20; education of mother – 0–2 years at secondary school; ethnicity – Maori; sex of child – boy; time of year – May–October; weight centile – not being recorded or decreasing.[98]

A 1982 report commented on the age of mother as a risk factor, explaining that 'Inexperience, combined with a lack of appropriate social support, has been linked to poor infant health'.[99]

In 1987 the *New Zealand Medical Journal* reported a two-year study by Hassall, together with Dr Edwin Mitchell, senior lecturer in paediatrics at Auckland University and later Professor of Child Health, and a pathologist, David Becroft, of infant deaths occurring in Auckland. Eighty of 134 infant deaths studied were attributed to cot death. Ninety per cent of the cases had certain 'notable factors'. These were 'young mothers, Maori, low socio-economic status, poor accommodation, frequent changes of address, maternal smoking, previous postneonatal death, poor antenatal care, male infant, low birth weight, twin, poor infant weight gain'.[100] Lesley Max, a journalist and author of *Children: Endangered Species?*, asked Mitchell to explain the difference between the low Pacific Island rate and high Maori rate, given their similar socio-economic circumstances. She wrote,

> Dr Mitchell stressed that he could only speak from his assumptions, but he believes that the difference can be partly accounted for by the heavier birth weight of the Pacific Island babies, the relative lack of maternal smoking, and the 'migrant' factor, involving 'get up and go' people. He believes the socio-economic rating can be misleading since it is based only on occupation and might not reflect lifestyle. The Maori infants, by contrast, were of low birth weight; many were born to mothers who smoked, and many were ex-nuptial.[101]

For her book, Max also consulted Dr Shirley Tonkin, a National Child Health Research Foundation medical officer, who founded the New Zealand Cot Death Association in 1979 (as a division of the Foundation) and was its national co-ordinator. Tonkin believed that in order to reduce the incidence of deaths from the syndrome, it was necessary to improve ante-natal care, to change attitudes towards baby care and to provide a specific assessment centre so that at-risk babies could be monitored during sleep and evaluated.[102] Hassall similarly believed the answer lay in 'defin[ing] a group of high risk infants using a scoring system based on risk factors . . . and tak[ing] special care of this group'.[103]

Max cited Hassall's reasoning that the 'essential factor' in cot death was genetic, environmental or related to infant care. Having discarded the first two possibilities, he settled on the latter. As Max wrote, 'This was greeted with anger by spokespeople for the support of cot death families, who resented what they saw as an unwarranted accusation against mothers.' Explaining that the cot death rate was five times that of countries spending a similar proportion of gross national product on health, Hassall believed the cause lay in the fact that 'A great many babies are in the care of mothers who have not been a part of a tradition of child-rearing and who are isolated in their task'.[104] He used this to argue for more support for mothers, specifically the Plunket in Neighbourhoods scheme which aimed to give all mothers with new babies the opportunity to link up with others, to provide mutual and baby-sitting support.[105] Max also reported that Tonkin had recently returned from an international conference on cot death with the information that New Zealand had the highest cot death rate among developed countries. Israel, 'where child-rearing was of high national significance and there is a strong mothering tradition', had the lowest. It might also be significant, Max added, that New Zealand's ex-nuptial birth rate was 23.8 per cent, as opposed to Israel's 2.5 per cent.[106] The National Cot Death Study (see below) noted in 1991 that 'The mothers of cases were significantly younger, less likely to be married, left school earlier and have lower socio-economic status than mothers of control infants'.[107]

At-risk epidemiology had led to the labelling of parents. An apparently objective measure, it nevertheless carried a moral dimension, that the perpetrators of risk might be held accountable in some way.[108] Identifying risk factors might also have served to control the anxiety evoked by a hitherto apparently haphazard and frightening danger, the reassurance that 'it only happened to others'.[109] In Britain, Virginia Berridge noted that the causes of cot death 'have been highly contentious' and before the 1990s were attributed to a range of factors from 'maternal ignorance' to inequalities in health.[110]

The New Zealand Cot Death Study ran from 1987 to 1990, at a time when New Zealand had the highest rate of cot deaths among Organisation for Economic Co-operation and Development (OECD) countries. Cot death was responsible for 32 per cent of all infant deaths in New Zealand, and the infant death rate for Maori was twice as high as for non-Maori.[111] The study, which included interviews with 393 SIDS parents and 1592 controls, was based on Mitchell's premise that different child care practices might cast light on SIDS. He admitted it was only by chance that he had included a question on sleeping positions in the study. He discovered, however, a very high incidence of prone (or tummy) sleeping among SIDS babies.[112] Other apparently significant factors included maternal smoking and the lack of breastfeeding. A 1991 Plunket study of more than 4000 babies nationwide found that a third of mothers smoked in pregnancy (an average of twelve cigarettes a day), and two-thirds of Maori mothers smoked while preg-

SAFE SLEEPING
for Your Baby—

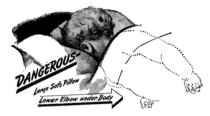

ADVICE TO PARENTS

A young baby has very little control of his muscles. He cannot hold up his head, sit erect or turn from side to side. You, his parents, have to do many things for him. To be sure he will sleep safely and peacefully carry out the following instructions.

1. *Provide him with his own bed —*
   Do not take him into yours.
2. *Lie him on a firm mattress.*
3. *If you give him a pillow,*
   see that it is small and FIRM.
4. *Having provided these, tuck baby down as follows—*

Tuck cuddly blankets around the shoulders only. *Place him* on his *side* in the cot. Bring forward the lower elbow. Tuck enveloping blankets over baby and under mattress. Next comes the sheet which should be tucked in about six inches at the top to prevent baby's face being irritated by the blankets. Any additional blanket should be light, as weight does not always ensure warmth.

Remember — DO NOT WRAP baby in the cuddly — Just tuck it round his shoulders. Bring his lower elbow FORWARD.

"HEALTH", the Official Bulletin of the Department of Health is available free to those who are interested in healthy living. If you belong to any women's organisation ask your secretary about it, if not, send your address to the Editor, Box 5013, Wellington.

ISSUED BY THE DEPARTMENT OF HEALTH   12.48

Plunket and the Health Department had long advised parents against allowing babies to sleep on their stomachs. This poster was issued in 1948 and reproduced in newspapers and magazines around New Zealand.

nant.[113] At three and six months breastfeeding rates were substantially higher among Pacific Islanders and Europeans than among Maori.[114]

Bed sharing was another modifiable risk factor identified by the New Zealand Cot Death Study.[115] This aroused debate among epidemiologists, and within the Maori and Pacific Island communities. Isolating bed sharing as a risk factor was queried by others such as the British *Sunday Times* which quoted leading scientists' claims that cot deaths were virtually unknown across 95 per cent of the world where infants generally slept close to their mothers.[116] Professor Barry Taylor, a paediatrician at the Otago Medical School and president of Paediatric Society of New Zealand, also pointed out that people in Japan and Hong Kong routinely shared beds with infants, yet their mortality rate from cot death was low.[117] It was generally agreed, however, that bed sharing, when associated with smoking, increased risks.

In 2001 Taylor called for the establishment of a database after Wellington coroner Garry Evans found bed sharing to be the common factor in three recent infant deaths. Speaking as a children's advocate, Taylor declared, 'It is absolutely necessary. If we don't have it, we are doing our children a disservice.' Dawn Elder, a consultant paediatrician with Wellington's Capital Coast Health, who wrote a comprehensive report for the coroner, also lamented that New Zealand's paediatricians had little data on topics such as how many babies were routinely sharing beds safely.[118]

Plunket nurses were ideally placed for data collection. Educated on risk factors, they were asked to identify high-risk families for 'more effective intervention'.[119] They were also involved in the three-year cot death study mentioned above, which Plunket proudly noted 'first identified risk factors', and another two-year National Cot Death Prevention Study 1991–3. In 1994 a 'SIDS risk factor study' was contracted to Plunket by the Public Health Commission, and 39,000 infants were surveyed by the nurses.[120] Plunket staff were also said to be 'front-line workers in the battle against SIDS by reinforcing risk factors to clients'. In 1995 Plunket joined forces with a Maori health promotion group, Hauora Runanga, and other health professional groups in the Wairarapa to educate the public. A study there had shown that, in the previous year, one in three women had smoked during pregnancy.[121]

Meanwhile, through their personal involvement with new mothers, Plunket nurses also found themselves in the role of counsellors in cases of

This photograph appeared in the Society's annual report for 1995/6, in a section headed 'Neighbourhood Support and Community Networks'.

cot death. From the 1980s they were given in-service training to deal with this situation, though they were already active in this area. Family Centres and local Plunket groups set up support groups. One such group, organised by the Pakuranga Plunket Committee, was reported in the press under the heading, 'Mothers, you're not alone':

> The idea of a support group came after a mother in the area who had lost a child in a cot death was unable to sleep because of anxiety about her new baby. The Plunket nurse arranged for someone to come in to babysit while the mother slept and the benefit was so obvious that it was decided to provide a service for mothers in need. A small group of mothers was formed to assist with anything from emotional problems, housework, transport, to helping with language difficulties for someone new to the country.[122]

Immunisation

In the areas of child abuse and cot death, paediatricians attempted to identify at-risk groups, and to modify parental behaviour accordingly. Attempts to persuade parents to act in a certain way for the protection of their children were also applied to immunisation, where it was believed that parents were either wilfully or inadvertently failing in their duty. Again, paediatricians saw themselves as children's advocates, and in this role they were fully supported and backed by the Plunket Society.

Begg's gentle persuasion-by-example approach to public health was gradually replaced by a move towards compulsion. Geddis noted, in his first annual report as Plunket's Medical Director in 1978, that 'the debate continues as to whether some form of financial inducement should be offered to parents to encourage them to ensure that children are protected. Sadly, it seems as though there may be no other way.'[123] The 1979 IYC Child and Health Committee studied ways of making the family benefit dependent upon up-to-date immunisation, looking to France and Canada as models.[124] In 1983, 1123 mothers of five-year-old children participating in the Christchurch Child Development Study were asked whether the family benefit should be linked to immunisation, and two-thirds agreed.[125] A 1986 *New Zealand Listener* article argued that it would be hard to find a health worker who did not agree. The writer cited Professor of Paediatrics Bob Elliott: 'I'm all for a few draconian measures. We've tried the velvet glove approach.'[126] This suggestion was never enacted and the benefit was abolished in 1991. But the debate over whether parents on income support should be 'encouraged' to have their children immunised continued.[127]

In 1988 the Paediatric Society of New Zealand suggested to the Minister of Health that no child should be admitted to school or pre-school without a document indicating that the child had been immunised or a declaration signed by the parents that they had chosen not to have their child immunised.[128] This was introduced by the Public Health Commission in 1995 under regulations which specified that early childhood centres and primary schools must ask parents to give them a copy of the immunisation certificate for children born after January 1995. Entry to these educational services was not dependent on immunisation, though unimmunised children could be excluded from schools during epidemics. Compulsory immunisation was rejected in favour of a requirement to select.

Many continued to slip through the net, however, which led paediatricians to demand a national register. This was advocated in 1979 by the newly appointed head of the Paediatrics Department at Auckland Medical School, Professor John Dower, formerly of the University of California, who claimed that New Zealand was about ten years behind the rest of the developed world in preventive health care for children. In particular he referred to New Zealand's poor immunisation record, noting that he still saw measles cases 'that should be unheard of in developed countries'. He advocated a computerised immunisation register as in Britain.[129] Twenty years later health specialists were 'infuriated' when the government rejected the latest call for a national immunisation database to track children.[130] Dr Nikki Turner, the Immunisation Advisory Centre Medical Director, advocated a central database to show which children had been vaccinated.[131] In 1999 the National government gave $135,000 for an integrated child health information system in Hamilton and Rotorua, but rejected a call for a national database. Regional health authorities were urged to form their own networks to keep track of children.[132]

The Plunket Society continued to offer support in local immunisation drives. In 1979 Hassall headed a Stamp out Measles campaign, in association with the Health Department. Plunket volunteers were mobilised to knock on doors, ask parents whether their children had been immunised and, if not, invite them to do so at a local clinic the following week. Apart from attacking measles – described as far more serious than people assumed – it was hoped the campaign would heighten awareness of immunisation against other diseases, such as polio, whooping cough, diphtheria and tetanus. By July 1979 about 20,000 children had been

The Immunisation Advisory Centre, founded in 1997, was supported by Plunket.

immunised against measles as a result of the campaign; this comprised 10 per cent of the one to five age group and 25 per cent of those previously unimmunised. Hassall enthused, 'If we relate this to recently published complication rates it means that at least 1000 children will not suffer from middle-ear infection – 800 will be spared pneumonia, 100 will not have convulsions, 20 will be protected from brain injury and the deaths of 5 children will be prevented as a result of campaign.'[133]

Reporting on the 1987 meningococcal meningitis campaign, Plunket's Director of Nursing Services Anne Cressey commended the input of volunteers: 'This type of programme highlights the value of having the support of a large team of women who create a permanent network that can be quickly and easily mobilised'.[134] The following year she noted that the Plunket Society had given high priority to the mass hepatitis B immunisation campaigns, and that voluntary members of the society had provided 'excellent backup and support'. Again, she stressed the importance of a permanent network of women, facilitated by Plunket.[135]

Anne Cressey also pointed out during the 1987 meningitis campaign that 'much media attention and misinformation' had been circulated relating to the disease and to immunisation. As a result, Plunket nurses had devoted 'countless hours of clinic and telephone time to answering queries on immunisation'.[136] They continued to support immunisation in the face of opposition such as that from Erwin Albert, spokesperson for the Vaccination Information Network, who argued that, 'Parents can, as always, freely choose whether to have their children injected with vaccines, a medical intervention we consider irresponsibly dangerous and of no proven benefit'.[137]

In 1995 a Plunket survey of several thousand children found that children particularly at risk of missing out on some of their immunisations were those born into already large, especially Maori and Pacific Island, families.[138] South Auckland continued to have one of the worst records. From 1979 to 1990, during which time Plunket was responsible for monitoring the health of all children under the age of five in South Auckland, Plunket nurses immunised the children and this led to a temporary increase in immunisation.[139] This, however, was not sustained. By the late 1990s immunisation rates were 56–76 per cent, compared with national rates of 83–87 per cent. Pam Williams, former principal Plunket nurse in South Auckland, attributed this to the fact that although immunisations were free, families often avoided GPs because they owed money from previous visits.[140] Health researcher Joy Simpson, who compiled a report on South Auckland in the late 1990s, pointed out that communicable diseases such as meningitis, measles, whooping cough and bronchial illnesses had all increased, particularly among Pacific Island families, and that the rates of some diseases equalled Third World levels.[141] Dower had declared in 1979 that measles should be unheard of in a developed country; a *Metro* reporter still found cases in South Auckland's Middlemore Hospital in 2000. The hospital's CEO, David Clark, informed the reporter that South Auckland's immunisation figures were 50 per cent compared with 72 per cent nationally.[142] In 1999 another report noted that New Zealand was lagging behind world immunisation rates for potentially fatal diseases such as measles and mumps. The immunisation rate for measles was 70 per cent, well below the WHO target of 90 per cent.[143] Plunket's networks were failing in some areas.

Accidents

Although the prevention of childhood accidents had been a longstanding concern, it was an area in which New Zealand's performance appeared to be lagging behind other countries. Geddis pointed out in 1985 that 'we continue to kill more children in accidents of various kinds than die from all other causes put together'.[144] The 1982 Board of Health report stated that accidents were currently one of the most important problems for child health. Not only were they the commonest cause of death in children over the age of one year, they accounted for 22 per cent of hospital admissions in the one to fifteen age group and around one in five children in the cities visited their local hospital each year as a result of an accident, often causing 'profound psychological effects'.[145] Geddis commented that 'the events are not "without apparent cause, unexpected, unforeseen or chance happenings" [dictionary definition]; rather they are events that happen for fairly predictable reasons in fairly predictable circumstances'.[146] Accidents have been a relatively neglected subject in historical research yet recent studies

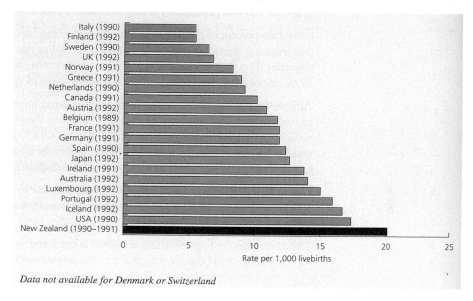

Italy (1990)
Finland (1992)
Sweden (1990)
UK (1992)
Norway (1991)
Greece (1991)
Netherlands (1990)
Canada (1991)
Austria (1992)
Belgium (1989)
France (1991)
Germany (1991)
Spain (1990)
Japan (1992)
Ireland (1991)
Australia (1992)
Luxembourg (1992)
Portugal (1992)
Iceland (1992)
USA (1990)
New Zealand (1990–1991)

0   5   10   15   20   25

Rate per 1,000 livebirths

Data not available for Denmark or Switzerland

In the early 1990s New Zealand had the poorest record of all 23 OECD countries for deaths due to unintentional injury for children aged 1–4. *Our Health, Our Future,* 1994

have found them to be socially and politically based, rather than 'natural' or 'neutral', as often assumed.[147] Advocates of child health saw accidents as a visual indicator of children's low status in society and as an issue demanding social and individual responsibility.

From the 1940s Helen Deem had advocated safety features for electric kettles and fire guards, with displays of available brands at Plunket rooms. Playpens were advocated as a safety measure.[148] Neil Begg focused on teaching parents safety in the home: the community had 'added greatly to the hazards of the toddler, and has not yet achieved the responsibility to legislate for his safety . . . so the responsibility devolves as a rule on the harassed mother'.[149] In 1976 the Accident Compensation Corporation set up the New Zealand Home Safety Advisory Council with Neil Begg as chair.[150] By the 1980s the focus had changed from restricting children's activities to providing a child-safe environment. Playpens, for example, were no longer socially acceptable; 'children must learn to adapt to the world, and exploration of their natural environment is to be encouraged'.[151] In 1980 a competition was launched with the goal of creating a child-safe environment. Called Design for Life: An AHI (Alex Harvey Industries Ltd)/ Plunket Community Project, its aim was to design a Plunket-Karitane family support unit that could double as a family home and would incorporate

Don't let <u>Flowing</u> garments
become <u>Flaming</u>
garments!

This 1960s Health Department poster chillingly illustrated the dangerous combination of nightdresses and unguarded electric heaters.

Tragedy can happen in a
split second!

features to prevent home accidents. Plunket's first purpose-built Family Centre in Rose Road, Grey Lynn, Auckland, used the winning design; it was opened in 1982.[152]

Just as the Plunket Society had funded visits from child abuse and cot death experts, so too in 1990 it invited an expert in childhood accidents, Professor Leif Svanstrom of Sweden. He outlined a community-based accident prevention programme that had cut injuries to those under three years old by 43 per cent.[153] Four years later, another expert, Dr Mike Hayes, director of the British Child Accident Prevention Trust, was invited to speak to the Plunket Society. This trust had been set up in 1976 specifically to lobby for legislative change to prevent accidents.[154] Hayes pointed out that approaches to accident prevention included first, education, second, modifying products, homes and playgrounds through engineering and environmental measures, and third, the introduction and enforcement of legislation, standards and codes of good practice, both nationally and through local by-laws.[155] Plunket was already abandoning Begg's gentle persuasion in favour of this three-pronged attack.

This purpose-built Plunket Family Support Centre at Grey Lynn in Auckland incorporated special safety features. It was the winning design in a contest, 'Design for Life: An AHI (Alex Harvey Industries Ltd)/Plunket Community Project'. Dr Ian Hassall is standing on the far left of the picture. Courtesy Ian Hassall.

From the 1960s attention had been drawn to the pre-school mortality rate from road accidents. The 1968 Plunket conference resolved that 'young mothers be made fully aware of the dangers of travelling with young children unharnessed in the front seat of the car'.[156] In the 1970s it was revealed that, although the pre-school mortality rate for motor vehicle accidents had been approximately the same in Sweden and New Zealand in 1959, Sweden had now halved its rate while New Zealand's had more than doubled.[157] Concern extended beyond the mortality statistics: a 1970s study of victims of motor vehicle accidents suggested that the emotional effects were often protracted.[158] Plunket decided to take up the issue and used its vast networks of volunteers to conduct a survey in 1979. Stationed on street corners throughout the country, they observed nearly 18,000 children travelling in cars. Their findings revealed that approximately one-third of infants under six months of age sat in the most dangerous position, on an adult's knee in the front seat. Over a quarter of all children aged between six months and four years sat unrestrained in the front seat and, as many observers noted, this frequently meant the child was sitting forwards on the seat with his or her face close to the dashboard and windscreen.[159] A Parliamentary Select Committee on Road Safety reacted to these findings by encouraging further efforts to educate parents.[160] The Traffic Department subsequently undertook an educational programme, assessed by Plunket in 1980. This time volunteers observed 21,000 children, and the results were much the same as before, suggesting that education was not enough.[161]

Because the cost and availability of child car restraints were identified as major problems, in 1981 Plunket launched a pilot child car seat rental scheme in Dunedin.[162] Within weeks, retailers of child car seats throughout the country reported increased sales owing to the publicity. Plunket itself contributed to that publicity. By early 1982, it had distributed 150,000 copies of a leaflet promoting child car seats.[163] Local Plunket committees did not wait for the results of the Dunedin pilot before setting up their own schemes: over 100 had started by 1982.[164] Two years later Plunket owned 14,000 car seats, worth $1.2 million and sufficient for 22 per cent of New Zealand children. Plunket president Myra Graham claimed that the failure to provide a child restraint was now socially unacceptable.[165] A decade later the number available had reached 36,000, with 280 voluntary committees operating the schemes.[166]

In 1986, following his return from an international conference, Geddis noted that New Zealand's scheme had been copied in several parts of Australia, and in England and Scotland. Its success had been marked by a congratulatory editorial in the American journal *Pediatrics* in which the editor noted that there was nothing comparable in the United States.[167] Geddis attributed the success of the New Zealand scheme to the Plunket network. After attending the first World Conference in Accident and Injury Prevention (1989), Geddis boasted, 'Clearly we are far advanced in the area of car seat rental schemes.'[168]

Plunket also lobbied to extend legislation relating to compulsory use of child seat belts, passing a resolution to that effect as its 1976 conference. At that time only children over the age of eight were legally required to wear a seat belt in the car, if one was fitted.[169] Plunket continued to pass resolutions,[170] and to lobby for change until new regulations were issued

Keith Hay, of Keith Hay Homes, surrounded by the 100 car seats his firm donated to Plunket. Plunket President Joan Hunt can be seen talking to guests behind Hay's right shoulder. Plunket Society Annual Report, 1988–89

in 1984 specifiying that children under eight had to wear a seat belt if sitting in the front seat.[171] Despite these regulations, a study of car restraint use among Auckland children three years later found that only 36 per cent of the sample was safely restrained. Reasons given for non-compliance included driver complacency and the cost and unavailability of child car seats.[172]

In 1993 further road traffic regulations were issued. Although the law remained the same for children aged five to fifteen – they had to use a seat belt if one was available or else travel in the rear seat – children under five were now required to use an appropriate child restraint. The new regulations applied to children under two years of age from 1 April 1994 and for children under five years of age from 1 April 1995.[173]

Despite Plunket's efforts to provide cheap rental child car seats, and the new regulations, some children were still unrestrained in cars. In 1996 Plunket's National Safety Adviser, Sue Campbell, began an educational campaign for Pacific Islanders, after it was discovered from hospital admissions that they were three times more likely than other children to be injured as an occupant in a car.[174] A 1998 survey of child car seat use in the Northland town of Kaikohe discovered that eight out of ten Kaikohe children travelled unrestrained. The results appalled the organiser of Kaikohe's Plunket car sear scheme, who attributed it to parental laziness. Plunket seats could be rented for $36 a year, with a negotiable bond, and help was also available through the Income Support Service. When a similar survey was conducted in the South Auckland suburb of Otara over a weekend the same year, out of 56 cars stopped, 53 contained children who were not strapped in.[175] Nor had the situation improved by 2001. Road deaths still accounted for 40 per cent of child deaths from accidental injury, and 60 per cent of those were passengers (the rest were pedestrians).[176] Northland had one of the worst rates of accidental child death in the developed world and road traffic injuries constituted the leading cause of the deaths.[177] By this time it was still estimated that, nationwide, only around 75 per cent of children were effectively restrained while travelling in cars.[178]

Plunket also took up the issue of water safety. In 1976 the society was invited to join the newly formed New Zealand Water Safety Council, on the basis that more Plunket members were involved in water safety issues than any other group represented.[179] In the 1980s Plunket began to lobby for the compulsory fencing of swimming pools. In 1980 a Local Government Amendment Act gave local authorities the power to legislate on the fencing of swimming pools, and the Safety Standards Association of New Zealand issued a model by-law. Geddis noted in 1982, when seventeen drownings had been recorded for the previous year, 'The issue is a simple one of little toddlers, mostly under the age of 3, falling into man-made holes in the ground and drowning. Yet some have seen in the proposed campaign to prevent such tragedies a threat to the basic fabric of our free society.'[180]

The 1984 national Plunket conference passed a remit urging the central government to pass legislation to make swimming pool fencing mandatory. Speaking to the remit, Mrs V. Mutton of Te Puke pointed out that accidents were the biggest cause of death of one- to four-year-olds, a third of these were drownings and half occurred in private swimming pools. She noted that only 50 of the 232 local authorities had enacted a by-law. Even where legislation existed, in some cases it was not enforced and in others the fences did not meet the standards set by the Safety Standards Association of New Zealand.[181]

A debate at one county council meeting in late 1982, which ended in the councillors voting four to three against a by-law, illustrated the objections. These included the additional regulations and controls involved, the many other hazards that would remain outside any regulation, the fact that no regulations could absolutely guarantee a child's safety and the difficulty of implementing by-laws. Commenting on the debate, the editor of the *Otago Daily Times* wondered whether there was 'an element of hysteria in singling out private pools as a target for administrative controls', but countered this with statistics showing New Zealand had a child drowning rate of 9.5 per 100,000 children, while the international average was 4.9. The editor pointed out that between 1979 and 1981, 32 out of 61 drownings occurred in private swimming pools, and that experience had shown that in parts of Australia, Sweden and the west coast of the United States the figures for pre-school drownings had dropped sharply following the introduction of mandatory fencing.[182]

During 1983 a bipartisan parliamentary committee investigated the high number of drownings of pre-schoolers and concluded that the adequate fencing of swimming pools was the only satisfactory means of prevention. It recommended, however, that responsibility should remain with local authorities.[183] Others disagreed. In May 1983 the Plunket Society conducted interviews throughout New Zealand with 8430 parents of one- to three-year-olds and found that 36 per cent of these children had access to pools, either on their own property or that of an immediate neighbour. Sixty-three per cent of the pools had no safety features. The survey further showed that 88 per cent of the interviewees were in favour of mandatory fencing.[184] Other surveys in Christchurch, Auckland and Wanganui showed that 86 per cent, 65 per cent and 80 per cent respectively of those interviewed favoured swimming pool fencing legislation.[185]

Finally, in 1987, the Labour government legislated for the compulsory fencing of swimming pools. Yet Hassall continued to lament the failure to achieve universal compliance.[186] The first prosecution for failing to fence in a private swimming pool was reported in Plunket's *Newsletter* in December 1989. A Huntly man was charged with manslaughter under the act and fined $1,000 when a neighbour's two-year-old daughter drowned in his pool. The newsletter noted that when members of the Plunket Society publicly criticised the attitudes of owners who failed to fence their pools, the latter retorted that guardians should take full responsibility for their children.[187]

A Plunket Society newsletter specifically devoted to child safety continued to draw attention to the incidence of pre-schoolers drowning.[188] Thousands of copies of a 'Keep Kids Safe Near Water' poster were issued, and a watching eye was kept on the fencing of pools. A Water Safety Council study in 1997 found that more than half of the country's 57,000 privately owned pools were still not fenced. Its director, Alan Muir, did not think this had changed much by 1999 when two Auckland lawyers escaped a manslaughter charge after an infant drowned in the pool of their rented property.[189] Yet the High Court later found the Auckland City Council at fault and that might have had a salutary effect on Auckland and others councils.[190] Increasingly the enclosure of pools became accepted as just another local authority building safety requirement.

Plunket lobbied hard for fencing around swimming pools. Plunket Society Annual Report 1993–94

Plunket had long seen itself as a watchdog on safety issues, lobbying authorities on matters such as fencing around state houses in the 1950s, the labelling of flammable children's nightwear and the import of Proban treated fabrics from the 1960s, and the introduction of child-resistant caps on medicines from the 1970s.[191] The society often used overseas examples to advance its cause; for instance, it was noted in 1976 that all aspirin and paracetamol sold in Britain had to be in child-resistant containers, a regulation that had reduced childhood poisonings by 30 per cent in a single year.[192] Two decades later they were still pressing for the mandatory use of child-resistant caps on medicines.[193] Although this was subsequently achieved, the society continued to stress parental education. Sue Campbell warned parents not to assume that any item with a child-resistant device was safe, and to keep all medicines, lighters and matches in a locked cupboard out of reach of children.[194]

In 1983 the new post of Marketing Officer (Child Safety) was created at Plunket's head office and local voluntary safety officers were appointed.[195] In the 1990s, when accidental injuries were still responsible for 42 per cent of all deaths between the ages of one and four,[196] Plunket launched a nationwide child safety campaign, with finance from the Public Health Commission. Based on a model devised by the WHO and used in Sweden from the 1970s, it aimed to motivate community groups to reduce hazards. In September 1997 Plunket joined other agencies in organising the country's first ever Kidsafe Week. The campaign, which became an annual event, focused on the prevention of unintentional injury, such as trampoline injuries, burns and scalds and road safety around schools.[197] Despite these efforts, a 2001 report by the United Nations Children's Fund, UNICEF, showed that New Zealand ranked 22 in a list of 26 OECD countries in terms of child injury death rates among children aged one to fourteen. The director of Kidsafe, which was run from Auckland's Starship Hospital, argued that New Zealand had to look seriously at reducing its child injury death rates through legislation, and regulate to create safer environments for children to travel, live and play in. She believed the UNICEF report was a 'timely wake-up call, which we as a country must heed'.[198] Despite Plunket's efforts, much clearly remained to be done.

Preventive paediatrics at the close of the century

Community paediatricians aligned themselves with others in a modern child protection movement.[199] Their focus on child health politicised them.

As Ian Hassall and Dr Russell Wills, then National Paediatrician for the Plunket Society, wrote in a 2000 paper entitled 'Advocacy for the General Paediatrician', 'Advocacy *is* our business, we are good at it and it is our belief that we, as paediatricians should be doing more of it.'[200]

In 2000 Dr Nikki Turner issued a 'Call for Action' to all child health providers, seeking to 'encourage all of New Zealand to participate in improving child health – from the personal to the community to the political level'. She referred to the United Nations Convention on the Rights of the Child which New Zealand signed in 1993; this spelled out the rights of children to survival, protection and development.[201] In her view, people 'should be yelling and screaming about the country's lousy record . . . We are ignoring our children. We have children with permanent brain damage from iron deficiency, dying from vaccine-preventable diseases, teeth falling out by the age of five, school dropouts from unrecognised deafness, children landing up as criminals and on the scrapheap.'[202] Other paediatricians were equally incensed by society's apparent indifference. In 1997 Dr Pat Tuohy, appointed as Plunket's National Paediatrician in 1992 in succession to Geddis, claimed that the perception of New Zealand as a good place to bring up children was a myth, since it had poorer child health statistics than several countries considered to be less free and more polluted: 'Children in New Zealand do have freedom but it is a freedom to be killed on the roads, to die from meningitis or rheumatic fever, or to be deafened by glue ear'. Further, he maintained, 'the lack of adequate parenting education for parents ultimately leads to our high rates of child abuse, youth offending, truancy and childhood injury'.[203]

Plunket volunteers had been heavily involved with infant car seat rental schemes, immunisation programmes, lobbying for legislation and enforcement relating to swimming pool fencing and other safety issues, support groups surrounding cot deaths, and research into preventive child health issues. Plunket nurses and Family Centres worked to monitor infant death, collect data for research purposes and offer support to new parents. Yet despite these endeavours Plunket was no longer the focal point of a country proud of its infant health record. Addressing the 1995 national Plunket conference, Hassall's successor as the Commissioner for Children, lawyer Laurie O'Reilly, urged the society to extend its role as an advocate for children: 'Maybe Plunket needs to be more upfront and confident about its track record and demand more resources'.[204]

CHAPTER 9

Plunket Nursing Services in the Late Twentieth Century

The nurses' view

By the 1980s the seventeen-week Plunket-nurse training course consisted of 350 hours of theory and 150 hours of supervised Plunket district nursing. Theory included child development (including 'Denver' developmental screening, which was introduced in 1979), common childhood disease, psychology and sociology of the family, parentcraft, community facilities, and sessions on multicultural diversity, child abuse, SIDS and alcoholism affecting the child and the family.[1] A conscious effort was made to break down barriers between nurses and their 'clients', or to 'de-professionalise' the nurses. In the mid-1980s the Plunket nurse uniform was discarded. The nurse was to assume the role of friend and facilitator.[2]

To many formerly uniformed Plunket nurses there was nothing new in this: they had simply learnt on the job. They were well aware that they were guests in their clients' houses and would soon be shown the door if they were not welcome. For many the encounter was interactive. For example, 'Rosaleen' remembered how, just after she graduated as a Plunket nurse in 1957, the mothers would sometimes laugh at her if she was too dogmatic about 'sticking to the book' (*Modern Mothercraft*), declaring that

The front cover of a 1970s Plunket recruitment booklet. Plunket Society, Auckland Branch archives

babies never stuck to rules. 'They'd tell me "You'll learn as you mature", and I did.'[3] 'Mary', another Plunket nurse who trained in the 1960s, claimed, 'My mothers were my best teachers. They always told me what had worked for them hoping I would pass it on to other people.'[4] After working for Plunket for 37 years, Eunice Ingold said, 'You can never underestimate how much mothers know. They're the true experts.'[5]

The nurses knew that mothers did not always follow their advice. As Plunket nurse Val Jones later explained, some mothers did deviate from her advice, though they often did not admit to it.[6] Plunket nurse Joan Meyer recalled that the best reference she ever had was that, 'they tell me around here they don't have to tell lies to you'. She also noted that mothers talked freely to her: 'I could have written a book,' she said.[7]

For some nurses Plunket was more than a job. 'Joan', who qualified in 1947, reflected, 'The best thing about Plunket was the friendships I made with the mothers. They were wonderful to me. Mothers I knew stop me today and talk to me . . . . Plunket was my life.' She was one of those nurses who sometimes took the baby home overnight to give the mother a break,

Plunket dress has become markedly less formal over the years.
TOP LEFT: Uniformed nurses, c. 1960. BOTTOM LEFT: Plunket nurse Eunice Ingold (left) at the Plunket family centre, Landscape Road, Mt Eden, Auckland, October 1994, with Alice Bulmer, her sons Albert and Tom Bannister, and Matthew Egbers. Plunket Society, Auckland Branch archives

Plunket nurses were true community figures. When Sister V. Ballance visited her new home in 1964, local committee members and their numerous children turned out to greet her. *Plunket News*, 1964

though she admitted that she always worried with someone else's baby in her care. She remembered the first time – she was up and down all night checking on the baby.[8] 'Gwen', who joined the service in 1978, foreshadowed Plunketline, 'I always gave my home phone number to all my mothers. Often I could help with phone advice . . . One of the advantages of being single, no husband to complain.'[9] Cressey noted that mothers always had access to Plunket nurses' after hours phone numbers.[10]

In rural New Zealand, Plunket nurses were respected community figures. 'Alma', who moved from the city to a farm in the 1980s and continued Plunket nursing on a part-time basis, recounted her rural experiences: 'The Plunket Nurse was someone in the community. "Our Plunket nurse", you were called . . . These women worked hard and many of them were lonely so they enjoyed a chat with the Plunket nurse.'[11] 'Iris', who nursed in rural central North Island and then Central Otago, gave an example of her multiple functions: 'I'd walk in the door and they'd say, "Nurse, the baby's okay but could you help us with the children's correspondence lessons?" So, I'd do a bit of both, check the baby and help with the correspondence lessons.'[12] 'Joan' worked on the West Coast of the South Island: 'Often I'd do shopping for the people who lived down there.' She stayed overnight on sheep stations as she travelled about, and found the people very hospitable. 'One lady asked, "Would you like a cup of tea?" "I've just had one," I said. "You always have time for everyone but me," she replied. I learned that I'd have to drink a cup of tea at every house.' She also flew once a month from Hokitika to Haast on a two-seater plane. 'We'd sit around and talk and laugh while I weighed and checked the babies. It was very nice. I stayed a couple of nights . . . There was no doctor down there . . . I think they came to see me because it was someone coming in from

Plunket reached out to the entire community. Here we see a Plunket nurse negotiating a remote rural landscape as part of her daily routine.
Plunket Society Annual Report 1987–88

Plunket nurse Robyn Dodds visits Ruia Hanuera-Brown, in remote Kaiwaka, Northland, 2000.
Plunket Society Archives

outside to see them and talk to them.'[13] 'Rosaleen', who also worked on the West Coast in the 1950s, was always given a pub lunch at Totara Flat on her visit there, though she had no idea who paid. She remembered visiting Stillwater during a storm, after which the local mill manager walked in front of her with a chainsaw to clear the road. 'Lorry drivers from the mill always looked out for us on home visiting days in case we were having problems with the car.' In the town area, she had the use of a dilapidated bicycle. She hoped that someone would steal it so that the committee would have to buy her a new one, but no one did. 'I suppose it would've been a rotten thing to do in the eyes of the community, pinching the Plunket nurse's bike.'[14] 'Gwen' explained, 'I liked working in country areas. I loved the friendly, welcoming people. Also it was a challenge. Kept you on your toes. A number of families were miles from the nearest doctor. Many times a Plunket or Public Health Nurse was the first person to see or diagnose an urgent situation.'[15]

In urban areas, too, Plunket nurses were frontline primary health workers. As Frieda Massey, a Plunket nurse in Auckland from 1967 to 1986 and Nurse Adviser for the Auckland area from 1970 to 1975, explained, 'We get to meet a very wide range of people, and for some, we may be the only visitor a mother has for days.'[16] Plunket nurses were well aware that needy mothers were not confined to any one socio-economic or cultural group. As 'Mary', part-Maori and with experience working in South Auckland from the 1960s to the 1980s, noted, 'A number of middle-class European mothers were anxious and lacked confidence.' She believed their need for help was just as great as that of Polynesians.[17] 'Judy', who worked in Auckland's more affluent areas in the 1970s and 1980s, recalled plenty of unsettled babies and stressed mothers: 'One woman rang the same time every night with some worry about the children. They'd ring because they were worried about their children, their husbands were working and they felt they had no one to turn to.'[18]

The nurses became involved with more practical problems when visiting poorer families. A 1984 *New Zealand Woman's Weekly* article noted that in some homes, 'Plunket is the only outside help tolerated'. In the words of Plunket's Director of Nursing Services, Anne Kerley (shortly to be Anne Cressey), 'Roll a social worker, housing officer, arbitrator, chauffeur, home economist, nurse and friend into just one person and you'll get an idea of the work the nurses do.' According to the *Woman's Weekly* journalist, it was the nurses' own descriptions of their work which 'explode[d] the myths about Plunket'. Besides nursing, along with their local supporters they set up play groups, ran mother support groups, gave talks on child health, petitioned the Housing Corporation and referred children and parents for specialist medical care.[19] One nurse commented that, as unemployment increased and general practitioner services became more expensive, parents often contacted her instead of the doctor. This nurse's other activities included writing letters in support of housing applications and dealing with council health inspectors over such problems as leaking toilets, rats, holes in the floor, 'mainly on behalf of people who have little command of English and less understanding of their landlords' responsibilities!'[20]

The contract Plunket was given by the government in 1977 to oversee the health of all under-five-year-olds in South Auckland was a real challenge to the nurses. A Plunket training school was set up in the area. About a third of the population of the area were Maori or Pacific Islanders and usually at the lower end of the socio-economic scale.[21] Under the contract

The Plunket Society has always been proud of its ability to maintain links with its clients. This photograph of the Patel family was captioned 'Every member of this fine Dannevirke family has been under Plunket supervision'. *Plunket News*, 1964

the number of nurses in the area increased from 30 to 54 in the first year, so that the number of babies under the care of each nurse dropped from 154 to 88. By 1988, there were 71 Plunket nurses in South Auckland. The contract was renewed three times, before it was absorbed into a national contract in 1991, when the number of nurses was reduced to 32.[22]

Some nurses coped better than others with this challenge. 'Patty', who was in the first batch of South Auckland trainees, commented that some left to work in other areas because they could not cope with the cultural differences. She stayed for over ten years. She recalled meeting members of the Mongrel Mob gang during her first week at work. 'I think if you don't try to be high and mighty and work at the same level that people are and talk in the same language they accept you. It's when you try to lord it over people that their backs go up. They don't like it. I learned to speak in a way people in the area understood.'[23] 'Mary', who worked in South Auckland for ten years from 1978 to 1988, explained her strategy of introducing herself by her tribal affiliation of Ngatiawa: 'They never questioned this in spite of my white skin, blonde hair and green eyes. Some families made me an honorary Auntie Mary, I was flattered and pleased.' She found Mongrel Mob members allied with her in persuading mothers not to take the babies to the pub. 'They'd take the baby to the pub for everyone to see. The baby would get overtired with all the handling, not feed well and lose weight. The Mongrel Mob would say, "You do as the nurse says and stay home."' She explained that they showed her respect because they were used to respecting the public health nurse who had looked after Maori family health in rural areas. When she visited Chinese and Indian families she would help their children with homework. The Indian families were very hospitable, sometimes inviting her to lunch on her rounds. She accepted this as an excellent way of getting to know their culture.[24]

Plunket nurses were aware of the practical problems many of the mothers faced, such as lack of transport. As 'Patty' explained, 'We'd pile them into our small Plunket Minis and take them to the hospital for their checks . . . Often we'd take them to the doctor for immunisations. We'd wait and drive them back again. I guess that took up a lot of our time, but we felt it was worth it.' She recalled the efforts that went into ensuring children were immunised in the 1970s and 1980s: 'Doing door-to-door knocking, having special immunisation days at clinics, driving families to these clinics, setting up immunisation caravans in streets . . . .'[25]

'Felicity', who trained as a Plunket nurse in South Auckland in 1984, noted a dilemma for some mothers she encountered: 'If you're a mother faced with a sick child and there's no food on the table, do you go and get your prescription filled or do you buy a loaf of bread? These were some of the awful things these poor mothers faced every single day of their life.' She was clearly impressed by their abilities and firmly believed that her own involvement helped: 'Some didn't know how to access a system. If you were there to go with them or speak on their behalf to Social Welfare or Housing Corps it made all the difference.' She became involved with the Child Protection Team for South Auckland, which posed some problems for her: 'Some families distrusted you if you brought in Social Welfare. They felt you had betrayed them and it was very difficult for you to work with them and give help.'[26] Others found their involvement in this delicate situation more appreciated. One nurse explained, 'When the child was brought to the house I had to be there as an observer to note how the father treated the child. The mother relied on me a lot. She'd come to the Clinic when I was there and tell me her troubles.'[27]

In 1984 Cressey noted how hard it was to maintain staffing levels in South Auckland. Nurses were demoralised by the number who did not turn up for appointments. There were practical problems such as a shortage of cars, which forced some nurses to do their rounds on foot. Dogs were a constant nuisance, as 'they do insist on biting Nurses, sometimes quite severely'.[28] The following year she reported that six nurses had been bitten at fortnightly intervals: one was a severe bite on the buttocks. Another nurse who had been attacked by three dogs required numerous sutures to bites on both arms and a leg, and lost the feeling in one hand.[29] In 1990 it was reported that at least one nurse was bitten each month and one nurse had recently been bailed up in the doorway of an Otara house for an hour and a half before being rescued by a neighbour. South Auckland Principal Nurse Pam Williams said some houses in the area were no longer being visited because of the dogs. Because many of these homes did not have a telephone there was no way of calling the mothers before the visit.[30] Vandalism of clinics was another problem: one clinic suffered at least one break-in a month.[31] There was also solvent abuse: nurses experienced some unpleasant situations when teenagers (up to 20 at a time) gathered outside Plunket clinics to sniff solvents. Police were called on several occasions. Involvement in child abuse and neglect cases placed added pressures on the nurses and their time, requiring referrals, attendance at case conferences and court and follow-ups. Cressey also sensed the frustration of the nurses that, despite their efforts, New Zealand was dropping behind in the league of infant mortality statistics, to a position below 20 other countries, and South Auckland was among the worst in New Zealand. For example, 45 per cent of cot deaths occurring in the Greater Auckland area during 1984 were South Auckland infants. Nurses recognised the problems as socio-economic, and felt frustrated at their inability to help.[32]

The nurses' problems were analysed by an English paediatric pathologist Professor John Emery during his 1986 visit to New Zealand. He wrote to Geddis, 'Not only are all of the nurses stretched to the limit but they realise that they are not able to control the situation and supply help where it is greatly needed.'[33] He commented on the high 'burn out' rate among Plunket nurses, which reached one in three each year in South Auckland. He understood that only one of a recent intake of ten survived a year, and personal domestic matters such as marriage, pregnancy and husbands moving jobs accounted for only a small proportion. He compared this with Sheffield, where the health visitor turnover was about 10 per cent per year, with only 1–2 per cent giving up because of the work. He concluded, 'The Plunket nurses are a remarkable, well trained and intelligent group of women – devoted both to children and to the Plunket Society and they are almost obsessively loyal to the local Plunket volunteers and also to their own seniors and the central organisation, but they are conscious of covering only part of the child care problem and feel that they are on a losing side.' Since they were immersed in routine child care, without the glamour of hospital therapeutics, they needed much more support than any other branch of nursing but were liable to be the most neglected and most isolated.[34]

A 1988 report on the South Auckland project, produced for the Minister of Health, found Plunket nurses complaining about feelings of isolation and stress, and what they called 'reality shock'.[35] Joyce Powell, a Plunket nurse of some experience who worked in the area, later commented that some of the young nurses approached the task as a mission, and were soon disappointed and frustrated by their rejection,[36] and upset to be sometimes greeted with hostility and suspicion. The nurses were concerned that in South Auckland the Plunket Society was seen as 'too much of a "Pakeha thing"'.[37] A 1986 market research exercise included the following statement from one Plunket nurse: 'There is definitely a negative attitude (towards Plunket) among Maori parents . . . I often get the impression that I am interfering in their autonomy by going to their homes and they resent anything I do.'[38] Plunket's 1987–8 Strategic Planning Sub-committee discovered a 'widespread feeling of low self-esteem among nurses'.[39]

A decade later, Plunket nurses were frustrated that their services were being cut back at the very time when there was a greater need for support owing to increased financial hardships.[40] In 1997, a local Auckland paper featured an article on Plunket in South Auckland. In Mangere only 9 per cent of Plunket's clients were white women, in Otara, 4 per cent. Pacific Island and Maori women dominated the South Auckland client list. 'Plunket nurses joked about being bitten by dogs on their rounds, of going home barefoot after dogs have taken their shoes and even having their car headlights smashed by dogs. They are a cheerful, energetic, sensible and positive bunch, Plunket nurses. They are realists without being whingers.' The problems, as nurses saw them, were the large number of transients, the absence of phones and the lack of transport. 'Plunket nurses talk of 20 people living in house-garage-caravan combos, sharing a kitchen and one toilet. A sure recipe for bad diet, poor hygiene and sickness, they say. TB is an ever-present risk.' Nurse Jenny Collard-Scruby commented, 'Most families want the best for their children and there are not many who don't want the Plunket nurse to call.'[41]

The doctors' view

Some doctors who wished to specialise in child health during the first half of the twentieth century resented the monopoly Plunket held on child health care. In 1950, following a recent visit to London, Dr Harold Turbott, who had offered positions to three young doctors interested in child hygiene, explained he was 'very anxious that the field most attractive to medical workers should be resourced for them, and not usurped by the Plunket Society'.[42] Plunket, however, had always enjoyed the support of some doctors who sat on its Medical Advisory Committee or acted as medical advisers to local branches. The record was undoubtedly held by 'Dr Bill', the husband of Dr Doris Gordon, who joined the Stratford Plunket Advisory Board in 1919 and was still serving in 1973, when he was awarded life membership of the society, only the third male to be so honoured.[43] When Plunket appeared to be threatened by the Health Department in the late 1950s, specialists in maternal and child heath, and the NZBMA itself, came out publicly in support of the society.[44] The NZBMA president, John Landreth, a Christchurch paediatrician, had been on Plunket's Medical Advisory Committee in 1938 and was a consultant to Christchurch's Karitane Hospital from 1934 to 1972. Speaking in support of Plunket during the 1959 inquiry, Landreth took the opportunity to suggest the immediate establishment of a chair of child health.[45] This had been urged by Truby King in the 1920s and Deem in the 1940s, and was finally achieved in 1967. The first incumbent was Dr Jim Watt, one of the four members of the 1959 Consultative Committee, who also became honorary consultant in medical education to the Plunket Society and sat on its Advisory Board.[46] Begg described Watt as 'a great acquisition to the University of Otago *and* the Plunket Society'.[47]

Paediatricians sought and held posts at Plunket's Karitane hospitals. Montgomery Spencer was not alone in losing his post following his denunciation of the society in 1938. In 1948 Dr Frederick Smale found that he was rejected in favour of another paediatrician at Auckland's Karitane hospital because, 'In the past he [had] made derogatory remarks about the Plunket Society'.[48] Yet some paediatricians had long and happy associations with the hospitals. At the time of the threatened closure, some, such as Neil MacKenzie, paediatric consultant to Wanganui Karitane hospital, and Alison Hunter at Auckland, fought to have the hospitals retained. The Family Centres, which were subsequently set up, appointed paediatricians on a part-time basis, though these services were increasingly subjected to cutbacks.

As in earlier decades, cordial relations in private practice were also sometimes maintained. During the 1938 infant feeding disputes (see Chapter 4), Dr Marie Buchler told Spencer that they were not the only doctors who disagreed with Plunket, 'but many pander to the P.N. [Plunket nurse] as it's good for business'.[49] Dr Edna Birkenshaw, who specialised in the health of women and children in her private practice, admitted in 1950 that the Plunket Society was her 'largest source of consultations'.[50] Yet other general practitioners continued to resent the nurses. Ten general practitioners interviewed by a medical student in 1951 felt that Plunket usurped the role of the general practitioner as 'Family Doctor', and detracted from the public image of the family doctor who looked after people's health 'from birth till death'.[51] This researcher found most 'family doctors' wanted to see more of the child, and argued that the 'Plunket care' took away the mother's initiative to visit the doctor.[52]

Breastfeeding was a major bone of contention between local doctors and Plunket nurses in the 1950s and 1960s. Some modern doctors were influenced by overseas authorities, such as Marriott and Clements, who did not favour breastfeeding.[53] Moreover, milk formulas now appeared perfectly safe and adequate. At least one commentator on breastfeeding in the early 1950s wondered whether the effort to breastfeed was worth it: 'Surely the milk of a placid cow, modified to suit the baby's digestion and requirements, is better than that of a nervous, overtired or temperamental mother'.[54] The association of breastfeeding with the natural childbirth movement might also have deterred some doctors from supporting it. Spencer had described prolonged breastfeeding in 1938 as a 'fetish'.[55] After 1939 women came into greater contact with local doctors, with free antenatal check-ups, free deliveries in hospital by a doctor, a free post-natal check-up and subsidised general practitioner services.

A 1941 study referred to a doctor who advised all his patients to discontinue breastfeeding after three months. The writer added, 'When the Plunket Nurse was asked by these mothers if she agreed with this advice she had to use the utmost tact to put forward the ideas of her Society without causing any offence to the medical profession',[56] something she probably did not achieve. When one woman consulted her doctor about mastitis following her return from hospital in 1954, she was told to 'stop all this silly nonsense and wean the baby'. His advice was: 'Tie yourself up tightly – don't drink any liquids just wash your mouth out if it gets dry – take a double dose of Epsom salts and that should fix it'. He also told the Karitane nurse present, 'Your mob are as helpful as a useless flea.'[57] When the nurse retorted that she would 'take the matter up', the local Plunket sister-in-charge commented, 'we feel that her enthusiasm for maintaining breast feeding had rather affected her correct attitude towards the medical profession'.[58] In 1963, another study recorded that, in three cases, the advice of the Plunket nurse to mothers had been 'in direct contradiction to that given by the family doctor'. In two cases, the difference had concerned breastfeeding problems.[59]

In 1937 the Plunket nurse for Timaru had commented that most local doctors were 'not very keen on us'.[60] Marion Shepherd, working in Rangiora, also commented on the nurses' need for tact in dealing with local doctors, adding, 'One I used to have a lot of arguments with'.[61] In 1951 medical student Margaret Woods found, when interviewing mothers, that although most had family doctors, the latter had not encouraged mothers to attend ante-natal classes or to call on Plunket after having their babies. She concluded that there was a poor relationship between general practitioners and Plunket nurses, though she added 'it must be realised that the Plunket Society is quite adequate in itself in recruiting new mothers to give service to'.[62] Plunket continued to appeal to the majority of mothers, with or without doctors' support.

The mothers' view

From around 1950, when Benjamin Spock's book was becoming popular, Plunket came under criticism from some mothers for its old-fashioned promotion of routines in child care.

That year one medical student, James Gilmour, reported that his observations 'proved the fallacy' of this criticism. In a study of 39 'Plunket mothers', he found 'the opposite of rigidity' in the feeding routines recommended by the nurses. The times and frequency of feeding were adjusted and readjusted according to the needs of the baby and mother.[63] A mother of three writing to the *Otago Daily Times* in 1952 similarly claimed that Plunket had never advised her to leave the baby to cry for more than five minutes, to fight over the 2am feed 'at first', to stick exactly to a rigid timetable for feeds or to wean the baby before it was 'unavoidable'.[64]

Gilmour's study was the start of a series of research projects into consumer responses to Plunket nursing services by medical students for their compulsory fifth-year public health dissertations. In 1961 Nigel Hamilton-Gibbs interviewed 50 new mothers and reported that 48 said they were 'on the same wavelength' as the nurse and were not annoyed by anything she suggested. Although many admitted that they did not always follow the advice, they fully realised that it was intended to help them and their babies. In response to the question, 'Did you feel a sense of inadequacy in looking after baby because of the nurse's attitude?', all the mothers said they had no such feeling. In fact many said that their nurses raised their confidence. The researcher noted that the two mothers who told the Plunket nurse not to call back would not admit that they rejected her because they were made to feel inadequate. 'But then no mother likes to admit

immunised, more likely to suffer an accident and more likely to be hospitalised for an illness. In trying to change attitudes, they said, the Plunket nurse might be perceived as 'being in conflict with some members of this group, no matter how hard she tries to get alongside them'.[79] The Dunedin Multidisciplinary Child Development Study was also used to evaluate client reaction to Plunket nurses. Of 982 mothers questioned, 83 per cent found the service to have been very helpful or of some help. Their criticisms revealed that they wanted more advice not less, and wished to use the nurse as a resource person on all aspects of child development.[80]

Mothers were also consulted for the 1988 report on Plunket services in South Auckland. Maori mothers regarded some Plunket nurses as helpful and others as far too officious and judgmental. Some said they felt uncomfortable because the nurses were generally white and middle-class, and they distrusted nurses without children of their own.[81] Pacific Islanders appeared to have a more positive view of Plunket, and welcomed the services provided by the society. They explained that many Pacific Island people did not need help with child-rearing because they were brought up from an early age to care for younger brothers and sisters. Yet some new arrivals to the country lacked self-confidence and the ability to cope with a new culture, and they turned to Plunket.[82] The report concluded that, despite criticisms, it would be a disaster if the services of Plunket nurses were withdrawn.[83]

Plunket's efforts to meet cultural demands

If Plunket were to survive in New Zealand in the 1980s, especially in Auckland, it had to meet criticisms of monoculturalism. Some individual nurses coped well with the new demands; others did not.

A milestone in the society's involvement with Maori health occurred in November 1987 when a child health hui, jointly organised by the Auckland branch of the Plunket Society and the Te Umere branch of the Maori Women's Welfare League, was held on Ngati Whatua Marae at Orakei. Plans for the hui were conceived during the meningitis vaccination campaign earlier that year when Plunket's executive councillor for Auckland, Lois McNaughton, met the league's Waireti Walters and they decided on a hui 'to bring everyone together'. As McNaughton explained, 'We didn't set any goals other than to come together and talk about child health.' About 80 people attended the hui, including Plunket nurses and members, representatives of the Maori Women's Welfare League and young Maori and

Pakeha mothers with babies. McNaughton recounted, 'At the beginning we just stood up and spoke about whatever we felt, . . . Maori women talked about their experience of Plunket nurses, and Plunket nurses talked about their work and that it mattered to them that they weren't reaching Maori families. There were tears. People were sharing some very deep personal things.' Among the recommendations coming out of the hui was the establishment of bursaries to increase the number of Maori Plunket nurses. The introduction of health workers to assist Plunket nurses in their work was also suggested.[84] Another hui, organised by the Maori Health Foundation, Te Puna Ora, was held four months later at Whare Tapere. Called to discuss the recent survey of Plunket in South Auckland, it recommended that nurses be further encouraged to 'de-emphasise their inspectoral role and to befriend clients'.[85]

In August 1987, in recognition of the imminent reorganisation of health services in New Zealand, Plunket's executive set up a Strategic Planning Sub-committee to investigate the society's future options.[86] Its strategic plan, issued the following year, announced that, 'The Plunket Society recognises and supports the current aspirations of the Maori people to improve the health of their children and families and it undertakes to keep under constant review the structures and the means whereby it offers its services to the Maori people to ensure that it continues to assist those aspirations to become reality'.[87] Plunket's annual report for 1990–1 reported enthusiastically that over two-thirds of Plunket branches now had child health programmes in partnership with local Maori groups such as iwi, the Maori Women's Welfare League, te kohanga reo and Maatua Whangai.[88] An increasing number of clinics and other services were based on local marae. Almost all Plunket staff now undertook training on their responsibilities under the Treaty of Waitangi.[89] McNaughton commented optimistically in 1990 that there was now a bicultural dimension to the nursing programme for new Plunket nurses and that administrators selected people with cultural sensitivity: she concluded that Plunket had begun the journey.[90]

An article in Plunket's February 1990 *Newsletter* was headed 'Rotorua Welcomes Maori Plunket Nurse'. Paea Hall, a Maori Plunket nurse already well-known for her work in West Auckland, was starting work in Rotorua. The local principal Plunket nurse, Marlene Cairns, believed this would 'help break down the false image of Plunket as solely white, middle-class'.[91] At that time 23 of Plunket's 445 nursing staff (5.2 per cent) described themselves as Maori. In some areas 8 per cent of Plunket staff were Maori.[92]

Plunket also attempted to involve Maori community workers or kaiawhina. In South Auckland, 1990 saw the opening of Te Rapu Ora at Papatoetoe, run by Plunket nurses and other community health workers including kaiawhina. In 1992, after consultation with the Maori Women's Welfare League, a new two-year in-service course for Maori health workers began to enable them to become certificated community Karitane nurses.[93] Plunket's first hui specifically for Maori health workers was held at Te Puea Marae in Mangere, Auckland, in November 1993. Both Maori and non-Maori Plunket staff attended.[94]

Some Maori Plunket nurses focused specifically on Maori health. In 1994 Rotorua's Plunket nurse Tuia Mahima began a programme that involved visiting 20 local kohanga reo six times a year for health checks. Wellington-based Plunket nurse Marama Parore-Katene took a leading role in a national glue ear prevention programme. The Public Health Commission contracted her to conduct a nationwide series of hui to update Maori health workers

Midday naptime at Gisborne's Te Whanau Aroha Kohanga Reo. By the early 1990s Plunket was working with te kohanga reo, the Maori Women's Welfare League, iwi and other Maori groups, including marae-based clinics. Plunket Society Annual Report 1990–1

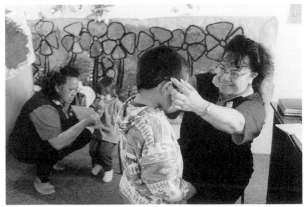

Plunket nurse Ripeka Mokaraka (right) and Plunket kaiawhina Diana Jensen visiting Nga Tai E Rua Kohanga Reo at Tuakau near Franklin in 2000. Plunket Society archives

Wellington-based Plunket nurse Marama Parore-Katene demonstrating educational resources at the launch of a national glue-ear prevention programme on Orangomai Marae in Upper Hutt. *Plunket News*, November 1994

on educational resources for preventing glue ear among Maori children. Almost all Plunket health workers attended the courses.[95]

From 1995 Plunket funded a new one-year course to train kaiawhina. Initially run by Marama Katene (later Parore-Katene), this started with a week on a marae where tikanga Maori (Maori customs) and race relations (specifically Treaty of Waitangi issues) were discussed. Katene explained the underlying philosophy in a *New Zealand Doctor* article in 1996: 'We look at barriers to health services for Maori people and how to convey information on topics like asthma, smoking, immunisation and nutrition'. There were then 70 kaiawhina throughout New Zealand.[96] In February 1997 a new position, the kaiawhina services co-ordinator, was created to enhance services to Maori, and Te Aomarama (Ozzie) Wilson was appointed to the post. In January 1997 Parore-Katene was replaced by Sandra Thompson as Plunket's national Maori clinical educator, responsible for managing the kaiawhina course. In 1999 Becky Fox, a Maori activist and former Waikato Polytechnic cultural safety educator, became Plunket's Maori adviser. She later commented that, 'Basically the HFA [Health Funding Authority] and the Ministry of Health were extremely sceptical about whether Plunket was able to deliver culturally appropriate services for Maori clients'.[97] The challenge and debates continued into the new century, when all Plunket nurses were required to attend 'cultural safety' workshops.[98]

Other ethnic groups were also among Plunket's clients. In 1993 a full-time adviser to Pacific Island communities was appointed.[99] At the local level, much depended on individual effort. For example, in 1990 Robyn Griffith, a Plunket nurse working in the Auckland suburb of Kingsland, explained that she did not force Plunket ideology on Pacific Island women

A hive of activity. 'Morningside Plunket Rooms', St Lukes, Auckland, 1990, with Plunket nurse Robin Griffith and Karitane Atele Iusitini.
Courtesy *Metro*

but rather referred mothers to older women in the Cook Island and Tongan communities with traditional health knowledge. Samoan clients were sometimes referred to a fofo (healer), and self-help health clinics in Kingsland were run according to 'fa'a Samoa' with 'mats and flowers and food and children'. In the 1980s the Kingsland Plunket clinic was made to look more culturally appropriate, with tapa wall hangings and Samoan mats scattered around the room. The success of the policy was reflected in an increased attendance: 'On busy days the children spill out the front doors and onto the pavement below'.[100] In a 1990 interview for *Plunket News*, Health Minister Helen Clark described Griffith as 'a model of the involved, community-aware, and committed nurse who goes beyond the call of duty to help her clients'.[101]

Many clinics in the South Auckland suburbs of Otara, Mangere and Otahuhu operated on an open clinic system with nurses available whenever mothers called.[102] The necessity for such a flexible system was spelled out in 1990 by *Metro* feature writer Nicola Legat: 'The Plunket nurse at the Otara clinic knows that you don't open the doors at 9am and expect people to show up on time for appointments. You don't, in fact, keep an appointment book. People turn up when they will. Generally that means

Waitakere Plunket on Wheels. Standing outside the bus are Karitane Diana Gasu (Pacific Islander), Plunket nurse Alison McTaggart (European) and Plunket kaiawhina Tania Chaney (Maori). Plunket Society Archives

later in the morning. Most don't have cars, so when it rains they may not come at all.'[103] Group sessions were also found to be more comfortable for Pacific Island women. Posters, such as those on infant car seats, were translated into Pacific Island languages. Support groups for other new immigrants, particularly South East Asians, were also started at local Plunket family centres. In 1994 a mobile child-health clinic was purchased for South Auckland, financed through grants and fund-raising, as part of 'a determined effort by Plunket to take the message of child health to those who need it most'.[104] Mobile clinics, known as 'Plunket on Wheels', were subsequently started for other areas. A 1999 University of Auckland study assessed its success in reaching Maori and Pacific Islanders. It found that while some appreciated the services, others did not think it catered for their people. Those who had strong family/whanau support explained that they relied little on professionals for infant care advice or support. Yet, in the Maori section of the report, it was noted, 'Although Plunket was perceived to be Pakeha, those who used the service were happy with it if the person they dealt with was kind, informative and supportive'.[105]

Support services: Family Centres and Plunketline

Plunket Karitane Family Centres were set up in place of the Karitane hospitals to provide daytime support for parents and babies in need. The first pilot centres started in Meadowbank (Auckland) and Porirua in 1978. Soon there were 27 centres nationwide. Each had a full-time Plunket nurse, two full-time Karitane nurses and a paediatrician employed part-time (one-tenth). In addition, to cater for mothers beyond the reach of the urban centres, Karitane nurses were employed to visit mothers at home.[106]

This brochure was produced in 1978 to advertise the Plunket–Karitane Family Support Service.

One of the early visitors to Meadowbank's Family Centre was Debbie La Hatte, a journalist from Southland's *Ensign* newspaper. After inspecting the new unit, she reported on its popularity, explaining that locals used it more than they would the 'old and very monolithic Karitane Hospital'. She attributed this to the fact that it was more casual, with no fuss over admissions and no bureaucracy. Friendliness was the keynote: 'Everyone smiles'. Advice was offered on 'breast feeding, parent education, weaning problems, family relationships, nervous exhaustion, sheer tiredness, budgeting, household hygiene or almost anything'.[107] The centre's Plunket nurse, Rosaleen Knell, explained that they had no set programme but encouraged mothers to rest and relax as much as possible. 'Many mothers are so desperately overtired when they are sent to us that they are quite incapable of taking anything in until they have had a few days complete rest.' This was why the unit had two beds in which to 'tuck our mums up for the day'.[108] Many of the problems encountered were reminiscent of those dealt with in the earlier Karitane hospitals. In 1993, for instance, Plunket nurse Penny Raybould reported that breastfeeding difficulties were 'a major portion of our work and one with which we have a great deal of success'. Support groups at the centre included a group for Asian mothers, one for those suffering from post-natal depression and one for grieving mothers.

An American parenting course known as STEP (systematic training for effective parenting) was started in 1992.[109]

Under the 1979 new funding agreement with the government, the latter paid Family Centre staff salaries and subsidised the purchase of cars. The upkeep and the running of the units were left to voluntary effort. From 1990 the capital cost of the cars was also met from voluntary funds. Knell mentioned in her first report that some mothers had cheerfully given not only cash but also vegetables, baking, jams, preserves and groceries. Some had done the mending and ironing while others had provided beautifully decorated cakes or donated some article for raffling. Still others came back 'just to attack the linen cupboard which is a nightmare at the best of times!'[110] A roster system organised by the sub-branches provided hot meals for mothers using the centre. This continued until 1992 when sub-branches were given the option of donating $200 instead. Voluntary drivers also helped with transporting mothers from time to time. The weekly paediatric clinic was axed as a cost-cutting measure in 1991.[111] Contracts with local paediatricians were replaced by contracts with three regional paediatricians for the 27 centres, who visited each centre once a month. Local paediatricians sometimes continued to visit on a voluntary basis.

In 1996 the centres in Tauranga, Gisborne, Hamilton and New Plymouth were closed to save money. They were replaced by a mobile service staffed by Karitane nurses or kaiawhina. Public petitions were drawn up to oppose the closures – 11,000 signatures in Hamilton and 9000 in Tauranga.[112] Threatened closure of Plunket's Family Centres in Auckland (Grey Lynn and Pukekohe) as a result of funding cuts by the local health authority also sparked a petition.[113] In September *New Zealand Doctor* noted that the closure of centres increased pressures on mental health services as new mothers sought help for depression: 'When the Plunket centre was open, they tended to deal with postnatal depression earlier on in the process. Now, by the time someone is seen, they are usually very unwell and dealing with what, in the beginning, might not have been a mental health issue.'[114] Plunket managed to raise funds to reopen the centres in New Plymouth and Hamilton later the same year.[115]

In 1998, when 24 of the original Plunket Karitane Family Centres were still operating, Plunket's National Nursing Advisor, Angela Baldwin, organised a client evaluation by means of a postal survey. Of the 836 clients (46 per cent of those approached) who replied, the great majority ranked Family Centre staff as very helpful (77 per cent). Twelve respondents found them less than moderately helpful and five considered them unhelpful. When asked to explain how staff were helpful, most appreciated their support, encouragement and reassurance, and the fact that they looked after the mother as well as the baby. The report concluded:

> Respondents highly valued staff qualities such as friendliness, professionalism, being non-judgemental, experienced, willing to listen, and knowledgeable . . . The holistic approach to providing family/whanau care and support is clearly effective and valued by Plunket clients. Clients also appreciated that staff did not rush or pressure them. The Family Centre itself was friendly, safe, encouraging, and available and accessible.[116]

They also appreciated the practical assistance, such as the equipment/videos and the food and drink provided. The facilities were applauded as unique.[117]

To reach those who could not get to the Family Centre or who needed help after hours, in 1990 Anne Cressey suggested a free phone helpline. She had just returned from an overseas research trip during which she had observed child health services in Australia, Britain, Sweden and Holland. She concluded that Plunket nurses provided more educational, supportive and screening services than elsewhere, 'but we lack a coordinated back-up service'. She was impressed by a 24-hour phone service in South and Western Australia.[118] Subsequently, Plunket's president, Joan Hunt, visited Adelaide's Child, Adolescent and Family Health Service under the direction of the Health Commission of South Australia. On her return she, too, recommended the establishment of a 24-hour telephone service.[119] One of the commonest suggestions among submissions to a Plunket survey in 1991 was for a national toll-free telephone service similar to that operated in Adelaide.[120]

Plunketline was launched in early 1994. Based in Wellington, it was funded by the Karitane Products Society, the Wellington branch of the Plunket Society and a Plunket Society fund. The new service was one of the society's major initiatives for the International Year of the Family, for which it was also given a grant of $20,000 by the IYF committee. Initially the line operated from 4pm to 1am but, to meet demand, it was extended in October to become a 24-hour service.[121] Expecting about 50 calls a day, they in fact received up to 250, or 83,000 a year.[122] Opposition Health spokesperson, Lianne Dalziel, claimed in Parliament that although there were about 15,000 calls a month, only 3000 could be answered owing to lack of funds.[123] Approaches to the regional health authorities (RHAs) for

The telephone helpline, manned by
Plunket nurse Antoinette Pheasant.
The figures in the background are
Plunketline manager Jenny Allan
and Plunket nurse Anne Riddell.
Plunket Society Annual Report 1993–94

funding were unsuccessful. Commenting in 1996 that New Zealand had
the fifth highest infant mortality rate of any OECD country, women's health
campaigner Sandra Coney pointed out that the government was cutting
back Plunket so that it could offer only a skeleton service (see below) and
refusing to finance the telephone helpline designed to fill the gap.[124]

Reducing the service to sixteen hours a day did not help the funding
problems.[125] In November 1997 it was announced that the service was
more than $500,000 in the red. Plunket's Chief Executive Officer, John
Thompson, noted its usefulness. He related the story of a mother in
Maungaturoto, about 60 kilometres south of Whangarei, whose eleven-
month-old baby had developed a temperature, and who phoned the
helpline. She was told how to get the temperature down quickly, and when
the Plunket nurse rang back 20 minutes later, she was advised to take the
baby to hospital where he was successfully treated for pneumonia: 'I
don't like to think what could have happened if they hadn't been there,'
commented Thompson. Discussing the government's failure to subsidise
the service, he continued, 'It shows once again the lack of willingness
by the Government to fund preventive services which can and do make
such a difference to child health.'[126] Referring to this in Parliament, Health
Minister Bill English reminded listeners that the government had never
funded the service. 'Plunket will have a much better understanding with
Government if it negotiates about the service it wants to provide, rather
than starting up new services that it knows it cannot maintain and trying
to force the Government into funding them.'[127] Nevertheless, in the middle
of 1999, with a general election pending, the government decided to

provide Plunket with $600,000 to restart Plunketline for sixteen hours a day.[128] There was much public support for this service: the Labour Party had collected 60,000 signatures on a petition calling for the restoration of the helpline.[129]

Government support for Plunket nursing services

The 1979 funding agreement whereby the government paid the salaries of a fixed number of Plunket nurses and other staff remained in force until 1990. That year a new agreement was negotiated, based on a fixed sum to provide specific services. Health Minister Helen Clark explained that the aim of the new contract was to measure output. Plunket was now contracted to deliver services 'on a performance output basis'.[130] Nine contacts between the nurse and her client from birth to the age of five were allowed for, and the requirement was to provide 90 per cent coverage for the birth to eighteen-month age group, and 60 per cent for those aged from two to four years. On that basis the contract provided $21.129 million for the 1990–1 year.

The new National government, elected to office in November 1990, continued this system. The contract amounted to $20.13 million in 1991–2, and $19.8 million for 1992–3. From 1 July 1993 the four RHAs and the Public Health Commission were responsible for purchasing health and disability services from providers, including hospitals and organisations such as Plunket. That year the Minister of Health instructed the RHAs to negotiate a single national contract with Plunket, but from the following year the society had to negotiate with individual RHAs and the Public Health Commission. Plunket's Director of Child Health Policy, Pat Tuohy, warned that the existence of four schedules could see New Zealand end up with a lack of consistency in child health services. In 1994–5 the four separate contracts amounted to $19 million in total. By 1995, $17.6 million a year was allocated to provide a comprehensive service to 93 per cent of all new babies in New Zealand. As John Thompson pointed out, that was less than half of one per cent of the health vote.[131]

Responding to concerns about the drop in funding for Plunket in 1991, Health Minister Simon Upton explained that the government was funding a new service in Rotorua, the Tipu Ora project.[132] Competitiveness was the ethos of the 1990s. In 1995 Health Minister Jenny Shipley explained that the service might be provided by a midwife or an organisation such as Plunket or the Tipu Ora Trust: 'There are many, many organisations that fulfil and provide well-child services. The Government currently requires regional health authorities to purchase such a service for every baby.'[133] While in 1990 Katherine O'Regan applauded Plunket as 'not just any voluntary organisation' but rather one which 'provided protection for mothers and babies throughout the whole of New Zealand', by 1996, as Associate Minister of Health, she viewed it differently. She now argued that, 'Plunket is not the sole provider of well-child services in New Zealand. The Southern Regional Health Authority, for example also contracts with family help trusts and the Pegasus Medical Group in Christchurch and the Anglican-Methodist Family Care Centre in Dunedin. The Northern Regional Health Authority purchases well-child services from a range of providers other than Plunket – and that is the point – including all the Crown health enterprises and several Maori health trusts.'[134] In 1997 English pointed out that he had just launched a new Pacific Island service for families in Auckland's Glen Innes area: 'So, while Plunket funding has not increased significantly, other groups are coming in alongside Plunket to offer similar services'.[135] The following year he said that other organisations also looked after children very effectively, and they became very concerned if politicians said that Plunket was to get all the money.[136] The competitive ethos of the 1990s was also seen in Education Minister Lockwood Smith's programme, Parents as First Teachers (PAFT), launched in 1991. Plunket successfully competed to run pilot schemes for three years in four areas: Northland, South Auckland, Gisborne East Coast and Dunedin. Thereafter it competed with other bodies, such as Barnardos. In 1993, it successfully tendered for four of the eight new PAFT schemes.[137]

Plunket nurses lamented the fact that cutbacks were occurring just as economic stresses were increasing. The new funding system introduced in 1990 led to nurse redundancies. At the end of 1992, 69 Plunket nurses were made redundant.[138] That year paediatrician Michael Watt commented that he had been 'getting a lot of feedback from mothers very distressed that they were unable to see their Plunket nurse as often as they needed'.[139] Plunket's Northern Regional Manager, Brett Austin, explained that nurses had to narrow their focus to resist being drawn into housing, education and welfare issues. Nor did they have time to follow up those who did not turn up for appointments. Plunket nurse Colleen Fakalogotoa (later Plunket's General Manager Operations Northern) said nurses had to see up to twelve families a day to perform to the contract: 'In the past we would work with families to improve their situation and could come back more than once'. They could no longer do that, and 'it makes you feel awfully hollow. As a nurse, it sticks in your throat.' She was also concerned about the long-term health impact on children from middle-class families who were getting less attention.[140]

Another retired Plunket nurse, Mary Fenton, felt strongly enough about the changes to write an article for *New Zealand Doctor* in 1996. She pointed out that the number of nurse contacts a family could have was now eight in five years (with four discretionary visits available), whereas not many years before first-time parents would have had eight contacts with the Plunket nurse by the time the baby was six months old. Indeed, in 1982 an average of 22 visits for each child under the age of five had been recorded.[141] At that time, 'Six per cent of the Plunket nurses made themselves available at all times, most Plunket nurses were available for telephone calls out of normal working hours, and nearly half sometimes made home visits out of working hours.'[142] The ethos had changed with the funding. Fenton declared that it was now accountants who decided how many times a baby and its family needed to be visited to maintain their health, and the result was graphically shown by the huge upsurge in baby and child hospital admissions. She asked whether the health authorities could not see that this increase might well be due to fewer home visits and less health surveillance by the Plunket nurses, where not only the baby's but the whole family's health and dynamics could be assessed.[143]

Returning from a conference in the United States in 1997, Tuohy declared that the clear message for policy-makers in New Zealand was that they were fortunate to have in place the core of a universal, non-targeted well child health system, delivered primarily by the trained child health nurses of the Plunket Society. He argued that the health reforms had seriously weakened the effectiveness of this organisation, by withholding adequate funding and attempting to replace the universal service with a fully targeted system. In his view this was 'a giant leap backwards'. 'We must build on and expand existing universal services, linking them closely with any new targeted services,' he declared.[144] Plunket's president Dianne Armstrong deplored the move to targeting, pointing out that caregivers with the labels 'white middle class' had just as many needs as others.[145]

Commenting on Prime Minister Jenny Shipley's proposed tax cuts in February 1999, Labour Party leader and future Prime Minister Helen Clark pointed out that instead of the cuts, 'people wanted the security of a police force, a proper health force and a Plunket service that was there for mothers who needed advice'.[146] Did the Plunket Society still have the political clout that it had had in earlier decades, when politicians were warned to ignore

Labour leader Helen Clark addressing Plunket's National Conference in 1995. Two years earlier she had described Plunket nurses as being 'among the unsung heroines of New Zealand's society. They work on the front line in providing a well child health service'. *Plunket News*, April–May 1995

it at their peril? Although its services were still valued and appreciated by most mothers, Plunket did not, as will be seen, have such a prominent public profile. Two years later, and under a Labour government, Plunket's CEO Paul Baigent still lamented low government spending on children, contrasting this with Australia and Canada which had invested $240 million and $5 billion on child health respectively over four years.[147]

CHAPTER 10

A Women's Society? Plunket's Changing Image from the 1970s

Taking responsibility

'Child health "a disgrace"', announced a *New Zealand Herald* headline in 2000. The article declared that 'Health professionals have challenged the public to stop burying their heads in the sand'. Dr Dwayne Crombie, Child Health Manager of Waitemata Health, commented, 'We are a total bloody cop-out as a nation', and even Health Minister Annette King agreed the country should be ashamed of its record in child health.[1] Had New Zealand come full circle from 1900, ripe for a repeat of the national concern that led to the founding of the Plunket Society?

In fact, there was one significant difference that made a replication of such events impossible. There was no longer an army of women waiting in the wings to embrace child health policy in the name of mothers and babies. As Erik Olssen argued in 1981, Plunket, with its promotion of the 'cult of domesticity', had given mothers a 'sense of cosmic importance' in the early twentieth century, and they embraced the new cause enthusiastically. The downside was, in Olssen's opinion, that the society, with its emphasis on domesticity, prevented women from entering the professions.[2] Yet it could also be argued that Plunket provided them with the means to wield considerable influence that they were otherwise denied. A hundred years later it no longer filled this role. Although women still supported Plunket and actively participated on its committees, they were younger and there was a greater turnover of members, as mothers re-entered the paid workforce or moved on to kindergarten and school committees as their children progressed.[3] Some areas found it hard to enlist volunteers at all.[4] This contrasted with the 1950s, for example, when 'Everybody belonged to Plunket' and when 'Plunket tended to attract the "top" people in the district'.[5] The reduced long-term commitment among modern committee members meant fewer opportunities to influence policy and left a gap in infant welfare leadership and advocacy. In 1990 children's advocate Lesley Max wrote, 'Any idea that someone, some agency, some individual, has any degree of oversight of the whole area of child health should be cast aside. There is no effective agency which gathers data, formulates a nation-wide policy, oversees regional implementation, and accepts responsibility for child health.'[6] She wrote indignantly, 'Yet somewhere in the Department of Health there must be someone with an overall perspective on children.'[7] The department was an obvious place to look for leadership, but in the past the Plunket Society, with considerable political support, had jealously guarded its right to oversee infant and pre-school child health in the face of departmental opposition. In a later section Max admitted that Plunket was 'By far the most significant agency with regard to child health in New Zealand',[8] yet clearly she did not credit it with having vision or leadership qualities in the field. Plunket's public image was changing.

In 1997 the *New Zealand Herald* discussed child health in New Zealand under the heading, 'Leading the world in ills that ravage the young'. 'The biggest complaint,' it noted, 'is that no one has taken charge of children's health. Within the Ministry of Health the issue has been handled by staff across different departments rather than by one specially focused team.' The report enthused that the ministry was about to create a new position of child adviser to look after child health, and a new Child Health Advisory Committee. There was no mention of Plunket in the article, despite the fact that it was accompanied by a picture captioned 'Preventive Medicine: Tupou Tonu aged four of Otara, awaits injections in the Plunket mobile child health care bus when it visited his street'.[9]

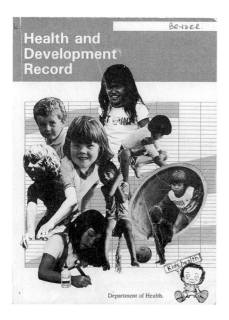

By the 1980s the *Plunket Baby Record Book* had become the *Health and Development Record* issued by the Department of Health.

From the mid-1970s Plunket no longer appeared to defend its right to lead initiatives in infant health. In contrast to its stance in 1960, it did not launch a public 'fighting' campaign when Health Minister Frank Gill set up a Board of Health Committee on Child Health in 1977, even though this was under the aegis of the Board of Health and closely associated with the Health Department. No objection was made, as in 1969, when Plunket's executive officers were excluded from the committee. The society was represented by its health professionals, David Geddis and Joy McMillan, two among the committee's 23 members. When regional co-ordinating committees were formed in 1980, the Health Department was represented by the medical officer of health and the principal public health nurse, despite Plunket's objections to the inclusion of the former in 1974.[10] In 1984 *Recording Child Health and Development: A Handbook for Professionals using the 'Health and Development Record Book'* was written and edited by Dr Murray Laugesen, Principal Medical Officer (Research) in the Health Department's Management Services and Research Unit. Although he consulted Ian Hassall and Maria Travers of the Plunket Society, there was only one reference to Plunket nurses in the index.

The changing balance of power within Plunket: maternalists give way

To some extent Plunket's altered public image was related to internal changes within the organisation: the balance of power was shifting. The president and her executive no longer reigned supreme. Meriel Johnstone, president 1984–6, commented in her retirement address in May 1986 that she definitely agreed with a recent public relations report that the president needed a higher profile: 'I had to ask to meet Professor Emery, a fact that did not escape his notice. Maybe this should be borne in mind when choosing a president – a media mouse like me is of little use.'[11] In reality it probably had little to do with her personality. The changing role of the president is indicated by a 1992 Management Consortium Report which noted the general view of the president and the medical director as strategists and as the only people in the society who had a vision for the future. The report commented that it was not appropriate for the president to take a chief executive officer role. 'Without leadership the Society will founder. The President cannot continue to be the CEO, it is not her legitimate role. She has assumed the role where there was a lack . . . the President and the Medical director (individually or jointly) in the absence of anyone else

[were] taking the role.'[12] The reviewers did not seem to realise that this had been precisely the expected role of the president and the medical director in the past. As Geddis later said, presidents 'very much ran things'.[13] Yet no one appeared to take issue with the 1992 report's conclusions. In March 1992 a former Air New Zealand chief executive, Jim Scott, was hired as transition manager to implement the report's proposals. Its recommendations for restructuring were enacted, including the appointment of a (male) chief executive officer and four regional managers (two of whom were male). A *North & South* article on Plunket in November of that year commented that 'a layer of grey-suited managers is sliding in'.[14]

In 1951 Elizabeth Bodkin had noted that, although Plunket was generally regarded as a women's society, with the 'burden of administration [falling] on the shoulders of women', help and advice were sought from prominent commercial and professional men.[15] Each branch was required to have a male Advisory Board, to be consulted on matters of finance.[16] In 1965 a male accountant, William (Bill) Hall, was employed as Plunket's national treasurer, a position he held until 1986, but other administrative posts had been held by women. From 1917, when the first paid secretary was appointed until the post was abolished in 1977, there were only four national secretaries: Gwen Hoddinott (1917–40), Mrs E. R. Batchelor (1940–5), Kathleen Rapps (1945–63) and Myra McKechie (later MacPherson) (1963–77). This had provided a remarkable continuity, and key people with considerable institutional memory. An indication that the society was changing, that it was no longer regarded as 'a woman's mission', was the appointment of a chartered accountant and B.Com. graduate, Peter Cressey, as director of administration in 1977 in place of the secretary. This followed a recommendation by PA Management Consultants Ltd, which reported on Plunket administration in 1975. In 1988 Geddis persuaded the council that his workload was enough to justify the appointment of a general manager. Des Watson was appointed.

Following the 1992 report, Plunket's executive was replaced by a board, which, along with its voluntary members, included a chief executive officer and directors of child health policy, nursing policy and corporate services. The directors were answerable to the CEO. Dr Pat Tuohy was appointed as Director of Child Health Policy in 1993.[17] From 1994 child health policy and nursing policy were amalgamated into a policy directorate, headed by Tuohy. Following protests from the nursing sector, the position of national nursing adviser was created to ensure that nursing policies and practices would be represented at a national level, and Angela Baldwin was appointed.[18] The post of director of Plunket nursing had previously been abolished in favour of a nursing adviser in 1934, when the executive felt threatened by its professional side. This time the position was subordinated not to the voluntary members, but to the paid CEO.

Women no longer headed the organisation; nor was there a medical voice of authority in a position of authority. Part of the reason for the demise of the medical director was opposition from the nursing sector of Plunket, which was gaining strength and confidence.[19] In 1991 Plunket nurses argued that Plunket was essentially a nursing service and that they should make nursing decisions. This culminated in a petition signed by 460 Plunket nurses and presented to the executive protesting the involvement of the medical director in the nursing service and expressing a vote of no confidence in him.[20] Objecting to the strong male medical model within Plunket, one group of nurses recommended that the position of medical director be abolished.[21] The society's concurrence suggests that it no longer felt its legitimacy depended on an authoritative medical voice. Eventually the post of General Manager Clinical Services was filled by a nurse, Angela Baldwin.

Plunket clearly felt the need to professionalise and modernise, in keeping with the market ideology of the 1980s. The cocktail of influential

A meeting of Plunket's Research and Education Unit, c. 1990. From left: Dr David Geddis (Chief Medical Director), Mary Stevenson (Research Nurse), Dr John Eastwood (Deputy Medical Director), Nicki Taylor (Executive Officer), Diane Sanders (Deputy Director of Nursing Services: Education), and Ruth Smith (Research Officer). Plunket Society Annual Report 1989–90

women volunteers and medical experts was no longer seen to be effective
or appropriate in the post-1970 world. Moreover, by this time women no
longer relied on Plunket to give them a niche in the public world. As it
became more acceptable for married women with families to enter paid
employment, they were less likely to channel their energies into voluntary
organisations like Plunket. Married women were now reaching high
positions in government departments, politics and the professions. The first
married woman to become Director of Nursing in the Health Department
was Shirley Bohm, who married shortly after her appointment in 1967 and
continued in the post until 1978.[22] Three decades later, in 1997, New
Zealand had its first female Prime Minister, Jenny Shipley, married with
two children. Before entering national politics in 1987 she was involved in
community associations such as Plunket and Playcentre. Rather than moving on to a position of prominence within the voluntary sector, as she might
have done in a previous era, she transferred those interests to national
politics. In 1989 she became Opposition associate spokesperson on education, with specific responsibility for early childhood.[23] In 1990 she
became Minister of Social Welfare and Minister of Women's Affairs, and
later Minister of Health. Prime Minister when Plunketline was relaunched
in 1999, she announced in the maternalist tradition, 'As a mother myself
and having raised two children . . . I feel proud to take the first call to
Plunketline from a parent wanting advice.'[24]

Another woman to successfully combine career and marriage was Sian
Elias, who married in 1970, the same year she became a barrister, and went
on to have two sons. In 1988 she became one of the first two women
Queen's Counsel, and subsequently became New Zealand's first female
Chief Justice.[25] If the opportunity to combine family and career had not
been available, she might very well have channelled her considerable
capabilities into the voluntary sector. Yet another woman who rose to prominence in the public world was Dame Catherine Tizard. The mother of four
children, she devoted her energies to local politics, and became Auckland's
first female mayor in 1983, a position she relinquished in 1990 on her
appointment as New Zealand's first female Governor-General. In *Who's
Who* (1991) Tizard listed among her interests health, education, child care
and child development.[26] While she became a patron to Plunket, indicating
her interest and support,[27] her political energies were directed elsewhere.

Plunket leaders of a former generation would, in all probability, have
grasped such opportunities had they been available. When Kate McGeorge
completed her three-year term as Plunket president in 1936 the council

minuted the fact that she brought to the presidency 'much administrative capability, a clever, clear-thinking mind, and an earnest comprehension of the responsibility that attaches to that important office'.[28] Elizabeth Bodkin was described as having 'a very clear, alert brain, a gift of speech, and a very optimistic and dauntless spirit'.[29] Sheila Horton claimed it was with some trepidation that she took on the Auckland presidency in 1957, including as it did the administration and the rebuilding of a hospital.[30] Auckland Mayor Sir Dove-Myer Robinson found her a formidable lobbyist.[31] The council said of her in 1973, 'It is women of the calibre of Mrs Horton who have made and are making the Plunket Society the strong and powerful organisation it is.'[32] On her retirement as president in 1978 the *Plunket Newsletter* wrote of Joy Reid that she was 'greatly admired by her colleagues – and those Parliamentarians and Government agencies she dealt with – and respected as a tough battler and formidable negotiator for Plunket'.[33] The society undoubtedly continued to attract women of high calibre. Bill Hall noted how the branch system created a 'tremendous management weeding out process. They have a degree in life, in caring, in consideration.'[34] Those who survived the promotion through the branch system probably possessed certain leadership qualities. Joyce Andrews, president 1978–81, was described by Gordon Parry as 'a natural leader', and Anne Cressey commented on her 'strong personality'.[35] Hall described Myra Graham, president 1981–4, as 'the most outstanding president the Plunket Society has ever had', and Geddis considered her definitely in the maternalist mould when he commented on her attitude to Cabinet ministers, 'who were "boys"'.[36] Pat Seymour, president 1990–3, was granted an OBE for services to the family and the community in 1995.[37] Yet these strong women no longer reigned supreme within the society. Nor did they claim the same media attention as had their predecessors.

Plunket opposes the 'permissive society'

From the 1970s Plunket's iconic status in New Zealand suffered a setback. In the new women's history of the 1970s the 'cult of domesticity' was denigrated as a product of middle-class male patriarchy. Any organisation that promoted motherhood was castigated by the new consciousness-raising feminist movement. Plunket fought a rearguard action. Sheila Horton, 56-year-old vice-president, told young women to 'keep your bras on, and enjoy being managing director of the hardest business of them all [the family]'.[38] In the crucial decade of the 1970s Plunket was not only filled with middle-

The Dominion Councillors' meeting in Wellington, 18–19 April 1972. Kneeling, fourth from left: Miss M. I. Nicholls, Director of Nursing Services; front row seated, second from left Miss M. K. McKechie (Dominion Secretary), Mrs T. E. M. Burton (Vice-President, Dunedin), Mrs W. H. Reid (President), Mrs I. C. Horton (Vice-President, Auckland). *Plunket News*, 1972

class middle-aged women who disapproved of the feminist movement, it was also led by the socially conservative Neil Begg and Margaret Liley.[39] Plunket's leaders opposed social trends associated with the 'permissive society'.

Begg expounded on the virtues of the nuclear family. One reviewer said of Begg's 1970 textbook, *The New Zealand Child and His Family*, commissioned by the Plunket Society to replace *Modern Mothercraft,* that it went 'far beyond infant care and studie[d] the importance of family and environment, stressing the point that parenthood is the ultimate test of maturity'.[40] Begg applauded the paediatric 'Thousand Family' study in Newcastle-upon-Tyne, England, and its plea for 'more responsible standards of family behaviour'. He agreed with its view that, until this was achieved, society would continue to pay the cost in 'emotional illness, family breakdown, maladjustment, delinquency, immature industrial relations and crime'.[41] His views were shared by Plunket Society president Joy Reid, who spoke out at the 1976 conference about an increase in problems of 'malnutrition, cruelty and the neglect of children', and referred to 'parent delinquency'.[42]

The 1970s witnessed an increase of solo parent families in New Zealand, aided or at least acknowledged by the introduction of the domestic purposes benefit for solo parents in 1973. That the Plunket Society did not

The New Zealand
CHILDand his FAMILY

NEIL BEGG
Director of Medical Services
N.Z. PLUNKET SOCIETY

Neil Begg's Plunket Society handbook, unlike its predecessors, highlighted the family.

entirely approve of this trend is indicated by the publication in its *News-letter* in 1977 of a statement by fourteen Wanganui health professionals who described themselves as 'social scientists, nurses and doctors', and claimed first-hand experience and knowledge of published sources about unmarried parents and their children. They held that marriage was the essential foundation for a stable and healthy society and that anything which tended to undermine it would destroy society itself. They contend-ed that the child of an unmarried parent was disadvantaged: 'The amount of *handicap* varies but can be severe'. In their view, steps should be taken to prevent such births, by educating young people about responsible parenthood, and unmarried mothers should be prevented from keeping their babies: 'We believe that, however unpopular it might be, the trend away from adoption should be reversed'.[43]

Others to comment on the breakdown of marriage and the family included Auckland branch president, Mary Kidd, who referred in 1972 to the 'insidious influences which are striving to destroy democracy as we know and enjoy it'.[44] One 'insidious' influence was *The Little Red School Book*, published in Wellington in 1972 and issued to schools.[45] This 'shocking' publication, with a very explicit chapter on sex ('fucking'), homosexuality, masturbation and contraception, was discussed at a 1972 Plunket council meeting. Reid believed that the book contained 'a phil-osophy which is both dangerous and destructive and poses a serious threat to our very way of life'. She spoke of the sanctity of marriage and the family unit as the basis of society.[46]

Mothers in paid employment and day care centres were subjects of concern. Addressing some 250 women at a provincial conference in Auckland in 1963, Begg maintained that a mother of young children in paid employment was 'one of the greatest threats in modern family life'.[47] Reid agreed, and opposed day care. She believed that up to the age of three children should stay at home with their mothers, and that many current problems stemmed from babies being placed in institutions, something other countries had realised too late.[48] An 'at home' allowance for full-time mothers was discussed at a council meeting in 1974.[49] This resulted in a Plunket Society submission to the Labour government's Select Committee on Women's Rights, advocating such an allowance.[50] Pointing out that the committee was chaired by a man, Reid considered it a gender division: 'We tried very hard to make them see the woman's point of view'.[51] At that time, however, there was no 'woman's point of view': women were divided into the usually younger feminists and the maternalists like Reid. The campaign for a mother's wage petered out.[52]

Margaret Liley, Plunket's deputy medical director from 1967, also held socially conservative views in the face of modern trends. In 1974 she commented disapprovingly on the current 'vociferous demands' to introduce contraceptives for under sixteens.[53] The following year, she pondered

In 1969 Dr Margaret Liley (left) spoke at a Ladies' Dinner in Gisborne, organised by the local Plunket committee and attended by 250 women. The other speakers were Mrs Susan Graham (centre), a well-known travel writer, and Miss Pare Hopa, an Oxford graduate and anthropologist. *Plunket News*, 1969

whether society was 'being progressive or retrogressive in encouraging the limitless appetite for young virgins by making them more available'.[54] Her fears appeared to be realised when the 1977 Report of the Royal Commission of Inquiry into Contraception, Sterilisation and Abortion in New Zealand recommended the repeal of the 1954 Police Offences Amendment Act, which had prohibited the sale of contraceptives and instruction on contraceptives to those under sixteen.[55]

Education in family planning had long been an issue for Plunket. The New Zealand Family Planning Association (NZFPA) dated back to the 1930s and had set up its first clinic in Auckland in 1954. It was around this time that it began to give talks to the Plunket Mothers' Clubs which had proliferated after the Second World War. Such talks were opposed on religious grounds by Nora Fitzgibbon, Plunket's Nursing Adviser and herself a Catholic. While she retired in 1945, she continued to wield some influence within the society and was active in the Catholic Women's League, serving as its first president, 1949–55.[56] In 1959 Plunket's council received a formal complaint from the league that NZFPA representatives were giving talks to Plunket Mothers' Clubs. One council member, Mrs A. J. Faith, believed the association was preventing some mothers from joining the clubs. A motion was carried that, 'No speaker should be invited to address a Plunket Mothers' Club on any subject likely to offend the religious beliefs of any members of the Club'. The NZFPA was ordered not to use the Plunket Society for the dissemination of its propaganda.[57] The ban was to avoid a Catholic withdrawal from Plunket, but in the event it proved useful for the NZFPA as the discussions drew attention to its existence.[58]

The issue did not go away. Delegates at the 1970 Plunket conference asked the council to review the society's policy concerning the NZFPA. The response reiterated the existing policy regarding religious beliefs.[59] Although it was laid down in 1969 that Plunket rooms were not to be used by 'organisations likely to upset any members' religious beliefs i.e. Family Planning',[60] it was agreed in 1972, after a 'long discussion' at an executive meeting, that the Aranui clinic could be used for a lecture on family planning, provided local doctors approved.[61] A remit passed at the 1972 conference ensured that addresses to Mothers' Clubs could include family planning. 'The clubs are non-political and non-sectarian and in such a responsible group of girls who know what they want there should be no restriction in choice of speakers,' said Joy Reid to a round of applause.[62] A more liberal stance may have evolved in this respect, but a second remit, that family planning advice should be incorporated into mothercraft classes, was lost. This was believed to be a professional matter between family and doctor, or a personal matter between husband and wife.

Plunket was forced to address the issue of Plunket nurses and family planning advice in 1972, once the Health Department's public health nurses were instructed to give such advice to parents.[63] Plunket's executive agreed unanimously that the society was not in favour of any family planning material being displayed in Plunket clinics.[64] This policy was reaffirmed at the 1972 conference. Alice Bush wrote to Reid, regretting the society's failure to allow nurses to undertake family planning education. 'As a doctor who works for the Plunket Society I will have difficulty in explaining to friends and colleagues why the Society has not kept in touch with community needs while New Zealand progresses rapidly toward a multi-racial society with all the problems of big cities, ignorance and social upheaval.'[65]

It took another two years before a general conference agreed that family planning literature could be displayed in Plunket rooms.[66] At the same time, a New Plymouth remit urging the society to extend its services to provide advice on contraception was defeated.[67] Yet, under the Contraception, Sterilisation and Abortion Act 1977, Plunket nurses were among those 'authorised' to provide advice on contraception. In 1980 the executive noted a newspaper article stating that Plunket staff, along with other nurses, had been authorised by the Minister of Health to give contraceptive advice to children under sixteen years of age. In response, Plunket's president Joyce Andrews stated that the society's policy 'remained the same . . . these types of matters were left entirely to the discretion and attitude of *individual nurses'.*[68] A more liberal interpretation of Plunket's role in family planning education had evolved under pressure.

Abortion, however, was an issue on which certain key Plunket officers would not give way. The *New Zealand Herald* announcement of Margaret Liley's appointment to the Plunket Society in 1966 commented that one of her recent contributions to infant welfare had been 'to focus attention on the often forgotten fact that the unborn baby is a real person with its own rights and privileges'.[69] The following year Begg told a group of medical students that abortion might possibly be justified if it meant saving a mother's life or if a child were abnormal to the extent where life could only be a burden.[70] Abortion was top of the feminist agenda of the early 1970s, and in 1970 the Society for the Protection of the Unborn Child (SPUC) was set up to forestall liberalisation of New Zealand's abortion laws, as had already happened in Britain and some states in Australia. Begg and Liley were members of SPUC. In 1978 Margaret Liley's husband, Sir

William, produced New Zealand's first film to examine life before birth. *I'd Love Her Back Though* 'looked at the choice that confronted many women who became pregnant – to deliver a child or to have an abortion'.[71] Liley provided the commentary, and there is no doubt which decision the film supported.

At the 1970 Plunket conference, Mrs Faith, who had been on the council since 1957, introduced a motion in support of SPUC: 'The aims and objects of the SPUC are so much akin to our own,' she said, noting that these included upholding the sanctity of human life and the right of all people to life, including the unborn child. Vice-president Sheila Horton opposed the motion, pointing out that the aims of the society which members were asked to support had been drawn up 60 years ago. Begg replied that his philosophy as a member of the Plunket Society was in line with that of SPUC: 'A child is a person with a continuum of life from the moment of conception,' he declared. An amended motion was passed: 'That this conference of the Plunket Society is sympathetic towards the aims and objects of the SPUC' was passed.[72] The feminist magazine, *Broadsheet*, described the 1978 revised edition of Begg's book, now titled *The Child and his Family,* as 'an undercover victory' for SPUC. Among the changes to the earlier version was a reference to Natural Family Planning Clinics but not to the Family Planning Association.[73]

At the 1974 conference Plunket's Geraldine branch proposed that the society should take a stand against legalised abortion. This remit was challenged on the basis that it might indicate rejection of the laws of the land. Reid upheld this point of order and thus avoided the expected heated debate.[74] Plunket Mothers' Clubs, representing a younger age group, did not necessarily agree with the society's leaders. At the 1976 conference, Mrs L. Mawby from Wellington proposed 'that the word Plunket be omitted from the title of Plunket Mother's Clubs'. She explained that she was in contact with a lot of mothers who considered the word 'Plunket' suggested stuffiness and women older than themselves, or just plain old-fashioned outlooks. She claimed that it had also been suggested that the word Plunket deterred the solo mother. The motion was lost.[75]

Plunket and women's support

In 1977 Trish Gribben wrote that it was easy to criticise: '"Plunket is a white middle-class weighing machine"; "Plunket is a revisionary upholder of the status quo", "Plunket is ladies in flower hats at fashion shows".' But, she argued, 'Plunket is also Polynesian mothers sitting around the nurse in a scruffy old RSA hall, talking about their babies; Plunket is haven for a mother no longer able to cope with drunk Dad and a baby that cries half the night; Plunket is a nurse who sees before anyone else that a mother is cracking up and enlists outside community help.'[76] Yet the socially conservative views of many Plunket leaders in the 1970s, promoting 'responsible parenting', had become the public face of the society.

Some feminist writers continued to support Plunket. In her 1983 PhD thesis on 'motherhood and self-definition', Robyn McKinlay argued that 'The Plunket Society perhaps changed more than the other organisations [Playcentre, Kindergarten, Parents' Centre, La Leche] in response to changing attitudes, as it has altered its services to offer more support for mothers'. She referred to the Plunket Family Units and the society's support of Trish Gribben's 1979 book *Pyjamas Don't Matter* (written in consultation with Geddis). This was 'based very firmly on the "life experience" paradigm of motherhood' which, in McKinlay's view, reflected Plunket's acceptance of this new ideology. She believed that the society was not as firmly attached to a particular ideology as the other organisations she studied. 'Today Plunket appears not to be concerned with spreading any particular child rearing philosophy, but to provide a practical response to what it sees as problems in the community.'[77] In 1988 feminist writer and director of Women's Health Action, Sandra Coney, began an article on 'Truby King's lasting legacy' with the words, 'It has become fashionable to knock the ideas of Plunket Society founder . . .' . She claimed that he had made a real contribution to child health in New Zealand.[78] As noted earlier, Coney deplored government cutbacks to Plunket's services, and continued to address Plunket audiences. In a keynote speech at the society's annual conference in 1997 she expressed her sadness that women's and children's interests now came second to those of the economy, business and the market. She issued a challenge to Plunket, with 'its supreme advantages of high credibility and being a household name throughout New Zealand', to speak up in the interests of women and children.[79]

Gribben's 1977 article noted that Plunket still enjoyed the support of 80,000 volunteers, not to mention the 46,205 new babies and their mothers who were visited that year. By the 1980s, however, women no longer had their predecessor's unerring confidence that, as women and mothers, they had a right to manage infant welfare services. It was Plunket's staff, not its voluntary workers, who petitioned Parliament in 1996 regarding cuts to services.[80] Many women still supported Plunket and its activities in a voluntary capacity, but not at the policy-making and governance level. Neighbourhood and local support groups remained important and dynamic and such involvement was still important to many women. Plunket provided mutual support at a particular time in their life cycle, as new mothers.[81] It was a temporary substitute for work, or a stepping stone to paid work. For those who reached the top, some of the traditional functions remained, giving them confidence in the public sphere. Dianne Armstrong, who became president in 1995, explained in 1997, 'The skills I've acquired through Plunket will take me back into the workforce. I came in as a young mother from the workforce, and in the time I've been with Plunket I've gained experience in management, contracting, negotiation, media and promotion.'[82] Granted a Queen's Service Order for her voluntary work in 2001, Plunket's 1997–9 president, Merle Newlove, explained, 'I learnt to handle myself in situations that arose, such as dealing with ministers and the media and being a health advocate for families.'[83] Gloria Longley, a local branch president in the 1960s and a council and executive member from 1969, described her involvement as 'a good learning exercise' and as 'something I wouldn't have missed for worlds'.[84]

In 2001 Plunket Society President Pam Murray chose the International Year of the Volunteer to speak out about Plunket's 'secret army' of 10,000 volunteers which played a vital role in New Zealand's health system and raised nearly $5 million each year.[85] Marg Hall, the Area Nurse Manager for South Canterbury, also spoke of Plunket's 'secret army' and wondered how the nursing services would survive without them.[86] Professor Virginia Hodgkinson of Georgetown University in Washington, DC, who addressed Plunket's 2001 national conference, calculated the value of Plunket's 10,000 volunteers as $46.8 million, substantially higher than the government's contribution of $19 million.[87] Such voluntary work was not, however, recognised in a market economy.

Sustaining this voluntary commitment was discussed by Ian Hassall in an address given to Plunket's 1993 national conference. He did not believe the society would continue to attract support if it were merely an agent of government or a business contracted by government. The 1990s funding changes affected Plunket's voluntary base. Hassall pointed out that, in this competitive funding system, Plunket was selling a product (its services) to the RHAs, which restricted its role as a consumer advocate: 'If Plunket makes a fuss on behalf of consumers the services it wishes to provide may not be funded'. Echoing Begg's demand that voluntary members have real power in order to retain their interest and commitment, Hassall argued that, 'Without the means of influencing what services they will receive, members become disillusioned and the membership falls away'. This, he said, was occurring at the very time when a strong consumer voice was needed. In his view, there was a danger of Plunket 'being seduced and bullied into becoming a mere service contractor'. Like Begg, he believed that 'in the field of population health individuals and groups fare best if they take an active role in identifying and dealing with threats to their health'.[88] This was Begg's 'citizen participation' concept, or Truby King's view that the Plunket Society's work should be 'left to the ladies'.[89]

Australia's feminist writer Kerreen Reiger has argued for a reconceptualisation of women's rights as sexually specific citizens to bring about an improvement in the supports for women in their child-bearing roles.[90] This would not have come as anything new to the women who founded Plunket. They had fought hard and successfully to gain public and government support for women in their role as mothers. They held a firm belief in women's entitlement to such support. The Plunket Society has a long history of advocacy for women as mothers and their infants. Hassall envisaged a continuing role for the society in advocacy: 'It either articulates and secures the needs of its constituency or it is history'.[91]

Notes

Introduction

1 Until 1980 its official title was the Royal New Zealand Society for the Health of Women and Children. For convenience throughout this book it will be referred to as the 'Plunket Society'.

2 *The Press*, 1 November 2001.

3 *Otago Daily Times (ODT)*, 26 June 1923.

4 Plunket Society, Deputation to George Forbes, 19 August 1930, H1 127 B.81 127, Archives New Zealand (ANZ).

5 *Mothercraft Training Society (MTS) Magazine* 34, December 1945, p. 507, Highgate Scientific and Literary Institution, London.

6 *New Zealand Parliamentary Debates (NZPD)*, Legislative Council, Vol. 285, 1949, p. 483.

7 Plunket Society, *Report of the Thirty-first General Conference 1952*, p. 7.

8 Erik Olssen, 'Towards a New Society', in G. W. Rice (ed.), *The Oxford History of New Zealand*, 2nd edn, Auckland, Oxford University Press, 1992, p. 263.

9 Philippa Mein Smith, 'Infant Welfare Services and Infant Mortality: A Historian's View', *Australian Economic Review*, 1, 1991, pp. 22–34; Philippa Mein Smith, *Mothers and King Baby: Infant Survival and Welfare in an Imperial World: Australia 1880–1950*, London, Macmillan, 1997.

10 Catherine Rollet, 'The Fight against Infant Mortality in the Past. An International Comparison', in Alain Bideau, Bertrand Desjardins, Hector Perez Brignoli (eds), *Infant and Child Mortality in the Past*, Oxford, Clarendon Press, 1997, p. 52.

11 Milton Lewis, 'The Problem of Infant Feeding', *Journal of History of Medicine and Allied Sciences*, 35, 1980, p. 185.

12 On reinstating a role for the infant welfare movement in the decline, see also Lara Marks, *Metropolitan Maternity: Maternity and Infant Welfare Services in Early Twentieth Century London*, Amsterdam, Rodopi, 1996.

13 Hoddinott to Stallworthy, 1 July 1930, 'Plunket Society General 1929–33', H.127, ANZ.

14 *New Zealand Herald (NZH)*, 14 September 1959.

15 Erik Olssen, 'Truby King and the Plunket Society: An Analysis of a Prescriptive Ideology', *New Zealand Journal of History (NZJH)*, 15, 1, 1981, pp. 3–23. For an example of its continuing place in the historical literature, see James Belich, *Paradise Reforged: A History of the New Zealanders from the 1880s to the Year 2000*, Auckland, Allen Lane, Penguin, 2001, p. 163.

16 Olssen, p. 14.

17 *Ibid.*, pp. 21–2.

18 See also L. Bryder, 'Perceptions of Plunket: Time to Review Historians' Interpretations?' in L. Bryder & D. A. Dow (eds), *New Countries and Old Medicine: Proceedings of an International Conference on the History of Medicine*, Auckland, Pyramid Press, 1995, pp. 97–103.

19 Anne Digby and John Stewart (eds), *Gender, Health and Welfare*, London, Routledge, 1996, p. 2; Jane Lewis, 'Gender, the Family and Women's Agency in the Building of "Welfare States": the British Case', *Social History*, 19, 1994, pp. 37–55.

20 Digby and Stewart, *Gender, Health and Welfare*, p. 2. See also Mein Smith, *Mothers and King Baby*, pp. 6, 139–61, 246; Bronwyn Dalley, *Family Matters: Child Welfare in Twentieth-century New Zealand*, Auckland, Auckland University Press, 1998, p. 7.

21 Two recent histories of state welfare are Margaret McClure, *A Civilised Community: A History of Social Security in New Zealand 1898–1998*, Auckland, Auckland University Press, 1998, and Dalley, *Family Matters*. See also Bronwyn Labrum, 'Family Needs and Family Desires: Discretionary State Welfare in New Zealand, 1920–1970', PhD thesis, Victoria University of Wellington, 2000; Alexander Davidson, *Two Models of Welfare: The Origins and Development of the Welfare State in Sweden and New Zealand, 1888–1988*, Uppsala, Academiae Ubsaliensis, 1989; Elizabeth Hanson, *The Politics of Social Security: The 1938 Act and Some Later Developments*, Auckland, Auckland University Press, Wellington, Oxford University Press, 1980. For a discussion of trends in welfare history, see David Thomson, 'Society and Social Welfare', in Colin Davis and Peter Lineham (eds), *The Future of the Past: Themes in New Zealand History*, Palmerston North, Department of History, Massey University, 1991, pp. 98–120. One noteworthy history of a voluntary organisation is Margaret Tennant, *Children's Health, the Nation's Wealth: A History of Children's Health Camps*, Wellington, Bridget Williams Books and Historical Branch, Department of Internal Affairs, 1994.

22 For general discussions of 'maternalism', see Theda Skocpol, *Protecting Soldiers and Mothers: The Political Origins of Social Policy in the United States*, Cambridge Mass., Belknap Press of Harvard University Press, 1992; Seth Koven and Sonya Michel (eds), *Mothers of a New World: Maternalist Politics and the Origins of Welfare States*, London and New York, Routledge, 1993, introduction; Lynn Weiner, 'International Trends: Maternalism as a Paradigm', *Journal of Women's History*, 5, 2, 1993, pp. 96–98; Molly Ladd-Taylor, *Mother-Work: Women, Child Welfare and the State, 1890–1930*, Urbana, University of Illinois Press, 1994. Melanie Nolan chose to use the label 'gynocentric feminism' to describe what others have called maternalism; see Melanie Nolan, *Breadwinning: New Zealand Women and the State*, Christchurch, Canterbury University Press, 2000, p. 33.

23 On the participation of women in 'active citizenship' or in a 'citizenship of contribution' through the voluntary organisations of health and social welfare in the nineteenth and early twentieth centuries, see Jane Lewis (ed.), *Women's Welfare, Women's Rights*, London, Croom Helm, 1983; Jane Lewis, *Women and Social Action in Victorian and Edwardian England*, Aldershot, Edward Elgar, 1991; Susan Pedersen, *Family Dependence and the Origins of the Welfare State: Britain and France 1914–1945*, New York & Cambridge, Cambridge University Press, 1993; Anne Digby, 'Poverty, Health and the Politics of Gender in Britain, 1870–1948', in Digby and Stewart, pp. 67–90.

24 Digby, 'Poverty, Health and the Politics of Gender', p. 67; Koven and Michel, *Mothers of a New World*, p. 21; Skocpol, *Protecting Soldiers and Mothers*, p. 522; Alisa Klaus, *Every Child a Lion: The Origins of Maternal and Infant Health Policy in the United States and France, 1890–1920*, Ithaca, Cornell University Press, 1993, p. 92.

25 See also Mein Smith, *Mothers and King Baby*, p. 5.

26 For example see Nolan, *Breadwinning*, Chapter 5.

27 Digby, 'Poverty, Health and the Politics of Gender', p. 84. I use 'maternalists' to distinguish those women who worked for women's rights as mothers from 'feminists' who worked to promote women's rights as men's equals. I do not see 'maternalist welfare' and 'paternalist welfare' as polar opposites; they both worked to promote the family. See also Jane Lewis, 'Women's Agency, Maternalism and Welfare', *Gender and History*, 6, 1, 1994, pp. 117–23, and Mein Smith, *Mothers and King Baby*, p. 246.

28 Sydney Halpern, *American Pediatrics: The Social Dynamics of Professionalism, 1880–1980*, Berkeley, University of California Press, 1988; Alexandra Minna Stern and Howard Markel (eds), *Formative Years: Children's Health in the United States 1880–2000*, Ann Arbor, University of Michigan Press, 2002.

29 H. C. Cameron, *The British Paediatric Association, 1928–1952*, London, British Paediatric Association, 1955, p. 9.

30   Honorary Secretary, New Zealand branch of the British Medical Association (BMA) to Plun-
     ket Society, 29 August 1910, AG7 11-5, Plunket Society Archives, Hocken Library (PSA).

31   Vida Jowett to Daisy Begg, 6 September 1938, 239, PSA.

32   M. W. Raffel, 'A Consultative Committee on Infant and Pre-school Health Services', *New
     Zealand Journal of Public Administration*, 28, 1, 1965, p. 48.

33   Helen Deem to Dr Basil Quin, 10 November 1950, 581, PSA.

34   See Christopher Lasch, *Haven in a Heartless World: The Family Besieged*, New York, Basic
     Books, 1977, and Barbara Ehrenreich and Deidre English, *For Her Own Good: 150 Years of
     the Experts' Advice to Women*, New York, Anchor Press/Doubleday, 1978; Ann Dally,
     Inventing Motherhood: The Consequences of an Ideal, London, Burnett Books, 1982, p. 82.
     Desley Deacon, 'Taylorism in the Home: The Medical Profession, the Infant Welfare Move-
     ment and the Deskilling of Women', *Australian New Zealand Journal of Sociology*, 21, 2, 1985,
     pp. 161–73, argued that the movement did not necessarily deskill women as mothers but
     denigrated their skills and undermined their confidence in the public sphere. For New
     Zealand examples see Helen May, *The Discovery of Early Childhood: The Development of
     Services for the Care and Education of Very Young Children, Mid Eighteenth Century Europe
     to Mid Twentieth Century New Zealand*, Auckland, Auckland University Press, Bridget
     Williams Books with New Zealand Council for Educational Research, 1997, pp. 142–3;
     Belinda Hitchman, 'Gender and Health: The Feminist Challenge to the Traditional Medical
     System', MA thesis, University of Auckland, 1987, pp. 67–8.

35   See for example J. Rodgers, '. . . A Good Nurse . . . A Good Woman', in R. Openshaw and
     D. McKenzie (eds), *Reinterpreting the Educational Past*, Wellington, New Zealand Council
     for Educational Research, 1987, pp. 54–63.

36   Plunket Society Council minutes (hereafter Council minutes), 10–11 April 1973, PSA.

37   See for example the report by George Salmond, discussed in Chapter 7: G. C. Salmond, *Mater-
     nal and Infant Care in Wellington: A Health Care Consumer Study*, Department of Health
     Special Report Series 45, Wellington, Government Printer, 1975.

38   See also L. Bryder, 'New Zealand's Infant Welfare Services and Maori, 1907–60', *Health and
     History*, 3, 1, 2001, pp. 65–86.

39   H.B. Turbott to N. Begg, 2 May 1962, Turbott memo to F. Cameron, 2 April 1962, H1 127
     32110, ANZ; 'Plunket Nurses', H1 127/4/5, ANZ.

40   For an institutional history of Plunket, see Gordon Parry, *A Fence at the Top: The First 75
     Years of the Plunket Society*, Dunedin, Plunket Society, 1982.

41   *Thursday*, 12 June 1975, p. 14. There are other examples, such as when K. V. Marriott asked
     women for a survey about 'infant welfare services' the response was invariably, 'you mean
     the Plunket Society': K. V. Marriott, 'The Plunket Society: Some Opinions', Public Health
     thesis, University of Otago, 1963, p. 8.

42   *NZH*, 16 July 2001.

Chapter 1: Founding the Society for Promoting the Health of Women and Children

1   *NZPD*, Legislative Council, Vol. 140, 1907, p. 636.

2   *NZPD*, House of Representatives, Vol. 117, 1901, p. 10.

3   Reported in *New Zealand Yearbook*, 1905, p. 253.

4   'Early Plunket', AG7-27, PSA. See also Editorial, *New Zealand Medical Journal* (*NZMJ*),
    7, November 1908, p. 22. In the United States progressive reformers sought an increase in
    birth rate only among the native-born white middle class, to counteract the effects of
    immigration: see Klaus, *Every Child a Lion*, p. 12.

5   See Deborah Dwork, *War is Good for Babies and Other Young Children: A History of the
    Infant and Child Welfare Movement in England 1898–1918*, London, Tavistock, 1987.

6   Klaus, *Every Child a Lion*, pp. 5, 31.

7   *NZPD*, Vol. 131, 1904, p. 481.

8 *NZH*, 3 February 1908.

9 *NZPD*, Vol. 140, 1907, p. 852.

10 'Save the Babies Week' Poster, 28 October, 2 November 1917, AG7/119, PSA.

11 Paul Baker, *King and Country Call: New Zealanders, Conscription and the Great War*, Auckland, Auckland University Press, 1988, pp. 110–5, 224.

12 'For the Sake of Women and Children' Public Health Department poster, Wellington, Government Printer, 1909, PSA.

13 *NZPD*, Vol. 128, 1904, p. 84.

14 *NZPD*, Vol. 140, 1907, p. 630.

15 *Ibid.*, p. 631.

16 This belief in man's capacity to control and modify his environment was also noted by Olssen, 'Truby King and the Plunket Society', p. 5.

17 Department of Public Health, Annual Report 1908, *Appendices to the Journals of the House of Representatives (AJHR)*, 1908, H-31, p. 10.

18 Newman was Chief Medical Officer of the Board of Education for England and Wales, 1907–19, and Chief Medical Officer of the Ministry of Health for England and Wales, 1919–35.

19 *NZPD*, Vol. 140, 1907, p. 655.

20 *NZPD*, Vol. 128, 1904, p. 78.

21 *NZPD*, Vol. 140, 1907, p. 661.

22 *New Zealand Observer*, 8 February 1908.

23 *NZPD*, Vol. 140, 1907, pp. 850–1.

24 Klaus, *Every Child a Lion*, p. 48.

25 Department of Public Health, Annual Report, *AJHR*, 1907, H-31, p. viii.

26 See Ernesto Lugaro, *Modern Problems in Psychiatry*, transl. by D. Orr and R. G. Rows, Manchester, Manchester University Press, 1909, pp. 230–8.

27 *AJHR*, 1906, H-7, p. 9; 1910, H-7, p. 17; F. Truby King, *Feeding and Care of Baby*, London, Macmillan, 1913, p. 151.

28 *NZPD*, Vol. 131, 1904, p. 481.

29 *NZPD*, Vol. 140, 1907, p. 632.

30 *NZPD*, Vol. 128, 1904, p. 69.

31 *NZPD*, Vol. 140, 1907, p. 856.

32 *Ibid.*, p. 661.

33 *AJHR*, 1907, H-31, p. 39.

34 Truby King's notebook, 89-098-29, PSA.

35 *NZH*, 3 February 1908; 'nursing' and 'suckling' were euphemisms for breastfeeding.

36 *NZPD*, Vol. 128, 1904, p. 77.

37 *NZPD*, Vol. 131, 1904, p. 481.

38 *NZPD*, Vol. 140, 1907, p. 655. The Public Health Department also lamented that 'for every profession and trade there has to be training save that of motherhood and fatherhood': Department of Public Health, Annual Report, *AJHR*, 1911, H-31, p. 249.

39 *NZPD*, Vol. 140, 1907, p. 661.

40 *Ibid.*, p. 622.

41 See David Hamer, *The Liberals: The Years of Power, 1891–1912*, Auckland, Auckland University Press, 1988, and W. H. Oliver, 'Social Welfare: Social Justice or Social Efficiency? Social Policy in the Liberal Period', *NZJH*, 13, 1, 1979, pp. 25–33.

42 *NZPD*, Vol. 140, 1907, p. 635.

43 Harry Hendrick, *Children, Childhood and English Society 1880–1990*, Cambridge, Cambridge University Press, 1997, p. 41.

44 On the general perceptions of children as 'social capital' at this time, see D. McDonald, 'The Paradox of Inequality: A Review of Child Welfare Policies in New Zealand', in P. Shannon and B. Webb (eds), *Social Policy and the Rights of the Child*, Dunedin, University of Otago, 1980, pp. 44–56, and Tennant, *Children's Health, the Nation's Wealth*, Chapter 1.

45 *NZPD*, Vol. 140, 1907, p. 637.

46 *Ibid.*, pp. 657–8.

47 *Ibid.*, pp. 661, 742, 745, 747.

48 *Ibid.*, p. 751.

49 Mein Smith, *Mothers and King Baby*, p. 87.

50 'Twenty Who Shaped a Nation', *NZH*, 1 January 2000; and on his international reputation, *Semi-Centennial Volume of the American Pediatric Society 1888–1938*, Wisconsin, George Banta Publishing Co., 1938, p. 393.

51 Keith Sinclair, *A Destiny Apart: New Zealand's Search for National Identity*, Wellington, Allen & Unwin, 1986, p. 223.

52 Truby King, American and English Notes 1918–19: Letter from Emmett Holt to King, 26 June 1919, 89-098-60, PSA.

53 Cathy Urwin and Elaine Sharland, 'From Bodies to Minds in Childcare Literature', in Roger Cooter (ed.), *In the Name of the Child: Health and Welfare 1880–1940*, London, Routledge, p. 177; see also Christina Hardyment, *Dream Babies: Three Centuries of Good Advice on Child Care*, New York, Harper & Row, 1983, p. 179 and Mabel Liddiard, *Mothercraft Manual*, London, Churchill, 1924, 6th edn, 1954. Visitors to the centre included Truby King and Anne Pattrick, and Liddiard visited New Zealand in 1926 further to study Plunket methods. The contacts were close until the Centre closed in 1951: MTS, *Annual reports*, Highgate Scientific and Literary Institution, London.

54 Chief Medical Officer to the Local Government Board, predecessor of Ministry of Health.

55 Lynne S. Milne, 'The Plunket Society: An Experiment in Infant Welfare', MA thesis, University of Otago, 1976, p. 19.

56 Cheryl Caldwell, 'Truby King and Seacliff Asylum 1889–1907', in Barbara Brookes and Jane Thomson (eds), *Unfortunate Folk: Essays on Mental Health Treatment, 1863–1992 / by Postgraduate History Students, University of Otago, 1972–2000*, Dunedin, Otago University Press, 2001, pp. 35–6.

57 Milne, 'The Plunket Society', p. 23

58 N. G. Falkner, 'Eliza Gordon', *Dictionary of New Zealand Biography (DNZB), Volume Four, 1921–1940*, p. 205; as Bella contracted rickets as a child, the Kings had no family of their own.

59 Milne, 'The Plunket Society', p. 26

60 See for example Dwork, *War is Good for Babies*.

61 G. F. McCleary, *Infantile Mortality and Infants' Milk Depots*, London, P. S. King & Son, 1905.

62 Letter from Alex R. Falconer to Watt, 3 February 1936, AG7 5-27, PSA.

63 F. T. King, *Feeding and Care of Baby*, Dunedin, Plunket Society, 1910, p. 140.

64 Plunket Society, *Report of the Fifth General Conference 1917*, p. 7.

65 *AJHR*, 1910 H-7, p. 17.

66 *AJHR*, 1908 H-7, p. 4.

67 Cited in *MTS Magazine*, Summer 1958, 49 (Sir Truby King Centenary issue); John Quinlan, 'Sir Truby King: Apostle of Mothercraft', *Nursing Times*, 54, 15, 1958, p. 414.

68 On the development of American paediatrics, see Stern and Markel (eds), *Formative Years*; Halpern, *American Pediatrics*; Richard A. Meckel, *Save the Babies: American Public Health Reform and the Prevention of Infant Mortality 1850–1929*, Baltimore, Johns Hopkins University Press, 1990; Rima M. Apple, *Mothers and Medicine: A Social History of Infant Feeding*, Madison, University of Wisconsin Press, 1987. On the influence of American paediatrics on Truby King, see also Mein Smith, *Mothers and King Baby*, pp. 93–5.

69 Halpern, *American Pediatrics*, p. 63.

70 This was said in 1938; Halpern, *American Pediatrics*, p. 63; Rima Apple, '"To be used only under the direction of a physician": Commercial Infant Feeding and Medical Practice, 1870–1940,' *Bulletin of the History of Medicine*, 54, 3, 1980, p. 311. For an illustration of the percentage method at its fullest, see five pages of equations for calculating percentages in T. M. Rotch, *Pediatrics: The Hygiene and Medical Treatment of Children*, London & Philadelphia, J. B. Lippincott, 1903. See also Hardyment, *Dream Babies*, p. 126.

71 Halpern, *American Pediatrics*, p. 64.

72 Kathleen Jones, 'Sentiment and Science: The Late Nineteenth Century Pediatrician as Mother's Advisor', *Journal of Social History*, 17, 1983, pp. 79–96; Apple, '"To be used only under the direction of a physician"', pp. 402–17; Meckel, *Save the Babies*, p. 57.

73 F. Truby King, 'Physiological Economy in the Nutrition of Infants', *NZMJ*, 6, November 1907, p. 82.

74 L. E. Holt, *The Care and Feeding of Children*, New York, Sidney Appleton, 1904; L. E. Holt, *The Diseases of Infancy and Childhood*, 3rd edn, London, Sidney Appleton, 1905.

75 F. Truby King, 'Physiological Economy in the Nutrition of Infants', *NZMJ*, 6, 1907, p. 102.

76 Also called Lactose, a dry powder extracted from milk.

77 *How to Reserve the Children: Plain Directions to Mothers*, Dunedin, Star Print, 1906, Auckland branch archives (ABA).

78 F. Truby King, *The Feeding of Plants and Animals* (Reprint from Pamphlet issued by New Zealand Farmers' Union), Wellington, Whitcombe & Tombs, 1905, p. 7.

79 Klaus, *Every Child a Lion*, p. 50.

80 See Nancy Tomes, *The Gospel of Germs: Men, Women and the Microbe in American Life*, Cambridge, Mass., Harvard University Press, 1998.

81 King, *The Feeding of Plants and Animals*, p. 6. In this he followed *The Care and Feeding of Infants* by Holt, who also wrote about producing the 'best grain or vegetables, cattle or horses': see Ehrenreich and English, *For Her Own Good*, p. 181.

82 J. S. Fairbairn, 'Natural Feeding of Infants', cited in King, Director of Child Health Report, Department of Health, Annual Report 1924–25, *AJHR*, 1925, H-31, pp. 27–8.

83 F. Truby King, *The Karitane Products Society. A Short Account of the Aims and Purposes of its Work in relation to the Plunket Society, the Medical Profession and the Public*, Wellington, L.T. Watkins Ltd, 1929, p. 2. Holt's statistics on New York were also cited in Truby King's 1907 *NZMJ* article, p. 79.

84 *Mother and Child*, March 1938, p. 454.

85 Irvine Loudon, 'Childbirth', in W. F. Bynum and Roy Porter, *Companion Encyclopedia of the History of Medicine*, Vol. 2, London & New York, Routledge, p. 1064.

86 Meckel, *Save the Babies*, p. 57.

87 *Ibid.*, p. 52.

88 King, *Natural Feeding of Infants*, with an introduction by Fairbairn issued by Babies of the Empire Society, London, Whitcombe & Tombs, 1918, p. 7.

89 King, *The Karitane Products Society*, p. 3; King, *NZMJ*, 6, 1907, pp. 80, 102.

90 Mary King, *Truby King: The Man, A Biography,* London, George Allen & Unwin, 1948, p. 204.

91 *Evening Star*, 22 December 1905, cited in Milne, p. 42.

92 Lynne S. Giddings, 'MacKinnon, Joanna', *DNZB, Volume Four, 1901–1920*, p. 306 (In Plunket Society sources it is spelt as 'McKinnon').

93 *New Zealand Observer*, 15 February 1908.

94 Neville Mayman, Commissioner, Report on the Inquiry into the Welfare of Mothers and Children in New Zealand, *New South Wales Parliamentary Papers*, Vol. 5, 1918, p. 309.

95 Molly Ladd-Taylor, *Mother-Work*, p. 43.

96 *ODT*, 15 May 1907.

97 *Ibid.*, 25 May 1907.

98 *NZH*, 29 January 1908.

99 Minutes of meeting 16 March 1908, Plunket Society Wellington branch minutes, AG 782 1/1, PSA.

100 See L. Bryder, *Not Just Weighing Babies: Plunket in Auckland 1908–1998*, Auckland, Pyramid Press, 1998, p. 1.

101 *Kai Tiaki*, 51, 1958, p. 153. Subsequently, as Lady Victoria Braithwaite, she maintained an active involvement in the London Society for many years as vice-chairman and vice-president in 1949. Her daughter-in-law, Lady Plunket, also became involved: MTS, *Annual reports*.

102 *NZH,* 29 January 1908.

103 Wellington branch minutes, 16 March 1908, PSA; Lady Plunket to Mason, 21 February 1908 & Mason to Lady Plunket, 2 March 1908, cited in Derek A. Dow, *Safeguarding the Public Health: A History of the New Zealand Department of Health*, Wellington, Victoria University Press, 1995, p. 66.

104 Plunket Society, *Annual report 1912–13*, p .7.

105 Parry, *A Fence at the Top*, p. 57.

106 Council minutes, 13 July 1917, AG7 1-2-1, PSA.

107 MTS, *Annual reports*, 1918–48.

108 Bryder, *Not Just Weighing Babies*, p. 34.

109 G. W. A. Bush, *Decently and in Order: The Centennial History of Auckland City Council*, Auckland, Collins, 1971, p. 527.

110 *Plunket News*, 10, 3, August 1973, p. 3.

111 Wellington branch minutes, 4 September 1908, PSA.

112 *Ibid.*, 16 March 1908.

113 Wellington branch, minutes of AGM, 16 August 1956, PSA; *Annual report 1951–52*, obituary of Mrs William Young, p. 6.

114 Truby King to Eileen Partridge, 1 June 1924, 1189, PSA.

115 Survey of Plunket branches, AG 2-76, PSA. Cited by Maureen Hickey, 'Negotiating Infant Welfare: The Plunket Society in the Interwar Period', MA thesis, University of Otago, 1999, p. 27.

116 Frances Porter, 'Atkinson, Lily May 1866–1921', *DNZB, Volume Two, 1870–1900*, pp. 15–16.

117 Raewyn Dalziel, 'Stout, Anna Paterson, 1858–1931', *DNZB, Volume Two, 1870–1900*, p. 483.

118 Frances Porter, 'Richmond, Mary Elizabeth, 1853–1949', *DNZB, Volume Three, 1901–1920*, p. 433.

119 Beryl Hughes, 'McVicar, Annie, 1862–1954', *DNZB, Volume Three, 1901–1920*, p. 317.

120 Wellington branch, minutes of AGM, 22 June 1939, PSA.

121 Wellington branch minutes, 1908, PSA.

122 Jessie Munro, *The Story of Suzanne Aubert*, Auckland, Auckland University Press & Bridget Williams Books, 1996, p. 265.

123 *Ibid.*, pp. 316, 362.

124 She was still elected vice-president 1925–26, then aged 90: Wellington branch, minutes of AGM, 7 June 1925, PSA.

125 J. S. Purdy, Report of Auckland District Health Officer, *AJHR*, H-31, 1908, p. 19; Wellington branch minutes, 16 March 1908, PSA.

126 See also Klaus, *Every Child a Lion*, p. 95.

127 Wellington branch minutes, 13 May 1908, PSA; Wellington branch, minutes of AGM, 22 June 1939, PSA.

128 Dorothy Page, 'Platts-Mills, Daisy Elizabeth, 1868–1956', *DNZB, Volume Three, 1901–20*, pp. 403–5.

129 Auckland branch minutes, 7 October 1912, ABA.

130 She was on the committee when the society was incorporated in February 1908. Truby King referred to her being on the 'Board' in 1910: Conference between Valintine and a Plunket Sub-committee, c.1910, p. 35, AG7 5-27, PSA.

131 Doris Gordon, *Backblocks Baby-Doctor: An Autobiography*, London, Faber & Faber, p. 162.

132 Heather McDonald, 'Boys-Smith, Winifred Lily', *DNZB, Volume Three, 1901–20*, pp. 60–1.

133 Maureen Hickey, 'Hanan, Susanna', *DNZB, Volume Three, 1901–20*, p.199.

Chapter 2: A Professional Organisation

1   Plunket Society, *Annual report 1912–3*, p.7.

2   Plunket Society Executive minutes (hereafter 'Executive minutes'), 1 July 1941, PSA.

3   Council minutes, 13 April 1917, AG7 1-2-1, PSA.

4   Hosking to Carr, 18 August 1916, AG7 3/174, items 13–16, 22, 23, PSA.

5 Council minutes, 14 September 1917, PSA.
6 See M. P. Belgrave, '"Medical Men" and "Lady Doctors": The Making of a New Zealand Profession, 1867–1941', PhD thesis, Victoria University of Wellington, 1985.
7 Auckland branch minutes, 6 October 1910, ABA.
8 *Dominion*, 1914, press cuttings, 6, PSA.
9 See for example Celia Davies, 'The Health Visitor as Mother's Friend: A Woman's Place in Public Health, 1900–14', *Social History of Medicine*, 1, 1, 1988, pp. 41–5; Seth Koven, 'Borderlands: Women, Voluntary Action and Child Welfare in Britain, 1840 to 1914', in Koven and Michel (eds), *Mothers of a New World*, p. 124; F. K. Prochaska, *Women and Philanthropy in Nineteenth-century England*, Oxford, Clarendon Press, 1980.
10 Plunket Society Deputation, Wellington, 10 June 1914, AG7 5-12, PSA.
11 Council minutes, 27 August 1919, PSA.
12 *British Nursing Journal*, 3 September 1910.
13 Plunket Society, *Annual report 1910–11*, p. 6.
14 Plunket Society, *Annual report 1911–12*, p. 8.
15 Porter, 'Richmond, Mary Elizabeth', p. 433.
16 Plunket Society, *Annual report 1911–12*, p. 8.
17 Plunket Society, *Report of the Fourth General Conference 1914*, p. 14.
18 James W. Barrett, 'Waste of Infant Life', *Kai Tiaki*, 7, 3, 1914, p. 119.
19 Wellington branch minutes, 2 September 1915, PSA.
20 Plunket Society, *Report of the Fifth General Conference 1917*, p. 14.
21 Council minutes, 21 May 1919, PSA.
22 Circular re. Recent Conference in Wellington, 1914, 120, PSA.
23 Rika Coleman to Jean Glendinning, 16 February 1915, 121, PSA.
24 Wellington branch minutes, 4 March 1915, PSA.
25 Plunket Society Deputation, 10 June 1914, AG7 5-12, PSA.
26 Auckland branch minutes, 7 September 1916; February & May 1917, ABA. Alison Henderson to Carr, 11 May 1916, 29 June 1917, 134, PSA.
27 Plunket Society, *Report of the Fifth General Conference 1917*, p. 15.
28 'Report of the National Baby Week Council', Box 79, SA/HVA/F3/3, Wellcome Library Archives and Manuscript Section (Wellcome). On American Baby Weeks, see also Klaus, *Every Child a Lion*, p.162.
29 Council minutes, 3 July 1917, AG7 1-2-1, PSA.
30 *New Zealand Observer*, 2 May 1908.
31 Council minutes, 11 January 1933, 1184, PSA.
32 Letter from Glendinning, 30 December 1916, quoted in Plunket Society, *Report of the Fifth General Conference 1917*, p. 22. The Auckland branch, for example, set up a businessmen's committee in 1928 with 25 members to tap the wealth of the business community: September 1928, AG7/1186, PSA.
33 Address by Frederic Truby King, Plunket Society, *Report of the Fifth General Conference 1917*, pp. 6–7.
34 Wellington branch, minutes of AGM, 18 October 1910, PSA.
35 J. Millar to Kathleen Hosking, 19 December 1907, AG7 11-3, PSA.
36 Plunket Society, *Annual report 1912–13*, p. 8.
37 Central Council, Deputation to Minister, February 1917, 124, PSA.
38 22 October 1917, AG7 3/174 items 13–16,22, 23, PSA.
39 Babies of the Empire Society, Report for 6 months ending 31 August 1918, p. 5, Highgate.
40 J. S. Purdy, 'Infant Mortality in New South Wales', *Medical Journal of Australia*, 11, 1922, p. 295.
41 Plunket Society, *Annual report 1912–13*, p. 8.
42 26 May 1914, AG 7, 3/174, items 13–16, 22, 23, PSA.
43 29 May 1914, AG 7, 3/174, items 13–16, 22, 23, PSA.
44 Letter from Glendinning, 30 December 1916, cited in Plunket Society, *Report of the Fifth General Conference 1917*, p. 22.

45 See Margaret Tennant, *Paupers and Providers: Charitable Aid in New Zealand,* Wellington, Allen & Unwin/ Historical Branch, 1989.

46 Plunket Society, *Annual report 1912–13,* p. 8.

47 Conference between Valintine and Plunket Society sub-committee, March 1913, AG7 5-27, PSA.

48 Report of the Commissioner, Mr Neville Mayman, on the Inquiry into the Welfare of Mothers and Children in New Zealand, *New South Wales Parliamentary Papers,* Vol. 5, 1918, 291, p. 10.

49 Plunket Society, *Report of the Fifth General Conference 1917,* p. 21.

50 *Ibid.,* p. 20.

51 See Bryder, 'New Zealand's Infant Welfare Services and Maori', pp. 65–86.

52 Russell to Carr, 11 September 1918, 131, PSA.

53 Carr to Russell, 26 September 1918, 124, PSA.

54 Glendinning to Heaton Rhodes, 12 May 1915, 120, PSA.

55 Council minutes, 8 August 1917, PSA.

56 *Auckland Star,* 15 October 1918, press cuttings, ABA.

57 Killick to Carr, 10 December 1918, 131, PSA.

58 See Dow, *Safeguarding the Public Health,* p. 91.

59 Josephine Baker, *Fighting for Life,* New York, Macmillan, 1939, cited in John Duffy, 'The American Medical Profession and Public Health: From Support to Ambivalence', *Bulletin of the History of Medicine,* 53, 1, 1979, p. 17 and Klaus, *Every Child A Lion,* p. 88. King was very impressed with Baker and her work, stating, 'Of all the women who had done great work for Child Welfare in our day, no one had done greater work than Dr Baker': Mary King, *Truby King,* p. 333.

60 Klaus, *Every Child A Lion,* p. 88; see also Robyn Muncy, *Creating a Female Dominion in American Reform 1890–1935,* New York, Oxford University Press, 1991, p. 143, and Kriste Lindenmeyer, *'A Right to Childhood': The US Children's Bureau and Child Welfare, 1912–46,* Urbana and Chicago, University of Illinois Press, 1997.

61 Auckland branch minutes, 19 August 1913, ABA. Letter from Lathrop printed in *The Plunket Magazine,* January 1915, p. 4, 26, PSA.

62 Meckel, *Save the Babies,* p. 205.

63 Council minutes, 27 September 1922, PSA.

64 Wellington branch minutes, 16 March 1908, PSA. On Fell see Rex Wright-St Clair, *A History of the New Zealand Medical Association: The First 100 Years,* Wellington, Butterworths, 1987, p. 74.

65 *NZMJ,* 7, 1908, p. 23.

66 *New Zealand Observer,* 27 June 1908.

67 Report of meeting 4 March 1910, AG7 11-4, PSA.

68 Nurse registration had been introduced into New Zealand in 1900.

69 1 April 1908, General Correspondence 1907–08, AG7 11-3, PSA.

70 *Kai Tiaki,* 1, 2, 1908, pp. 32–3.

71 Letter to editor, *ODT,* 11 March 1910.

72 Hon. Secretary BMA Otago Branch, to Plunket Society, 29 August 1910, AG7 11-5, PSA.

73 Wellington branch minutes, 20 November 1908, 4 December 1908, 18 December 1908; Wellington branch, first AGM, 7 May 1909, PSA.

74 Plunket Society, *Report of the Fourth General Conference 1914,* p. 11.

75 Auckland branch minutes, 2 April 1915, ABA.

76 Plunket Society, *Report of the Fourth General Conference 1914,* p. 21.

77 Auckland branch minutes, 5 June 1914, ABA.

78 *NZMJ,* 8, August 1910, pp. 78, 80.

79 Auckland branch minutes, 5 May 1910, ABA.

80 *Ibid.,* 1 December 1910.

81 *Ibid.,* 2 March 1911.

82 Wellington branch minutes, 1908–10, PSA.

83 Truby King to Lily Atkinson, 20 June 1910, 89-098-58, PSA.
84 Glendinning, hon. secretary Plunket Society, letter of condolence to Dr Batchelor jnr on death of father, September 1915, 120, PSA.
85 Wellington branch minutes, PSA; Obituary, *NZMJ*, 1934, pp. 328–31; *Lancet*, 2, 1934, p. 387.
86 'The Plunket Society and the Department: Infant-feeding and the Training of Maternity Nurses', *Journal of Public Health*, 3, September 1917, pp. 41–2.
87 Auckland branch minutes, 6 March 1913, ABA.
88 *Ibid.*, 1910–21.
89 Plunket Society, *Annual report 1912–13*, p. 4.
90 *Ibid.*
91 Plunket Society, *Annual report 1908–09*, p. 4.
92 Plunket Society, *Annual report 1912–13*, p. 11.
93 *Otago Daily Times and Witness* to Carr, 9 February 1915, AG 7, 3/174 Items 13-16, 22, 23, PSA.
94 Plunket Society, *Annual report 1911–12*, p. 5.
95 Plunket Society, *Annual report 1912–13*, p. 11.
96 Plunket Society, *Annual report 1911–12*, p. 9; *1912–13*, p. 12.
97 Muncy, *Creating a Female Dominion*, pp. 112–13.
98 J. Ilott, Wellington agent for Glaxo to *Otago Daily Times*, 27 January 1915, AG 7, 3/174 Items 13-16, 22, 23, PSA. According to Douglas Myers, his grandmother was among them: personal communication.
99 Katherine Arnup, *Education for Motherhood: Advice for Mothers in Twentieth-century Canada*, Toronto, University of Toronto Press, 1994, p. 28. See for example Plunket Society, *Annual report 1911–12*, p. 4, *1912–13*, p. 12.
100 Plunket Society, *Annual report 1908–09*, p. 6. Lady Margaret Talbot was the wife of the then Governor of Victoria. Victorians co-opted the aims and objects of New Zealand's Plunket Society: see Mein Smith, *Mothers and King Baby*, p. 84.
101 Neville Mayman, Commissioner, Report on the Inquiry into the Welfare of Mothers and Children in New Zealand, *New South Wales Parliamentary Papers*, Vol. 5, 1918, p. 310.
102 Auckland branch minutes, 5 February 1920, ABA.
103 Robert M. Woodbury, *Infant Mortality and Preventive Work in New Zealand*, reprinted from the *Transactions of the Eleventh Annual Meeting of the American Child Hygiene Association*, St Louis, October 11–13, 1920.

Chapter 3: Plunket Becomes a Household Word

1 Muncy, *Creating a Female Dominion*, p. 96.
2 Ladd-Taylor, *Mother-Work*, p.177.
3 Charles Webster, *The Health Services Since the War. Volume 1. Problems of Health Care. The National Health Service Before 1957*, London, HMSO, 1988, p. 7.
4 Mein Smith, *Mothers and King Baby*, p. 84.
5 Arnup, *Education for Motherhood*, p. 28. On the First World War and social policy, see also Dalley, *Family Matters*, p. 67.
6 Plunket Society, *Report of the Sixth General Conference 1920*, p. 6.
7 G. W. Rice, 'The Making of New Zealand's 1920 Health Act', *NZJH*, 22, 1, 1988, p. 4.
8 'Memorandum being on the Appointment of Dr Truby King as Director of Child Welfare', February 1920, AG7 5-12, PSA.
9 Dow, *Safeguarding the Public Health*, pp. 93–4.
10 'Memorandum being on the Appointment of Dr Truby King', 23 July 1920, AG7 5-12, PSA.
11 *NZMJ*, 21, 1922, p. 80. Along with his wife, Young was a close friend of Truby King; he had been present at the founding of the Wellington Plunket branch and 50 years later became a patron of the branch: Wellington branch, *Annual report 1951–52*, obituary of Mrs William Young; Wellington branch, AGM, 16 August 1956, PSA.

12 'Memorandum being on the Appointment of Dr Truby King', 31 August 1920, AG7 5-12, PSA.
13 4 January 1921, AG7 5-12, PSA.
14 8 February 1921, AG7 5-12, PSA.
15 *Dominion*, 27 April 1922.
16 Cited by King in letter to Massey, 28 July 1922, AG7 5-12, PSA, and also in Plunket Society, *Report of the Eighth General Conference 1922*, pp. 116–17.
17 King to Massey, 28 July 1922, AG7 5-12, PSA.
18 Memo by Parr to Massey, 11 August 1922, AG7 5-12, PSA.
19 Health Department Annual Report, Child Welfare, *AJHR*, 1924, H-31, pp. 26–7.
20 Barbara Brookes has commented that it was probably with some relief that King was side-lined into mental health services in 1924: Barbara Brookes, 'Truby King, Frederic', *DNZB, Volume Two, 1880–1899*, p. 258. In 1924 he was appointed acting Inspector-General of Mental Defectives; from 1925 to 1927 he was Inspector-General of Mental Defectives.
21 Dalley, *Family Matters*, p.94.
22 May, *The Discovery of Early Childhood*, p.141.
23 Sue Kedgley, *Mum's the Word: The Untold Story of Motherhood in New Zealand*, Auckland, Random House, 1996, p. 90.
24 Michael H. Watt, 'The Rest of the Day to Myself', unpublished autobiography (deposited in Health Department), pp.56–7.
25 Plunket Society, *Report of the Sixth General Conference 1920*, pp. 18–19.
26 *NZPD*, House of Representatives, Vol. 189, 1920, p. 623.
27 Plunket Society, *Report of the Eighth General Conference 1922*, p. 23.
28 Council minutes, 1–3 November 1939, PSA.
29 Yvonne M. Wilkie, 'Stewart, Mary Downie', *DNZB, Volume Three,1901–1920*, pp. 487–8.
30 Wellington branch, minutes of AGM, 24 April 1922, PSA; *Evening Post*, 26 April 1922.
31 Plunket Society, *Condensed Summaries of Conference Reports 1914–1926*, p. 69B.
32 *Dominion*, 22 June 1926; Wellington branch AGM, 21 June 1926, Wellington branch, 1913–38, H-1 127/21 13358A, ANZ.
33 Plunket Society, *Report of the Twenty-third General Conference 1936*, p. 10.
34 Plunket Society, *Report of the Fourteenth General Conference 1928*, pp. 73–4.
35 Memo, Ministry of Health to Valintine, 23 June 1921, 89-098-68, ANZ.
36 M. H. Watt, 'Infant Mortality in New Zealand,' *New Zealand Journal of Health and Hospitals*, 4, 4, 1921, pp. 88–94.
37 Hoddinott to Stallworthy, 13 June 1930, H1/127/54 (17775), ANZ.
38 Stallworthy to Hoddinott, 18 June 1930, and Valintine's annotation, H1/127/54 (17775), ANZ.
39 Stallworthy to Hoddinott, 18 June 1930, 'Plunket Society General 1929–33', H1 127 B.81 127, ANZ.
40 Valintine to Stallworthy, 16 June 1930, 'Plunket Society General 1929–33', H.127, ANZ.
41 Valintine to Hoddinott, 16 June 1930, 'Plunket Society General 1929–33', H.127, ANZ.
42 Hoddinott to Stallworthy, 1 July 1930, 'Plunket Society General 1929–33', H.127, ANZ.
43 Plunket Society, Deputation to G. Forbes, 19 August 1930, H1 127 B.81 127, ANZ.
44 *Dominion*, 19 November 1930.
45 Council minutes, 18 August 1931, PSA. The subsidies were reduced from £125 to £112 10s to £106 10s.
46 Memo by Watt, 28 July 1936, H1 127 9251 127, ANZ.
47 Final Report of the National Expenditure Commission, *AJHR*, B-4A, 1932, p. 72.
48 *NZPD*, Vol. 233, 1932, pp. 288–9, 308.
49 *Dominion*, 24 March 1933.
50 Watt, memo on Plunket Society, 28 July 1936, H1 127 9251 127, ANZ.
51 Begg to Fraser, 22 May 1937, H1 127 925127, ANZ.
52 Hilary Stace, 'Fraser, Janet', *DNZB, Volume Four, 1921–1940*, p. 182.

53 Wellington branch minutes, letter from Fraser to Begg, 8 June 1937, read at meeting 3 September 1937, PSA; *Evening Post*, 22 July 1937.

54 *Evening Post*, 22 July 1937.

55 H. Deem, N. Fitzgibbon, *Modern Mothercraft: A Guide to Parents, The Official Handbook of the Royal New Zealand Society for the Health of Women and Children (inc) (Plunket Society)*, Dunedin, Plunket Society, 1945, p. 7.

56 Plunket Society, *Report of the Twenty-third General Conference 1936*, p. 7.

57 Plunket Society, *Report of the Twenty-fifth General Conference 1938*, p. 6.

58 D. G. McMillan, *A National Health Service: New Zealand of Tomorrow*, Wellington, The New Zealand Worker, 1934, pp. 6, 11.

59 Memo by Watt, Deputy Director General, 21 January 1931, H1 127 B.81 127, ANZ.

60 Tweed to Hoddinott, 25 October 1935, 231, PSA.

61 Cited in Watt's unpublished autobiography, pp.124–5. M. H. Watt, *Report of the Director-General of Health Reviewing Public-Health Administration in North America, the United Kingdom and Scandinavia, with Consequent Proposals for the Development of the New Zealand System*, Wellington, Government Printer, 1940, pp. 30–1.

62 Muncy, *Creating a Female Dominion*, p.121.

63 On the Karitane Products Society see Chapter 4.

64 Auckland branch, *Annual report 1931*, ABA.

65 Guy H. Scholefield, *Who's Who in New Zealand and the Western Pacific*, 2nd end. Masterton, 1925, p.117, 3rd edn, Wellington, Rangatira Press, 1932, p. 214.

66 Council minutes, 1 November 1933, PSA.

67 *Ibid.*, 28 April 1937.

68 *Ibid.*, 12 December 1930.

69 Letter from McGeorge, Council minutes, 12 December 1930, PSA.

70 *Kai Tiaki*, 15 September 1934, p. 151.

71 Challis Hooper, *Anne Pattrick, Director of Plunket Nursing New Zealand 1920–1934: A Memoir*, Dunedin, Training School for Plunket Nurses, 1958, p. 2.

72 *Kai Tiaki*, 11, 1918, pp. 14, 111.

73 *Kai Tiaki*, 11, 1918, p. 192.

74 Hooper, *Anne Pattrick*, p. 2.

75 *Kai Tiaki*, 13, 1920, p. 150; 14, 1921, p. 89.

76 Truby King to Valintine, 13 June 1920, AG7 5-12, PSA.

77 Plunket Society, *Report of the Tenth General Conference 1924*, p. 46.

78 He did not state that women were not capable doctors, though this was the view of his friend and colleague in the earlier twentieth century, Dr Ferdinand Batchelor, 'Society for the Promotion of the Health of Women and Children. Address by Dr F.C. Batchelor', 1909, University of Auckland Library.

79 Obituary, *Kai Tiaki*, 30, 1937, p. 248.

80 Hooper, *Anne Pattrick*, p. 7; *Kai Tiaki*, 30, 1937, p. 248; 32, 1939, p. 205.

81 Hooper, *Anne Pattrick*, p. 5.

82 Council minutes, 20 August 1928, PSA.

83 *Kai Tiaki*, 18, 1925, p. 47.

84 Council minutes, 22 November 1930, PSA.

85 *Ibid.*, 12 December 1930.

86 *Ibid.*, 3 May 1932.

87 *Ibid.*, 30 March 1933.

88 *Ibid.*, 2 November 1933; copy of letter from Hoddinott to Pattrick, 30 November 1933, in Wellington branch minute book, PSA.

89 Wellington branch minutes, letter, 18 December 1933, PSA.

90 *Ibid.*, 5 December 1930; 3 March 1931.

91 *Ibid.*, 25 January 1934, 19 February 1934.

92 *Kai Tiaki*, 27, 1, 1934, p. 26.

93   *Ibid.*
94   Cited in Auckland branch, *Twenty-sixth annual report 1933–34*, p. 28.
95   *Kai Tiaki*, 27, 1, 1934, p.28.
96   Noeline de Courcy, *Nora Philomena Fitzgibbon 1889–1979: A Biography of an Outstanding New Zealand Woman*, Dunedin, N. de Courcy, 1990.
97   *Kai Tiaki*, 27, 4, 1934, p.153
98   *Kai Tiaki*, 27, 1, 1934, p. 6; 27, 4, 1934, p. 154.
99   Maureen Hickey, 'Negotiating Infant Welfare: The Plunket Society in the Interwar Period', MA thesis, University of Otago, 1999, p.122.
100 The 1917 constitution established a council of fifteen members, seven of whom were Dunedin branch members who made up the executive. From 1931 there were fifteen council members, three from each provincial district (Auckland, Wanganui, Wellington, Christchurch and Dunedin), as well as seven members of the executive drawn from Dunedin.
101 'Unofficial Provincial Conference – to discuss proposed alterations to Rules in preparation for General Conference in Wellington in July', 27 April 1934, ABA.
102 *Kai Tiaki*, 27, 4, 1934, p. 196; Challis, *Anne Pattrick*, p. 4.
103 *Kai Tiaki*, 28, 3, 1935, p. 124; 28, 4, 1935, p. 163.
104 *Kai Tiaki*, 34, 3, 1941, p. 124.
105 Plunket Society, *Report of Interim Conference 1925*, p.16.
106 Charles Hercus and Gordon Bell, *The Otago Medical School under the First Three Deans*, Edinburgh, Livingstone, 1964, p. 271; Plunket Society, *Annual report 1948–49*, pp. 6–8; Obituary, *NZMJ*, 53, 1954, p. 80.
107 Plunket Society, *Report of Interim Conference 1925*, pp. 34–40.
108 Plunket Society, *Report of the Twelfth General Conference 1926*, p. 25; Council minutes, 18 March 1927, PSA.
109 Truby King to Valintine, 13 June 1920, AG7 5-12, PSA.
110 Mary King, *Truby King*, p. 305.
111 Helen MacMurchy to W. Jenkins, 3 May 1927, AG 782-6/13, PSA.
112 Mary White (nee King), interview, Plunket Society Oral History Project, 1992.
113 Barbara Brookes, 'Truby King, Frederic', *DNZB, Volume Two, 1880–1899*, p. 258.
114 Mary King, *Truby King*, p. 334. However, according to the conference report he received a 'very warm welcome', *Mother and Child*, 1, 6 September 1930, p. 215.
115 Mary King, *Truby King*, pp. 339–40; see also Mein Smith, *Mothers and King Baby*, Chapter 5.
116 Plunket Society, *Annual report 1928–29*, p.15.
117 Council minutes, 12 December 1930, PSA.
118 *Ibid.*, 14 December 1921.
119 *Ibid.*, 18 August 1931.
120 See Hickey, 'Negotiating Infant Welfare', p. 62.
121 Letter to Judge Blair, Council minutes, 4 July 1932, PSA.
122 *Dominion*, 19 and 22 October 1932.
123 Council minutes, 25 October 1932, PSA.
124 Truby King to Tweed, 4 September 1933, 231, PSA.
125 Hoddinott statement for McGeorge, 2 April 1933, Plunket Society General and Administration 1929–33, H1 127 B.81 127, ANZ.
126 See for example *Evening Post*, 14 February 1938, with depictions of his state funeral.
127 Mary White, interview, Plunket Society Oral History Project, 1992.
128 See Chapter 4.
129 Executive minutes, 1 November 1933, PSA.
130 Watt to Secretary Treasury, 25 June 1934, H1 127 9251 127, ANZ. On Karitane Products Society, see Chapter 4.
131 Executive minutes, 7 December 1934, 25 June 1935, 4 July 1935, 7 August 1935, PSA.
132 *Ibid.*, 1 June 1937.
133 Sidey to Hunt, 8 December 1936, 234, PSA.

134 Confidential circular to members of Dominion Council, 12 March 1937, 234, PSA.

135 Council minutes, 28 April 1937, PSA.

136 Executive minutes, 28 September 1937, PSA.

137 *Ibid.*

138 Council minutes, 29 March 1938, PSA.

139 Olssen, 'Truby King and the Plunket Society', pp. 3–23.

140 This was evident in the dispute re the update of *The Feeding and Care of Baby*: 'Feeding and Care of Baby 1936–40', AG7 11-21, PSA.

141 *Mother and Child*, 19, 11, February 1949, p. 252.

142 Kathleen W. Jones, '"Mother Made Me Do It": Mother-Blaming and the Women of Child Guidance', in Molly Ladd-Taylor and Lauri Umansky, *'Bad' Mothers: The Politics of Blame in Twentieth-Century America*, New York, New York University Press, 1998, p.108. See also Lasch, *Haven in a Heartless World*, and Ehrenreich and English, *For Her Own Good*.

143 Claudia Knapman, 'Reconstructing Mothering: Feminism and the Early Childhood Centre', *Australian Feminist Studies*, 18, 1993, p. 122.

144 For further discussion of this, see Linda Bryder, 'Perceptions of Plunket', pp. 97–103. Apple also argued that, in the United States, 'scientific motherhood' 'denied [women] control over child-rearing': R. M. Apple, 'Constructing Mothers: Scientific Motherhood in the Nineteenth and Twentieth Centuries', *Social History of Medicine*, 8, 2, 1995, pp. 161–78.

145 Olssen, 'Truby King and the Plunket Society', pp. 3–23.

146 May, *The Discovery of Early Childhood*, pp. 142–3.

147 Hitchman, 'Gender and Health', pp. 67–8.

148 Cited in Mein Smith, *Mothers and King Baby*, pp. 128–9.

149 Montgomery Spencer to Tweed, 12 November 1937, cited in Christine Daniell, *A Doctor at War: A Life in Letters, 1914–43*, Masterton, Fraser Books, 2001, p.157; see also Daniell, *A Doctor at War*, pp. 166, 184, 185.

150 Health Department, Annual Report 1938–39, *AJHR*, 1939, H-31, p. 102.

151 Quin to Deem, 25 October 1950, 595, PSA.

152 Lynne Giddings, in Anne Else (ed.), *Women Together: A History of Women's Organisations in New Zealand: Nga Ropu Wahine o Te Motu*, Wellington, Historical Branch, Department of Internal Affairs and Daphne Brasell Associates Press, 1993, p. 259.

153 Partridge to Pattrick, February 1932, 378, PSA.

154 Circular letter to Plunket nurses, 26 July 1945, 579, PSA.

155 *NZH*, 11 August 1962.

156 *Ibid.*

157 Auckland branch minutes, 7 April 1921, ABA.

158 *Auckland Star*, 29 June 1933.

159 M. Tweed, 'Report on Wellington District Plunket Nursing Service in relation to reduction of staff, 1934', AG7 2-306, PSA.

160 Rona Adshead (ed.), *Some of My Yesterdays. The Autobiography of Marion Shepherd ('Maisie')*, Invercargill, Craig Printing, 1989, pp. 120–1.

161 Interview, Marion Shepherd, Plunket Society Oral History Project, 1992.

162 *Ibid.*, p. 131.

163 See for example Auckland branch, *Twenty-sixth annual report 1933–34*, pp. 15, 20.

164 Kedgley, *Mum's the Word*, pp. 89–94.

165 Jane Lewis, *The Politics of Motherhood, Child and Maternal Welfare in England, 1900–1939*, London, Croom Helm, 1980.

166 Wellington branch minutes, 2 December 1915, PSA.

167 Auckland branch, *Eighteenth annual report 1925–26*, p. 23.

168 Auckland branch, *Nineteenth annual report 1926–27*, p. 28.

169 *NZH Supplement*, 6 March 1936.

170 Auckland branch minutes, 2 October, 6 November 1919, ABA.

171 Council minutes, 12 July 1932, PSA.

172 Wellington branch, minutes of AGM, 7 May 1909, PSA.

173 Auckland branch minutes, 4 December 1919, ABA.

174 *Dominion*, 10 February 1934.

175 Philippa Mein Smith, 'Mothers, Babies and the Mothers' and Babies' Movement: Australia through Depression and War', *Social History of Medicine*, 6, 1, 1993, pp. 68, 73.

176 See Desley Deacon, 'Taylorism in the Home: The Medical Profession, the Infant Welfare Movement and the Deskilling of Women', *Australian New Zealand Journal of Sociology*, 21, 2, 1985, p. 169.

177 G. C. Jennings, 'The Royal New Zealand Society for the Health of Women and Children', Public Health thesis, University of Otago, 1936, p. 17.

178 Auckland branch, *Twenty-fourth annual report 1931–32*, p. 24. This was also the view of two medical students in 1940: S. K. Watson and A. E. Walton, 'A study in antenatal care', Public Health thesis, University of Otago, 1940, p. 23.

179 H. Main and V. Scantlebury, 'Report to the Minister of Public Health on the Welfare of Women and Children', Department of Public Health, Victoria, 1926, p. 11, *Victorian Parliamentary Papers*, 9, 2, 1926.

180 Nolan, *Breadwinning*, p.126.

181 J. R. Gilmour, 'The Mother, the Baby, and the Plunket Sister', Public Health thesis, University of Otago, 1950, p. 30.

182 Meckel, *Save the Babies*, p. 47; Ehrenreich and English, *For Her Own Good*, p. 181. Both Holt and Spock produced books on parenting which proved extremely popular in their respective generations.

183 Mein Smith, *Mothers and King Baby*, p. 10; Kathleen V. Lynch, *An Annotated Bibliography of the Royal New Zealand Society for the Health of Women and Children (Inc) "Plunket Society"*, Wellington, Wellington Library School, 1975.

184 Council minutes, 17 September 1924, PSA.

185 Plunket Society, *Report of the Eighth General Conference 1922*, pp. 17, 18.

186 MTS, *Annual report 1937–38*, p. 20.

187 Doris Odlum, 'Bringing up Baby the Modern Way', *Family Doctor*, BMA, August 1953, p. 445, cited in *MTS Newsletter*, Autumn 1953, p. 13.

188 Olssen, 'Truby King and the Plunket Society', p.15. See also James Belich, *Paradise Reforged*, p.159.

189 F. Truby King, *Feeding and Care of Baby*, Macmillan, London, 1913, pp. 102–3; F. Truby King, *Feeding and Care of Baby*, Dunedin, Plunket Society, Dunedin, 1940, p. 42.

190 King, *Feeding and Care of Baby*, 1913, p. 3.

191 Mein Smith, *Mothers and King Baby*, p. 96.

192 King, *Feeding and Care of Baby*, 1913, pp. 1, 62.

193 *Ibid.*, p. 111.

194 *Ibid.*, pp. 111–5.

195 *ODT*, 8 November 1936.

196 See Olssen, 'Truby King and the Plunket Society', p. 14.

197 Plunket Society, *Report of the Eighth General Conference 1922*, p. 10.

198 Olssen, 'Truby King and the Plunket Society', p. 16, Mein Smith, *Mothers and King Baby*, p. 96.

199 *ODT*, 9 August 1938.

200 *ODT*, 11 February 1936, 21 June 1938.

201 See, for example, Tomes, *The Gospel of Germs*.

202 *Auckland Star*, 1 October 1952; 'Grandmother writes, "Nature also intends a mother to get a little rest and sleep, which is impossible if a baby has to be fed every few minutes."': *NZH*, 1 October 1952.

203 Reiger, *The Disenchantment of the Home*, p. 151.

204 *NZH*, 25 June 1934.

205 *Dominion*, 10 February 1934.

206 Jennings, 'The Royal New Zealand Society for the Health of Women and Children', p. 17.
207 Gilmour, 'The Mother, the Baby, and the Plunket Sister', p. 16.
208 Cited in Daniell, *A Doctor at War*, p. 188.
209 Editorial, *NZMJ*, 37, 1938, pp. 185–7.
210 Mein Smith, 'Infant Welfare Services and Infant Mortality', pp. 22–34.
211 *NZ Observer*, 28 July 1938.

Chapter 4: Complementary or Competing Services

1 Sheila Rothman, *Woman's Proper Place: A History of Changing Ideals and Practices, 1870 to the Present*, New York, Basic Books, 1978, p. 142. See also Alexandra Stern and Howard Markel, 'Introduction', Stern and Markel (eds), *Formative Years*, pp. 9–10; Alexandra Stern, 'Better Babies Contests at the Indiana State Fair: Child Health, Scientific Motherhood, and Eugenics in the Midwest, 1920–35', Stern and Markel (eds), *Formative Years*, p. 130.
2 Cited in Watt's unpublished autobiography, pp.124–5. Watt, *Report of the Director-General of Health Reviewing Public-Health Administration*, pp. 30–1.
3 Tweed to Hoddinott, 29 September 1932, 231, PSA.
4 Hoddinott to Tweed, 30 April 1934.04.30, 231, PSA.
5 Allen to Hilda Bloomfield, 1920, 1188, PSA.
6 Delepine to Bloomfield, 21 November 1920, 1188, PSA.
7 Main and Scantlebury, 'Report to the Minister of Public Health', p. 30.
8 Truby King to Mrs Parkes, 20 March 1924, AG7/119, PSA.
9 Council minutes, 28 June 1924, PSA.
10 S.L. Ludbrook, 'Paediatrics in New Zealand', *NZMJ*, 75, 1972, p. 259; Obituary, *NZMJ*, 38, 1939, p. 296.
11 See for example G. Bruton Sweet, *Lectures on the Management of Infants in Health and Sickness*, Auckland, Whitcombe & Tombs, 1920; his book, *Infant Mortality*, was referred by J. S. Purdy, 'Infant Mortality in New South Wales', *Medical Journal of Australia*, 1, 11, 1922, p. 296.
12 F. Truby King, *The Application of Science, Simplicity and Economy to the Everyday Practice of Artificial Feeding during Infancy*, Wellington, Wellington Publishing Company, 1921, pp. 9–10, 1183, PSA; G. Bruton Sweet, 'Some remarks on infant feeding. A reply to Dr Truby King', *NZMJ*, 20, 1921, pp. 104–112.
13 Bruton Sweet, *The Management of Infants in Health and Sickness*, pp. 6, 46.
14 Auckland branch, *Annual reports,* 1930s, e.g. 1934 Plunket Nurse's Report, pp.35–7.
15 Cited in Purdy, 'Infant Mortality in New South Wales', p. 296.
16 Partridge to Pattrick, 16 November 1922, 722, PSA.
17 Bruton Sweet to Partridge, 22 November 1928, 1186, PSA.
18 Partridge to Bruton Sweet, 24 November 1928, 1186, PSA.
19 Bruton Sweet to Partridge, 26 November 1928, 1186, PSA.
20 Eileen Partridge to Hoddinott, 11 May 1933, 231, PSA.
21 Goulstone to Hooper, 8 July 1930, 359, PSA.
22 Chapman, 7 July 1931, 379, PSA.
23 Auckland branch, *Twenty-fifth annual report 1932–33*, p. 31.
24 Pattrick to Johnstone, 30 May 1931, 174, PSA.
25 Wellington branch minutes, 18 December 1923, PSA; *Evening Post*, 26 April 1922, 23 November 1923.
26 Wellington branch, minutes of AGM, 25 June 1928, PSA; *Sir Truby and Lady King Plunket/Karitane Hospital, Wellington, Golden Jubilee 1927–77*, booklet, Wellington, 1977.
27 Marie Stringer Buchler, 'The Premature Baby', *Kai Tiaki*, 31, 2, 1938, p. 80. Now 'special care' or premature babies are defined as those weighing less than 1.5 kilograms at birth.
28 *New Zealand Observer*, 1931, press cuttings, ABA.
29 Auckland branch, *Seventeenth annual report 1924–25*, p. 24.

30 Beatrice E. Nelson, 'Wellington Karitane Hospital and Mothercraft Home, Melrose, Wellington', Public Health thesis, University of Otago, 1936, p. 56.

31 *Ibid.*, p. 54.

32 Obituary, *NZMJ*, 84, 1976, p. 415.

33 Examination of Nurse Carmichael, Acting Matron, Karitane Hospital, Auckland, 1931, 1190, PSA; Carmichael to Truby King, 17 June 1931, AG7 1190, PSA.

34 Pattrick to Johnstone, 25 May 1931, 174, PSA.

35 Ludbrook to Partridge, 1 June 1931, 1190, PSA.

36 Tweed to Helena Sidey, 1 June 1936, 234, PSA.

37 Partridge to Hoddinott, 11 May 1933, 231, PSA.

38 Parkes to Tweed, 24 May 1933, 231, PSA.

39 *Ibid.*

40 Tweed to Parkes, 5 June 1933, 231, PSA.

41 Hoddinott to Tweed, 27 June 1933, 231, PSA.

42 Council minutes, 25 March 1936, PSA.

43 Wellington branch minutes, letter from T. F. Corkill, 7 September 1934, PSA.

44 Wellington branch minutes, 13 December 1933, 19 February 1934, PSA.

45 Tweed to Hoddinott, 22 March 1934, 231, PSA.

46 Wellington branch minutes, Report of Rule Revision Committee, 27 July 1934, PSA.

47 Council minutes, 7 December 1934, PSA.

48 Tweed, notes from Executive meeting, 1936, AG7 2-306, PSA.

49 On the new concern with malnutrition in the United States see Jeffrey Bosco, 'Weight Charts and Well Child Care: When the Paediatrician Became the Expert in Child Health', in Stern and Markel (eds), *Formative Years*, pp. 91–120.

50 Cited by B. Wyn Irwin, 'Preliminary Report of an Investigation of Pre-school Children in New Zealand 1934–35', AG7 1-8-12, PSA.

51 See, for example, F. M. Spencer, 'Malnutrition and a C3 Population Part 1', *NZMJ*, 36, 1937, p. 19; Part 2, 37, 1938, p. 136.

52 Meckel, *Save the Babies*, p. 61.

53 King to Parr, 14 January 1921, AG89-098-68, PSA.

54 Memo on Karitane Emulsion Factory for Truby King, 21 February 1927, AG7 5-38, PSA.

55 Council minutes, 20 August 1928, 3 December 1929, PSA.

56 Valintine to Secretary Treasury, 25 June 1934, H1 127 9251 127, ANZ.

57 Statement from acting Matron, Joan Carmichael, to Pattrick, 23 May 1931, 1190, PSA.

58 Mein Smith, *Mothers and King Baby*, p.129.

59 Scantlebury Brown, Diary, 14 January 1924, University of Melbourne Archives.

60 V. Sanson, Christchurch, to Mr Roach, 5 March 1935, AG7/229, PSA.

61 Fitzgibbon to Pattrick, 21 February 1933, 375, PSA.

62 Irwin, 'Preliminary Report'; F. M. Spencer, 'Modern Principles in Infant Nutrition', *NZMJ*, 31, 1932, p. 166; Elspeth Fitzgerald, 'Some Practical Experiences in Modern Infant Feeding', *NZMJ*, 32, 1933, p. 167; E. J. Cronin, 'Lactic Acid Milk in the Feeding of Infants', *NZMJ*, 32, 1933, p. 169.

63 Editorial, *NZMJ*, 34, 1935, p. 365. Fitzgerald's paper was published as 'Modern Infant Feeding', *NZMJ*, 34, 1935, pp. 388–95.

64 Editorial, *NZMJ*, 37, 1938, p. 187.

65 Account by Parkes, cited by Truby King to Partridge, 31 May 1931, AG7 1190, PSA.

66 E. H. Williams, 'Infant Feeding and the Plunket Society', *NZMJ*, 32, 1933, p. 331.

67 Council minutes, 1 November 1933, PSA.

68 Formation of Medical Advisory Committee, 1936, 234, PSA. These were all child specialists; in her account of the dispute between Montgomery Spencer and Plunket, Daniell incorrectly writes: 'It should be noted that the Medical Advisory Board had not one member who was a paediatrician or child specialist', *A Doctor at War*, p. 170.

69 Council minutes, 16 October 1934, PSA; Tweed to Wyn Irwin, 1 October 1934, 231, PSA.

70 Wyn Irwin, 'Preliminary Report'.
71 *Ibid.*
72 *Dominion*, 22 June 1938.
73 *NZH*, 23 June 1938.
74 Cited in Wyn Irwin, 'Preliminary Report'; Williams McKim Marriott, *Infant Nutrition: A Text-book of Infant Feeding for Students and Practitioners of Medicine*, St Louis, C.V. Mosby, 1930.
75 Report of Medical Advisory Committee Meeting to Re-examine Plunket Feeding, 17 June 1938, AG7 11-49, PSA.
76 Leonard G. Parsons and Seymour Barling (eds), *Diseases of Infancy and Childhood*, London, Oxford University Press, 1933; cited in *NZH*, 29 June 1934.
77 Wellington branch minutes, 5 October 1934, PSA.
78 Spencer to Plunket President and Council, 18 December 1937, 239, PSA; also cited in Daniell, *A Doctor at War*, p. 161.
79 *Dominion*, 22 June 1938.
80 Spencer to Central Council, 18 December 1937, 239, PSA; also cited in Daniell, *A Doctor at War*, p. 162.
81 Spencer to Begg, 26 February 1938, 239, PSA; also cited in Daniell, *A Doctor at War*, p. 168.
82 Report of Medical Advisory Committee Meeting, p. 41.
83 Spencer to President and Council, 18 December 1937, 239, PSA.
84 Begg to Spencer, 2 February 1938, 239, PSA.
85 Daniell, *A Doctor at War*, p. 171.
86 Cited in Daniell, *A Doctor at War*, p. 159.
87 Daniell, *A Doctor at War*, p.176.
88 *Ibid.*, p.175.
89 *Dominion*, 20 May 1938. My emphasis.
90 Daniell, *A Doctor at War*, pp. 175–6.
91 *Dominion*, 20 June 1938.
92 H. E. A. Washbourn, 'A Criticism of Some Features of the Propaganda and Methods of the Royal New Zealand Society for the Health of Women and Children', *NZMJ*, 20, 1921, p. 114.
93 See Apple, *Mothers and Medicine*.
94 *Dominion*, 22 June 1938.
95 Council minutes, 25 May 1938, PSA.
96 Wellington branch minutes, 1 December 1933, PSA.
97 Corkill to Begg, 5 June 1938, 229, PSA. As an indication of his respect within the profession, after he died prematurely in the Second World War, a Spencer Memorial Lecture was established by the New Zealand Paediatric Society; Ludbrook gave the 1949 Spencer Memorial Lecture, and Corkill gave the 1950 lecture: *NZMJ*, 50, 1951, pp. 1–13.
98 Ewart to Begg, 22 June 1938, 229, PSA.
99 *Dominion*, 22 June 1938.
100 *NZH*, 22 & 23 June 1938.
101 Daniell, *A Doctor at War*, pp. 170, 188.
102 *Ibid.*, p. 186.
103 Report of Medical Advisory Committee Meeting, p. 28.
104 *Ibid.*, p. 47.
105 Council minutes, 20 July 1938, PSA.
106 *Ibid.*, 25 June 1938
107 William Hunt to Dominion Council, 26 July 1938, PSA.
108 By 1957 the KPS was paying one-sixteenth of the medical director's salary: Karitane Products Society Grants, 28 November 1957, AG7 2-416, PSA.
109 Expressed for example by Mrs David (Simone) Nathan at the Auckland Provincial Council, 27 April 1934, ABA.
110 Mary King to Fitzgibbon, 28 June 1936, 664, PSA.
111 See Daniell, *A Doctor at War*, pp. 170, 179, 184, 185, 187, 188, 197.

112 *NZH*, 23 June 1938.
113 H. C. D. Somerset, *Child Nutrition in a Rural Community*, Christchurch, New Zealand Council for Educational Research, 1941, p. 7.
114 *Dominion*, 10 May 1935.
115 Spencer to Jowett, 3 November 1938, cited in Daniell, *A Doctor at War*, p. 203.
116 Buchler to Spencer, 15 June 1938, 26 June 1938, cited in Daniell, *A Doctor at War*, pp. 181, 189.
117 Hilary Marland, 'The Medicalisation of Motherhood: Doctors and Infant Welfare in the Netherlands, 1901–1930', in V. Fildes, L. Marks and H. Marland (eds), *Women and Children First: International Maternal and Infant Welfare, 1870–1945*, London, Routledge, 1992, p. 77.
118 Obituary, *NZMJ*, 32, 1933, pp. 292–3.
119 Obituary, *NZMJ*, 36, 1937, pp. 140–1.
120 Eleanor Rose to Fitzgibbon, 22 June 1934, 373, PSA; letter to editor, *NZH*, 9 June 1934.
121 Letter to editor, *NZH*, 18 June 1934.
122 *NZH*, 30 June 1934.
123 Report of Medical Advisory Committee Meeting, p. 3.
124 *Ibid.*
125 *Ibid.*, p. 18.
126 Wellington branch minutes, 30 June 1938, PSA.
127 *Ibid.*, 14 July 1938.
128 Council minutes, 20 July 1938, PSA.
129 Wellington branch minutes, 16 September 1938, PSA.
130 Jowett to Begg, 6 September 1938, 239, PSA.
131 Begg to Jowett, 29 September 1938, 239, PSA.
132 Spencer to Jowett, 3 November 1938, 239, PSA.
133 Begg to Jowett, 10 November 1938, 239, PSA; Council minutes, 14 November 1938, PSA.
134 Wellington branch minutes, 3 March 1939, PSA; Wellington branch, *Annual report 1938–39,* p. 26.
135 Council minutes, 20 July 1938, PSA.
136 *NZH*, 24 June 1938; committee composition announced *NZH*, 23 June 1938.
137 Watt to Malcolm, 8 August 1938, H1 127/5/6, ANZ.
138 Report of Medical Advisory Committee Meeting.
139 Mary Lambie to Miss Selbie, South Africa, 7 September 1938, H1 127 B.81 127, ANZ; unlike some other members of the Health Department, Lambie applauded Plunket, see Mary Lambie, *My Story: Memoirs of a New Zealand Nurse*, Christchurch, Peryer, 1956, p. 169.
140 *NZ Observer*, 28 July 1938.
141 Philippa Mein Smith, *Maternity in Dispute, New Zealand 1920–1939*, Wellington, Historical Branch, Department of Internal Affairs, 1986.
142 Walter Radcliffe, *Milestones in Midwifery*, Bristol, John Wright, 1967, p. 98.
143 Lewis, *The Politics of Motherhood*, p. 35.
144 Janet McCalman, *Sex and Suffering: Women's Health and a Women's Hospital*, Melbourne, Melbourne University Press, 1998, p. 159.
145 Ann Oakley, *The Captured Womb: A History of the Medical Care of Pregnant Women*, Oxford, Blackwell, 1984, pp. 51–2.
146 Plunket Society, *Report of the Fifth General Conference 1917*, p. 7.
147 Plunket Society, *Report of the Seventh Interim Conference, 1921*, p. 4; in Wellington the Plunket nurse noted work with 'expectant mothers' for the first time in 1913: Wellington branch minutes, 7 June 1913, PSA.
148 Council minutes, 6 December 1926, PSA.
149 Health Department Annual Report, Child Welfare, *AJHR*, H-31, 1924, pp. 26–7.
150 Mein Smith, *Maternity in Dispute*, p. 26.
151 *AJHR*, 1929, H-31, p. 40.
152 Auckland branch, *Fifteenth annual report 1922–23,* p. 10.

153 Mein Smith, *Maternity in Dispute*, p. 97.
154 Auckland branch, *Thirty-second annual report 1940*, p. 36. Watson and Walton, 'A Study in Antenatal Care', p. 23. A similar description was given of Christchurch Plunket 'ante-natal clinic' in 1940: H. Stringer and C. Morkane, 'Ante and Post-natal Work in Christchurch', Public Health thesis, University of Otago, 1940, pp. 60–1.
155 Stringer and Morkane, 'Ante and Post-natal Work in Christchurch', p. 63.
156 Watson and Walton, 'A Study in Antenatal Care', p. 76.
157 Plunket Society, *Report of the Fourteenth General Conference 1928*, p. 68.
158 Mein Smith, *Maternity in Dispute*, p. 96.
159 Cited by Tweed, evidence to 1937 Committee of Inquiry into Maternity Services, Vol. 1, 21 May 1937, MS78, Museum Library Auckland.
160 Tweed to McGeorge, 22 May 1933, 231, PSA; Council minutes, 1 November 1933, 1184, PSA; Wellington branch minutes, circular from Dunedin, 6 April 1934, PSA.
161 Evidence by Miss O'Shea, 18 May 1937.
162 Evidence by Miss Barnett, 19 May 1937.
163 Evidence by Plunket Society, 21 May 1937.
164 Ogden and Chapman to Pattrick, 8 July 1932, 377, PSA.
165 Auckland branch, *Thirty-fourth annual report 1941–42*, p. 11.
166 Auckland branch, *Thirty-eighth annual report 1945–46*, p. 13. Gabrielle Fortune also noted that in her interviews with 'war brides' many commented appreciatively and without prompting on the support from Plunket nurses: G. Fortune, 'War brides in New Zealand', PhD thesis in progress, History Department, University of Auckland.
167 Wellington branch, *Annual report 1946–47*, p. 11.

Chapter 5: Helen Deem and Paediatrics

1 Council minutes, 1–3 November 1955, PSA.
2 Council minutes, 14 November 1938, 18 November 1938, PSA.
3 Allan to Begg, 19 October, 28 November 1938, 236, PSA.
4 Application by Helen Deem for Position of Medical Adviser to Plunket Society, 23 September 1938, 236, PSA.
5 Robertson to Williams, 23 November 1938, 236, PSA.
6 Application by Deem; 'Observations on the Milk of New Zealand Women', *Archives of Disease in Childhood*, 6, 1931, pp. 53–70.
7 Rose to Fitzgibbon, 25 May 1934, 373, PSA.
8 Reference by H. B. Turbott for Deem, 20 September 1938; reference by M. H. Watt for Deem, 5 September 1938, 236, PSA.
9 Deem to Ludbrook, 11 June 1948, 581, PSA.
10 *NZMJ*, 46, 1947, p. 47.
11 Ludbrook to Deem, 14 January 1946, 581, PSA.
12 Ludbrook to Deem, 19 July 1948, 581, PSA.
13 Deem to Ludbrook, 17 August 1948, 581, PSA.
14 Quin to Deem, 25 October 1950, 595, PSA; see also Dr Harold Pettit, Plunket Society Deputation to Watts, 17 April 1951, H1 127 26040, ANZ.
15 Deem to Alice Bush, 14 March 1952, 581, PSA.
16 Executive minutes, 15 June 1943, PSA.
17 Executive minutes, 31 July 1946, PSA.
18 Executive minutes, 21 September 1943, PSA.
19 Council minutes, 19–20 April 1950, PSA.
20 Council minutes, 18–19 April 1951, PSA.
21 Plunket Society, *Annual report 1942–43*, p. 16.
22 Executive minutes, 11 August 1943, PSA.
23 Plunket Society, *Annual report 1947–48*, p. 28.

24 Plunket Society, *Report of Twenty-eighth General Conference 1946*, p.16.

25 Joyce Powell, 'Keep Pumping Those Brakes Nurse', transcript of oral interviews, c1997.

26 Deem to Ludbrook, 11 June 1948, 581, PSA.

27 Council minutes, 21–22 July 1948, PSA.

28 Deem to Ludbrook, 13 April 1949, 581, PSA; Ludbrook to Deem, 19 September 1949, 581, PSA.

29 See Fay Hercock, *Alice: The Making of a Woman Doctor 1914–1974*, Auckland, Auckland University Press, 1999.

30 Deem to Alice Bush, 14 March 1952, 581, PSA.

31 Deem to Ludbrook, 16 May 1950, 595, PSA.

32 Plunket Society, *Annual report 1947–48*, pp. 15, 16.

33 Deem to Ludbrook, 16 May 1950, 595, PSA.

34 Ludbrook to Deem, 25 May 1950, 595, PSA.

35 Quin to Deem, 25 October 1950, 595, PSA.

36 This referred to Professor McKim Marriott, see note 41 below and Chapter 4.

37 Deem to Quin, 10 November 1950, 581, PSA.

38 Plunket Society, *Annual report 1950–51*, p. 20; Deem to J. Dilworth Matthews, Honorary Secretary, Paediatric Society of New Zealand, 25 June 1951, 588, PSA.

39 F. W. Clements, *Infant Nutrition: Its Physiological Basis*, Bristol, John Wright, London, Simpkin Marshall, 1949, p. 185.

40 Ewart to Begg, 10 June 1938, 229, PSA.

41 Williams McKim Marriott, *Infant Nutrition: A Textbook of Infant Feeding for Students and Practitioners of Medicine*, 3rd edn, London, Henry Kimpton, 1942, p. 138.

42 E. H. Williams to Deem, 15 July 1946, 595, PSA; US Children's Bureau pamphlet on breast-feeding advised that at two weeks breastfeeding should be supplemented by cod liver oil (or something containing vitamin D) and orange juice; by 2 months the supplement should consist of half a measuring cup a day: AG7 4-103, PSA; Marriott, *A Textbook of Infant Feeding*, 2nd edn 1930, p. 110, 3rd edn 1942, p. 138.

43 Deem to Ludbrook, 20 December 1952, 581, PSA.

44 Deem to M. Bevan-Brown, 1 October 1945, 581, PSA.

45 Deem to The Organiser, Book Reviews, Station 4ZB, Dunedin, 7 August 1950, 577, PSA.

46 M. Bevan-Brown, *The Sources of Love and Fear, with Contributions by Members of the Christchurch Psychological Society*, Wellington, Reed, 1950, p. 85.

47 Obituary, *NZMJ*, 67, 1967, p. 329.

48 See Ernest Beaglehole, *Mental Health in New Zealand*, Wellington, New Zealand University Press, 1950, p. 68.

49 Mary Dobbie, *The Trouble with Women: The Story of Parents' Centre New Zealand*, Whatamongo Bay, Queen Charlotte Sound, 1990, pp. 2, 88; *The Parents' Centre Bulletin*, 1967.

50 Dobbie, *The Trouble with Women*.

51 Kedgley, *Mum's the Word*, p. 177.

52 *Ibid.*

53 Sigmund Freud, *The Standard Edition of the Complete Psychological Works of Sigmund Freud, VII: Three Essays on the Theory of Sexuality (1901–05)*, transl. J. Strachey, London, Hogarth Press, 1953, p. 182.

54 Bevan-Brown, *The Sources of Love and Fear*, pp. 18, 20, 24, 27.

55 *Report of Advisory Committee on Mother and Young Children on The Breast Feeding of Infants*, London, Ministry of Health, HMSO, 1944, pp. 9–10.

56 Plunket Society, *Report of the Thirty-first General Conference 1952*, p. 23.

57 *Dominion*, 21 November 1952; the results were published after Deem's death, *NZMJ*, 57, 1958, pp. 530–56.

58 Wellington branch minutes, 18 August 1938, PSA.

59 Plunket Society, *Report of the Twenty-ninth General Conference 1948*, p. 15.

60 Margaret Woods, 'Plunket Nursing in the Invercargill Area', Public Health thesis, University of Otago, 1951, p. 30.

61 A. G. Strayer to Deem, Takapuna, 13 July 1953, 576, PSA.

62 O. K. Orris to Deem, Pukekohe, 17 July 1953, 576, PSA.

63 Gwen Johnson to Deem, Matamata, 22 July 1953, 576, PSA.

64 Gwen Evans to Deem, Wanganui, 23 July 1953, 576, PSA.

65 Plunket nurse to Deem, Otaki, 13 July 1953, 576, PSA.

66 Kathleen Lee to Deem, North Canterbury, 31 July 1953, 576, PSA.

67 Doris L. Williams to Deem, Devonport, 20 July 1953, 576, PSA; in 1937 one Plunket nurse had suggested that a bonus be given to all mothers who breastfed: Evidence to Committee of Inquiry into Maternity Services 1937, Nurse Arnott, 11 August 1937.

68 See Chapter 9 on medical attitudes to breastfeeding in the 1950s.

69 Nolan, *Breadwinning*, p. 216.

70 See Chapter 7.

71 Breastfeeding also declined in Britain in the post-war years: *MTS Magazine*, Spring 1950, p. 849.

72 Plunket Society, *Report of the Twenty-ninth General Conference 1948*, p. 15; *MTS Magazine*, Autumn 1953, p. 9, reprinted from the *Times*, 17 October 1953.

73 Grantly Dick Read to Mrs Charlotte (and Gayle) Aiken, refers to 'my acrimonious correspondence with him' about his not helping breast feeding, 14 September 1951, Dick Read Papers, DD/GDR/D.269, Wellcome. Grantly Dick Read officially hyphenated his name, to Dick-Read, in 1958.

74 Mein Smith, *Mothers and King Baby*, p. 173; J. E. Meckling, 'Advice to Historians on Advice to Mothers', *Journal of Social History*, 9, 1, 1975, pp. 44–63; Margaret A. Ribble, *The Rights of Infants: Early Psychological Needs and their Satisfaction*, New York, Columbia University Press, 1943; Reiger, *The Disenchantment of the Home*, Chapter 7.

75 Bevan-Brown, p. xvi.

76 A. and M. Aldrich, *Babies are Human Beings*, New York, Macmillan, 1938, republished in Britain as *Understanding Your Baby*, London, Black, 1939, cited in Urwin and Sharland, 'From Bodies to Minds in Childcare Literature', pp. 187–8.

77 Beaglehole, *Mental Health in New Zealand*, pp. 59–60.

78 Plunket Society, *Report of the Twenty-ninth General Conference 1948*, pp.16–17; Deem to Ludbrook, 13 September 1949, 581, PSA.

79 Deem to Roberton, 5 June 1951, 581, PSA.

80 Deem to Bush, 9 May 1951, 581, PSA.

81 Jacqueline H. Wolf, 'Don't Kill Your Baby: Feeding Infants in Chicago, 1903–1924', *Journal of the History of Medicine and Allied Sciences*, 53, 1998, p. 238. Jacqueline H. Wolf, *Don't Kill Your Baby: Public Health and the Decline of Breastfeeding in the Nineteenth and Twentieth Centuries*, Columbus, Ohio State University Press, 2001.

82 For example, Deem wrote to Miss M. Neumann in 1954, 'It is inefficient emptying of the breast which is so often responsible for the cessation of the supply': Deem to M. Neumann, 15 February 1954, 576, PSA.

83 *Nursing Times*, 21 March 1958.

84 Plunket Society, *Report of the Twenty-ninth General Conference 1948*, pp. 35–6.

85 Dally, *Inventing Motherhood*, pp. 84–97.

86 John Bowlby, *Maternal Care and Mental Health*, Geneva, WHO Technical Monograph Series 2, 1951; John Bowlby, *Child Care and the Growth of Love*, London, Penguin Books, 1953.

87 Urwin and Sharland, 'From Bodies to Minds in Childcare Literature', p.194.

88 Jane Lewis, 'Anxieties about the Family and the Relationships between Parents, Children and the State in Twentieth Century England', in Martin Richards and Paul Light (eds), *Children of Social Worlds: Development in a Social Context*, Cambridge, Mass., Harvard University Press, 1986, p. 44.

89 See also Ladd-Taylor and Umansky (eds), *'Bad' Mothers*, p. 14.

90 Plunket Society, *Annual report 1947–48*, p. 24.

91 Plunket Society, *Annual report 1948–49*, p. 26; on Spence's views, see also Lewis, 'Anxieties

about the Family', pp. 40–3. Spence's work was also applauded by Bevan-Brown, *The Sources of Love and Fear*, p. 34.

92 See for example A. Gesell and H. Thomson, *The Psychology of Early Growth*, New York, Macmillan, 1938.

93 Ehrenreich and English, *For Her Own Good*, p. 195.

94 Plunket Society, *Annual report 1949–50*, p. 21

95 Deem to Moncrieff, 26 August 1955, 585, PSA.

96 A decade later, Spock attempted to present 'a more balanced view'; he now thought there was 'more chance of a conscientious parent's getting into trouble with permissiveness than with strictness': Benjamin Spock, *Baby and Child Care*, London, Bodley Head, new and enlarged edition 1958, p.12. Deem, however, believed that even the early Spock had much to offer. When it seemed that he might visit New Zealand in 1952, she suggested arranging conferences of 'hand-picked nurses . . . to enable them to hear this eminent speaker who could help them greatly with pre-school problems': Executive minutes, 24 September 1952, PSA.

97 Wellington branch minutes, 5 May 1949, PSA.

98 Wellington branch, *Annual report 1948–49*, p. 12.

99 Plunket Society, *Annual report 1948–49*, p. 28.

100 *MTS Nurses League Newsletter*, 1965, p.8 – Obituary Dr C. V. Pink, Pioneer of Natural Childbirth; Violet Melchett Infant Welfare Centre, Chelsea, *Annual report 1933–34*, p. 16, Wellcome.

101 Wellington branch, *Annual report 1936–37*,H1 127/21 13358, ANZ; Wellington branch, *Annual report 1939–40*, p. 16.

102 Stringer and Morkane, 'Ante and Post-natal Work in Christchurch', pp. 61, 95; Plunket Society, Christchurch branch, *Annual report 1954–55*, p. 14.

103 Auckland branch, *Thirty-third annual report 1940–41*, pp. 21–2; *Thirty-fifth annual report 1942–43*, p. 16; Margaret Morris in collaboration with M. Randell *Maternity and Post-operative Exercises in Diagrams and Words*, London, Heinemann, 1936.

104 Dobbie, *The Trouble with Women*, pp. 14, 16.

105 T. F. Corkill, *Lectures on Midwifery and Infant Care: A New Zealand Course*, 6 edns from 1932 to 1958, Auckland, Coulls, Somerville, Wilkie, 1932, Wellington, Banks, 1940, Christchurch, Whitcombe & Tombs, 1946, 1951, 1954.

106 After 1953 he continued to publish widely, for example, Grantly Dick Read, *Antenatal Illustrated: The Natural Approach to Happy Motherhood*, London, Heinemann, 1955. See Mary Thomas (ed.), *Post-War Mothers: Childbirth Letters to Grantly Dick-Read, 1946–1956*, Rochester, University of Rochester Press, 1997. On the diffusion of Read's ideas to Australia, see Kerreen M. Reiger, *Our Bodies, Our Babies: The Forgotten Women's Movement*, Melbourne, Melbourne University Press, 2001.

107 Bevan-Brown referred to Dick Read in his book several times, *The Sources of Love and Fear*, pp.34, 130, 137, 141.

108 Bevan-Brown, *The Sources of Love and Fear*, pp. 53–4.

109 See Thomas, *Post-War Mothers*, introduction.

110 Dick Read reply to Mrs B. R. Clarke, 22 January 1952, Dick Read to Mr Rankin, 1953, Grantly Dick Read Papers, Correspondence New Zealand, PP/GDR/D94, Wellcome.

111 Report of Conference of Group Mothercraft Teaching to Expectant Mothers, Wellington, 21 April 1950, 601, PSA.

112 *Ibid.*

113 Dobbie, *The Trouble with Women*, p. 21.

114 *Ibid.* p. 23.

115 *Ibid.*, p. 32.

116 Brew to Deem, 20 May 1952, 599, PSA.

117 Dobbie, *The Trouble with Women*, p. 18.

118 *Ibid.*

119 Helen Heardman, *A Way to Natural Childbirth: A Manual for Physiotherapists and Parents-to-be,* Edinburgh, E. & S. Livingstone, 1948 (reprint 1949, 1950, 1951, 1952, 1954, 1956, 1958, 1961, rev. 1964).

120 Mrs Christine Cole to Secretary, Plunket headquarters, 15 May 1952, 599, PSA; Brew to Deem, 20 May 1952, 599, PSA.

121 Wellington branch, *Annual report 1948–49,* p. 12.

122 Wellington branch, *Annual report 1950–51,* p. 17; Wellington branch, *Annual report 1951–52,* p. 18.

123 Simpson to Deem, 3 November 1952, 599, PSA.

124 Dobbie, *The Trouble with Women,* p. 23.

125 Simpson to Deem, 3 November 1952, and Deem to Simpson, 5 November 1952, 599, PSA.

126 Deem to Clayton, 17 October 1952, 599, PSA.

127 Simpson to Deem, 22 October 1952, 599, PSA.

128 Brew to Deem, 20 October 1952, 599, PSA.

129 Deem to Corkill, 24 October 1952, 599, PSA.

130 Simpson to Deem, 3 November 1952, 599, PSA.

131 Plunket Society, *Report of the Thirty-First General Conference 1952,* p. 17.

132 Dobbie, *The Trouble with Women,* p. 23. On Mrs Irving Robertson, see also *MTS Nurses' League Newsletter,* Winter 1959, p. 12.

133 Deem to Simpson, 5 November 1952, 599, PSA.

134 Lusk to Clayton, 24 February 1953, 599, PSA.

135 Dobbie, *The Trouble with Women,* pp. 24, 33.

136 *Ibid.,* p. 32.

137 Rapps to Barnett, Plunket rooms, Hamilton, 8 March 1956, 793, PSA.

138 Corkill to Dick Read, 15 January 1957, Correspondence New Zealand, PP/GDR/D189, Wellcome.

139 Rapps to Barnett, Plunket rooms, Hamilton, 8 March 1956, 793, PSA; Executive minutes, 1 May 1957, PSA.

140 Bevan-Brown, *The Sources of Love and Fear,* pp. 51–2.

141 Dobbie, *The Trouble with Women,* p. 21.

142 Report of Conference of Group Mothercraft Teaching to Expectant Mothers, Wellington, 21 April 1950, 601, PSA.

143 Dobbie, *The Trouble with Women,* p. 21.

144 Council minutes, 26–28 July 1944, PSA.

145 *NZH,* 18 October 1950. Plunket nurse Marion Shepherd also related a story of her 'winning over' a husband: *Some of My Yesterdays,* p. 121.

146 *NZH,* 30 June 1934.

147 Letter to editor, *NZH,* 25 March 1944.

148 Plunket Society, *Report of the Twenty-eighth General Conference 1946,* p. 25. Ralph LaRosse also found that letters to the US Children's Bureau in the first half of the twentieth century indicated that fathers were 'more involved with infants than most historical accounts would have us believe': Ralph LaRossa, *The Modernization of Fatherhood: A Social and Political History,* Chicago, University of Chicago Press, 1997, pp. 70, 80, 195.

149 Hygeia, 'Our Babies', from *ODT,* 4 December 1940.

150 See also Chapter 7 on Karitane nurses.

151 *Plunket Newsview,* October 1948.

152 Deem and Fitzgibbon, *Modern Mothercraft,* p. 63.

153 *Ibid.,* pp. 52–3.

154 Report of Conference of Group Mothercraft Teaching; the Maternity Center Association of New York had held classes for expectant fathers since the 1930s: LaRosse, *The Modernization of Fatherhood,* photo, p. 88.

155 Auckland branch, *Forty-first annual report 1948–49,* p. 17.

156 *Dominion,* 18 March 1950.

157 *The Press*, 10 June 1950.
158 Christchurch branch, *Annual report 1950–51*, p. 13, *1951–52*, p. 13, *1953–54*, p. 12, *1954–55*, p. 13.
159 Report of Conference of Group Mothercraft Teaching to Expectant Mothers, 21 April 1950, 601, PSA.
160 See Gael Ferguson, *Building the New Zealand Dream*, Palmerston North, Dunmore Press, 1994, on house building in the 1950s.
161 Auckland branch, *Thirty-eighth annual report 1945–46*, p. 13.
162 *Kai Tiaki*, 39, 2, 1946, p. 143.
163 *Auckland Star*, 9 August 1949.
164 Plunket Society, *Report of the Twenty-eighth General Conference 1946*, p. 39.
165 Plunket Society, *Annual report 1953–54*, p. 23.
166 Auckland Provincial Conference, 5 August 1953, ABA.
167 Dobbie, *The Trouble with Women*, p. 43.
168 *NZH*, 16 December 1957.
169 Plunket Society, *Annual report 1954–55*, p. 44.
170 See also Ehrenreich and English, *For Her Own Good*, p. 218.
171 Arnup, *Education for Motherhood,* p. 99.
172 Auckland Provincial Conference, 5 August 1953, ABA.
173 On the school medical service, see M. Tennant, '"Missionaries of health": the School Medical Service during the Inter-war Period', in L. Bryder, (ed.), *A Healthy Country: Essays on the Social History of Medicine in New Zealand*, Wellington, Bridget Williams Books, 1991, pp. 129–48.
174 McMillan, *A National Health Service*, pp. 11–12.
175 Executive minutes, 13 June 1939, PSA.
176 Plunket Society, *Annual report 1939–40*, p. 24.
177 Mein Smith argues that while Australia had its Lady Gowrie Centres, New Zealand introduced school milk: Mein Smith, *Mothers and King Baby*, p. 225.
178 24 December 1940, 586, PSA; Deem kept up her contacts, visiting the Lady Gowrie Centres again in 1954: Council minutes, 28 April 1954, 579, PSA.
179 Plunket Society, *Annual report 1953–54*, pp. 25–6.
180 Mein Smith, *Mothers and King Baby*, pp. 226–7.
181 Executive minutes, 13 June 1939, PSA.
182 Plunket Society, *Annual report 1939–40*, p. 24.
183 *Evening Star*, 8 November 1947.
184 *Free Lance*, 25 February 1955.
185 Plunket Society, *Annual report 1954–55*, pp. 37–41.
186 Plunket Society, *Annual report 1954–55*, p. 44.
187 T. C. Svenson and B. E. Tomlinson, 'Survey of the Dunedin Karitane Hospital', Public Health thesis, University of Otago, 1952, p. 63.
188 *Ibid.*, p. 64.
189 See also Kedgley, *Mum's the Word*, pp. 180–1.
190 Mein Smith, *Mothers and King Baby,* p. 226.
191 Plunket Society, *Annual report 1950–51*, p. 25.
192 Deem to Ludbrook, 13 April 1949, 581, PSA.
193 Eleanor Alden, Helen (Val) Jones, Plunket Society Oral History Project, 1992.
194 F. W. Clements to Deem, 24 August 1955, 585, PSA.
195 Howard Williams to Deem, 25 August 1955, 585, PSA.

Chapter 6: Plunket and the Government

1 Plunket Society, *Report of the Twenty-seventh General Conference 1944*, p. 5.
2 Auckland branch, *Thirty-ninth annual report 1946–47*, p. 9.

3 Health Department Memo, Lennane, Kennedy, Sheppard, 19 February 1957, H1 127/5/9/1 37999, ANZ.

4 See Ferguson, *Building the New Zealand Dream*, pp. 117–76.

5 Plunket Society, *Report of the Twenty-eighth General Conference 1946*, p. 44.

6 Plunket Society, *Report of the Twenty-seventh General Conference 1944*, p. 5.

7 Evidence to 1937 Committee of Inquiry into Maternity Services, Mrs Begg, 21 May 1937, Mrs Bodkin, 28 May 1937; Plunket Society, *Report of the Twenty-seventh General Conference 1944*, p. 13; see also Nolan, *Breadwinning*, pp. 213–6.

8 M. I. Elliott and M. D. Rohan, 'Infant Feeding', Public Health thesis, University of Otago, 1941, p. 10.

9 Auckland Provincial Conference, 11 August 1942, ABA; Wellington Provincial Conference, 18 August 1942, PSA.

10 *NZ Listener*, 1 September 1944, pp.18–19.

11 Plunket Society, *Report of the Twenty-ninth General Conference 1948*, p. 11.

12 *Ibid.*, pp. 12–13; *Plunket News*, 15 November 1948, p. 2.

13 Auckland branch, *Thirty-sixth annual report 1943–44*, p. 16.

14 Plunket Society, *Report of the Twenty-eighth General Conference 1946*, p. 20.

15 Auckland branch, *Thirty-ninth annual report 1946–47*, p. 13. See also Wellington branch, *Annual report 1946–47*, p. 11.

16 Plunket Society, *Report of the Twenty-eighth General Conference 1946*, p. 20–1.

17 Nolan, *Breadwinning*, p. 194.

18 Plunket Society, *Report of the Thirtieth General Conference 1950*, p. 6. Yet Elizabeth Bodkin was elected in her own right. She had served a long apprenticeship with Plunket, having been a foundation member of the Central Otago branch in 1915. When she retired from the executive in 1959, a tribute was paid to her commitment. It was noted that, to attend the fortnightly executive meetings in Dunedin, Bodkin, who lived in Alexandra, travelled 137 miles each way by bus. While serving as Dominion President, Bodkin had also travelled extensively throughout New Zealand, and had given great encouragement to branches, especially those in scattered rural areas.

19 Memo for Cabinet by Minister of Health, February 1957, 'Plunket Society 1951–57', MH, H1 127 26040, ANZ.

20 D. J. Sheppard, Chief Accountant, Department of Health, 'Report and Recommendations on the Plunket Society's Application for an Increase in the Rate of Hospital Benefit for Karitane Hospitals', Treasury Report, 1 October 1958, p. 7, H1 127/5/9/1 37999, ANZ.

21 Health Department, Annual Report, *AJHR*, 1941, H-31, p. 20.

22 Health Department, Annual Report, *AJHR*, 1943, H-31, p. 5.

23 Health Department, Annual Report, *AJHR*, 1950, H-31, p. 55.

24 Rapps to Director-General of Health, 18 December 1947, H1 127 23201 127, ANZ.

25 Memo by H. Turbott, Deputy Director-General of Health, 28 February 1950, H1 127 26040, ANZ.

26 H. Turbott, 3 August 1950, H1 127 23201 127, ANZ; see also Council minutes, 28 June 1950, PSA.

27 Health Department, Annual Report, *AJHR*, 1952, H-31, p. 45.

28 Council minutes, 7 June 1950, PSA.

29 Rapps to Director-General of Health, 7 July 1953, 'Plunket Society 1951–57', H1 127 26040, ANZ.

30 Deputation to Minister of Health J. R. Marshall, 4 March 1954, 'Plunket Society 1951–57', H1 27 26040, ANZ.

31 *Ibid.*

32 Cited in Watt's unpublished autobiography, pp. 124–5. Watt, *Report of the Director-General of Health Reviewing Public-Health Administration*, pp. 30–1.

33 Council minutes, 20 November 1940, PSA.

34 'Plunket Society General', H1 127 23201, ANZ.

35 Council minutes, 5–7 November 1957, PSA.

36   Jocelyn Ryburn to Walter Nash, 6 September 1958, AAFB 127 acc w3464 127/3/8 27691, ANZ. This function of the local committees was something Neil Begg chose to stress (see Chapter 7).

37   Turbott, memo for Minister of Health, 3 August 1950, H 127 23201, ANZ.

38   Turbott, 3 August 1950, H 127 23201, ANZ.

39   Lambie, *My Story*, p.152.

40   Plunket Society Submission to the Consultative Committee on Infant and Pre-School Health Services, 1959, p. 46, PSA.

41   Lusk to Lambie, 30 September 1949, 1192, PSA.

42   Secretary, Gisborne Plunket Society, to Lusk, 28 September 1949, AG7/1192, PSA.

43   Secretary, Kaitaia Branch of Plunket Society, to Mrs Phillpotts, Secretary, Kaikohe Branch of Plunket Society, 10 October 1949, AG7/1192, PSA.

44   Plunket Society, *Report of the Ninth Provincial Conference, 1949*, ABA.

45   Watts to Rapps, 11 May 1950, Health Department H1 127/4/5 25988, ANZ.

46   Executive minutes, 23 March 1955, PSA.

47   See A. McKegg, 'The Maori Health Nursing Scheme: An Experiment in Autonomous Health Care', *NZJH*, 26, 2, 1992, pp. 145–60.

48   Plunket Society, *Report of Interim Conference 1945*, ABA.

49   Turbott, memo, 29 October 1953, H1 127 26040, ANZ.

50   Turbott to MOH, Auckland, 23 November 1955, H1 127/4/5 25988, ANZ.

51   W. E. Henley, 'A Survey of the Clinical and Nutritional Status of 1076 Infants Aged 6 Months from the Urban Area of Auckland, New Zealand, 1939–40', University of Otago, 1944, AG7 1-8-13, PSA. Henley graduated in medicine at Oxford University in 1935, and was registered in New Zealand in 1940. He went on to become Superintendent in Chief of Auckland Hospital Board, 1961–73.

52   See *New Zealand Population Census, 1936, Vol.3: Maori Census*, Wellington, Government Printer, 1940, p.2; *Vol.9: Race*, 1945, p.4.

53   Deem, Executive minutes, 28 November 1951, PSA.

54   Council minutes, 14–16 November 1945, PSA.

55   Council minutes, 28–30 April 1953, PSA.

56   Hamilton Grieve, *Sketches from Maoriland*, London, Robert Hale, 1939, pp. 55–7, cited in Derek A. Dow, *Maori Health and Government Policy 1840–1940*, Wellington, Victoria University Press in association with the Historical Branch, Department of Internal Affairs, p. 202. On the history of Native schools, see J. M. Barrington and T. H. Beaglehole, *Maori Schools in a Changing Society: An Historical Review*, Wellington, New Zealand Council for Educational Research, 1974; Judith Simon et al., *Nga Kura Maori: The Native Schools System 1867–1969*, Auckland, Auckland University Press, 1998.

57   Executive minutes, 3 July 1942, 25 August 1942, PSA.

58   Deem to Ludbrook, 10 December 1952, 581, PSA.

59   Memo, re J. R. McKenzie Trust, November 1952, MA 1 243 12/866, ANZ.

60   Lusk to Lambie, 1 December 1945, H1 20414 127/1/2, ANZ.

61   Council minutes, 14–16 November 1945, PSA; Dow, *Maori Health and Government Policy*, p. 207.

62   Council minutes, 10–12 April 1946, PSA.

63   Nothing was done before the mid-1950s: D. Dow, personal communication, 10 February 2003.

64   Council minutes, 1–3 November 1949, PSA.

65   Turbott later claimed that he had responsibility for all facets of the Department's work, see Dow, *Safeguarding the Public Health*, p. 179.

66   Council minutes, 3–5 November 1953, PSA.

67   *Ibid.*

68   Rex Mason to Jocelyn Ryburn, 13 March 1958, H1 127 32110, ANZ.

69   The problem for Dunedin's Karitane Hospital was compounded by Plunket nurse training costs. Until 1942 Plunket nurse trainees paid a fee of £15 for the seventeen-week training

course at the Hospital, and supplied their own uniform. The fee was abolished that year, and from 1950 nurses were paid a bursary at the salary rate of a first-year trained nurse. This was largely because Health Department nurses who took the training were still on full salary, which meant that those not attached to the Health Department felt disadvantaged.

70 Ryburn to W. Nash, 6 September 1958, AAFB 127 acc w3464 127/3/8 27691, ANZ.
71 N. E. Kirk to R. Mason, 14 August 1958, AAFB 127 acc w3464 127/3/8 27691, ANZ.
72 Council minutes, 4–7 November 1958, PSA.
73 Hunn, Deputy Director-General of Health Administration, memo 15 January 1959, AAFB 127 acc w3464 127/3/8 27691, ANZ.
74 *NZH*, 6 November 1958.
75 Executive minutes, 4 March 1959, PSA.
76 *Report of the Consultative Committee on Infant and Pre-school Health Services*, Wellington, Government Printer, 1960, p. 40. On Mason see Dobbie, *The Trouble with Women*, p. 59.
77 Plunket Society, *Annual report 1966–67*, p. 2.
78 See Chapter 7.
79 *NZH*, 27 July 1959.
80 L. Bryder, 'Begg, Neil Colquhoun', *DNZB, Volume Four, 1941–1960*, pp. 47–8.
81 Council minutes, 9–11 April 1957, PSA.
82 Neil Begg, *The Intervening Years: A New Zealand Account of the Years between the Last Two Visits of Halley's Comet*, Dunedin, John McIndoe, 1992, p. 105.
83 Plunket Society Submission to Consultative Committee on Infant and Pre-school Health Services, p. 112, PSA.
84 Editorial, *NZH*, 27 July 1959.
85 *Auckland Star*, 22 July 1959.
86 *Ibid*. In 1960 Matthews joined the consultant staff at Auckland's Karitane Hospital. He was later described as New Zealand's first full-time neonatal paediatrician: Dr Ross Howie, talk to Auckland Medical History Society, 4 July 2002.
87 *Evening Post*, 1 July 1959.
88 *Report of the Consultative Committee*, p. 12.
89 Council minutes, 4 November 1959, PSA.
90 Editorial, *NZH*, 27 July 1959.
91 Plunket Society Submission, p. 37.
92 *Report of the Consultative Committee*, p. 7.
93 Plunket Society Submission, p. 54. Also cited in *NZH*, 27 June 1959.
94 Evidence of W. Herewini, *Dominion*, 19 August 1959.
95 *Report of the Consultative Committee*, pp. 35, 39.
96 *NZH*, 22 December 1959.
97 *Daily Telegraph*, 7 July 1960.
98 Dobbie, *The Trouble with Women*, p. 59.
99 Begg to Mrs A. Rose, 29 June 1956, 1176c, PSA.
100 Begg to Edward B. Watts, Wellington Parents' Centre, 29 June 1956, 1176c, PSA.
101 Fay Hercock, 'Professional Politics and Family Planning Clinics', in L. Bryder (ed.), *A Healthy Country: Essays on the Social History of Medicine in New Zealand*, Wellington, Bridget Williams, 1991, pp. 181–97.
102 Bush to Begg, 1 April 1958, 1176c, PSA.
103 Begg to Bush. 9 April 1958, 1176c, PSA.
104 *Parents' Centre Bulletin*, 13 June 1959, p. 3.
105 See for example Hercock, *Alice*, p.142.
106 NZBMA approval was revoked in September 1959, then restored in June 1961. Dobbie, *The Trouble with Women*, pp. 6, 78.
107 *Report of the Consultative Committee*, p. 8.
108 *Ibid.*, p. 9.
109 Begg, *Intervening Years*, p.107.

110 'Review of Maternal and Child Health in New Zealand', Report of the Department of Health for the Year ended March 1969, *AJHR*, 1969, H-31, Appendix 2, p. 113.
111 Council minutes, 3 April 1960, PSA.
112 *Auckland Star*, 17 June 1960, referred to Minister's 6 April statement; 'Fighting File – Health Department – Plunket Society, 1960', PSA.
113 *Auckland Star*, 17 June 1960.
114 Council minutes, 3 May 1960, PSA; see Health Department, Annual Report, *AJHR*, 1961, H-31, p.16 for composition of council.
115 J. E. Raine, honorary general secretary, NZBMA, to Deputy Prime Minister, Tom Skinner, 17 May 1960, 'Child hygiene 1941–61', H1 35/26/1 35100, ANZ.
116 Executive minutes, 5 April 1960, PSA.
117 Executive minutes, 1 June 1960, PSA.
118 *NZH*, 7 July 1960.
119 Health Department, Annual Report, *AJHR*, 1961, H-31, p.16.
120 Begg, *Intervening Years*, p.108.
121 Executive minutes, 1 June 1960, PSA.
122 Council minutes, 13 July 1960; 27 July 1960, PSA.
123 *Ibid.*, 30 November 1960.

Chapter 7: Neil Begg and Social Paediatrics

1 Council minutes, 27–28 April 1971, 18–19 April 1972, PSA.
2 *NZH*, 6 July 1963.
3 Begg to Turbott, 12 March 1962, H1 127 32110, ANZ.
4 J. K. Hunn, *Report on the Department of Maori Affairs*, Wellington, Government Printer, Wellington, 1960.
5 M. P. K. Sorrenson, 'Modern Maori: The Young Maori Party to Mana Motuhake', in Keith Sinclair (ed.), *The Oxford Illustrated History of New Zealand*, Auckland, Oxford University Press, 1990, p. 339.
6 Turbott to Begg, 2 May 1962, H1 127 32110, ANZ.
7 Turbott to Cameron, 2 April 1962, H1 127 32110, ANZ.
8 Executive minutes, 26 June 1968, PSA.
9 *Ibid.*, 21 June 1969.
10 *Plunket News*, 9, 3, 1972, p. 3.
11 Obituary, *ODT*, 7 April 1980.
12 *Plunket Newsletter*, 13 February 1980.
13 Council minutes, 30–31 October 1973, PSA; Plunket Society, *Annual report 1973–74*, p. 3.
14 See also Sheila Horton, *Memoirs of a Colonial Goose*, Auckland, Shoal Bay Press, 1984.
15 Plunket Society, *Annual report 1970–71*, p. 13.
16 On Salmond, see Dow, *Safeguarding the Public Health*, p. 210.
17 Minutes of Steering Committee meeting, 6 September 1972, Steering Committee Plunket minute book, 1970–83, AAFB 786 Box 2, ANZ.
18 G. C. Salmond, *Maternal and Infant Care in Wellington A Health Care Consumer Study*, Department of Health Special Report Series 45, Wellington, Government Printer, 1975 ('Salmond Report'), Appendix 3, p. 90.
19 Executive minutes, 30 May 1973, PSA.
20 Salmond Report, p. 4.
21 Salmond Report, pp. 69–70; J. T. Hart, 'The Inverse Care Law', *Lancet*, 1, 1971, 405–12; Marshall Marinker, '"What is Wrong" and "How We Know It"': Changing Concepts of Illness in General Practice', in I. Loudon, J. Horder and C. Webster (eds), *General Practice under the National Health Service 1948–1997*, London, Clarendon Press, 1998, p. 85.
22 Salmond Report, p. 73.

23 *Ibid.*, pp. 70–2.
24 *Ibid.*, p. 76.
25 On page 71, Salmond wrote, 'Further evidence concerning the nursing services is confined to the activities of Plunket nurses, the reason being that only 12 per cent of mothers were supervised by public health nurses', though this was not the case for Porirua.
26 Salmond Report, p. 85.
27 G. C. Salmond, 'Social Needs for Medical Services: The Inverse Care Law in New Zealand', *NZMJ*, 80, 1974, pp. 396–403, and *NZH*, 13 November 1974.
28 Salmond Report, p. 55.
29 See for example his address to the Auckland Provincial Conference, Kaikohe, 1 July 1975, p. 3, AG 7 1-5-20, PSA.
30 Executive minutes, 13 August 1974, PSA.
31 N.C. Begg, 'Correspondence. Medical Services', *NZMJ*, 80, 1974, p. 566.
32 Executive minutes, 13 August 1974, PSA. On the growth of these instant communities, see also Bronwyn Labrum, 'Persistent Needs and Expanding Desires: Pakeha Families and State Welfare in the Years of Prosperity', in Bronwyn Dalley and Bronwyn Labrum (eds), *Fragments: New Zealand Social and Cultural History,* Auckland, Auckland University Press, 2000, pp. 190–1.
33 G.C. Salmond, 'Correspondence: Medical Services', *NZMJ*, 81, 1975, p.217.
34 Salmond, memo 1975, p. 9, AAFB Acc W3463 127 46835, ANZ.
35 Salmond Report, p. 79.
36 *Ibid.*, pp. 83–4.
37 Board of Health, Public Health Nursing Report, p. 6, cited in Executive minutes, 13 May, 10 June 1970, PSA.
38 Memo to all MPs, 13 June 1970, H1 127 37391 Box 59, ANZ.
39 *NZ Truth*, 23 June 1970; see also *ODT*, 24 June 1970, 25 June 1970, *Dunedin Evening Star*, 25 June 1970, *Taranaki Daily News*, 25 June 1970; *The Press*, 13 July 1970, *Timaru Herald*, 13 July 1970, which led to a debate in Parliament, 17 July 1970.
40 *NZ Truth*, 7 July 1970.
41 *Dunedin Evening Star*, 25 June 1970.
42 *NZPD*, Vol. 366, 1970, p.1349.
43 Joint Steering Committee minute book, 1970–83, AAFB 786 Box 2, ANZ.
44 Executive minutes, 30 May 1973, PSA.
45 *Ibid.*, 8 September 1976.
46 *Ibid.*, 15 December 1976.
47 *NZPD*, Vol. 366, 1970, p. 1356.
48 K. Holyoake to Mrs P. L. McKenzie , Pahiatua, 14 August 1970, H1 127 37391 box 59, ANZ.
49 E. Heggie, Deputy Director-General (Administration) to Dr Mackay, 27 April 1971, H1 127 37391 Box 59, ANZ.
50 *NZPD*, Vol. 367, 1970, p. 1981.
51 Plunket Society, *Annual report 1971–72*, p. 4.
52 *NZPD*, Vol. 366, 1970, p.1355.
53 Council minutes, 10–11 April 1973, PSA.
54 Michael Bassett, *The Third Labour Government: A Personal History*, Palmerston North, Dunmore Press, 1976, p. 197.
55 Letter from Tizard to Reid, 1 August 1974, AAFB Acc W3463 127 46835, ANZ.
56 Council minutes, 3 December 1974, PSA; *Hawke's Bay Herald-Tribune*, 6 December 1974.
57 Reid to Tizard, 14 August 1974, ABA.
58 Neil Begg, 'A Decade of Change', manuscript, 11 April 1975, ABA.
59 Plunket Society, *Annual report 1976–77*, pp. 19–20
60 N.C. Begg, 'Yesterday and Tomorrow in Child Health', *NZMJ*, 75, 1972, p. 265.
61 *Ibid.*

62 N. C. Begg, 'A Partnership Child Care in a New Zealand Suburb', *Australian Paediatric Journal*, Supplement 3, 1975, p. 46.

63 Begg, 'A Partnership', p. 45. See also Begg, *Intervening Years*, p. 150.

64 Truby King to Valintine, 13 June 1920, AG7 5-12, PSA. Valerie Norton argued in 1990 that the work of lay people as providers of health care was only just being recognised. However, this clearly has a longer history than is generally appreciated: Valerie Norton, 'Access to Health: Women's Experiences of Providing Health Care for Their babies', MA thesis, University of Canterbury, 1990, p. 6.

65 Begg, *Intervening Years*, p. 143.

66 *Ibid.*, p. 144.

67 *Ibid.*, p. 148.

68 Council minutes, 15–16 April 1975, PSA.

69 Bassett, *The Third Labour Government*, p. 198.

70 Auckland branch, *Seventy-second annual report 1975–76*, p. 7.

71 *NZPD*, Vol. 366, 1970, p. 1361.

72 Mr Cameron, Dunedin, Conference report, Council minutes, 3 November 1936, PSA.

73 Plunket Society, *Annual report 1952–53*, p. 19.

74 Council minutes, 13 October 1943, 26–28 July 1944, 3–5 May 1948, 1–4 November 1948, 19–20 April 1950, PSA.

75 Council minutes, 4 November 1959, PSA.

76 Neil Begg, 'Te Wero or A Crisis of Priorities', Silver Jubilee Course, Postgraduate School of Obstetrics and Gynaecology, Auckland, 2 August 1976, p. 7, ABA.

77 F. S. Maclean, *Hydatid Disease in New Zealand: An Account of the Events Leading to the Establishment of the National Hydatids Council, and the Methods Adopted to Eradicate the Disease*, Wellington, National Hydatids Council, 1964, pp. 26–7. Neil Begg, 'Te Wero', p. 7.

78 Maclean, *Hydatid Disease*, p. 30.

79 *Ibid.*, pp. 28, 30.

80 Plunket Society, *Annual report 1957–58*, p. 14.

81 Plunket Society, *Annual report 1958–59*, p. 11.

82 Plunket Society, *Annual report 1962–63*, p. 10; Plunket Society, *Annual report 1963–64*, p. 9; Plunket Society, *Annual report 1965–66*, pp. 15–16.

83 Plunket Society, *Annual report 1957–58*, p. 15.

84 Dow, *Safeguarding the Public Health*, p. 171.

85 *NZH*, 21 October 1963.

86 *Ibid.*, 10 July 1962.

87 *Ibid.*, 2 October 1964.

88 Plunket Society, *Annual report 1962–63*, p. 10.

89 Plunket Society, *Annual report 1963–64*, p. 9.

90 *NZH*, 6 November 1964.

91 *Ibid.*, 5 May 1964.

92 Plunket Society, *Annual report 1958–59*, p.11; N.C. Begg, 'Immunisation Procedures in Infancy', *NZMJ*, 57, 1958, pp. 372–3. On the history of New Zealand's immunisation schedule, see also D. A. Dow and O. Mansoor, 'New Zealand Immunisation Schedule History', *NZMJ*, 109, 1996, pp. 209–12.

93 Plunket Society, *Annual report 1957–58*, p. 14.

94 Plunket Society, *Annual report 1962–63*, p. 9.

95 Kennedy to Begg, 4 May 1962, 'Plunket Society 1957–66', H1 127 32110, ANZ.

96 *ODT*, 1 November 1966.

97 *Auckland Star*, 29 June 1966.

98 Dow, *Safeguarding the Public Health*, pp. 195–6; S. Hickling, 'Immunisation against Diphtheria, Tetanus and Whooping Cough in Childhood', *NZMJ*, 65, 1966, pp. 357–62; S. Hickling, 'Immunisation in Childhood', letter to editor, *NZMJ*, 69, 1969, pp. 108–9.

99 Council minutes, 8–19 April 1972; Executive minutes, 2 May 1973, PSA.
100 'Eve' (the Plunket nurse referred to was Mrs MacDonald), *Auckland Star*, March 1972, press cuttings, ABA.
101 Council minutes, 30–31 October 1973, PSA.
102 Executive minutes, 27 June 1973, PSA.
103 *Christchurch Star*, 15 November 1962.
104 *The Press*, 16 November 1962.
105 *Auckland Star*, 22 November 1962.
106 Nolan, *Breadwinning*, p. 220.
107 M. J. Kral, 'The Decline of Breast Feeding', Public Health thesis, University of Otago, 1963, pp. 33–4.
108 Lynley J. Hood, Julia A. Faed, P. A. Silva, Patricia M. Buckfield, 'Breast Feeding and Some Reasons for Electing to Wean the Infant: A Report from the Dunedin Multidisciplinary Child Development Study', *NZMJ*, 88, 1978, pp. 275.
109 L. Weiner, 'Reconstructing motherhood: The La Leche League in Postwar America', *Journal of American History*, 80, 4, 1994, pp. 1357–81.
110 Begg, *Intervening Years*, p. 145.
111 *Ibid.*, p.149.
112 Executive minutes, 20 October 1971, PSA; see also Sandra Coney, 'Health Organisations', in Else (ed.), *Women Together*, p. 248, and Kedgley, *Mum's the Word*, pp. 204–5. On local branch support see Auckland branch, *Annual reports*, *1966*, p. 9., *1967*, p. 9, *1971*, p. 10, *1972*, p. 10, *1973*, p. 10, *1974*, p. 15, *1975*, p. 16, *1976*, p. 11, *1977*, p. 14, *1978*, p. 13, *1979*, p. 15.
113 Janette Briggs and Allan Bridget, *Maternal and Infant Care in Wellington 1978: A Health Care Consumer Study in Replication*, Department of Health Special Report Series 64, Wellington, Government Printer, 1983, pp. 56–7.
114 *Ibid.*, p. 56; Hood *et al.*, 'Breast Feeding', pp. 273–6.
115 See Reiger, *Our Bodies, Our Babies*, pp. 62–5; Wolf, *Don't Kill Your Baby*, p. 197.
116 Plunket Society, *Annual report 1966–67*, pp. 16–17.
117 *Auckland Star*, 23 October 1972.
118 Hercock, *Alice*, p. 125; Dow, *Safeguarding the Public Health*, p. 169.
119 Report of the Special Committee on Moral Delinquency in Children and Adolescents ('Mazengarb Report'), *AJHR*, 1954, H-47, p. 42.
120 Sandra Coney, *Every Girl: A Social History of Women and the YWCA in Auckland 1885–1985*, Auckland, Auckland YWCA, 1986, p. 255.
121 William Liley, a physiologist, also worked at National Women's Hospital where he pioneered the science of foetology and was knighted for his work in 1973.
122 *Auckland Star*, 20 September 1972.
123 Plunket Society, *Annual report 1971–72*, p. 21.
124 Sorrenson, 'Modern Maori', pp. 339, 345.
125 Mary Boyd, 'New Zealand and the Other Pacific Islands', in Sinclair (ed.), *The Oxford Illustrated History of New Zealand*, p. 314.
126 Sorrenson, 'Modern Maori', pp. 345–6.
127 *Weekly News*, 17 August 1971.
128 *Auckland Star*, 17 July 1971.
129 Morag Hardy, 'Malnutrition in Young Children at Auckland', *NZMJ*, 75, 1972, pp. 291–6; *NZH*, 3 October 1972.
130 *NZH*, 3 October 1972; *NZH*, 4 October 1972.
131 Editorial, 'Malnutrition in Auckland Children', *NZMJ*, 76, 1972, pp. 200–1.
132 *NZH*, 12 July 1972.
133 Executive minutes, 28 October 1970 (his post was honorary though Plunket paid his petrol costs), *New Zealand Woman's Weekly (NZWW)*, 5 July 1971.
134 *Weekly News*, 2 August 1971.
135 *Ibid.*

136 *NZH*, 23 May 1973.

137 Executive minutes, 28 July 1976, PSA.

138 Plunket Society, *Report of Forty-third General Conference 1976*, p. 55.

139 Plunket Society, *Annual report 1977–78*, p. 6.

140 *Courier*, 10 May 1978, press cuttings, ABA.

141 Executive minutes, 7–8 November 1978, PSA.

142 A 1997 thesis did, however, argue that the report indirectly affected Plunket funding: M. D. Favell, 'Plunket Nursing in a Social, Political and Historical Context: Clients' Perspective of Mothering and Nursing', Master of Health Sciences thesis, University of Otago, 1997, pp. 3, 43, 63.

143 Plunket Society, *Report of the Forty-fourth General Conference 1978*.

144 Briggs and Bridget, *Maternal and Infant Care*, pp. 76, 77.

145 *Ibid.*, pp. 50, 70.

146 *Ibid.*, pp. 75–6.

147 Executive minutes, 16–17 July 1975, PSA.

148 The Council was fully aware of this – see Council minutes, 18–19 April 1972, PSA.

149 Plunket Society, *Annual report 1972–73*, p. 7; Plunket Society, *Annual report 1973–74*, p. 31. The largest was Auckland which took 18 mothers and babies in the mothercraft section and 40 babies in the hospital.

150 Plunket Society, The Plunket Karitane Hospitals. Submission to the Caucus Committee, August 1973, ABA.

151 See for example Auckland branch, *Forty-third annual report 1950–51*, p. 25.

152 Auckland Branch, Karitane Nurses' Club, Annual Report 1936, ABA.

153 Karitane Nurses' Club Annual Report 1964, p. 8.

154 *The League of Mothercraft Nurses Newsletter*, 1967, p. 8.

155 *NZH*, 16 June 1964.

156 Auckland branch, *Seventieth annual report 1972–73*, p. 18.

157 Memo from Turbott to Minister of Health, 20 September 1949, 'Plunket Society 1943–1953', H1 127/4/1 24627, ANZ; *NZ Listener,* 12 May 1944, p. 7, 25 May 1944, p. 16.

158 Auckland branch, *Forty-fourth annual report 1951–52*, p. 18.

159 Memo from Turbott to Minister of Health, 20 September 1949, 'Plunket Society 1943–1953', H1 127/4/1 24627, ANZ.

160 Deem, 22 November 1949, 592, PSA.

161 M. C. Wilson, 'Breast Feeding', Public Health thesis, University of Otago, 1949, p. 11.

162 Auckland branch, *Forty-second annual report 1949–50*, p. 28.

163 Letter from Mrs E. M. Southcombe, Otaki, to Plunket Headquarters, 1956, AG7 2-416, PSA.

164 *NZ Listener*, 26 May 1944, p. 16.

165 *Ibid.*, 1948, p. 19.

166 Dickie to Deem, 26 October 1946; Deem to Dickie, 15 November 1946, 581, PSA.

167 Hercock, *Alice*, pp. 61, 80, 116.

168 Circular 14/1950/51, 18 December 1950, 579, PSA.

169 Executive minutes, 18–21 November 1952, PSA.

170 Deem and Lusk, Circular to Plunket Nurses, C.5.51, 17 July 1951, 587, PSA.

171 Circular to Plunket Nurses V.10.55, 9 December 1955, 579, PSA.

172 Executive minutes, 31 October 1961, PSA.

173 *City News*, 16 October 1974, press cuttings, ABA.

174 Council minutes, 2–3 April 1974, PSA; see also Lambie, *My Story*, p. 33.

175 Confidential Report on Plunket Karitane Hospitals, by Director of Nursing Services, 11 November 1977, ABA.

176 Conference on Karitane hospitals between Drs G.A.Q. Lennane and D.P. Kennedy, 15 June 1955, p. 9, 18 June 1956, H1 26040 127, ANZ.

177 *NZ Listener*, 12 May 1944, p. 7.

178 Executive minutes, 30 April 1975, 29 October 1975, 15 December 1976, PSA.

179 Plunket Society, *Annual report 1972–73*, p. 7.
180 *NZH*, 28 June 1973.
181 Tizard to Reid, 26 July 1974, Circular for Councillors and Chairmen of Hospital Boards, Ref. C10/74, ABA.
182 Re. Submission to Caucus Committee – letter from Basil Quin to Myra McKechie, 25 June 1972, ABA.
183 Executive minutes, 4 September 1974, PSA; see also Reid to Tizard, 5 July 1974, ABA.
184 Begg, Memo to Council, 11 April 1975, ABA.
185 Executive minutes, 12 March 1975, PSA.
186 Margaret Lynch, Derek Steinberg, Christopher Ounsted, 'Family Unit in a Children's Psychiatric Hospital', *British Medical Journal (BMJ)* 2, 1975, pp. 127–9.
187 Plunket Society, *Annual report 1963–64*, p. 11.
188 M. R. Chalmers, '"Karitane Babies" and their Families', Public Health thesis, University of Otago, 1971, p. 5.
189 Plunket Society, *Report of Forty-third General Conference 1976*, p. 8; Plunket Society, *Annual report 1975–76*, p. 20.
190 Council minutes, 15–16 April 1975, PSA.
191 Executive minutes, 9 April 1975, PSA; Begg, Auckland Provincial Conference, 1 July 1975, ABA.
192 Executive minutes, 25 June 1975, 10 December 1975, PSA.
193 Council minutes, 11–15 October 1976, PSA.
194 Meeting, Plunket and Health Department; 28 October 1976, C. A. Oram, Acting Director, Department of Social Welfare, to Director-General Department of Health, 7 December 1976, AAFB Acc W3463 127 4683, ANZ.
195 See for example Halpern, *American Pediatrics*.
196 Chalmers, 'Karitane Babies', p. 39.
197 Council minutes, 18–19 April 1972, PSA.
198 *Ibid.*, 6–7 April 1976.
199 *Ibid.*
200 Council minutes, 30–31 October 1973, PSA.
201 Auckland branch, *Annual report 1975*, pp. 19, 22.
202 Council minutes, 18–19 April 1972, PSA.
203 *Ibid.*, 21–23 October 1975.
204 *Ibid.*, 6–7 April 1976.
205 Executive minutes, 8 September 1976, PSA.
206 Parry, *Fence at the Top*, p. 160.
207 *Plunket Newsletter 3*, May 1977, p. 1.
208 David Geddis, Confidential Report on Karitane Hospitals, 11 November 1977, ABA.
209 Joy McMillan, Confidential Report on Karitane Hospitals, 11 November 1977, ABA.
210 *Auckland Star*, 3 April 1978.
211 McMillan, Confidential Report.
212 On the wider implication for Plunket of this administrative change, see Chapter 11.
213 Peter K. Cressey, 11 November 1977, Confidential Report on Karitane Hospitals, 11 November 1977, ABA.
214 Council minutes, 22 March 1978, PSA; see also Parry, *Fence at the Top*, pp. 160–1.
215 Parry, *Fence at the Top*, p. 162.
216 *Auckland Star*, 3 April 1978.
217 Pauline Rout, Plunket Society Oral History Project, 1992.
218 Council minutes, Special Conference, 2 May 1978, PSA.
219 *Ibid.*
220 Parry, *Fence at the Top*, p. 159
221 Lynley Hood, 'Karitane: Southland's Pride', *NZ Listener*, 5 April 1980, pp. 43–4.
222 Council minutes, 6–7 April 1976, PSA.

223 Executive minutes, 12–13 December 1978, 31 January 1979, PSA.
224 Council minutes, Special Conference, 31 January 1980, PSA.
225 Hood, 'Karitane: Southland's Pride', pp. 43–4.
226 *Ibid.*, p. 44.
227 Horton, *Memoirs of a Colonial Goose*, p. 83.
228 Council minutes, 9 October 1978, PSA.

Chapter 8: Community Paediatrics

1 Committee on Child Health, *Child Health and Child Health Services in New Zealand*, Board of Health Report Series 31, Wellington, Government Printer, 1982, pp. 2, 3.
2 Plunket Society, *Annual report 1968–69*, pp. 12–13.
3 Plunket Society, *Annual report 1970–71*, pp. 17–18.
4 See for example R. J. Rose, *Infant and Foetal Loss in New Zealand*, Department of Health Special Report Series 17, Wellington, Government Printer, 1964, pp. 5, 10, 17.
5 'Deaths in Infancy', *NZMJ*, 83, 1976, p. 20; *Plunket Newsletter*, 4, August 1977, p. 1.
6 *Child Health and Child Health Services*, p. 2; J. Fraser, *Post-neonatal Mortality: Results of a National Survey 1978–79*, Special Report Series 61, Wellington, Government Printer, 1982, p. 1.
7 *Child Health and Child Health Services*, p. 10.
8 Virginia Berridge, 'History in Public Health: A New Development for History', *Hygiea Internationalis*, 1, 1, 1999, pp. 30–3.
9 Stevi Jackson and Sue Scott, 'Risk Anxiety and Social Construction of Childhood', in Deborah Lupton (ed.), *Risk and Sociocultural Theory: New Directions and Perspectives*, Cambridge, Cambridge University Press, 1999, p. 95. In her history of child welfare, Dalley discusses the dual perception of children as victims of society and threats to it from the early twentieth century. Dalley, *Family Matters*, p. 5. Child health professionals contributed to the entrenchment of the former.
10 *Child Health and Child Health Services,* p.27.
11 See D. M. Ferguson, L.J. Howood, F.T. Shannon, 'Child Health: Attitudes of Mothers of Five-year-old Children to Compulsory Child Health Provisions', *NZMJ*, 96, 1983, p.338–40.
12 Plunket Society, *Report of the Forty-sixth General Conference 1982*, p. 13.
13 Harry Hendrick, *Child Welfare: England 1872–1989*, London, Routledge, 1994, p. 243.
14 R. E. Helfer and C. H. Kempe (eds), *The Battered Child*, Chicago, University of Chicago Press, 1968; R. E. Helfer and C. H. Kempe (eds), *Helping the Battered Child and His Family*, Philadelphia, Lippincot, 1972, p. x.
15 Helfer and Kempe, *Helping the Battered Child*, p. xi.
16 Hendrick, *Child Welfare*, p. 244; Nigel Parton, *The Politics of Child Abuse*, Basingstoke, Macmillan, 1985, pp. 52–4.
17 D. L. Griffiths and F. J. Moynihan, 'Multiple Epiphysieal Injuries in Babies ("Battered Baby Syndrome"), *BMJ*, 2, 1963, pp. 1558–61; *BMJ*, leader, 21 December 1963, pp. 1544–5. See also the Special Standing Committee on Accidents in Childhood of the British Paediatric Association, 'The Battered Baby', *BMJ*, 1, 1966, p. 601.
18 Standing Medical Advisory Committee for the Central Health Services Council, the Secretary of State for Social Services and the Secretary of State for Wales, *The Battered Baby*, London, HMSO, 1970, p. 3.
19 Hendrick, *Child Welfare*, p. 245.
20 *Ibid.*, pp. 244–9.
21 *Ibid.*, p. 253.
22 Press report, 6 November 1964, Press Cuttings, ABA.
23 *NZH*, 12 February 1965.
24 Council minutes, 31 March 1965, PSA.
25 Letter from Margaret Nicholls, *League of Mothercraft Nurses Newsletter*, 1968, p. 21.

26 'Review of Maternal and Child Health in New Zealand', Report of the Health Department for the year ending March 1969, Appendix 2, *AJHR*, 1969, H-31, p. 113.

27 Plunket Society, *Annual report 1973–74*, p. 22.

28 District reports, Executive minutes, 4 October 1973, PSA.

29 *Ibid.*, 3 July 1974.

30 Auckland branch, *Seventieth annual report 1977–78*, p. 15.

31 *NZH*, 5 May 1978.

32 *Ibid.*, 21 January 1975.

33 *NZ Listener*, 3–9 June 1978, p. 9.

34 *Ibid.*, p. 9.

35 Executive minutes, 23–4 April 1979, PSA.

36 Plunket Society, *Annual report 1979–80*, pp. 10–11.

37 *NZH*, 4 December 1978.

38 Plunket Society, *Annual report 1982–83*, p. 12. He thanked the Society for allowing him to spend time on the issue again in his second annual report: Plunket Society, *Annual report 1979–80*, pp. 11–12.

39 Max Abbott (ed.), *Child Abuse Prevention in New Zealand: The Edited Proceedings of the National Symposium on Child Abuse Prevention, Palmerston North, 9–11 November 1982*, Auckland, Mental Health Foundation of New Zealand, 1983.

40 D.C. Geddis, 'Leading Article: New Developments Concerning Child Abuse', *NZMJ*, 97, 1984, p. 404.

41 Standing Medical Advisory Committee for the Central Health Services Council, the Secretary of State for Social Services and the Secretary of State for Wales, *The Battered Baby*, London, HMSO, 1970, p. 9.

42 Jackson and Scott, 'Risk Anxiety and Social Construction of Childhood', p. 89.

43 *NZ Listener*, 3–9 June 1978, p. 10.

44 *Ibid.*

45 Gail de Boer, Juanita Saxby, Michael Soljak, *Child Health Profile 1989*, Health Services Research and Development Unit, National Health Statistics Centre, Wellington, Department of Health, 1990, p. 57.

46 *Ibid.*, p. 57.

47 Abbott, *Child Abuse Prevention in New Zealand*, p. 25.

48 *NZ Listener*, 18 February 1989, pp. 16–17, 33–41.

49 Plunket Society, *Annual report 1984–85*, p. 13.

50 I. Johnston and D. C. Geddis, 'Child Abuse and Neglect – Reform of the Law', *NZMJ*, 97, 1984, pp. 367–70.

51 *NZ Listener*, 3–9 June 1978, p.10. On the development of child protection teams, see Dalley, *Family Matters*, pp. 345–50.

52 Plunket Society, Submission to the Royal Commission on Social Policy, 1987, p. 8, ABA.

53 Dalley, *Family Matters*, p. 354.

54 See Chapter 9.

55 Plunket Society, *Annual report 1988–89*, p. 11.

56 Plunket Society, *Annual report 1989–90*, p. 12. See also Pauline Tapp, David Geddis, Nicola Taylor, 'Protecting the Family', in Mark Henaghan and Bill Atkin (eds), *Family Law Policy in New Zealand*, Oxford, Oxford University Press, 1992, pp. 168–97.

57 Hendrick, *Child Welfare*, p. 242.

58 David Geddis, 'Children and Violence' in Pauline Tapp (convener), 'The Needs and Rights of Children – Papers Presented at a Series of Lectures offered by the Centre of Continuing Education, University of Auckland, June–August 1978'.

59 Plunket Society, *Annual report 1977–78*, pp. 13–14.

60 IYC Report of Child and Health Committee, p. 6, ABA.

61 Plunket Society, *Annual report 1989–90*, p. 12.

62 Hendrick, *Child Welfare*, p. 242. For the defining of child sexual abuse as a medical problem

in the United States see Hugh Evans, 'The Discovery of Child Sexual Abuse in America', in Stern and Markel (eds), *Formative Years*, pp. 233–59.

63 Edited Proceedings of the National Symposium on Child Abuse Prevention, 1982, p. 1.

64 Plunket Society, *Annual report 1986–87*, p. 13.

65 Plunket Society, *Annual report 1988–89*, p. 11; D. C. Geddis, 'Leading Article. The Diagnosis of Sexual Abuse of Children', *NZMJ*, 102, 1989, pp. 99–100.

66 Lynley Hood, *A City Possessed: The Christchurch Civic Crèche Case: Child Abuse, Gender Politics and the Law*, Dunedin, Longacre Press, 2001.

67 Nigel Parton, *Governing the Family: Child Care, Child Protection and the State*, Basingstoke, Macmillan, 1991, p. 214.

68 *Plunket News. Special Issue*, April 1993, p. 2.

69 *NZH*, 24 August 1998.

70 *Ibid.*, 27 May 1999.

71 *Ibid.*, 16 September 1996. The following year, however, Tuohy reported an evaluation of the scheme which concluded that a non-targeted universal Well Child Service would be a more effective way of providing needed resources to the appropriate people at the appropriate time: P. Tuohy, 'Conference Report Responding to Child Maltreatment – The Prevention of Child Abuse', Plunket Society, *Annual report 1996–97*, p. 12.

72 Phil A. Silva, *Annotated Bibliography of Publications and Reports from the Dunedin Multidisciplinary Health and Development Research Unit, 1975 to 1985*, Dunedin, The Unit, 1986; see also Phil A. Silva and Warren R. Stanton (eds), *Child to Adult: The Dunedin Multidisciplinary Health and Development Study*, Auckland, Oxford University Press, 1996.

73 *NZH*, 16 September 1996.

74 *Ibid.*

75 Plunket Society, *Annual report 1987–88*, p. 25.

76 *Evening Post*, 7 November 1992.

77 *NZH*, 5 August 2000.

78 *Dominion*, 15 February 2001.

79 *NZH*, 12–13 August 2000, 2 February 2001.

80 Virginia Berridge, *Health and Society in Britain since 1939*, Cambridge & New York, Cambridge University Press, 1999, p. 30.

81 *Child Health and Child Health Services*, p. 16.

82 A. B. Bergman, J. B. Beckwith, C. G. Ray (eds), *The Sudden Infant Death Syndrome: Proceedings of the Second International Conference on Causes of Sudden Death in Infants, Seattle, 1969*, Seattle, University of Washington Press, 1970; Abraham B. Bergman, *The "Discovery" of Sudden Infant Death Syndrome: Lessons in the Practice of Political Medicine*, New York, Praeger, 1986.

83 R. R. Robinson (ed.), *SIDS 1974: Proceedings of the Francis E. Camps International Symposium on Sudden and Unexpected Deaths in Infancy*, Toronto, University of Toronto Press, 1974, p. xvii.

84 Plunket Society, *Annual report 1911–12*, p. 3.

85 Deem to Dr Jennings, Christchurch, 13 May 1944, 589, PSA.

86 Bush to Deem, 22 November 1949, 581, PSA.

87 *League of Mothercraft Nurses Newsletter*, Winter 1958, pp.11–12; reprinted from *Cambridge Daily News*, 5 July 1958.

88 Neil Begg, *The New Zealand Child and His Family*, Christchurch, Whitcombe & Tombs, 1970, p.128.

89 *League of Mothercraft Nurses Newsletter*, 1966, p.11.

90 *Ibid.*, 1969, p. 15.

91 R. J. Rose, *Infant and Foetal Loss in New Zealand*, Department of Health Special Report Series 17, Wellington, Government Printer, 1964.

92 Plunket Society, *Annual report 1971–72*, p. 18.

93 Plunket Society, *Annual report 1973–74*, p. 15.

94 *Plunket Newsletter*, 4 August 1977, p. 1.

95 I. B. Hassall, 'Leading Article: Sudden Infant Death Syndrome – A Serious New Zealand Health Problem', *NZMJ*, 99, 1986, pp. 233–4; P. D. Gluckman (ed.), *Workshop on Post-Neonatal Mortality and Cot Death, Auckland, 3–7 September 1984*, Auckland, Joint Committee on Child Health Research, 1985.

96 *Report of National Steering Committee on Cot Death*, Wellington, The Committee, 1985; *NZMJ*, 99, 1986, p. 120; on consumer pressure, see for example, Lorraine Webb, *Cot Death in New Zealand: Unfolding the Mystery*, Auckland, David Bateman, 1986, p. 70.

97 John L. Emery, Confidential Report to the Royal Plunket Society, Sheffield Health Authority, 11 June 1986, p. 3, ABA.

98 Department of Health, *Recording Child Health and Development: A Handbook for Professionals using the 'Health and Development Record' Book*, Wellington, Department of Health, 1984, pp. 131, 133. My emphasis.

99 J. Fraser, *Post-neonatal Mortality: Results of a National Survey 1978–79*, Department of Health Special Report Series 61, Wellington, Government Printer, 1982.

100 E. A. Mitchell, I. B. Hassall, D. M. O. Becroft, 'Postneonatal Mortality Review in Auckland: Two Years' Experience', *NZMJ*, 100, 1987, p. 269.

101 Lesley Max, *Children: Endangered Species?: How the Needs of New Zealand Children are being Seriously Neglected: A Call for Action*, Auckland, Penguin, 1990, p. 37.

102 *Ibid.*, p. 37.

103 Hassall, 'Sudden Infant Death Syndrome', p. 234.

104 Max, *Children: Endangered Species?*, p. 38. Hassall later explained that he was taken to task for implying that mothers were incompetent, but still believed that it was a step forward to examine childrearing practices rather than physiological causes: personal communication, 15 July 2002.

105 *NZH*, 24 October 1986.

106 Max, *Children: Endangered Species?*, pp. 38–9.

107 E. A. Mitchell, R. Scragg, A. W. Stewart, D. M. O. Becroft, B. J. Taylor, R. P. K. Ford, I. B. Hassall, D. M. J. Barry, E. M. Allen, A. P. Roberts, 'Cot Death Supplement: Results from the First Year of the New Zealand Cot Death Study', *NZMJ*, 104, 1991, p. 75.

108 Nick J. Fox, 'Postmodern Reflections on "Risk", "Hazards" and "Life Choices"', in Lupton (ed.), *Risk and Sociocultural Theory*, p. 12.

109 See also Helene Joffe, *Risk and 'the Other'*, Cambridge, Cambridge University Press, 1999, p. 7.

110 Berridge, *Health and Society in Britain since 1939*, p. 7. Yet see also James J. McKenna, 'Sudden Infant Death Syndrome: Making Sense of Current Research', *Mothering*, 81, 1996, pp. 74–80, in which the author noted that the majority of infants who died from SIDS worldwide had no known risk factors: cited in Ladd-Taylor & Umansky, *'Bad' Mothers*, p. 24.

111 *Our Health – Our Future. The State of Public Health in New Zealand*, Wellington, Public Health Commission, 1994 (Professor David Skegg, chair), p. 95.

112 *North & South*, March 1996, p. 55; 'New Professor', *University of Auckland News*, 31, 8, 2001, p. 6.

113 *Plunket Newsletter*, May 1992, p. 7; also cited in *Tamariki Ora: A Consensus Development Conference Report on Well Child Care to the National Advisory Committee on Core Health and Disability Support Services and the Public Health Commission*, Wellington, Public Health Commission, 1993, p. 17.

114 *Our Health – Our Future*, p. 46.

115 E. A. Mitchell *et al.*, 'Four Modifiable and other Major Risk Factors for Cot Death: The New Zealand Study', *Journal of Paediatric Child Health*, 1992, Supplement 1.

116 Cited in *Sunday Star Times*, 15 October 1995.

117 *Bay of Plenty Times*, 10 March 2001; see also *North & South*, March 1996, p. 57.

118 *Bay of Plenty Times*, 10 March 2001; *Dominion*, 14 March 2001.

119 Plunket Society, *Annual report 1987–88*, pp. 25–6.

120 Plunket Society, *Annual report 1989–90*, p. 27; *Plunket News*, September 1995, p.1.

121 *Plunket News*, September 1995, p.3.

122 *NZH*, 25 September 1979.

123 Plunket Society, *Annual report 1978–79*, p. 11.

124 *NZH*, 3 April 1979.

125 Ferguson *et al.*, 'Child Health: Attitudes of Mothers of Five-year-old Children', p. 338.

126 Brian Rudman, 'Our Third World Child Health Care', *NZ Listener*, 27 September 1986, p. 18.

127 Jenny Shipley and Winston Peters, 'Towards a Code of Social and Family Responsibility. He Kaupapa Kawenga Whanau, Kawenga Hapori. Public Discussion Document', February 1998, p. 11.

128 Max, *Children: Endangered Species?*, p. 36.

129 *NZ Listener*, 15 December 1979, p. 24; *Auckland Star*, 2 March 1979;

130 *NZH*, 18 August 1999.

131 *Ibid.*, 9 June 1999.

132 *Ibid.*, 14 April 2000.

133 *Ibid.*, 12 July 1979.

134 Plunket Society, *Annual report 1987–88*, p. 28.

135 Plunket Society, *Annual report 1988–89*, p. 28.

136 Plunket Society, *Annual report 1987–88*, p. 25.

137 *NZH*, 18–19 December 1999.

138 *Plunket News*, September 1995, p. 8.

139 *Northern Advocate*, 11 October 1979.

140 Sally Jackman, *Child Poverty in Aotearoa/New Zealand: A Report from the New Zealand Council of Christian Social Services*, Wellington, The Council, 1993.

141 *NZH*, 23 August 1999.

142 Geraldine Johns, 'Suffer the Little Children', *Metro*, April 2000, pp. 70–8.

143 *NZH*, 12–13 June 1999.

144 Plunket Society, *Annual report 1984–85*, p. 12.

145 *Child Health and Child Health Services*, p. 107.

146 Plunket Society, *Annual report 1984–85*, p. 12.

147 See Roger Cooter and Bill Luckin (eds), *Accidents in History*, Amsterdam, Rodopi, 1997, Introduction, pp. 1–16.

148 'Safety First' Campaign, Dunedin, described by Deem in Plunket Society, *Report of the Twenty-eighth General Conference 1946*, p. 16; Plunket Society, *Annual report 1948–49*, p. 21.

149 *League of Mothercraft Nurses Newsletter*, Winter 1956, p. 13.

150 Council minutes, 19–20 April 1977, PSA.

151 *Child Health and Child Health Services*, p. 114.

152 Bryder, *Not Just Weighing Babies*, pp. 103–4.

153 *Plunket Newsletter*, December 1990, p. 2.

154 Donald Court and Eva Alberman, in John O Forfar (ed.), *Child Health in a Changing Society*, Oxford, Oxford University Press, 1988, p. 21, and Chapter 5.

155 Plunket Society, Northern Regional Conference Minutes, 15 March 1994, p. 6, ABA.

156 Plunket Society, *Report of the Thirty-ninth General Conference 1968*, p. 20.

157 Plunket Car Safety Survey, May 1979, p. 2, ABA.

158 *Child Health and Child Health Services*, p. 123; see also Tord Kjellstrom *et al.*, 'A Survey of Children's Protection against Accident Injuries in Cars in New Zealand', Department of Community Health, University of Auckland, 1979, and Tord Kjellstrom *et al.*, 'The Traffic Disease in Children: Epidemiology and Case Histories: Detailed Results of Interviews with Parents of 284 Children Admitted to Hospital 1970–77', Department of Community Health, University of Auckland, 1980.

159 Plunket Car Safety Survey, May 1979, ABA; D. C. Geddis, 'Children in Cars: Results of an Observational Study in New Zealand', *NZMJ*, 90, 1979, pp. 468–71.

160 Plunket Society, *Annual report 1979–80*, p. 10.

161 Plunket Society, *Annual report 1980–81*, p. 11; D. C. Geddis and I. C. Appleton, 'Use of Restraint Systems by Preschool Children in Cars', *Archives of Disease in Childhood*, 57, 1982, pp. 540–60.

162 *Plunket Newsletter*, 18, May 1981.

163 Ibid., 21, February 1982.

164 Plunket Society, *Annual report 1981–82*, p. 16.

165 Plunket Society, *Report of the Forty-seventh General Conference 1984*, p. 6.

166 Plunket Society, *Annual report 1992–93*, p.14.

167 Plunket Society, *Annual report 1985–86*, p. 15.

168 Plunket Society, *Annual report 1989–90*, p. 13.

169 Plunket Society, *Report of the Forty-third General Conference 1976*, p. 84.

170 See for example, Plunket Society, *Report of the Forty-sixth General Conference 1982*, p. 23. See also *Child Health and Child Health Services*, p. 108, and Plunket Society, *Annual report 1982–83*, p. 11.

171 de Boer, Saxby, Soljak, *Child Health Profile 1989*, p. 51.

172 *Ibid.*

173 *Plunket Child Safety Newsletter*, December 1993.

174 *Plunket in Touch*, October 1996, p. 4.

175 *NZH*, 18 March 1998.

176 *Ibid.*, 10 October 2001.

177 *Northern Advocate*, 26 February 2001.

178 *Nelson Mail*, 4 August 2000.

179 Executive minutes, 20 October 1976, PSA.

180 Plunket Society, *Annual report 1981–82*, p.17; NZWSC statistics, Hassall, personal papers.

181 Plunket Society, *Report of the Forty-seventh General Conference 1984*, p. 65.

182 *ODT*, 29 November 1982.

183 New Zealand Parliament, Local Bills Committee, *Report on Fencing Private Swimming Pools*, Wellington, Government Printer, 1983, pp. 8, 9, 60–1.

184 D. C. Geddis, 'Child Health: The Exposure of Pre-school Children to Water Hazards and the Incidence of Potential Drowning Accidents', *NZMJ*, 97, 1984, pp. 223–6.

185 Plunket Society, *Report of the Forty-seventh General Conference 1984*, p. 66; for Christchurch, see Ferguson *et al.*, 'Child Health: Attitudes of mothers', pp. 338–9. See also I. B. Hassall, 'Drownings in Private Swimming Pools', *NZMJ*, 95, 1982, pp. 129–30, Geddis, 'Child Health: The Exposure of Pre-school Children to Water Hazards', pp. 223–6.

186 Hassall, Report to Council, 1989, ABA; I. B. Hassall, 'Swimming Pool Fencing At Last', *NZMJ*, 100, 1987, p. 637; I. B. Hassall, 'Thirty Six Consecutive Under 5 Year Old Domestic Swimming Pool Drownings', *Australian Paediatric Journal*, 25, 1989, pp. 1430–6; I. B. Hassall, *Under Five Year Old Domestic Swimming Pool Drownings since the 1987 Fencing of Swimming Pools Act: A Briefing Paper from the Office of the Commissioner for Children*, Wellington, The Office, 1991.

187 *Plunket Newsletter*, December 1989, p. 2.

188 *Plunket Child Safety Newsletter*, June–July 1994.

189 *NZH*, 29 May 1999.

190 Hassall, personal communication, July 2002; *NZH*, 24 September 2000.

191 Council minutes, 10–11 April 1973, PSA.

192 Council minutes, 6–7 April 1976, PSA.

193 *Plunket Child Safety Newsletter*, June–July 1994, p. 2.

194 *NZH*, 3 August 2000.

195 Executive minutes, 6–7 December 1983, 4–5 December 1984, PSA.

196 *Our Health – Our Future*, 1994, p. 95.

197 Caroline Coggan, Pam Patterson, Rhonda Hooper, *Evaluation of Kidsafe Week 1999*, Injury Prevention Research Centre, Department of Community Health, University of Auckland, 1999.

198 *Northern Advocate*, 26 February 2001.

199 See for example, Sylvia Ann Hewlett, *Child Neglect in Rich Nations*, New York, United Nations Children's Fund, 1993, which Ian Hassall drew my attention to.

200 Ian Hassall and Russell Wills, 'Advocacy for the General Paediatrician', Paediatric Update, Starship Children's Hospital, 19 March 2000, Hassall, personal papers; see also Evans, in Stern and Markel (eds), *Formative Years*, p. 251.

201 N. Turner, memo to All Child Health Colleagues, 30 June 2000, in author's possession.

202 *NZH*, 10 May 2000.

203 *Ibid.*, 22 May 1997.

204 *Plunket News*, April–May 1995, p. 4.

Chapter 9: Plunket Nursing Services in the Late Twentieth Century

1 *Child Health and Child Health Services in New Zealand*, p. 366. A 1983 report argued that new emphases on psychological, educational and social aspects of child development had been incorporated into Plunket training in 1975: Briggs & Allan, *Maternal and Infant Care in Wellington 1978*, p. 75. However, Begg had already stressed developmental aspects in 1959: *Born in New Zealand*, Plunket Society film, New Zealand National Film Unit, 1959.

2 Max, *Children: Endangered Species?*, p.52. Joan Lambert argued that the discarding of the uniform was driven by the nurses between 1985 and 1987. She cited one nurse: 'By . . . 1987 most of us were out of uniform full stop. We weren't meant to be. We just refused to wear them': Joan Lambert, ' "They Can't See What We See": Voices and Standpoint of Twelve Plunket Nurses', M. Phil. thesis, Massey University, 1984, p. 184. On the nurses' perception of themselves as facilitators, see also Lambert, pp. 108–12, 126–9.

3 Rosaleen, in Joyce Powell, 'Keep those Brakes Pumping Nurse', transcripts of interviews, c1997 (Christian names only were used by Powell).

4 Mary, in Powell, transcript.

5 *NZH*, 11 October 1994.

6 Helen (Val) Jones, interview, Plunket Society Oral History Project, 1992.

7 Joan Myer, interview, Plunket Society Oral History Project, 1992.

8 Joan, in Powell, transcript.

9 Gwen, in Powell, transcript.

10 Anne Cressey, interview, Plunket Society Oral History Project, 1992.

11 Alma, in Powell, transcript.

12 Iris, in Powell, transcript.

13 Joan, in Powell, transcript.

14 Roslaeen, in Powell, transcript.

15 Gwen, in Powell, transcript.

16 Adele Follick, 'Frieda Massey: Far from a Battleaxe!', *NZWW*, 6 October 1986, p.17.

17 Mary, in Powell, transcript.

18 Judy, in Powell, transcript.

19 Favell noted that Plunket nurses did not have the right to make referrals directly to most hospital departments and specialists, though they sometimes did so, and in one of the cases she interviewed, this resulted in the saving of the baby's life: Favell, pp. 101, 117.

20 Claire O'Brien, 'They See the Darker Side of NZ Life', *NZWW*, 22 October 1984, pp. 33–5.

21 Michael Clinton, 'Child Health Services in South Auckland Project: Report to the Hon Mr David Caygill, Minister of Health. June 1988', Victoria University of Wellington, Wellington, 1988, p. 43. Maori constituted 17.1 per cent of the population and 12.7 per cent were Pacific Islanders.

22 Jenny Chamberlain, 'Babes in Arms: Plunket's Fight for Life', *North & South*, November 1992, p. 108.

23 Patty, in Powell, transcript.

24 Mary, in Powell, transcript.

25 Patty, in Powell, transcript.
26 Felicity, in Powell, transcript.
27 Patty, in Powell, transcript.
28 Plunket Society, *Annual report 1983–84*, p. 17.
29 Plunket Society, *Annual report 1984–85*, p. 15.
30 *Plunket Newsletter*, December 1990, p. 1.
31 Vandalism was not exclusively a South Auckland problem; see comment on Christchurch in *Plunket Newsletter*, December 1990, p. 1.
32 Plunket Society, *Annual report 1986–87*, Report of Director of Nursing Services, p.14; Brian Rudman, 'Our Third World Child Health Care', *NZ Listener*, 27 September 1986, p. 17.
33 John Emery, Sheffield Health Authority, 'Confidential Report to David Geddis on Plunket Society', 11 June 1986, p. 4, ABA.
34 *Ibid.*, pp. 5–6.
35 Clinton, 'Child Health Services in South Auckland Project', p. 17.
36 Interview with Joyce Powell, May 2000.
37 Clinton, 'Child Health Services in South Auckland Project', p. 33.
38 M. C. Brennan, 'The Public Image of Plunket Society', Market Research Centre, Massey University, January 1986, ABA.
39 Plunket Society, Strategic Planning Sub-committee, 'Discussion Paper on Service Options', 24 February 1988, p. 2, ABA.
40 Pam Williams, cited in Jackman, *Child Poverty in Aotearoa/ New Zealand,* p. 23. See below for further discussion of cutbacks.
41 *East and Bays Courier,* 17 December 1997.
42 Turbott, 3 August 1950, H1 127 23201 127, ANZ; see also Council minutes, 28 June 1950, PSA.
43 *Plunket News,* 10, 5, 1973, p. 18.
44 See section on Consultative Committee, Chapter 6.
45 *Evening Post,* 1 July 1959; *Plunket News,* 10, 2, 1973, p. 33.
46 Plunket Society, *Annual report 1966–67*, p. 4.
47 Plunket Society, *Annual report 1966–7*, p.15 (my emphasis).
48 Deem to Harold Pettit, 11 June 1948, 595, PSA.
49 M. P. Buchler to Spencer, 22 March 1938, cited in Daniell, *A Doctor at War*, p.171.
50 Edna Birkenshaw to Deem, 31 May 1950, 581, PSA.
51 Woods, 'Plunket Nursing in the Invercargill Area', p. 37.
52 *Ibid.*, p. 43.
53 Although Clements, the acknowledged authoritative source for the New Zealand Paediatric Society, regarded breastfeeding as every child's 'birthright', he added that it was no longer essential to life, and in some cases it was 'unsuitable for the infant': Clements, *Infant Nutrition*, p.207; Marriott, *A Textbook of Infant Feeding,* 3rd edn 1942.
54 *Daily Times,* 9 October 1954.
55 *Dominion,* 22 June 1938.
56 Elliott and Rohan, 'Infant Feeding', p. 25.
57 H. McMullen to A. W. S. Thompson, 3 July 1954, 580, PSA.
58 M. I. Nicholls to Thompson, 7 July 1954, 580, PSA.
59 K. V. Marriott, 'The Plunket Society: Some Opinions', Public Health Dissertation, University of Otago, 1963, p. 11.
60 Evidence to 1937 Committee of Inquiry into Maternity Services, Miss Barnett, Timaru, 19 May 1937.
61 Interview, Marion Shepherd, Plunket Society Oral History Project, 1992.
62 Woods, 'Plunket Nursing in the Invercargill Area', p. 21.
63 J. R. Gilmour, 'The Mother, the Baby, and the Plunket Sister', Public Health thesis, University of Otago, 1950, p. 28
64 *ODT,* 13 October 1952.

65 N. N. Hamilton-Gibbs, 'The Work of the Plunket Society', Public Health thesis, University of Otago, 1961, p. 28.

66 Alan Webster and Mervyn Hancock, in Stewart Houston (ed.), *Marriage and the Family in New Zealand*, Wellington, Sweet & Maxwell, 1970, p. 231.

67 J. Y. Yee, 'To Help the Mothers and Save the Babies', Public Health thesis, University of Otago, 1962, pp. 20–2.

68 Marriott, 'The Plunket Society: Some Opinions', pp. 20, 36.

69 Joyce Thorpe, interview, Plunket Society Oral History Project, 1992.

70 William James Reeder, 'The Plunket Tradition and Today's Mother', Public Health thesis, University of Otago, 1969, p. 18.

71 *Ibid.*, pp. 36–7.

72 See also Chapter 7.

73 Salmond Report, p. 76.

74 *Ibid.*, p. 85. It was not made clear whether it was a Plunket or a public health nurse who was being referred to, but it was generally assumed to be the former.

75 *Ibid.*, p. 55.

76 Briggs and Allan, *Maternal and Infant Care in Wellington 1978*, p. 70.

77 *Ibid.*, pp. 47, 49.

78 D. M. Ferguson, A. L. Beautrais, F. T. Shannon, 'Maternal Satisfaction with Primary Health Care', *NZMJ*, 94, 1981, pp. 291–4.

79 I. B. Hassall and D. C. Geddis, 'The Plunket Nurse', *NZMJ*, 94, 1981, p. 249.

80 D. C. Geddis, P. A. Silva, 'The Plunket Society: A Consumer Survey', *NZMJ*, 90, 1979, pp. 507–9; Phil A. Silva, 'Health and Development in the Early Years', in P.A. Silva and W. R. Stanton (eds), *Child to Adult: The Dunedin Multidisciplinary Health and Development Study*, Auckland, Oxford University Press, 1996, p. 44.

81 Clinton, 'Child Health Services in South Auckland Project', p. 43.

82 *Ibid.*, p. 45.

83 *Ibid.*

84 Nicola Legat, 'Suffer the Children', *Metro*, February 1990, pp. 47–8.

85 Clinton, 'Child Health Services in South Auckland Project', p. 65.

86 Plunket Society, *Annual report 1987–88*, p. 5.

87 Plunket Society, *Annual report 1989–90*, p. 9.

88 On the development of the Maatua Whangai programme, see Dalley, *Family Matters*, pp. 329ff.

89 Plunket Society, *Annual report, 1990–91*, p. 12.

90 Legat, 'Suffer the Children', p. 48.

91 *Plunket Newsletter*, February 1990, p. 1.

92 Plunket Society, *Annual report 1990–91*, p. 12.

93 *Plunket News*, February 1994, p. 2.

94 *Ibid.*, December 1993, p. 1.

95 *Ibid.*, November 1994, p. 9.

96 *New Zealand Doctor*, 10 July 1996, p. 12.

97 Anne Manchester, 'Delivering a Safe and Accessible Service to Maori', *Kai Tiaki*, 8, 3, 2002, p. 16.

98 *Sunday Star Times*, 30 June 2002.

99 Plunket Society Board, *Newsbrief*, 10 August 1993.

100 Legat, 'Suffer the Children', p. 41.

101 *Plunket News*, April 1990, p. 1.

102 Clinton, 'Child Health Services in South Auckland Project', p. 32.

103 Legat, 'Suffer the Children', p. 49.

104 *NZH*, 13 May 1994.

105 Sally Abel, Michele Lennan, Julie Park, David Tipene-Leach, Sitaleki Finau, Carol Everard, *Infant Care Practices: A Qualitative Study of the Practices of Auckland Maori, Tongan,*

Samoan, Cook Islands, Niuean, Pakeha Caregivers of Under 12 Month Old Infants, Auckland, The Infant Care Practices Study Team, Department of Maori and Pacific Health, University of Auckland, 1999, pp. 34–5, 74–5, 114, 183, 245.

106 I. B. Hassall and Anne Cressey, 'A Report on the Plunket Karitane Family Centres', March 1989, ABA.

107 *Ensign*, 10 March 1979; see also *NZH*, 24 April 1979.

108 Meadowbank Family Centre, Rosaleen Knell, Annual Report for the Year ending 31 March 1980, ABA.

109 Reports of Meadowbank Family Centre and Minutes of Management Committee, 1990s, ABA.

110 Meadowbank Family Centre, Rosaleen Knell, Annual Report for the Year ending 31 March 1980, ABA.

111 Meadowbank Family Centre, Report 18 November 1991, ABA.

112 *NZH*, 22 April 1996.

113 *Sunday Star Times*, 25 August 1996.

114 *New Zealand Doctor*, 4 September 1996.

115 *NZH*, 13 August 1996; Janet Gafford, Tracy J. Riddler, Trinie Moore, Angela Baldwin, *Client Evaluation. Plunket Karitane Family Centres. Policy Unit Occasional Paper 22*, Wellington, Plunket Society, 1998; also cited in *Plunket Care Delivery News*, April 1997, pp. 1–4.

116 *Client Evaluation*, p. 82.

117 *Ibid.*, pp. 79, 88. On positive responses, including some from Maori clients, see also Abel *et al.*, *Infant Care Practices: A Qualitative Study*, pp. 35, 214–5.

118 Anne Cressey, Report to Executive, 4 September 1990, ABA.

119 Joan Hunt, 'Report on Visit to the Office of Child, Adolescent and Family Health Services, Adelaide, South Australia', 19 October 1990, ABA.

120 Nicola Taylor, 'Regional Meeting Series – May 1991: Review of the Minutes of the Meetings', July 1991, p. 42, ABA.

121 *Plunket News*, November 1994.

122 *NZH*, 21 November 1997.

123 *NZPD*, Vol. 542, 1994, p. 3670.

124 *Sunday Star Times*, 25 August 1996.

125 *Plunket At Work,* April 1997, p.2.

126 *NZH*, 5 November 1997.

127 *NZPD*, Vol. 565, p. 5661.

128 *Ibid.*, Vol. 579, 1999, p. 18587.

129 Editorial, *NZH*, 7 May 1999.

130 Questions on Notice, No. 11, 1 March 1990, Plunket Society Funding, *NZPD*, 1990, p. 4725.

131 *Plunket News*, April–May 1995, p. 2.

132 *NZPD,*Vol. 521, 1991, p. 5760.

133 *Ibid.*, Vol. 551, 1995, p. 9841.

134 *NZPD*, Vol. 505, 1990, pp. 331–2, Vol. 557, 1996, p. 14181.

135 *Ibid.*, Vol. 565, 1997, p. 5661.

136 *NZPD*, Vol. 574, 1998, p. 13702.

137 Plunket Society Board, *Newsbrief*, 29 October 1993; *Plunket News*, December 1993, p. 3. On the PAFT scheme, see also Helen May, *Politics in the Playground: The World of Early Childhood in Postwar New Zealand,* Wellington, Bridget Williams Books with New Zealand Council of Educational Research, 2001, pp. 222–6.

138 *NZPD*, Vol. 531, 1992, p. 12304.

139 Meadowbank Family Centre, Committee minutes, 17 August 1992, ABA.

140 *East and Bays Courier*, 6 December 1995.

141 *Child Health and Child Health Services*, p. 213. Lambert commented that, in the interviews she conducted with twelve Plunket nurses, 'The reduction of home visits was of such concern to the nurses that they returned to it again and again': Lambert, p. 111.

142 *Child Health and Child Health Services*, p. 214.

143 *New Zealand Doctor*, 7 August 1996, p. 4.
144 *Plunket in Touch*, March 1997, p. 12.
145 Sandra Coney, 'Plunket's Universal Service Threatened by Health Reforms', *Women's Health Watch Newsletter*, 41, July 1997, Women's Health Action Trust.
146 *NZH*, 5 February 1999.
147 *Evening Post*, 18 April 2001.

Chapter 10: A Women's Society?

1   *NZH*, 10 May 2000.
2   Erik Olssen, 'Breeding for Empire', *NZ Listener*, 12 May 1979, p. 19.
3   Frieda Massey, cited in *NZWW*, 6 October 1986, p. 17
4   *Taupo Times*, 15 May 2002; *Nelson Mail*, 20 June 2002.
5   Myra Graham, interview, Plunket Society Oral History Project, 1992.
6   Max, *Children: Endangered Species?*, p. 26.
7   *Ibid.*, p. 30.
8   *Ibid.*, p. 52.
9   *NZH*, 19 June 1997.
10 It was recorded in the minutes of the Steering Committee, 12 February 1974, in relation to the proposed Co-ordinating Committees: 'The Society felt that the Medical Officer of Health could be a threat to its autonomy in making its own policy', AAFB 786 Box 2 Steering Committee Plunket minute book 1970–83, ANZ; 'Guidelines for Regional Co-ordinating Committees of Department of Health and Plunket Society', 15 July 1980, ABQU 632 Acc W4415/104 35-30-4 53144, ANZ.
11 M. B. Johnstone, 'Future Direction of Plunket Society: Paper Presented to New Zealand Executive, 27 May 1986', p. 6, A.24(b), ABA. At 46, she was also said to be the society's youngest president to date: *Plunket Newsletter*, November 1984, 14.
12 Management Consortium, 'Report. Royal Plunket Society Management Reviews, 19 February 1992', pp. 18–19, ABA.
13 David Geddis, interview, Plunket Oral History Project, 1992.
14 Jenny Chamberlain, 'Babes in Arms: Plunket's Fight for Life', *North & South*, November 1992, pp. 105, 107.
15 Deputation to J. T. Watts, 17 April 1951, p.1, H1 127 26040, ANZ.
16 Health Department memo, 13 July 1951, H1 127 26040, ANZ.
17 *Plunket News*, August 1993.
18 Favell, 'Plunket Nursing in a Social, Political and Historical Context', pp. 3–4.
19 This must be seen in the context of changes in nursing in general, for example with independent nurse practices being set up in the 1980s: *NZWW*, 2 March 1987, p. 11.
20 Chamberlain, *North & South*, p. 110; Favell, p. 34.
21 Nicola Taylor, 'Regional Meeting Series – May 1991', ABA.
22 Dow, *Safeguarding the Public Health*, p. 180.
23 Lambert, Max (ed.), *Who's Who in New Zealand*, 12th edn, Auckland, Reed, 1991, p. 575.
24 'Russell Brown's Hardnews', 20 August 1999, NZNews.net.nz/hardnews/1999/19990820.html
25 Lambert, *Who's Who in New Zealand*, p. 182.
26 *Ibid.*, p. 640.
27 See *Plunket News*, February 1994, p. 1.
28 Council minutes, 28 April 1937, PSA.
29 Auckland Provincial Conference, 6 August 1957, ABA.
30 Horton, *Memoirs of a Colonial Goose*, pp. 77–8.
31 Nd, Press cuttings, 1964, ABA.
32 Council minutes, 30–31 October 1973, PSA; Plunket Society, *Annual report, 1973–74*, Dunedin, 1974, p. 3. See also obituary, *Sunday Star-Times*, 22 December 1996.

33 *Plunket Newsletter*, 13, 13 February 1980.
34 Bill Hall, Interview, Plunket Society Oral History Project, 1992.
35 Parry, *Fence at the Top*, p. 147; interview with Anne Cressey, Plunket Society Oral History Project, 1992.
36 Interviews with Bill Hall and David Geddis, Plunket Society Oral History Project, 1992.
37 *Plunket News*, April–May 1995.
38 Report of Auckland Provincial Conference, 1970, ABA.
39 See Chapter 8.
40 Auckland branch, *Sixty-third annual report 1970–71*, p. 7.
41 Begg, 'Te Wero', pp. 9–10. The Newcastle study had been initiated by Professor Sir James Spence in 1947 and continued for twenty years under the guidance of Drs F. J. W. Miller and S. D. M. Court.
42 Plunket Society, *Report of the Forty-third General Conference 1976*, p. 5.
43 *Plunket Newsletter*, August 1977. My emphasis.
44 Auckland branch, *Sixty-fourth annual report 1971–72*, p. 9.
45 *Plunket News*, 9, 3, 1972, p. 23; Soren Hansen and Jesper Jensen, *The Little Red Schoolbook*, translated from Danish by Bent Thornberry, Wellington, A. Taylor, 1972. The first edition in London, 1969, had been declared 'obscene' by a British magistrate under its Obscene Publications Act.
46 Council minutes, 18–19 April 1972, PSA.
47 *Auckland Star*, 30 July 1963.
48 Council minutes, 30–31 October 1973, PSA.
49 *Ibid.*, 2–3 April 1974.
50 Women's Rights Committee, Report June 1975 (Chair N. V. Douglas), *AJHR*, I.13, 1975, p. 66.
51 Plunket Society, *Report of the Forty-second General Conference 1974*, p. 14.
52 Kedgley, *Mum's the Word*, p. 268.
53 Foreword, Auckland branch, *Sixty-sixth annual report 1973–74*, p. 6.
54 Foreword, Auckland branch, *Sixty-seventh annual report 1974–75*, p. 6.
55 *Royal Commission of Inquiry, Contraception, Sterilisation and Abortion, Report*, Wellington, Government Printer, 1977, pp. 76–9.
56 Helen Smyth, *Rocking the Cradle: Contraception, Sex and Politics in New Zealand*, Wellington, Steele Roberts, 2000, p. 83.
57 Council minutes, 4–7 November 1959, PSA.
58 Smyth, *Rocking the Cradle*, p. 83.
59 Council minutes, 27–28 April 1971, PSA.
60 *Ibid.*, 21–22 April 1969.
61 Executive minutes, 25 August, 13 December 1972, PSA.
62 *NZH*, 2 November 1972.
63 *AJHR*, 1971, H-31, p. 26.
64 Executive minutes, 20 September, 18 October 1972, PSA.
65 Hercock, *Alice*, p. 166.
66 Plunket Society, *Report of the Forty-second General Conference 1974*, p. 28.
67 *Ibid.*, pp. 28–9.
68 Executive minutes, 22–3 May 1980, PSA. My emphasis.
69 *NZH*, 1 April 1966.
70 Press cutting, 2 March 1967, ABA.
71 *North Shore Times Advertiser*, 24 October 1978.
72 *Christchurch Star*, 6 November 1970; *NZH*, 6 November 1970.
73 J. Steincamp, 'The Undercover Victory', *Broadsheet*, September 1978, pp. 15–16.
74 Plunket Society, *Report of the Forty-second General Conference 1974*, p. 59; *ODT*, 11 October 1974.
75 Plunket Society, *Report of the Forty-third General Conference 1976*, pp. 58–9.
76 Trish Gribben, 'Plunket's Plight', *NZ Listener*, 1 October 1977, p. 14.

77 Robyn McKinlay, 'Where would we be without them? Motherhood and Self-definition in New Zealand', PhD thesis, Victoria University of Wellington, 1983, pp. 257–8.

78 Sandra Coney, 'Truby King's Lasting Legacy', *Dominion*, 4 February 1988.

79 Coney, 'Women's Health Watch'.

80 *New Zealand Doctor*, 4 September 1996, p. 7.

81 On the benefits for modern women to be involved in voluntary associations, see also Reiger, *Our Bodies, Our Babies*, pp.157–8.

82 *Plunket At Work*, April 1997.

83 *Dargaville News*, 7 June 2001.

84 Gloria Longley, interview, Plunket Society Oral History Project, 1992.

85 *East and Bays Courier*, 29 June 2001, p. 15.

86 *Timaru Herald*, 16 April 2001.

87 *Dominion,* 17 May 2001.

88 Hassall, 'The Plunket Society as an Advocate for Children and Families', paper delivered to 51st National Conference of the Royal NZ Plunket Society, 1993.

89 Neil Begg's ' citizen participation' concept was recently adopted in a Maori context. The success of Tipu Ora, for Maori caregivers and their children up to the age of five in the Waiariki region, has been attributed to its practice being based on kaupapa Maori framework, 'where spirituality, knowledge of tikanga, understanding of community and the acknowledgement of commonality are all important': Alison Blaiklock, 'Children's Health in the Next Five Years: Commentary to the Seminar on Children's Policy, 19–20 July 2000', www.msp.govt.nz/agendaforchildren/docs.

90 Reiger, *Our Bodies, Our Babies*, p. 288.

91 Hassall, 'The Plunket Society as an Advocate', p. 8.

Bibliography

Archives and manuscripts

Plunket Society archives

The bulk of the Plunket Society archives before the mid-1980s are deposited in the Hocken Library at the University of Otago. This collection consists primarily of records generated by the society's headquarters. The library also holds the Wellington branch records. Most of the Christchurch branch records were on loan to the Hocken Library from 1978 until 1998, when they were transferred to the Canterbury Museum. The latter's collection now comprises the surviving records of Christchurch, Canterbury and West Coast branches and sub-branches from 1907 to 1992. The Auckland records were retained by branch officials until 2003, when they were deposited in the University of Auckland Manuscripts Department.

Records consulted included minutes of the Central (later Dominion) Council 1917–80; executive minutes 1933–84; annual and branch reports 1907–98; reports of the general conferences 1914–93; general correspondence, memoranda, circulars and deputations 1903–70; secretary's correspondence with branches and with the Department of Health; Auckland branch minutes 1909–22, 1953–77; reports of Auckland provincial conferences 1927–75; Wellington branch minutes 1908–57; Auckland branch Karitane Nurses' Club minutes and annual reports 1934–61; admission register of the Karitane Hospital, Wellington 1971–77; papers of Frederic Truby King; papers and correspondence of Helen Deem; correspondence of the Director of Nursing and the Nursing Adviser; notes relating to Lady King scholars and the Karitane Products Society; *Plunket Magazine* 1915; *Plunket Newsview* 1948; *Plunket News* 1945–76, *Plunket Newsletter* 1977–92; *Plunket Child Safety Newsletter* 1993–4; *Plunket in Touch* 1996–7; *Plunket Care Delivery News* 1997; *Plunket at Work* 1997; newspaper clippings and scrapbooks. As the Hocken Library's collection was recatalogued subsequent to my first visit in 1993, some of the file reference numbers may differ from current codes.

Copies of the following unpublished reports are held by the Auckland branch:

Brennan, M. C., 'The Public Image of the Plunket Society', Market Research Centre, Massey University, January 1986.

Emery, John, Sheffield Health Authority, Confidential Report to David Geddis on Plunket Society, 11 June 1986.

Geddis, D. C., Cressey, P. K., McMillan, J. H., Confidential Reports on Plunket Karitane Hospitals, 11 November 1977.

Hunt, Joan, 'Report on Visit to the Office of Child, Adolescent and Family Health Services, Adelaide, South Australia', 19 October 1990.

Johnstone, Meriel, 'Future Direction of the Plunket Society: Paper presented to New Zealand Executive', 27 May 1986.

Management Consortium, 'Report. Royal NZ Plunket Society Management Review', January 1992.

Mark-Woods, G. M., 'Auckland Region – Submission to Child Health Taskforce', 13 June 1990.

Plunket Society Board Newsbrief: Information for Plunket Volunteers and Staff, 1993–7.

Strategic Planning Sub-committee, Plunket Society, 'Discussion Paper on Service Options', 24 February 1988.

Taylor, Nicola, 'Regional Meeting Series May 1991: Review of the Minutes of the Meetings', July 1991.

Tekiela, Izabela, 'Stakeholder Research on The Royal New Zealand Plunket Society', Auckland University 71.410, Futures Research, unpublished paper, 1990.

New Zealand Health Department files, Archives New Zealand, Wellington

Series H1-127, relating to the Plunket Society and local branches 1913–83; minute books of the Plunket and Health Department Steering Committee 1970–83; Child Health Council minute book 1960–73.

Plunket Society Oral History Project, 1992 (OHColl 0314), Alexander Turnbull Library, Wellington

This collection includes: interviews by Jim Sullivan with Eleanor Alden, Joyce Andrews, Neil Begg, Anne Cressey, Margaret Francis, David Geddis, Myra Graham, Bill Hall, Val Jones, Gloria Longley, Ruby Pierson, Jessie Preston, Pauline Rout, Marion Shepherd, Joyce Thorpe, Mary White; interviews by Sarah Dalton with Mary Bayne, Irene Cornwell, Joan Meyer, and Molly McGovern.

Library Archives, Auckland Museum

Evidence to the 1937 Committee of Inquiry into Maternity Services, Vol.1–2, MS78.

Wellcome Library Archives and Manuscript Section, Wellcome Institute for the History of Medicine, London

Records of the Health Visitors' Association, the National Birthday Trust Fund, and the personal papers of Eric Pritchard, John Bowlby, Grantly Dick Read and Hugh Jolly.

Highgate Literary and Scientific Institution, London

Records of the Mothercraft Training Society, London, including annual reports 1918–50; *Mothercraft Training Society Magazine* 1925–52; *League of Mothercraft Nurses Newsletter* 1952–74.

Tavistock Clinic, London

Annual reports 1929–53, and other miscellaneous papers.

Hassall, Ian, private papers

'The Plunket Society as an Advocate for Children and Families', paper presented by Dr I. B. Hassall, Commissioner for Children, at 51st National Conference of the Royal NZ Plunket Society, Wellington, 22 April 1993.

Hassall, I. to M. Bassett, Proposal for Evaluation of Community Health Care Plunket/ Public Health, South Auckland Health District, 8 August 1986.

'A Chronology of the Campaign in New Zealand to Prevent Toddler Pool Drownings', nd.

Some selected Papers to Contribute to a History of the Plunket Society, 19 July 2002.

Miscellaneous
Watt, M. H., 'The Rest of the Day to Myself', unpublished autobiography, deposited in Health Department.

Powell, Joyce, 'Keep Pumping Those Brakes Nurse', manuscript based on oral history, c.1997, in possession of author.

Interview with Joyce Powell, 24 & 31 July 2000.

Brown, Vera Scantlebury, Diaries, University of Melbourne Archives.

Official publications
Department of Health, Annual Reports, H-31, *Appendices to the Journals of the House of Representatives (AJHR)*, 1907–75.

New Zealand Parliamentary Debates (NZPD), 1901–99.

New Zealand Official Yearbook, 1902–96.

Official reports
Briggs, Janette and Allan, Bridget, *Maternal and Infant Care in Wellington 1978: A Health Care Consumer Study in Replication*, Department of Health Special Report Series 64, Wellington, Government Printer, 1983.

Committee on Child Health, *Child Health and Child Health Services in New Zealand*, Board of Health Report Series 31, Wellington, Government Printer, 1982.

de Boer, Gail, Juanita Saxby, Michael Soljak, *Child Health Profile 1989*, Health Services Research and Development Unit, National Health Statistics Centre, Wellington, Department of Health, 1990.

Department of Health, *Recording Child Health and Development: A Handbook for Professionals using the 'Health and Development Record' Book*, Wellington, Department of Health, 1984.

Douglas, N. V. (Chairman), Report of Women's Rights Committee, 1975, *AJHR*, I.13, 1975.

Final Report of the National Expenditure Commission, *AJHR*, B-4A, 1932.

Fraser, J., *Post-neonatal Mortality: Results of a National Survey 1978–79*, Special Report Series 61, Wellington, Government Printer, 1982.

Hassall, I. B., *Under Five Year Old Domestic Swimming Pool Drownings since the 1987 Fencing of Swimming Pools Act: A Briefing Paper from the Office of the Commissioner for Children*, Wellington, The Office, 1991.

Hunn, J. K., *Report on the Department of Maori Affairs*, Wellington, Government Printer, 1960.

Main, H. and Scantlebury, V., 'Report to the Minister of Public Health on the Welfare of Women and Children', Department of Public Health, Victoria, 1926, *Victorian Parliamentary Papers*, 9, 2, 1926.

Mayman, Neville, Report on the Inquiry into the Welfare of Mothers and Children in New Zealand, *New South Wales Parliamentary Papers*, 5, 1918, pp. 291–310.

Ministry of Health (England and Wales), *Report of Advisory Committee on Mother and Young Children on 'The Breast Feeding of Infants'*, London, HMSO, 1944.

New Zealand Parliament, Local Bills Committee, *Report on Fencing Private Swimming Pools*, Wellington, Government Printer, 1983.

Report of the Consultative Committee on Infant and Pre-school Health Services, Wellington, Government Printer, 1960.

Report of the Royal Commission of Inquiry, Contraception, Sterilisation and Abortion, Wellington, Government Printer, 1977.

Report of the Special Committee on Moral Delinquency in Children and Adolescents, *AJHR*, 1954, H-47.

Rose, R. J., *Infant and Foetal Loss in New Zealand*, Department of Health Special Report Series 17, Wellington, Government Printer, 1964.

Salmond, G. C., *Maternal and Infant Care in Wellington A Health Care Consumer Study*, Department of Health Special Report Series 45, Wellington, Government Printer, 1975.

Shannon, F. T., *Research into Post-neonatal Mortality in New Zealand: A Report to the Medical Research Council*, Wellington, Medical Research Council, 1987.

Skegg, David (Chairman), *Our Health – Our Future: The State of Public Health in New Zealand*, Public Health Commission, Wellington, Government Printer, 1994.

Watt, M. H., *Report of the Director-General of Health Reviewing Public-Health Administration in North America, the United Kingdom, and Scandinavia, with Consequent Proposals for the Development of the New Zealand System*, Wellington, Government Printer, 1940.

Books and articles

Abel, Sally, Frances Campbell, David Jansen, Ripipeti Haretuku, David Tipene-Leach, *Maori Infant Care Practices: A Qualitative Study of the Practices of Auckland Maori Caregivers of Under 12 Month Old Infants*, Auckland, The Infant Care Practices Study Team, Department of Maori and Pacific Health, University of Auckland, 1999.

Abel, Sally, Michele Lennan, Julie Park, David Tipene-Leach, Sitaleki Finau, Carol Everard, *Infant Care Practices: A Qualitative Study of the Practices of Auckland Maori, Tongan, Samoan, Cook Islands, Niuean, Pakeha Caregivers of Under 12 Month Old Infants*, Auckland, The Infant Care Practices Study Team, Department of Maori and Pacific Health, University of Auckland, 1999.

Abbott, Max (ed.), *Child Abuse Prevention in New Zealand: The Edited Proceedings of the National Symposium on Child Abuse Prevention, Palmerston North, 9–11 November 1982*, Auckland, Mental Health Foundation of New Zealand, 1983.

Adshead, Rona (ed.), *Some of My Yesterdays: The Autobiography of Marion Shepherd ('Maisie')*, Invercargill, Craig Printing, 1989.

Aldrich, A. and M., *Babies are Human Beings*, New York, Macmillan, 1938, republished in Britain as *Understanding Your Baby*, London, Black, 1939.

Allen, Ann Taylor, *Feminism and Motherhood in Germany, 1880–1914*, New Brunswick, New Jersey, Rutgers University Press, 1991.

Apple, Rima M., '"To be Used Only Under the Direction of a Physician"': Commercial Infant Feeding and Medical Practice, 1870–1940,' *Bulletin of the History of Medicine*, 54, 3, 1980, pp. 402–17.

Apple, Rima M., *Mothers and Medicine: A Social History of Infant Feeding*, Madison, University of Wisconsin Press, 1987.

Apple, Rima M., 'The Medicalization of Infant Feeding in the United States and New Zealand: Two Countries, One Experience', *Journal of Human Lactation*, 10, 1, 1994, pp. 23–9.

Apple, Rima M., 'A Century of Infant Feeding in the United States and New Zealand', in S. Atkins, K. Kirkby, P. Thomson and J. Pearn (eds), *"Outpost Medicine": Australasian Studies on the History of Medicine*, Tasmania, Australian Society of the History of Medicine, 1994, pp.303–10.

Apple, Rima M., 'Constructing Mothers: Scientific Motherhood in the Nineteenth and Twentieth Centuries', *Social History of Medicine*, 8, 2, 1995, pp. 161–78.

Arnup, Katherine, *Education for Motherhood: Advice for Mothers in Twentieth-century Canada*, Toronto, University of Toronto Press, 1994.

Auckland Plunket Nurses, *From the Pen of F. Truby King; His Life and Work by Rita R. Snowden, Infant Loss in New Zealand by Helen Deem*, Auckland, Whitcombe & Tombs, c.1940.

Baker, Paul, *King and Country Call: New Zealanders, Conscription and the Great War*, Auckland, Auckland University Press, 1988.

Barrett, James W., 'Waste of Infant Life', *Kai Tiaki*, 7, 3, 1914.

Barrington, J. M. and T. H. Beaglehole, *Maori Schools in a Changing Society: An Historical Review*, Wellington, New Zealand Council for Educational Research, 1974.

Bassett, Michael, *The Third Labour Government: A Personal History*, Palmerston North, Dunmore Press, 1976.

Bassett, Michael, *Tomorrow Comes the Song: A Life of Peter Fraser*, Auckland, Penguin, 2000.

Beaglehole, Ernest, *Mental Health in New Zealand*, Wellington, New Zealand University Press, 1950.

Begg, N. C., 'Immunisation Procedures in Infancy', *NZMJ*, 57, 1958, pp. 372–3.

Begg, Neil, *The Plunket Society of New Zealand*, Dunedin, Plunket Society, 1968.

Begg, Neil, *The New Zealand Child and His Family*, Christchurch, Whitcombe & Tombs, 1970.

Begg, Neil, *The Child and His Family*, Christchurch, Whitcoulls, 1972.

Begg, N. C., 'Yesterday and Tomorrow in Child Health', *NZMJ*, 75, 1972, pp. 263–6.

Begg, N. C., 'Correspondence. Medical Services', *NZMJ*, 80, 1974, pp. 566–7.

Begg, N. C., 'A Partnership Child Care in a New Zealand Suburb', *Australian Paediatric Journal*, Supplement 3, 1975, pp. 42–6.

Begg, N. C., 'Child Health and Sickness', *NZMJ*, 81, 1975, pp. 100–5.

Begg, Neil, *The Intervening Years: A New Zealand Account of the Period between the 1910 Visit of Halley's Comet and its Reappearance in 1986*, Dunedin, John McIndoe, 1992.

Bergman, A. B., J. B. Beckwith, C. G. Ray (eds), *The Sudden Infant Death Syndrome. Proceedings of the Second International Conference on Causes of Sudden Death in Infants, Seattle, 1969*, Seattle, University of Washington Press, 1970.

Bergman, Abraham B., *The 'Discovery' of Sudden Infant Death Syndrome: Lessons in the Practice of Political Medicine*, New York, Praeger, 1986.

Berridge, Virginia, *Health and Society in Britain since 1939*, New York, Cambridge University Press, 1999.

Berridge, Virginia, 'History in Public Health: A New Development for History', *Hygiea Internationalis*, 1, 1, 1999, pp. 23–36.

Bevan-Brown, Maurice, *The Sources of Love and Fear, with Contributions by Members of the Christchurch Psychological Society*, Wellington, Reed, 1950.

Bowlby, John, *Maternal Care and Mental Health*, Geneva, WHO Technical Monograph Series No. 2, 1951.

Bowlby, John, *Child Care and the Growth of Love*, London, Penguin Books, 1953.

Boyd, Mary, 'New Zealand and the Other Pacific Islands', in Keith Sinclair (ed.), *The Oxford Illustrated History of New Zealand*, Auckland, Oxford University Press, 1990, pp. 295–322.

Bryder, Linda, 'Perceptions of Plunket: Time to Review Historians' Interpretations?', in L. Bryder and D. A. Dow (eds), *New Countries and Old Medicine: Proceedings of an International Conference on the History of Medicine*, Pyramid Press, Auckland, 1995, pp. 97–103.

Bryder, Linda, *Not Just Weighing Babies: Plunket in Auckland 1908–1998*, Auckland, Pyramid Press, 1998.

Bryder, Linda, 'New Zealand's Infant Welfare Services and Maori, 1907–60', *Health and History*, 3, 1, 2001, pp. 65–86.

Buchler, Marie Stringer, 'The Premature Baby', *Kai Tiaki*, 31, 2, 1938, pp. 80–4.

Bush, G. W. A., *Decently and in Order: The Centennial History of Auckland City Council*, Auckland, Collins, 1971.

Callan, Louise, 'Plunket – Who Holds the Baby?', *Thursday*, 12 June 1975, pp. 12–14.

Cameron, Hector Charles, *The British Paediatric Association, 1928–1952*, London, The Association, 1955.

Chamberlain, Jenny, 'Babes in Arms', *North & South*, November 1992, pp. 104–11.

Chick, Norma and Rodgers, Jan (eds), *Looking Back, Moving Forward: Essays in the History of New Zealand Nursing and Midwifery*, Palmerston North, Massey University, 1997.

Clements, F. W., *Infant Nutrition: Its Physiological Basis*, Bristol, John Wright; London, Simpkin Marshall, 1949.

Clinton, Michael, *Child Health Services in South Auckland Project: Report to the Hon Mr David Caygill, Minister of Health. June 1988*, Wellington, Victoria University of Wellington, 1988.

Coggan, Caroline, Pam Patterson, Rhonda Hooper, *Evaluation of Kidsafe Week 1999*, Auckland, Injury Prevention Research Centre, Department of Community Health, University of Auckland, 1999.

Coney, Sandra, *Every Girl. A Social History of Women and the YWCA in Auckland 1885–1985*, Auckland, Auckland YWCA, 1986.

Coney, Sandra, 'Health Organisations', in Anne Else (ed.), *Women Together: A History of Women's Organisations in New Zealand: Nga Ropu Wahine o Te Motu*, Wellington, Historical Branch, Department of Internal Affairs and Daphne Brasell Associates Press, 1993, pp. 241–53.

Coney, Sandra, *Standing in the Sunshine: A History of New Zealand Women Since They Won the Vote*, Auckland, Penguin, 1993.

Coney, Sandra (ed.), 'Plunket's Universal Service Threatened by Health Reforms', *Women's Health Watch Newsletter*, 41, July 1997, www.womens-health.org.nz/whwjul97.htm#plunket.

Cooter, Roger and Bill Luckin (eds), *Accidents in History*, Amsterdam, Rodopi, 1997.

Corkill, T. F., *Lectures on Midwifery and Infant Care: A New Zealand Course* (6 editions from 1932 to 1958), Auckland, Coulls, Somerville, Wilkie, 1932; Wellington, Banks, 1940; Christchurch, Whitcombe & Tombs, 1946, 1951, 1954.

Corkill, T. F., 'The Montgomerie Spencer Memorial Lecture: The Quest Continues – Earlier Steps in Infant Life Saving', *NZMJ*, 50, 1951, pp. 1–13.

Cronin, E. J., 'Lactic Acid Milk in the Feeding of Infants', *NZMJ*, 32, 1933, pp. 149–59.

Dalley, Bronwyn, *Family Matters: Child Welfare in Twentieth-century New Zealand*, Auckland, Auckland University Press, 1998.

Dally, Ann, *Inventing Motherhood: The Consequences of an Ideal*, London, Burnett Books, 1982.

Davies, Celia, 'The Health Visitor as Mother's Friend: A Woman's Place in Public Health, 1900–14', *Social History of Medicine*, 1, 1, 1988, pp.39–59.

Davin, Anna, 'Imperialism and Motherhood', *History Workshop Journal*, 5, 1978, pp. 9–65.

de Courcy, Noeline, *Nora Philomena Fitzgibbon 1889–1979: A Biography of an Outstanding New Zealand Woman*, Dunedin, N. de Courcy, 1990.

Deacon, Desley, 'Taylorism in the Home: The Medical Profession, the Infant Welfare Movement and the Deskilling of Women', *Australian and New Zealand Journal of Sociology*, 21, 2, 1985, pp. 161–73.

'Death of Truby King', *Kai Tiaki*, 31, 2, 1938, pp. 52–3.

Deem, Helen, 'Observations on the Milk of New Zealand Women', *Archives of Disease in Childhood*, 6, 31, 1931, pp. 53–70.

Deem, Helen, 'Infant Loss in New Zealand', *NZMJ*, 46, 1947, pp. 475–85.

Deem, Helen, 'The Management of the New-Born', *NZMJ*, 48, 1949, pp. 45–9.

Deem, Helen E. and Nora P. Fitzgibbon, *Modern Mothercraft: A Guide to Parents. Official Handbook of the Royal New Zealand Society for the Health of Women and Children*, Dunedin, Plunket Society, 1945, 2nd revised edn, 1953.

Deem, Helen and Murray McGeorge, 'Breast Feeding', *NZMJ*, 57, 1958, pp. 539–56.

Dick Read, Grantly, *Antenatal Illustrated: The Natural Approach to Happy Motherhood*, London, W. Heinemann, 1955.

Digby, Anne and John Stewart (eds), *Gender, Health and Welfare*, London, Routledge, 1996.

Dobbie, Mary, *The Trouble with Women: The Story of Parents' Centre New Zealand*, Queen Charlotte Sound, Whatamongo Bay, Cape Catley, 1990.

Donley, J., *Save the Midwife*, Auckland, New Women's Press, 1986.

Dow, Derek A., *Annotated Bibliography for the History of Medicine & Health in New Zealand*, Dunedin, Hocken Library, University of Otago, 1994.

Dow, Derek A. *Safeguarding the Public Health: A History of the New Zealand Department of Health*, Wellington, Victoria University Press, 1995.

Dow, Derek A., *Maori Health and Government Policy 1840–1940*, Wellington, Victoria University Press in association with the Historical Branch, Department of Internal Affairs, 1999.

Dow, Derek A., O. Mansoor, 'New Zealand Immunisation Schedule History', *NZMJ*, 109, 1996, pp. 209–12.

Duffy, John, 'The American Medical Profession and Public Health: From Support to Ambivalence', *Bulletin of the History of Medicine*, 53, 1, 1979, pp. 1–22.

Dwork, Deborah, *War is Good for Babies and Other Young Children: A History of the Infant and Child Welfare Movement in England 1898–1918*, London, Tavistock, 1987.

Ehrenreich, Barbara and Deirdre English, *For Her Own Good: 150 Years of the Experts' Advice to Women*, New York, Anchor Press/Doubleday, 1978.

Fenton, Mary, 'What Ever Happened to the Plunket Nurse?', *New Zealand Doctor*, 7 August 1996, p. 4.

Ferguson, D. M., A. L. Beautrais, F. T. Shannon, 'Maternal Satisfaction with Primary Health Care', *NZMJ*, 94, 1981, pp. 291–4.

Ferguson D. M., L. J. Horwood, F. T. Shannon, 'Child Health: Attitudes of Mothers of Five-year-old Children to Compulsory Child Health Provisions', *NZMJ*, 96, 1983, pp.338–40.

Ferguson, Gael, *Building the New Zealand Dream*, Palmerston North, Dunmore Press, 1994.

Fildes, Valerie, Lara Marks and Hilary Marland (eds), *Women and Children First: International Maternal and Infant Welfare, 1870–1945*, London & New York, Routledge, 1992.

Fitzgerald, Elspeth, 'Some Practical Experiences in Modern Infant Feeding', *NZMJ*, 32, 1933, pp. 21–33.

Fitzgerald, Elspeth, 'Modern Infant Feeding', *NZMJ*, 34, 1935, pp.388–95.

Follick, Adele, 'Frieda Massey: Far from a Battleaxe!' *New Zealand Women's Weekly* (*NZWW*), 6 October 1986, p. 17.

Freud, Sigmund, *The Standard Edition of the Complete Psychological Works of Sigmund Freud, VII: Three Essays on the Theory of Sexuality (1901–05)*, transl. J. Strachey, London, Hogarth Press, Institute of Psycho-analysis, 1953.

Gafford, Janet, Tracy J. Riddler, Trinie Moore, Angela Baldwin, *Client Evaluation. Plunket Karitane Family Centres. Policy Unit Occasional Paper 22*, Wellington, Plunket Society, 1998.

Gardiner, Cedric E., 'Maori Infant Mortality', *NZMJ*, 58, 1959, pp. 321–40.

Geddis, D. C., 'Children in Cars: Results of an Observational Study in New Zealand', *NZMJ*, 90, 1979, pp. 468–71.

Geddis, D.C., 'Day Care, Working Mothers and the Pre-school Child', *NZMJ*, 92, 1980, pp. 201–4.

Geddis, D. C., 'Child Health: The Exposure of Pre-school Children to Water Hazards and the Incidence of Potential Drowning Accidents', *NZMJ*, 97, 1984, pp. 223–6.

Geddis, D. C., 'Leading Article: New Developments Concerning Child Abuse', *NZMJ*, 97, 1984, p. 404.

Geddis, D. C., 'Leading Article: The Diagnosis of Sexual Abuse of Children', *NZMJ*, 102, 1989, pp. 99–100.

Geddis, D. C. and I. C. Appleton, 'Use of Restraint Systems by Preschool Children in Cars', *Archives of Disease in Childhood*, 57, 1982, pp. 540–60.

Geddis, D. C. and P. A. Silva, 'The Plunket Society: A Consumer Survey', *NZMJ*, 90, 1979, pp. 507–9.

Gesell, A. and H. Thomson, *The Psychology of Early Growth*, New York, Macmillan, 1938.

Giddings, Lynne, 'Plunket Society', in Anne Else (ed.), *Women Together*, pp. 257–61.

Gluckman, P. D. (ed.), *Workshop on Post-Neonatal Mortality and Cot Death, Auckland, 3–7 September 1984*, Auckland, Joint Committee on Child Health Research, 1985.

Gordon, Doris, *Backblocks Baby-Doctor: An Autobiography*, London, Faber & Faber, 1955.

Gordon, Linda, 'Putting Children First: Women, Maternalism and Welfare in the Early

Twentieth Century', in Linda Kerber, Alice Kessler-Harris and Kathryn Kish Sklar (eds), *US History as Women's History: New Feminist Essays*, Chapel Hill & London, University of North Carolina Press, 1995, pp. 238–69.

Gorham, Deborah and Florence Kellner Andrews, 'La Leche League: A Feminist Perspective', in Katherine Arnup, Andree Levesque, Ruth Roach Pierson (eds), *Delivering Motherhood: Maternal Ideologies and Practices in the 19th and 20th Centuries*, London & New York, Routledge, 1990, pp. 238–69.

Gribben, Trish, 'Plunket's Plight', *New Zealand Listener*, 1 October 1977, pp.14–16.

Gribben, Trish with David Geddis and Roy Muir, *Pyjamas Don't Matter, or, What Your Baby Really Needs*, Auckland, Heinemann, 1979.

Griffiths D. L. and F. J. Moynihan, 'Multiple Epiphysical Injuries in Babies ("Battered Baby Syndrome")', *British Medical Journal*, 1963, pp. 1558–61.

Gustafson, Barry, *The First 50 Years. A History of the New Zealand National Party*, Auckland, Reed Methuen, 1986.

Halpern, Sydney, *American Pediatrics: The Social Dynamics of Professionalism, 1880–1980*, Berkeley, University of California Press, 1988.

Hamer, David, *The Liberals: The Years of Power, 1891–1912*, Auckland, Auckland University Press, 1988.

Hansen, Soren and Jesper Jensen, *The Little Red Schoolbook*, translated from Danish by Bent Thornberry, Wellington, A. Taylor, 1972.

Hardy, Morag, 'Malnutrition in Young Children at Auckland', *NZMJ*, 75, 1972, pp. 291–6.

Hardyment, Christina, *Dream Babies: Three Centuries of Good Advice on Child Care*, New York, Harper & Row, 1983.

Hart, J. T., 'The Inverse Care Law', *Lancet*, i, 1971, pp. 405–12.

Hassall, I. B. 'Drownings in Private Swimming Pools', *NZMJ*, 95, 1982, pp. 129–30.

Hassall, I. B., 'Leading Article: Sudden Infant Death Syndrome – A Serious New Zealand Health Problem', *NZMJ*, 99, 1986, pp. 233–4.

Hassall, I. B., 'Swimming Pool Fencing at Last', *NZMJ*, 100, 1987, p. 637.

Hassall, I. B., 'The Cot Death Enigma', *Medical Journal of Australia*, 147, 1987, pp. 214–16.

Hassall, I. B., 'Thirty Six Consecutive Under 5 Year Old Domestic Swimming Pool Drownings', *Australian Paediatric Journal*, 25, 1989, pp. 143–46.

Hassall I. B. and D.C. Geddis, 'The Plunket Nurse', *NZMJ*, 94, 1981, pp. 249–30.

Heardman, Helen, *A Way to Natural Childbirth: A Manual for Physiotherapists and Parents-to-be*, Edinburgh, E. & S. Livingstone, 1948 (reprint 1949, 1950, 1951, 1952, 1954, 1956, 1958, 1961, rev. 1964).

Helfer, R. E. and C. H. Kempe (eds), *The Battered Child*, Chicago, University of Chicago Press, 1968.

Helfer, R. E. and C. H. Kempe (eds), *Helping the Battered Child and His Family*, Philadelphia, Lippincot, 1972.

Helly, Dorothy O., Susan M. Reverby (eds), *Gendered Domains: Rethinking Public and Private in Women's History: Essays from the Seventh Berkshire Conference on the History of Women*, Ithaca, Cornell University Press, 1992.

Hendrick, Harry, *Child Welfare: England 1872–1989*, London, Routledge, 1994.

Hendrick, Harry, *Children, Childhood and English Society, 1880–1990*, New York, Cambridge University Press, 1997.

Hercock, Fay, 'Professional Politics and Family Planning Clinics', in L. Bryder (ed.),

A Healthy Country: Essays on the Social History of Medicine in New Zealand, Wellington, Bridget Williams, 1991, pp. 181–97.

Hercock, Fay, *Alice: The Making of a Woman Doctor 1914–1974*, Auckland, Auckland University Press, 1999.

Hercus, Charles and Gordon Bell, *The Otago Medical School under the First Three Deans*, Edinburgh, Livingstone, 1964.

Hickling, S., 'Immunisation against Diphtheria, Tetanus and Whooping Cough in Childhood', *NZMJ*, 65, 1966, pp. 357–62.

Hickling, S., 'Immunisation in Childhood', letter to editor, *NZMJ*, 69, 1969, pp. 108–9.

Holt, L. Emmett, *The Diseases of Infancy and Childhood: For the Use of Students and Practitioners of Medicine*, New York, Appleton, 2nd rev. edn, 1902.

Holt, L. Emmett, *The Care and Feeding of Children: A Catechism for the Use of Mothers and Children's Nurses*, New York, Appleton, (1st edn c.1894), 8th rev. edn 1915.

Hood, Lynley, 'Karitane: Southland's Pride', *NZ Listener*, 5 April 1980, pp. 43–4.

Hood, Lynley, *A City Possessed: The Christchurch Civic Crèche case: Child Abuse, Gender Politics and the Law*, Dunedin, Longacre Press, 2001.

Hood, Lynley J., Julia A. Faed, P. A. Silva, Patricia M. Buckfield, 'Breast Feeding and Some Reasons for Electing to Wean the Infant: A Report from the Dunedin Multi-disciplinary Child Development Study', *NZMJ*, 88, 1978, pp. 273–6.

Hooper, Challis, *Anne Pattrick, Director of Plunket Nursing New Zealand 1920–1934: A Memoir*, Dunedin, Training School for Plunket Nurses, 1958.

Horton, Sheila, *Memoirs of a Colonial Goose*, Auckland, Shoal Bay Press, 1984.

Houston, Stewart (ed.), *Marriage and the Family in New Zealand*, Wellington, Sweet & Maxwell, 1970.

How to Reserve the Children: Plain Directions to Mothers, Dunedin, Star Print, 1906.

Jackman, Sally, *Child Poverty in Aotearoa/New Zealand: A Report from the New Zealand Council of Christian Social Services*, Wellington, The Council, 1993.

Johns, Geraldine, 'Suffer the Little Children', *Metro,* April 2000, pp. 70–8.

Johnston, I. and D. C. Geddis, 'Child Abuse and Neglect – Reform of the Law', *NZMJ*, 97, 1984, pp. 367–70.

Jones, Kathleen, 'Sentiment and Science: The Late Nineteenth Century Pediatrician as Mother's Advisor', *Journal of Social History*, 17, 1983, pp. 79–96.

Kedgley, Sue, *Mum's the Word: The Untold Story of Motherhood in New Zealand*, Auckland, Random House, 1996.

King, F. Truby, *The Feeding of Plants and Animals* (Reprint from Pamphlet issued by New Zealand Farmers' Union), Wellington, Whitcombe & Tombs, 1905.

King, F. Truby, 'Physiological Economy in the Nutrition of Infants', *NZMJ*, 6, 1907, pp. 71–102.

King, F. Truby, *Feeding and Care of Baby*, Dunedin, Plunket Society, 1910.

King, F. Truby, *Feeding and Care of Baby*, London, Macmillan, 1913 (reprinted annually to 1932); revised and enlarged edition, 1940.

King, F. Truby, *Natural Feeding of Infants*, Dunedin, Plunket Society, 1917, London, Whitcombe & Tombs, 1918.

King, F. Truby, 'The Application of Science, Simplicity and Economy to the Everyday Practice of Artificial Feeding during Infancy', *NZMJ*, 20, 1921, pp. 33–48.

King, F. Truby, *The Karitane Products Society: A Short Account of the Aims and Purposes of its Work in relation to the Plunket Society, the Medical Profession and the Public*, Wellington, L.T. Watkins Ltd, 1929.

King, F. Truby, *The Expectant Mother and Baby's First Month: For Parents and Nurses,* Wellington, Government Printer, 4th edn, 1935; 6th edn, 1939; English edition, London, Macmillan, 1924.

King, F. Truby, *The Story of the Teeth and How to Save Them*, Auckland, Whitcombe & Tombs Ltd, 1935.

King, Mary, *Mothercraft*, Sydney, Angus & Robertson, 1934.

King, Mary, *Truby King: The Man, A Biography*, George Allen & Unwin, London, 1948.

Klaus, Alisa, *Every Child a Lion: The Origins of Maternal and Infant Health Policy in the United States and France, 1890–1920*, Ithaca, Cornell University Press, 1993.

Knapman, Claudia, 'Reconstructing Mothering: Feminism and the Early Childhood Centre', *Australian Feminist Studies*, 18, 1993, pp. 111–31.

Koven, Seth and Sonya Michel (eds), *Mothers of a New World: Maternalist Politics and the Origins of Welfare States*, London & New York, Routledge, 1993.

Labrum, Bronwyn, 'Persistent Needs and Expanding Desires: Pakeha Families and State Welfare in the Years of Prosperity', in Bronwyn Dalley and Bronwyn Labrum (eds), *Fragments: New Zealand Social and Cultural History,* Auckland, Auckland University Press, 2000, pp. 188–210.

Ladd-Taylor, Molly, 'Women's Health and Public Policy', in Rima D. Apple (ed.), *Women, Health and Medicine in America: A Historical Handbook*, New York, Garland, 1990, pp. 139–410.

Ladd-Taylor, Molly, 'Toward defining Maternalism in U.S. History', *Journal of Women's History*, 5, 2, 1993, pp. 110–13.

Ladd-Taylor, Molly, *Mother-Work: Women, Child Welfare and the State, 1890–1930*, Urbana, University of Illinois Press, 1994.

Ladd-Taylor, Molly and Lauri Umansky (eds), *'Bad' Mothers: The Politics of Blame in Twentieth-century America*, New York, New York University Press, 1998.

Lambert, Max (ed.), *Who's Who in New Zealand,* twelfth edition, Auckland, Reed, 1991.

Lambie, Mary, *My Story: Memoirs of a New Zealand Nurse*, Christchurch, Peryer, 1956.

Lasch, Christopher, *Haven in a Heartless World: The Family Besieged*, New York, Basic Books, 1977.

Legat, Nicola 'Suffer the Children', *Metro*, February 1990, pp. 37–51.

Lewis, Jane, 'Anxieties about the Family and the Relationships between Parents, Children and the State in Twentieth-century England', in Martin Richards and Paul Light (eds), *Children of Social Worlds: Development in a Social Context*, Cambridge, Massachusetts, Harvard University Press, 1986, pp. 31–54.

Lewis, Jane, *The Politics of Motherhood: Child and Maternal Welfare in England, 1900–1939*, London, Croom Helm, 1980.

Lewis, Jane (ed.), *Women's Welfare, Women's Rights*, London, Croom Helm, 1983.

Lewis, Jane, *Women and Social Action in Victorian and Edwardian England*, Aldershot, Edward Elgar, 1991.

Lewis, Jane, 'Gender, the Family and Women's Agency in the Building of "Welfare States": The British Case', *Social History*, 19, 1, 1994, pp. 37–55.

Lewis, Jane, 'Women's Agency, Maternalism and Welfare', *Gender and History*, 6, 1, 1994, pp. 117–23.

Lewis, Milton, 'The Problem of Infant Feeding: The Australian Experience from the Mid-nineteenth Century to the 1920s', *Journal of the History of Medicine and Allied Sciences*, 35, 2, 1980, pp. 174–87.

Lewis, Milton, 'The "Health of the Race" and Infant Health in New South Wales:

Perspectives on Medicine and Empire', in Roy McLeod and Milton Lewis (eds), *Disease, Medicine and Empire: Perspectives on Western Medicine and the Experience of European Expansion*, London & New York, Routledge, 1988, pp. 301–15.

Liddiard, Mabel, *Mothercraft Manual: Or the Expectant and Nursing Mother and Baby's First Two Years*, London, Churchill, 1st edn, 1924, 12th edn, 1954.

Lindenmeyer, Kriste, '*A Right to Childhood': The US Children's Bureau and Child Welfare 1912–46*, Urbana and Chicago, University of Illinois Press, 1997.

Loudon, Irvine, 'Childbirth', in W. F. Bynum and Roy Porter (eds), *Companion Encyclopedia of the History of Medicine, 2*, London, Routledge, 1993, pp. 206–20.

Ludbrook, S. L., 'Paediatrics in New Zealand', *NZMJ*, 75, 1972, pp. 259–62.

Lugaro, Ernesto, *Modern Problems in Psychiatry*, transl. by D. Orr and R. G. Rows, 2nd edn, Manchester, Manchester University Press, 1913.

Lynch, Kathleen V., *An Annotated Bibliography of the Royal New Zealand Society for the Health of Women and Children (Inc) "Plunket Society"*, Wellington, Wellington Library School, 1975.

Lynch, Margaret, Derek Steinberg, Christopher Ounsted, 'Family Unit in a Children's Psychiatric Hospital', *British Medical Journal*, 2, 1975, pp. 127–9.

Mackay, Joan, 'The Contribution of the Department of Health to Child Health, *NZMJ*, 75, 1972, pp. 299–302.

Maclean, F. S., *Hydatid Disease in New Zealand: An Account of the Events Leading to the Establishment of the National Hydatids Council, and the Methods Adopted to Eradicate the Disease*, Wellington, National Hydatids Council, 1964.

'Malnutrition in Auckland Children', Editorial, *NZMJ*, 76, 1972, pp. 200–1.

Marshall, Marinker, '"What is Wrong" and "How We Know It": Changing Concepts of Illness in General Practice', in I. Loudon, J. Horder and C. Webster (eds), *General Practice under the National Health Service 1948–1997*, London, Clarendon Press, 1998, pp. 65–91.

Marks, L., *Metropolitan Maternity: Maternal and Infant Welfare Services in Early Twentieth Century London*, Amsterdam, Rodopi, 1996.

Marland, Hilary, 'The Medicalisation of Motherhood: Doctors and Infant Welfare in the Netherlands, 1901–1930', in V. Fildes, L. Marks and H. Marland (eds), *Women and Children First: International Maternal and Infant Welfare, 1870–1945*, London, Routledge, 1992, pp. 74–96.

Marland, Hilary, 'A Pioneer in Infant Welfare: The Huddersfield Scheme 1903–1920', *Social History of Medicine*, 6, 1, 1993, pp. 25–50.

Marriott, Williams McKim, *Infant Nutrition: A Textbook of Infant Feeding for Students and Practitioners of Medicine*, St Louis, C. V. Mosby, 1930.

Max, Lesley, *Children: Endangered Species?: How the Needs of New Zealand Children are being Seriously Neglected: A Call for Action*, Auckland, Penguin, 1990.

May, Helen, 'Motherhood in the 1950s: An Experience of Contradiction', in S. Middleton (ed.), *Women and Education in Aotearoa*, Wellington, Allen & Unwin, Port Nicholson Press, 1988, pp. 57–71.

May, Helen, *Minding Children, Managing Men: Conflict and Compromise in the Lives of Postwar Pakeha Women*, Wellington, Bridget Williams Books, 1992.

May, Helen, *The Discovery of Early Childhood: The Development of Services for the Care and Education of Very Young Children, Mid-eighteenth-century Europe to Mid-twentieth-century New Zealand*, Auckland University Press, Bridget Williams Books, New Zealand Council for Educational Research, 1997.

May, Helen, *Politics in the Playground: The World of Early Childhood in Postwar New Zealand*, Wellington, Bridget Williams Books with New Zealand Council of Educational Research, 2001.

McCalman, Janet, *Sex and Suffering: Women's Health and a Women's Hospital*, Melbourne, Melbourne University Press, 1998.

McCleary, G. F., *Infantile Mortality and Infants' Milk Depots*, London, P. S. King & son, 1905.

McClure, Margaret, *A Civilised Community: A History of Social Security in New Zealand 1898–1998*, Auckland, Auckland University Press, 1998.

McDonald, Dugald, 'Children and Young Persons in New Zealand Society', in Peggy Koopman-Boyden (ed.), *Families in New Zealand Society*, Wellington, Methuen, 1980, pp. 44–56.

McMillan, D. G., *A National Health Service, New Zealand of Tomorrow*, Wellington, New Zealand Worker, 1934.

Meckel, Richard A., *Save the Babies: American Public Health Reform and the Prevention of Infant Mortality 1850–1929*, Baltimore, Johns Hopkins University Press, 1990.

Mechling, Jay, 'Advice to Historians on Advice to Mothers', *Journal of Social History*, 9, 1, 1975, pp. 44–63.

Mein Smith, Philippa, *Maternity in Dispute, New Zealand 1920–1939*, Wellington, Historical Branch, Department of Internal Affairs, 1986.

Mein Smith, Philippa, 'Truby King in Australia: A Revisionist View of Reduced Infant Mortality', *New Zealand Journal of History*, 22, 1, 1988, pp. 23–43.

Mein Smith, Philippa, 'Infant Welfare Services and Infant Mortality: A Historian's View', *Australian Economic Review*, 1, 1991, pp. 22–34.

Mein Smith, Philippa, '"That Welfare Warfare": Sectarianism in Infant Welfare in Australia, 1918–1939', in Valerie Fildes, Lara Marks and Hilary Marland (eds), *Women and Children First: International Maternal and Infant Welfare, 1870–1945*, London & New York, Routledge, 1992, pp.230–56.

Mein Smith, Philippa, 'Mothers, Babies and the Mothers' and Babies' Movement: Australia through Depression and War', *Social History of Medicine*, 6, 1, 1993, pp. 51–83.

Mein Smith, Philippa, *Mothers and King Baby: Infant Survival and Welfare in an Imperial World: Australia 1880–1950*, London, Macmillan, 1997.

Mitchell, E. A. *et al.*, 'Four Modifiable and other Major Risk Factors for Cot Death: The New Zealand Study', *Journal of Paediatrics and Child Health*, 28, 1992, Supplement 1.

Mitchell, E. A, I. B. Hassall, D. M. O. Becroft, 'Postneonatal Mortality Review in Auckland: Two Years Experience', *NZMJ*, 100, 1987, pp. 269–72.

Mitchell, E. A., R. Scragg, A. W. Stewart, D. M. O. Becroft, B. J. Taylor, R. P. K. Ford, I. B. Hassall, D. M. J. Barry, E. M. Allen, A. P. Roberts, 'Cot Death Supplement. Results from the First Year of the New Zealand Cot Death Study', *NZMJ*, 104, 1991, p. 75.

Morris, Margaret in collaboration with M. Randell, *Maternity and Post-operative Exercises in Diagrams and Words*, London, Heinemann, 1936.

Muncy, Robyn, *Creating a Female Dominion in American Reform 1890–1935*, New York, Oxford University Press, 1991.

Munro, Jessie, *The Story of Suzanne Aubert*, Auckland, Auckland University Press & Bridget Williams Books, 1996.

New Zealand Health Department, *The Maori Mother and Her Child*, Wellington, Government Printer, new edn, 1942.

New Zealand National Film Unit, *Born in New Zealand* (Plunket Society film), 1959.

Nolan, Melanie, *Breadwinning: New Zealand Women and the State*, Christchurch, Canterbury University Press, 2000.

O'Brien, Claire, 'They See the Darker Side of NZ Life', *NZWW*, 22 October 1984, pp. 33–5.

Oakley, Ann, *The Captured Womb: A History of the Medical Care of Pregnant Women*, Oxford, Blackwell, 1984.

Oliver, W. H., 'Social Welfare: Social Justice or Social Efficiency? Social Policy in the Liberal Period', *New Zealand Journal of History*, 13, 1, 1979, pp. 25–33.

Olssen, Erik, 'Breeding for Empire', *NZ Listener*, 12 May 1979, pp.18–19.

Olssen, Erik, 'Producing the Passionless People', *NZ Listener*, 19 May 1979, pp. 20–1.

Olssen, Erik, 'Truby King and the Plunket Society: An Analysis of a Prescriptive Ideology', *New Zealand Journal of History*, 15, 1, 1981, pp. 3–23.

Orange, Claudia, general editor, *Dictionary of New Zealand Biography, Volumes Two to Five*, Auckland University Press & Historical Branch, Wellington, 1993–2000.

'Paediatric Society of New Zealand', Editorial, *NZMJ*, 75, 1972, p. 303.

Parry, Gordon, *A Fence at the Top: The first 75 years of the Plunket Society*, Dunedin, Plunket Society, 1982.

Parsons, Leonard G. and Seymour Barling (eds), *Diseases of Infancy and Childhood*, London, Oxford University Press, 1933.

Parton, Nigel, *The Politics of Child Abuse*, Basingstoke, Macmillan, 1985.

Parton, Nigel, *Governing the Family: Child Care, Child Protection and the State*, Basingstoke, Macmillan, 1991.

Pedersen, Susan, *Family Dependence and the Origins of the Welfare State: Britain and France 1914–945*, New York & Cambridge, Cambridge University Press, 1993.

'The Plunket Dietary', Editorial, *NZMJ*, 34, 1935, pp. 365–6.

Plunket Society, *Condensed Summaries of Conference Reports 1914–1926*, Dunedin, Plunket Society, 1927.

'The Plunket Society', Editorial, *NZMJ*, 37, 1938, pp. 185–7.

'The Plunket Society and the Department. Infant-feeding and the Training of Maternity Nurses', Editorial, *Journal of Public Health*, 3, 1917, pp. 40–3.

Pomare, Maui, *Ko Nga Tamariki Me Nga Kai Ma Ratou, Infants and their Foods*, Wellington, Department of Health, 1916.

Pool, D. Ian, *Te Iwi Maori: A New Zealand Population, Past, Present & Projected*, Auckland, Auckland University Press, 1991.

Porter, Dorothy, '"Enemies of the Race": Biologism, Environmentalism and the Public Health in Edwardian England', *Victorian Studies*, 34, 2, 1991, pp. 159–78.

Powell, Joyce, 'To Help the Mothers and Save the Babies', *New Zealand Memories*, June/July 2002, pp. 39–44.

Prochaska, F. K., *Women and Philanthropy in Nineteenth-century England*, Oxford, Clarendon Press, 1980.

Public Health Department, *Baby's First Month*, Wellington, Government Printer, 1913.

Purdy, J. S., 'Infant Mortality in New South Wales', *Medical Journal of Australia*, 1, 11, 1922, pp. 287–96.

Pybus, Marion (ed.), *The Nurse in the Community. Community Health Nursing in New Zealand*, Auckland, McGraw-Hill, 1983.

Radcliffe, Walter, *Milestones in Midwifery*, Bristol, John Wright, 1967.

Raffel, Marshall W., 'A Consultative Committee on Infant and Pre-school Health Services', *New Zealand Journal of Public Administration*, 28, 1, 1965, pp. 37–79.

Raffel, Marshall W., 'Plunket Society-Health Dept. A Controversy Revisited', *New Zealand Journal of Public Administration*, 39, 2, 1977, pp. 7–17.

Raftery, Judith, '"Mainly a Question of Motherhood": Professional Advice-giving and Infant Welfare', *Journal of Australian Studies*, 45, 1995, pp. 66–78.

Reiger, Kerreen, *The Disenchantment of the Home: Modernizing the Australian Family, 1880–1940*, Melbourne, Oxford University Press, 1985.

Reiger, Kerreen, *Our Bodies, Our Babies: The Forgotten Women's Movement*, Melbourne, Melbourne University Press, 2001.

Report of National Steering Committee on Cot Death, Wellington, The Committee, 1985.

Ribble, Margaret A., *The Rights of Infants: Early Psychological Needs and their Satisfaction*, New York, Columbia University Press, 1943.

Rice, G. W., 'The Making of New Zealand's 1920 Health Act', *New Zealand Journal of History*, 22, 1, 1988, pp. 3–22.

Rice, G. W., *The Annotated Biography of the Hon. Sir R. Heaton Rhodes (1861–1956)*, Christchurch, Hawthorne Press, 2001.

Ritchie, Jane and James, *Child Rearing Patterns in New Zealand*, Wellington, Reed, 1970.

Robinson R. R.,(ed.), *SIDS 1974. Proceedings of the Francis E. Camps International Symposium on Sudden and Unexpected Deaths in Infancy*, Toronto, University of Toronto Press, 1974.

Rollet, Catherine, 'The Fight Against Infant Mortality in the Past: An International Comparison', in Alain Bideau, Bertrand Desjardins, Hector Perez Brignoli (eds), *Infant and Child Mortality in the Past*, Oxford, Clarendon Press, 1997.

Rotch, Thomas Morgan, *Pediatrics: The Hygiene and Medical Treatment of Children*, 5th edn, London, Lippincott, 1906.

Rothman, Sheila, *Woman's Proper Place: A History of Changing Ideals and Practices, 1870 to the Present*, New York, Basic Books, 1978.

Royal New Zealand Society for the Health of Women and Children (Inc.), *Report of General Conference*, Dunedin, The Society, 1914–99.

Royal New Zealand Society for the Health of Women and Children (Inc.), *Rules of the Royal New Zealand Society for the Health of Women and Children (Inc.)*, Dunedin, Otago Daily Times & Witness Newspapers Co., 1926.

Royal New Zealand Society for the Health of Women and Children (Inc.), *Rules and Guiding Lines for Plunket Nurses*, Dunedin, Stone, Son & Co., rev. 1938, rev. 1943, rev. 1948, rev. 1953, rev. 1963.

Royal New Zealand Society for the Health of Women and Children (Inc.), *Rules Regarding the Engagement and Duties of Karitane Baby Nurses. For the Guidance of Mothers and Nurses*, Dunedin, Stone, Son & Co., rev. 1938, rev. 1942, rev. 1947, rev. 1950.

Royal New Zealand Society for the Health of Women and Children (Inc.), *A Short History of the Origin and Development of the Work of the Society*, Dunedin, The Society, 1939.

Royal New Zealand Society for the Health of Women and Children (Inc), *The Work of the Plunket Society in New Zealand: For the Mother and Baby and Pre-school Child*, Dunedin, The Society, 1945.

Royal New Zealand Society for the Health of Women and Children (Inc.), *Guide Book for Infant Welfare Nurses*, Dunedin, The Society, new edition, 1963.

Royal New Zealand Society for the Health of Women and Children (Inc.), *The Plunket Society*, Dunedin, The Society, 1967.

Rudman, Brian, 'Our Third World Child Health Care', *NZ Listener*, 27 September 1986, pp. 15–18.

Salmond, G. C., 'Social Needs for Medical Services: The Inverse Care Law in New Zealand', *NZMJ*, 80, 1974, pp. 396–403.

Salmond, G. C., 'Correspondence: Medical Services', *NZMJ*, 81, 1975, p. 217.

Sargison, Patricia, *Notable Women in New Zealand Health. Te Hauora ki Aotearoa: Ona Wahine Rongonui*, Auckland, Longman Paul, 1993.

Scholefield, Guy H., *Who's Who in New Zealand and the Western Pacific*, 2nd edn, Masterton, 1925, 3rd edn, Wellington, The Rangatira Press, 1932.

Semi-Centennial Volume of the American Pediatric Society 1888–1938, Wisconsin, George Banta Publishing Co., 1938.

Shannon, F. T., 'Paediatric Teaching in Retrospect and Prospect', *NZMJ*, 81, 1975, pp. 168–71.

Silva, Phil A., *Annotated Bibliography of Publications and Reports from the Dunedin Multidisciplinary Health and Development Research Unit, 1975 to 1985*, Dunedin, The Unit, 1986.

Silva Phil A. and Warren R. Stanton (eds), *Child to Adult: The Dunedin Multidisciplinary Health and Development Study*, Auckland, Oxford University Press, 1996.

Simon, Judith (ed.), *Nga Kura Maori: The Native Schools System 1867–1969*, Auckland, Auckland University Press, 1998.

Sinclair, Keith, *A Destiny Apart: New Zealand's Search for National Identity*, Wellington, Allen & Unwin, 1986.

Sir Truby and Lady King Plunket/ Karitane Hospital, Wellington, Golden Jubilee 1927–77, Wellington, Plunket Society, 1977.

Skocpol, Theda, *Protecting Soldiers and Mothers: The Political Origins of Social Policy in the United States*, Cambridge, Mass., Belknap Press of Harvard University Press, 1992.

Smith, Valerie, *Nurse at Large*, Wellington, GP Publications, 1992.

Smyth, Helen, *Rocking the Cradle: Contraception, Sex and Politics in New Zealand*, Wellington, Steele Roberts, 2000.

Society for the Health of Women and Children (Plunket Society), *What Baby Needs*, Dunedin, Plunket Society, 1912.

Sorrenson, M. P. K., 'Modern Maori: The Young Maori Party to Mana Motuhake', in Keith Sinclair (ed.), *The Oxford Illustrated History of New Zealand*, Auckland, Oxford University Press, 1990, pp. 323–52.

Spencer, F. Montgomery, 'Modern Principles in Infant Nutrition', *NZMJ*, 30, 1931, pp. 393–400.

Spencer, F. Montgomery, 'Malnutrition and a C3 Population Part 1', *NZMJ*, 36, 1937, pp. 4–20.

Spencer, F. Montgomery, 'Malnutrition and a C3 Population Part 2', *NZMJ*, 37, 1938, pp. 115–36.

Spock, Benjamin, *Baby and Child Care*, London, Bodley Head, new and enlarged edition, 1958.

Steincamp, Jacqueline, 'An Undercover Victory', *Broadsheet*, 62, September 1978, pp. 15–16.

Stern, Alexandra Minna and Howard Markel (eds), *Formative Years: Children's Health in the United States 1880–2000*, Ann Arbor, University of Michigan Press, 2002.

Sweet, G. Bruton, *Lectures on the Management of Infants in Health and Sickness*, Auckland, Whitcombe & Tombs, 1920.

Sweet, G. Bruton, 'Some Remarks on Infant Feeding. A Reply to Dr Truby King', *NZMJ*, 20, 1921, pp. 104–12.

Tennant, Margaret, *Paupers and Providers: Charitable Aid in New Zealand*, Wellington, Allen & Unwin/Historical Branch, 1989.

Tennant, Margaret, '"Missionaries of health": the School Medical Service during the Inter-war Period', in L. Bryder (ed.), *A Healthy Country: Essays on the Social History of Medicine in New Zealand*, Wellington, Bridget Williams Books, 1991, pp. 128–48.

Tennant, Margaret, *Children's Health, the Nation's Wealth: A History of Children's Health Camps*, Wellington, Bridget Williams Books and Historical Branch, Department of Internal Affairs, 1994.

The Plunket Society New Zealand, Dunedin, Plunket Society, 1961.

Thomas, Mary (ed.), *Post-War Mothers: Childbirth Letters to Grantly Dick-Read, 1946–1956*, Rochester, University of Rochester Press, 1997.

Tomes, Nancy, *The Gospel of Germs: Men, Women and the Microbe in American Life*, Cambridge, Mass., Harvard University Press, 1998.

Urwin, Cathy and Sharland, Elaine, 'From Bodies to Minds in Childcare Literature', in Roger Cooter (ed.), *In the Name of the Child: Health and Welfare, 1880–1940*, London & New York, Routledge, 1992, pp. 174–99.

Walker, Anne, *The Karitane Products Society Ltd*, Wellington, Karitane Products Society Ltd, 1968.

Washbourn, H. E. A., 'A Criticism of Some Features of the Propaganda and Methods of the Royal New Zealand Society for the Health of Women and Children', *NZMJ*, 20, 1921, pp. 113–6.

Watt, J. M., *Practical Paediatrics: A Guide for Nurses*, Christchurch, Peryer, 1964.

Watt, M. H., 'Infant Mortality in New Zealand,' *New Zealand Journal of Health and Hospitals*, 4, 4, 1921, pp. 88–94.

Webb, Lorraine, *Cot Death in New Zealand: Unfolding the Mystery*, Auckland, David Bateman, 1986.

Webster Alan and Mervyn Hancock, in Stewart Houston (ed.), *Marriage and the Family in New Zealand*, Wellington, Sweet & Maxwell, 1970.

Weiner, Lynn, 'International Trends: Maternalism as a Paradigm, Defining the Issues', *Journal of Women's History*, 5, 2, 1993, pp. 96–8.

Weiner, Lynn, 'Reconstructing Motherhood: The La Leche League in Postwar America', *Journal of American History*, 80, 4, 1994, pp. 1357–81.

Williams, E. H., 'Infant Feeding and the Plunket Society', *NZMJ*, 32, 1933, pp. 330–5.

Wilson, Mollie, 'Client Centred Approach to Community and Family Care: A Descriptive Account of Social Support Services Provided by Plunket Nurses in the Central Region', *Nursing Praxis in New Zealand*, 11, 1, 1996, pp. 12–18.

Wolf, Jacqueline H., 'Don't Kill Your Baby': Feeding Infants in Chicago, 1903–1924', *Journal of the History of Medicine and Allied Sciences*, 53, 1998, pp. 219–53.

Wolf, Jacqueline H., *Don't Kill Your Baby: Public Health and the Decline of Breastfeeding in the Nineteenth and Twentieth Centuries*, Columbus, Ohio University Press, 2001.

Woodbury, Robert M., *Infant Mortality and Preventive Work in New Zealand*, Reprinted from the *Transactions of the Eleventh Annual Meeting of the American Child Hygiene Association*, St Louis, October 11–13, 1920.

Woods, Sybil, 'Tried and True', *NZ Listener*, 16 June 1979, pp. 44–5.

Wright-St Clair, Rex, *A History of the New Zealand Medical Association: The First 100 years*, Wellington, Butterworths, 1987.

Unpublished theses

Belgrave, Michael P., '"Medical Men" and "Lady Doctors": The Making of a New Zealand Profession, 1867–1941', PhD thesis, Victoria University of Wellington, 1985.

Calder, J. A., '"Non-Plunket" Mothers and Aspects of Welfare', Public Health thesis, University of Otago, 1969.

Chalmers, M. R. '"Karitane Babies" and their Families', Public Health thesis, University of Otago, 1971.

Coop, D. H., 'Problems of Breast Feeding at Richmond', Public Health thesis, University of Otago, 1951.

Courtney, Lesley, '"An Excellent Preparation for Marriage and Families of Their Own": Karitane Nursing in New Zealand 1959–1979', MA thesis, Massey University, 2001.

Cox, Elizabeth, 'Plunket Plus Commonsense: Women and the Plunket Society, 1940–1960', MA thesis, Victoria University of Wellington, 1996.

Elliott, M. I. and M. D. Rohan, 'Infant Feeding', Public Health thesis, University of Otago, 1941.

Favell, Margaret D., 'Plunket Nursing in a Social, Political and Historical Context: Clients' Perspectives of Mothering and Nursing', Master of Health Sciences thesis, University of Otago, 1997.

Frengley, J. D., 'A Study of the Balclutha Branch of the Plunket Society', Public Health thesis, University of Otago, c1960.

Gibbons, Anita Helen, 'The Mothercraft Training Society: Its Origins, Development and Demise', BSc thesis, University of London, 1985.

Gilmour, J. R. 'The Mother, the Baby, and the Plunket Sister', Public Health thesis, University of Otago, 1950.

Hamilton-Gibbs, N. N., 'The Work of the Plunket Society', Public Health thesis, University of Otago, 1961.

Hickey, Maureen, 'Negotiating Infant Welfare: The Plunket Society in the Interwar Period', MA thesis, University of Otago, 1999.

Hill, M., 'Attitudes to Breast Feeding – Comparisons Between a Rural and Urban Community', Public Health thesis, University of Otago, 1970

Hitchman, Belinda, 'Gender and Health: The Feminist Challenge to the Traditional Medical System', MA thesis, University of Auckland, 1987.

Hosking, M N, 'Aspects of Breast Feeding', Public Health thesis, University of Otago, 1968.

Houghton, 'Antenatal Hygiene', Public Health thesis, University of Otago, 1926.

Jennings, G. C. 'The Royal New Zealand Society for the Health of Women and Children', Public Health thesis, University of Otago, 1936.

Knox, H., 'Feminism, Femininity and Motherhood in Post-World War Two New Zealand', MA thesis, Massey University, 1995.

Kral, M. J., 'The Decline of Breast Feeding', Public Health thesis, University of Otago, 1963.

Kyd, G., 'Breast Feeding', Public Health thesis, University of Otago, 1965.

Lambert, Joan, '"They Can't See What We See": Voices and Standpoint of Twelve Plunket Nurses', MPhil. thesis, Massey University, 1994.

Lewis, M. J., '"Populate or Perish": Aspects of Infant and Maternal Health in Sydney, 1870–1939', PhD thesis, Australian National University, 1976.

Marriott, K. V. 'The Plunket Society: Some Opinions', Public Health thesis, University of Otago, 1963.

Maxwell, Sean, J. 'Mothers and Plunket: A Study of Infant Care in Auckland, 1950–1975', MA research essay, University of Auckland, 1993.

McCafferty, J. F. and J. G. Perry, 'Antenatal Training', Public Health thesis, University of Otago, 1957.

McGettigan, J. F., 'Breast Feeding and Bottle Feeding in the Community', Public Health thesis, University of Otago, 1971.

McKinlay, R. M., 'Where Would We Be Without Them? Motherhood and Self-definition in New Zealand', PhD thesis, Victoria University of Wellington, 1983.

Milne, Lynne S., 'The Plunket Society: An Experiment in Infant Welfare', BA (Hons) thesis, University of Otago, 1976.

Nash, M. D. and A. H. Paul, 'A Survey of the Truby King-Harris Hospital, Dunedin', Public Health thesis, University of Otago, 1950.

Nelson, Beatrice E. 'Wellington Karitane Hospital and Mothercraft Home, Melrose, Wellington', Public Health thesis, University of Otago, 1936.

Norton, Valerie, 'Access to Health: Women's Experiences of Providing Health Care for their Babies', MA thesis, University of Canterbury, 1990.

Reeder, William James, 'The Plunket Tradition and Today's Mother', Public Health thesis, University of Otago, 1969.

Salkeld, H. F., 'The New Zealand Plunket Society: Its Origin and Development', Public Health thesis, University of Otago, 1948.

Shief, B. and A. G. Roberts, 'The Normal Breast-fed Child and its Mother', Public Health thesis, University of Otago, 1942.

Stringer, H. and C. Morkane, 'Ante and Post-natal Work in Christchurch', Public Health thesis, University of Otago, 1940.

Svenson, T. C. and B. E. Tomlinson, 'Survey of the Dunedin Karitane Hospital', Public Health thesis, University of Otago, 1952.

Tennant, Margaret, 'Matrons with a Mission: Women's Organizations in New Zealand, 1893–1915', MA thesis, Massey University, 1976.

Watson S. K. and A. E. Walton, 'A Study in Antenatal Care', Public Health thesis, University of Otago, 1940.

Wilson, M. C., 'Breast Feeding', Public Health thesis, University of Otago, 1949.

Woods, Margaret, 'Plunket Nursing in the Invercargill area', Public Health thesis, University of Otago, 1951.

Yee, J. Y. 'To Help the Mothers and Save the Babies', Public Health thesis, University of Otago, 1962.

Index

abortion, 192, 202, 271–2
Accident and Injury Prevention, first World Conference, 1989, 226
Accident Compensation Corporation, 223
accident prevention: xi, 222–30, *223*, *224*, 246; child-resistant medicine caps, 230; playpens, 223; road traffic accidents, xi, 202, 204, 225, 231; swimming pools, fencing of, 227–9, *229*, 231
Adams, Mrs J. M., 206
Adams-Schneider, Lance, 207
adoption, 195, 197, 268
Agriculture: Department of, 179; Minister of, 142, 178
Albert, Erwin, 221
Alden, Eleanor, 139
Aldrich, C. Anderson, 122–3
Aldrich, Mary, 122–3
Alexandra Home for Unmarried Mothers, Wellington, 107
Allan, Irene, 110–11
Allan, Jenny, *255*
Allen, James, 21, 27, 32, 35
Allen, Mrs James, 21, 27, 32, 35
Allen, Olive, 22
Allen, Sydney, 22, 83
American Child Hygiene Association, 33
American Medical Association on Diseases of Children, 12
American Medical Association, 177; Operation Reach Out, 177
American Pediatric Society, 9, 12, 13
Anderson, Mary P., x
Andrews, Joyce, 195, 204, 266, 271
Anglican-Methodist Family Care Centre, Dunedin, 257
ante-natal care: 45, 48, 64, 74, 106–9, *107*, 115, 126–7, 133–6, 184, 215, 242–4; Margaret Morris exercises, 126; conference on teaching, 1950, 132, 134. *See also* natural childbirth
Appleton, Mrs W., 141
Armitage, Rachelina H., 23, 49
Armstrong, Dianne, 258, 274
Armstrong, William, 32
Arnup, Katherine, 136
Atkinson, Lily, 23, 39

Aubert, Mary J., 23
Auckland Hospital, children's wards, 84, 88
Auckland Karitane Nurses' Club, 189
Auckland Medical Research Foundation, 185
Auckland University: chair of child health, 215, 219; Paediatrics Department, 220
Austin, Brett, 257
Australia: comparisons with, x, xiii, 1, 34, 43–4, 45, 68–9, 73, 80, 106, 137, 197, 202–3, *203*, *223*, 226, 228, 254, 259; Health Commission of South Australia, Child, Adolescent and Family Health Service, 254; Lady Gowrie Child Centres, 137, 138; Lady Talbot Pure Milk Depot, Melbourne, 43–4; New South Wales Legislative Council inquiry into welfare of mothers and babies in New Zealand, 34; Royal Society for the Welfare of Mothers and Babies, Sydney, 45; Victorian Baby Health Centres Association, Melbourne, 45; Victorian Council of Women, 43
Averill, Alfred, 22
Averill, Mary, 22

Babies of the Empire: campaign, *46*; Society, 9
baby weeks, 30–1, 86
baby-farming, 7
Bagnall, Eva, 21
Bagnall, Lemuel, 21
Baigent, Paul, 259
Bailey, Ronald, 178
Baker, Eleanor, 24
Baker, Jacqueline, 186
Baker, Josephine, 36
Baldwin, Angela, 253, 263, 264
Ballance, V., *234*
Ballantyne, John W., 106
Bannister/Bulmer family, *233*
Barker, Mrs, 29
Barnett, Miss, *107*, 109
Barr, John, 8
Barrowclough, C. B., 103
Bassett, Michael, 177
Batchelor, Ferdinand, 40
Batchelor, Mrs E. R., 263
Batt, Dorothy, *111*
battered baby syndrome *see* child abuse